2ⁿᵈ EDITION

Ventures 3

TEACHER'S EDITION

Gretchen Bitterlin   Dennis Johnson   Donna Price   Sylvia Ramirez

K. Lynn Savage (Series Editor)

with Lois Miller

CAMBRIDGE
UNIVERSITY PRESS

CAMBRIDGE
UNIVERSITY PRESS

University Printing House, Cambridge CB2 8BS, United Kingdom

One Liberty Plaza, 20th Floor, New York, NY 10006, USA

477 Williamstown Road, Port Melbourne, VIC 3207, Australia

4843/24, 2nd Floor, Ansari Road, Daryaganj, Delhi – 110002, India

79 Anson Road, #06–04/06, Singapore 079906

Cambridge University Press is part of the University of Cambridge.

It furthers the University's mission by disseminating knowledge in the pursuit of education, learning and research at the highest international levels of excellence.

www.cambridge.org
Information on this title: www.cambridge.org/9781107652170

First published 2008
Reprinted 2017

Printed in Italy by Rotolito Lombarda S.p.A.

A catalogue record for this publication is available from the British Library

ISBN 978-1-107-68472-0 Student's Book with Audio CD
ISBN 978-1-107-64001-6 Workbook with Audio CD
ISBN 978-1-139-88472-3 Online Workbook
ISBN 978-1-107-65217-0 Teacher's Edition with Assessment Audio CD / CD-ROM
ISBN 978-1-107-66076-2 Class Audio CDs
ISBN 978-1-107-64952-1 Presentation Plus

Additional resources for this publication at www.cambridge.org/ventures

Art direction, book design, photo research, and layout services: Q2A / Bill Smith
Audio production: CityVox, LLC

Contents

To the teacher

What is *Ventures*?

Ventures is a six-level, four-skills, standards-based, integrated-skills series that empowers students to achieve their academic and career goals.

- This most complete program with a wealth of resources provides instructors with the tools for any teaching situation.
- The new Online Workbook keeps students learning outside the classroom.
- Easy-to-teach materials make for a more productive classroom.

What components does *Ventures* have?

Student's Book with Audio CD

Each of the core **Student's Books** contains ten topic-focused units, interspersed with five review units. The main units feature six skill-focused lessons.

- **Lessons** in the Student's Book are self-contained, allowing for completion within a one-hour class period.
- **Review lessons** recycle and reinforce the listening, vocabulary, and grammar skills developed in the two prior units and include a pronunciation activity.
- **Self-assessments** in the back of the book give students an opportunity to reflect on their learning. They support learner persistence and help determine whether students are ready for the unit test.
- **Reference charts**, also in the back of the book, provide grammar paradigms and rules for spelling, punctuation, and grammar.
- References to the **Self-study audio CD** that accompanies the Student's Book are indicated in the Student's Book by an icon and track number: Look for the audio icon and track number to find activities with self-study audio. "STUDENT" refers to the self-study audio, and "CLASS" refers to the class audio. A full class audio is available separately.

  STUDENT TK 10
  CLASS CD1 TK 14

- A **Student Arcade**, available online at www.cambridge.org/venturesarcade, allows students to practice their skills with interactive activities and download self-study audio.

Teacher's Edition with Assessment Audio CD / CD-ROM

The interleaved **Teacher's Edition** includes easy-to-follow lesson plans for every unit.

- Tips and suggestions address common areas of difficulty for students and provide suggestions for expansion activities and improving learner persistence.
- A **More Ventures** chart at the end of each lesson indicates where to find additional practice material in other *Ventures* components such as the Workbook, Online Teacher's Resource Room (see below), and Student Arcade.
- Unit, midterm, and final tests, which include listening, vocabulary, grammar, reading, and writing sections, are found in the back of the Teacher's Edition.
- The **Assessment Audio CD / CD-ROM** that accompanies the Teacher's Edition contains the audio for each unit, midterm, and final test. It also features all the tests in customizable format so teachers can customize them to suit their needs.

Online Teacher's Resource Room (www.cambridge.org/myresourceroom)

Ventures 2nd Edition offers a free Online Teacher's Resource Room where teachers can download hundreds of additional worksheets and classroom materials including:

- A *placement test* that helps place students into appropriate levels of *Ventures*.
- A *Career and Educational Pathways* solution that helps students identify their educational and career goals.
- *Collaborative activities* for each lesson in Levels 1–4 that develop cooperative learning and community building within the classroom.
- *Writing worksheets* that help Literacy-level students recognize and write shapes, letters, and numbers, while alphabet and number cards promote partner and group work.
- *Picture dictionary cards and worksheets* that reinforce vocabulary learned in Levels Basic, 1, and 2.
- *Extended readings and worksheets* that provide added reading skills development for Levels 3 and 4.
- *Add Ventures* worksheets that were designed for use in multilevel classrooms and in leveled classes where the proficiency level of students differs.

Log on to www.cambridge.org/myresourceroom to explore these and hundreds of other free resources.

Workbook with Audio CD

The **Workbook** provides two pages of activities for each lesson in the Student's Book and includes an audio CD.

- If used in class, the Workbook can extend classroom instructional time by 30 minutes per lesson.
- The exercises are designed so learners can complete them in class or independently. Students can check their answers with the answer key in the back of the Workbook. Workbook exercises can be assigned in class, for homework, or as student support when a class is missed.
- Grammar charts at the back of the Workbook allow students to use the Workbook for self-study.

Online Workbooks

The self-grading **Online Workbooks** offer programs the flexibility of introducing blended learning.

- They provide the same high-quality practice opportunities as the print Workbooks and give students instant feedback.
- They allow teachers and programs to track student progress and time on task.

Unit organization

Each unit has six skill-focused lessons:

LESSON A Listening focuses students on the unit topic. The initial exercise, *Before you listen*, creates student interest with visuals that help the teacher assess what learners already know and serve as a prompt for the unit's key vocabulary. Next is *Listen*, which is based on conversations. Students relate vocabulary to meaning and relate the spoken and written forms of new theme-related vocabulary. *After you listen* concludes the lesson by practicing language related to the theme in a communicative activity, either orally with a partner or individually in a writing activity.

LESSONS B AND C focus on grammar. The lessons move from a *Grammar focus* that presents the grammar point in chart form; to *Practice* exercises that check comprehension of the grammar point and provide guided practice; and, finally, to *Communicate* exercises that guide learners as they generate original

answers and conversations. These lessons often include a *Culture note*, which provides information directly related to the conversation practice (such as the use of titles with last names), or a *Useful language* note, which introduces useful expressions and functional language.

LESSON D Reading develops reading skills and expands vocabulary. The lesson opens with a *Before you read* exercise, designed to activate prior knowledge and encourage learners to make predictions. A *Reading tip*, which focuses on a specific reading skill, accompanies the **Read** exercise. The reading section of the lesson concludes with *After you read* exercises that check comprehension. In Levels Basic, 1, and 2, the vocabulary expansion portion of the lesson is a *Picture dictionary*. It includes a *word bank*, pictures to identify, and a conversation for practicing the new words. The words expand vocabulary related to the unit topic. In Books 3 and 4, the vocabulary expansion portion of the lesson uses new vocabulary from the reading to build skills such as recognizing word families, selecting definitions based on the context of the reading, and using clues in the reading to guess meaning.

LESSON E Writing provides practice with process writing within the context of the unit. *Before you write* exercises provide warm-up activities to activate the language needed for the writing assignment, followed by one or more exercises that provide a model for students to follow when they write. A *Writing tip* presents information about punctuation or paragraph organization directly related to the writing assignment. The *Write* exercise sets goals for the student writing. In the *After you write* exercise, students share with a partner.

LESSON F Another view has three sections. *Life-skills reading* develops the scanning and skimming skills used with documents such as forms, charts, schedules, announcements, and ads. Multiple-choice questions (modeled on CASAS[1] and BEST[2]) develop test-taking skills. *Grammar connections*, in Levels 1–4, contrasts grammar points and includes guided practice and communicative activities. Finally, *Wrap up* refers students to the self-assessment page in the back of the book, where they can check their knowledge and evaluate their progress.

---

[1] The Comprehensive Adult Student Assessment System. For more information, see www.casas.org.

[2] The Basic English Skills Test. For more information, see www.cal.org/BEST.

Scope and sequence

UNIT TITLE TOPIC	FUNCTIONS	LISTENING AND SPEAKING	VOCABULARY	GRAMMAR FOCUS
Welcome pages 2–5	■ Discussing goals ■ Filling out a goal form ■ Discussing past and future events	■ Listening and asking about goals ■ Asking about daily routines ■ Listening about events in the past and future	■ Review of time phrases	Verb tense review: ■ present and present continuous ■ past and future
Unit 1 **Personal information** pages 6–17 Topic: **Personality traits**	■ Describing and comparing likes and interests ■ Describing and discussing personality types	■ Asking about and comparing preferences ■ Describing personality types	■ Personal interests ■ Personality types ■ Adjectives that describe people	■ Verbs + gerunds ■ Comparisons with *more than*, *less than*, *as much as* ■ *must* for logical conclusions
Unit 2 **At school** pages 18–29 Topic: **Study skills**	■ Discussing study problems and learning strategies ■ Offering advice ■ Inquiring about people's experiences	■ Asking about study problems and learning strategies ■ Asking about someone's recent past	■ Study problems ■ Learning strategies	■ Present perfect with *how long*, *for*, *since* ■ Present perfect questions with *ever*; short answers ■ Simple past and present perfect
Review: Units 1 and 2 pages 30–31		■ Understanding a conversation		
Unit 3 **Friends and family** pages 32–43 Topic: **Neighbors**	■ Offering help ■ Agreeing and disagreeing ■ Giving reasons ■ Making a complaint	■ Asking about and describing problems ■ Giving reasons ■ Discussing borrowing and lending	■ *borrow* vs. *lend* ■ Two-word verbs	■ *because of* phrases and *because* clauses ■ *too* and *enough* ■ *be able to*
Unit 4 **Health** pages 44–55 Topic: **Healthy habits**	■ Discussing healthy foods and exercise ■ Describing events in the recent past ■ Describing past habits	■ Asking about staying healthy ■ Asking about past and present health habits	■ Healthy habits and routines ■ Beneficial plants	■ Present perfect with *recently* and *lately* ■ *used to* ■ Reported commands
Review: Units 3 and 4 pages 56–57		■ Understanding a conversation		
Unit 5 **Around town** pages 58–69 Topic: **Community resources and events**	■ Discussing future plans ■ Describing actions based on expectations ■ Describing community events	■ Asking about people's plans ■ Asking about people's expectations ■ Talking about community events	■ Entertainment ■ Positive and negative adjectives	■ Verbs + infinitives ■ Present perfect with *already* and *yet* ■ Verbs + infinitives and verbs + gerunds

READING	WRITING	LIFE SKILLS	PRONUNCIATION
■ Reading a paragraph about goals	■ Writing your goal and steps to reach it	■ Talking about your goal and steps to reach it	■ Pronouncing key vocabulary
■ Reading an article about personality and jobs ■ Predicting content from titles and pictures	■ Writing a descriptive paragraph with a topic sentence and supporting sentences ■ Using adjectives	■ Understanding a bar graph ■ Scanning a Web page for information	■ Pronouncing key vocabulary
■ Reading an article about strategies for learning English ■ Using context to identify parts of speech ■ Locating examples that support statements	■ Writing a paragraph with examples to support ideas ■ Using examples to support your ideas	■ Reading and understanding tips for taking tests ■ Talking about strategies for learning English	■ Pronouncing key vocabulary
			■ Stressing content words
■ Reading a newsletter about a neighborhood watch ■ Identifying the main idea, facts, and examples	■ Writing a letter of complaint ■ Supporting the main idea with examples	■ Reading and understanding an ad for volunteers ■ Writing a letter of complaint	■ Pronouncing key vocabulary
■ Reading an article about beneficial plants ■ Identifying the topic from the introduction and conclusion ■ Identifying parts of word families	■ Writing a descriptive paragraph ■ Writing a topic sentence ■ Completing a chart	■ Completing a medical history form ■ Talking about how to stay healthy	■ Pronouncing key vocabulary
			■ Voiced and voiceless *th* sounds
■ Reading a review of a concert ■ Using context to distinguish between positive and negative words	■ Writing an e-mail ■ Completing a graphic organizer	■ Reading and understanding announcements about community events ■ Talking about community events	■ Pronouncing key vocabulary

UNIT TITLE TOPIC	FUNCTIONS	LISTENING AND SPEAKING	VOCABULARY	GRAMMAR FOCUS
Unit 6 **Time** pages 70–81 Topic: **Time management**	■ Prioritizing ■ Discussing how to manage time ■ Giving advice ■ Describing habits	■ Prioritizing tasks ■ Asking about habits and daily activities ■ Contrasting qualities and habits of good and weak time managers	■ Time-management ■ Prefixes meaning *not* ■ Idioms with time	■ Adverb clauses with *when* ■ Adverb clauses with *before* and *after* ■ *one / some / any* and *it / them*
Review: Units 5 and 6 pages 82–83		■ Understanding a conversation		
Unit 7 **Shopping** pages 84–95 Topic: **Saving and spending**	■ Making suggestions ■ Asking for and giving advice ■ Discussing financial concerns ■ Comparing banking services	■ Asking and answering questions about buying on credit ■ Making suggestions and giving advice	■ Banking and finances ■ Compound nouns	■ *could* and *should* ■ Gerunds after prepositions ■ Collocations with *get* and *take*
Unit 8 **Work** pages 96–107 Topic: **Finding a job**	■ Discussing work-related goals ■ Discussing ways to find a job ■ Identifying procedures involved with a job interview	■ Talking about a job interview ■ Asking about ongoing activities	■ Employment ■ Separable phrasal verbs	■ Present perfect continuous ■ Separable phrasal verbs ■ Present continuous and present perfect continuous
Review: Units 7 and 8 pages 108–109		■ Understanding a conversation		
Unit 9 **Daily living** pages 110–121 Topic: **Community action**	■ Describing past activities ■ Describing past events	■ Describing a crime ■ Describing past actions ■ Asking about an emergency ■ Discussing safety items	■ Crimes ■ Emergency situations ■ Time phrases	■ Past continuous ■ Past continuous and simple past with *when* and *while* ■ Three uses of the present continuous
Unit 10 **Free time** pages 122–133 Topic: **Vacation plans**	■ Describing future possibility ■ Describing a sequence of events in the future	■ Describing vacation plans ■ Asking about future possibility ■ Describing the sequence of future events	■ Travel and vacation	■ Future real conditionals ■ Future time clauses with *before* and *after* ■ Three uses of the present perfect
Review: Units 9 and 10 pages 134–135		■ Understanding a news report		

READING	WRITING	LIFE SKILLS	PRONUNCIATION
■ Reading an article about cultural time rules ■ Recognizing dashes that introduce examples ■ Identifying words with prefixes meaning *not*	■ Writing a descriptive paragraph about a good or weak time manager ■ Using a signal before the conclusion	■ Reading and understanding a pie chart ■ Talking about how to manage time	■ Pronouncing key vocabulary
			■ Initial *st* sound
■ Reading an article about credit card debt ■ Identifying problems and solutions discussed in a text	■ Giving advice about saving money ■ Using *first*, *second*, *third*, and *finally* to organize ideas	■ Reading and understanding a brochure comparing checking accounts ■ Talking about credit, credit cards, and debt	■ Pronouncing key vocabulary
■ Reading a blog about a job search ■ Scanning for specific information ■ Using a dictionary to select the best definition for a context	■ Writing a formal thank-you letter ■ Understanding what to include in a thank-you letter	■ Reading and understanding a chart comparing job growth ■ Preparing for a job interview ■ Reading and understanding a blog	■ Pronouncing key vocabulary
			■ Linking sounds
■ Reading an article about an emergency ■ Recognizing time phrases ■ Guessing meaning from context	■ Writing about an emergency ■ Using *Who*, *What*, *When*, *Where*, *Why*, and *How*	■ Reading and understanding a chart comparing safety in various U.S. states ■ Talking about emergency situations	■ Pronouncing key vocabulary
■ Reading an article about Alcatraz ■ Using clues to guess the meaning of words	■ Writing about a tourist attraction ■ Using complex sentences to add variety	■ Reading and understanding hotel brochures ■ Talking about travel arrangements	■ Pronouncing key vocabulary
			■ Unstressed vowel sound

Correlations

UNIT	CASAS Competencies	NRS Educational Functioning Level Descriptors *Oral BEST: 42–50 (SPL 4)* *BEST Plus: 439–472 (SPL 4)* *BEST Literacy: 47–53 (SPL 4)*
Unit 1 **Personal information** Pages 6–17	0.1.2, 0.1.4, 0.1.5, 0.1.6, 0.2.1, 0.2.4, 4.1.7, 4.6.1, 4.8.1, 4.8.2, 6.0.1, 7.1.1, 7.1.4, 7.2.1, 7.2.3, 7.2.4, 7.4.1, 7.5.1	■ Asking and answering common questions ■ Expressing basic needs ■ Engaging in routine social conversations ■ Reading simple material on familiar subjects ■ Understanding simple and compound sentences in single or linked paragraphs ■ Writing simple notes and messages ■ Basic computer literacy
Unit 2 **At school** Pages 18–31	0.1.2, 0.1.4, 0.1.5, 0.2.1, 0.2.4, 2.3.1, 2.3.2, 4.1.2, 4.6.1, 4.8.1, 4.8.2, 6.0.1, 7.1.1, 7.1.2, 7.1.3, 7.1.4, 7.2.1, 7.2.2, 7.2.4, 7.2.6, 7.3.1, 7.3.2, 7.3.4, 7.4.1, 7.4.2, 7.5.1, 7.5.6	■ Common words, simple phrases, and sentences ■ Asking and answering common questions ■ Expressing basic needs ■ Engaging in routine social conversations ■ Understanding simple and compound sentences in single or linked paragraphs ■ Practicing writing with correct grammar ■ Interpreting simple directions and schedules
Unit 3 **Friends and family** Pages 32–43	0.1.2, 0.1.3, 0.1.4, 0.1.5, 0.2.1, 0.2.3, 0.2.4, 1.4.1, 1.4.7, 1.7.4, 2.3.1, 2.3.2, 3.4.2, 4.8.1, 4.8.2, 4.8.4, 5.3.7, 5.6.1, 5.6.2, 6.0.1, 7.1.4, 7.2.1, 7.4.2, 7.5.1, 8.2.6, 8.3.2	■ Common words, simple phrases, and sentences ■ Asking and answering common questions ■ Engaging in routine social conversations ■ Reading simple material on familiar subjects ■ Writing simple notes and messages ■ Practicing writing with correct grammar ■ Interpreting simple directions and schedules
Unit 4 **Health** Pages 44–57	0.1.2, 0.1.3, 0.1.5, 0.1.7, 0.2.4, 2.3.2, 3.1.1, 3.2.1, 3.3.3, 3.4.2, 3.5.2, 3.5.4, 3.5.5, 3.5.8, 3.5.9, 4.8.1, 6.0.1, 7.1.4, 7.2.1, 7.3.2, 7.4.1, 7.4.2, 7.5.1, 8.1.1, 8.2.1	■ Asking and answering common questions ■ Expressing basic needs ■ Engaging in routine social conversations ■ Expanding understanding of grammar ■ Reading simple material ■ Practicing writing with correct grammar ■ Filling out simple forms
Unit 5 **Around town** Pages 58–69	0.1.2, 0.1.4, 0.1.5, 0.2.1, 0.2.4, 2.3.1, 2.3.2, 2.6.1, 2.6.2, 2.6.3, 2.7.6, 4.8.1, 6.0.1, 7.1.1, 7.1.2, 7.1.4, 7.2.1, 7.4.2, 7.4.3, 7.5.1	■ Asking and answering common questions ■ Engaging in routine social conversations ■ Expanding understanding of grammar ■ Writing simple notes and messages ■ Practicing writing with correct grammar ■ Filling out simple forms ■ Basic computer literacy

All units of *Ventures 2nd Edition* meet most of the EFF content standards and provide overall BEST test preparation. The chart above lists areas of particular focus.

For more details and correlations to other state standards, go to: www.cambridge.org/myresourceroom

EFF	Florida Adult ESOL Low Intermediate	LAUSD ESL Low Intermediate Competencies
■ Conveying ideas in writing ■ Cooperating with others ■ Listening actively ■ Reading with understanding ■ Speaking so others can understand ■ Taking responsibility for learning ■ Understanding and working with pictures	4.01.02, 4.01.03, 4.03.07, 4.03.10, 4.03.11, 4.03.13, 4.03.15	I. 1 II. 3 IV. 29 VIII. 48, 50, 51, 52
■ Attending to oral information ■ Guiding others ■ Monitoring comprehension and adjusting reading strategies ■ Paying attention to conventions of spoken English ■ Solving problems ■ Cooperating with others ■ Speaking so others can understand	4.01.02, 4.01.04, 4.03.07, 4.03.10, 4.03.11, 4.03.13	II. 3, 6 VIII. 50, 51, 52 IX. 64
■ Organizing and presenting information to serve the purpose, context, and audience ■ Paying attention to conventions of spoken English ■ Selecting appropriate reading strategies ■ Solving problems ■ Speaking so others can understand ■ Testing out new learning in real-life applications ■ Cooperating with others	4.01.02, 4.01.3, 4.03.01, 4.03.07, 4.03.10, 4.03.11, 4.03.15, 4.04.05, 4.05.02, 4.07.01	I. 1 II. 3, 41, 5a, 6, 9 IV. 23 VIII. 50, 51, 52
■ Attending to oral information ■ Conveying ideas in writing ■ Listening actively ■ Offering clear input on own interests and attitudes ■ Paying attention to conventions of written English ■ Speaking so others can understand ■ Cooperating with others	4.01.02, 4.03.07, 4.03.10, 4.03.11, 4.05.01, 4.05.02	I. 2 II. 3 VI. 36, 38, 41 VIII. 50, 51, 52
■ Attending to oral information ■ Cooperating with others ■ Listening actively ■ Monitoring progress toward goals ■ Paying attention to conventions of written English ■ Reading with understanding ■ Understanding and working with pictures ■ Speaking so others can understand	4.01.02, 4.01.03, 4.01.04, 4.01.08, 4.02.08, 4.03.07, 4.03.10, 4.03.11, 4.03.13, 4.03.15	II. 3 VIII. 50, 51, 52

UNIT	CASAS Competencies	NRS Educational Functioning Level Descriptors *Oral BEST: 42–50 (SPL 4)* *BEST Plus: 439–472 (SPL 4)* *BEST Literacy: 47–53 (SPL 4)*
Unit 6 **Time** Pages 70–83	0.1.2, 0.1.4, 0.1.5, 0.2.1, 0.2.4, 1.1.3, 2.3.1, 2.7.2, 2.7.3, 4.1.7, 4.4.1, 4.4.3, 4.4.5, 4.8.1, 6.0.1, 6.7.4, 7.1.1, 7.1.2, 7.1.4, 7.2.1, 7.2.3, 7.2.4, 7.3.2, 7.4.1, 7.4.2, 7.4.8, 7.5.1	▪ Common words, simple phrases, and sentences ▪ Asking and answering common questions ▪ Engaging in routine social conversations ▪ Expanding understanding of grammar ▪ Reading simple material on familiar subjects ▪ Practicing writing with correct grammar ▪ Interpreting simple directions and schedules
Unit 7 **Shopping** Pages 84–95	0.1.2, 0.1.3, 0.1.5, 0.1.6, 0.2.1, 1.1.6, 1.2.1, 1.2.2, 1.2.5, 1.3.1, 1.4.1, 1.8.2, 4.8.1, 6.0.1, 6.5.1, 7.1.1, 7.1.4, 7.2.1, 7.2.3, 7.2.6, 7.3.1, 7.3.2, 7.4.2, 7.5.1, 7.5.5	▪ Common words, simple phrases, and sentences ▪ Engaging in routine social conversations ▪ Expanding understanding of grammar ▪ Understanding simple and compound sentences in single or linked paragraphs ▪ Writing simple notes and messages ▪ Practicing writing with correct grammar ▪ Interpreting simple directions and schedules
Unit 8 **Work** Pages 96-107	0.0.1, 0.1.2, 0.1.3, 0.1.5, 0.2.1, 2.3.1, 2.3.2, 2.4.1, 4.1.2, 4.1.5, 4.1.6, 4.1.7, 4.1.8, 4.4.3, 4.5.1, 4.6.1, 4.6.2, 4.8.1, 4.8.2, 6.0.1, 7.1.1, 7.1.4, 7.2.1, 7.4.1, 7.4.2, 7.4.4, 7.5.1, 7.5.2, 7.5.6	▪ Engaging in routine social conversations ▪ Expanding understanding of grammar ▪ Writing simple notes and messages ▪ Interpreting simple directions and schedules ▪ Practicing entry-level job-related writing ▪ Practicing entry-level job-related speaking ▪ Basic computer literacy
Unit 9 **Daily living** Pages 110–121	0.1.2, 0.1.4, 0.1.5, 0.2.1, 0.2.4, 1.4.1, 2.3.1, 2.5.1, 2.7.3, 3.4.2, 4.8.1, 5.3.7, 5.6.1, 5.6.2, 6.0.1, 7.1.1, 7.2.1, 7.4.2, 7.5.1, 8.3.2	▪ Common words, simple phrases, and sentences ▪ Asking and answering common questions ▪ Expressing basic needs ▪ Engaging in routine social conversations ▪ Expanding understanding of grammar ▪ Reading simple material on familiar subjects ▪ Practicing writing with correct grammar
Unit 10 **Free time** Pages 122–133	0.1.2, 0.1.4, 0.1.5, 0.2.1, 0.2.4, 1.2.2, 1.2.5, 2.1.8, 2.3.1, 2.3.2, 2.3.3, 2.7.1, 4.8.1, 6.0.1, 6.5.1, 7.1.1, 7.2.1, 7.2.2, 7.2.3, 7.2.6, 7.4.1, 7.4.2, 7.5.1	▪ Asking and answering common questions ▪ Engaging in routine social conversations ▪ Reading simple material on familiar subjects ▪ Understanding simple and compound sentences in single or linked paragraphs ▪ Practicing writing with correct grammar ▪ Interpreting simple directions and schedules ▪ Basic computer literacy

All units of *Ventures 2nd Edition* meet most of the EFF content standards and provide overall BEST test preparation. The chart above lists areas of particular focus.

For more details and correlations to other state standards, go to: www.cambridge.org/myresourceroom

EFF	Florida Adult ESOL Low Intermediate	LAUSD ESL Low Intermediate Competencies
■ Conveying ideas in writing ■ Cooperating with others ■ Listening actively ■ Reading with understanding ■ Solving problems ■ Speaking so others can understand	4.01.02, 4.01.5, 4.03.06, 4.03.07, 4.03.10, 4.03.11	II. 3 IV. 22 VIII. 50, 51, 52
■ Attending to oral information ■ Guiding others ■ Monitoring comprehension and adjusting reading strategies ■ Paying attention to conventions of written English ■ Selecting an alternative that is most appropriate to goal, context, and available resources ■ Understanding and working with pictures and numbers ■ Cooperating with others ■ Speaking so others can understand	4.01.02, 4.03.07, 4.03.10, 4.03.11, 4.04.01, 4.04.02, 4.04.03, 4.04.04, 4.04.07, 4.04.08, 4.04.09	II. 3, 5a IV. 23, 25c, 25d VIII. 49, 50, 51, 52
■ Anticipating and identifying problems ■ Conveying ideas in writing ■ Listening actively ■ Monitoring comprehension and adjusting reading strategies ■ Seeking input from others in order to understand their actions and reaction ■ Speaking so others can understand ■ Testing out new learning in real-life applications ■ Cooperating with others	4.01.02, 4.02.02, 4.02.06, 4.03.02, 4.03.04, 4.03.07, 4.03.10, 4.03.11, 4.03.13, 4.03.15	I. 1 II. 3, 4a, 5a VII. 44a VIII. 50, 51, 52
■ Attending to oral information ■ Monitoring progress toward goals ■ Paying attention to conventions of written English ■ Reading with understanding ■ Reflecting and evaluating ■ Taking responsibility for learning ■ Understanding and working with pictures and numbers ■ Cooperating with others ■ Speaking so others can understand	4.01.02, 4.02.05, 4.03.07, 4.03.10, 4.03.11, 4.06.04, 4.07.01	II. 3 IV. 23 VIII. 50, 51, 52
■ Attending to oral information ■ Interacting with others in ways that are friendly, courteous, and tactful ■ Listening actively ■ Monitoring comprehension and adjusting reading strategies ■ Paying attention to conventions of written English ■ Speaking so others can understand ■ Taking stock of where one is ■ Cooperating with others	4.01.02, 4.01.03, 4.03.07, 4.03.10, 4.03.11, 4.03.15, 4.04.03	II. 3 VIII. 50, 51, 52

Features of the Student's Book

The Most Complete Course for Student Success

Ventures empowers students to achieve their academic and career goals.

- The most complete program with a wealth of resources provides instructors with the tools for any teaching situation.
- The new Online Workbook keeps students learning outside the classroom.
- Easy-to-teach materials make for a more productive classroom.

The Big Picture

- Introduces the unit topic and provides rich opportunities for classroom discussion.
- Activates students' prior knowledge and previews the unit vocabulary.

Unit Goals

- Explicit unit goals ensure student involvement in the learning process.

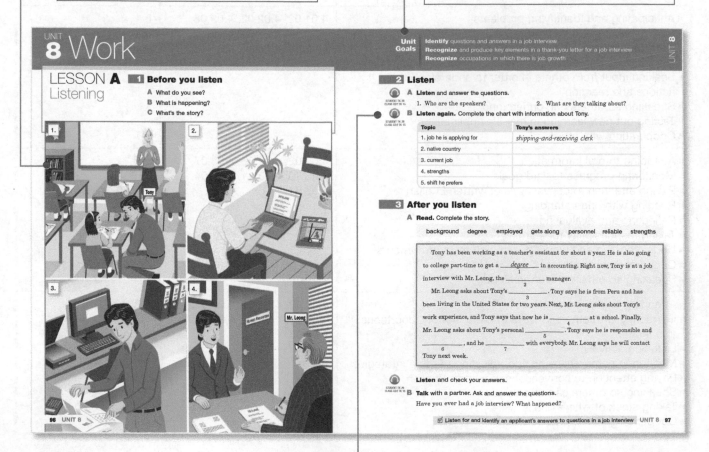

Two Different Audio Programs

- Class audio features over 100 minutes of listening practice and improves listening comprehension.
- Self-study audio encourages learner persistence and autonomy.
- Easy navigation between the two with clear track listings.

Grammar Chart

- Clear grammar charts with additional grammar reference in the back of the book allow for greater teacher flexibility.

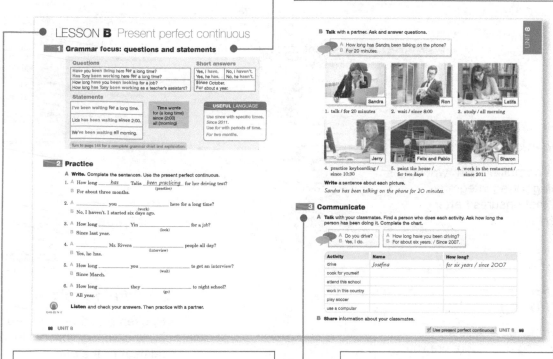

Natural Progression

- Students gain fluency and confidence by moving from guided practice to communicative activities.

Real-life Practice

- Meaningful application of the grammar allows for better student engagement.

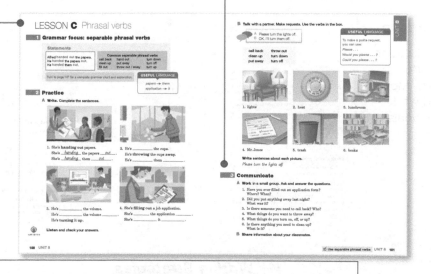

Every unit has two grammar lessons that follow the same structure.

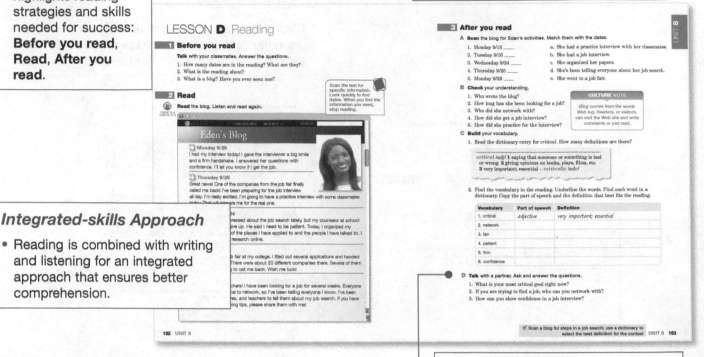
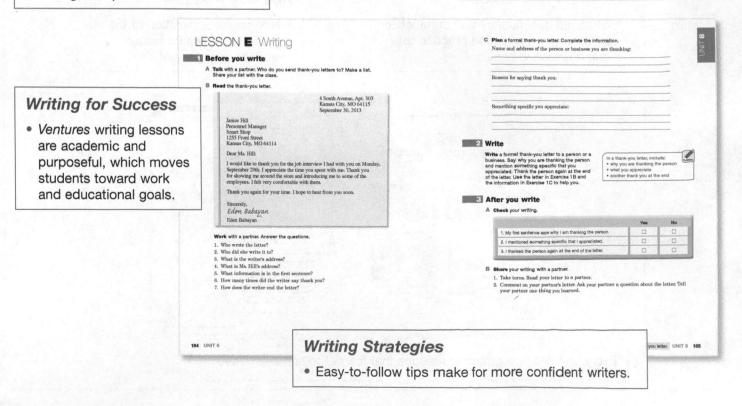

Document Literacy

- Explicit practice with authentic-type documents builds real-life skills.

Grammar Connections

- Contrasting two grammar forms in a communicative way helps with grammar accuracy.

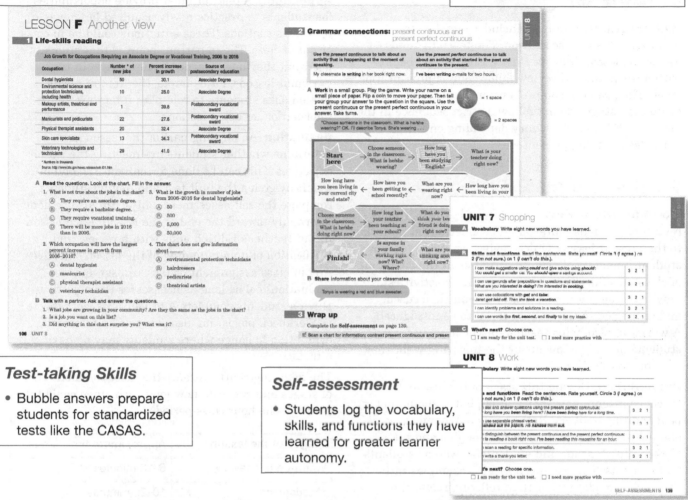

Test-taking Skills

- Bubble answers prepare students for standardized tests like the CASAS.

Self-assessment

- Students log the vocabulary, skills, and functions they have learned for greater learner autonomy.

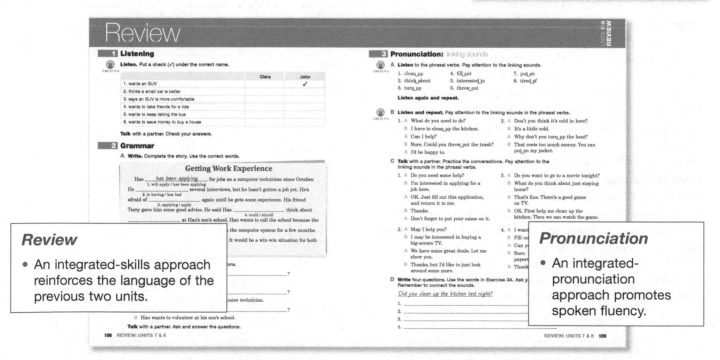

Review

- An integrated-skills approach reinforces the language of the previous two units.

Pronunciation

- An integrated-pronunciation approach promotes spoken fluency.

Features of the Teacher's Edition

Introduction

Ventures Teacher's Edition includes step-by-step teaching notes for each lesson. The teaching notes divide the lesson into six stages. Each lesson begins with a warm-up and review followed by a presentation stage. The practice, comprehension, application, and evaluation stages do not follow a strict sequence in the Teacher's Edition. They vary depending on the content of the lesson being presented.

Stages of a lesson

Warm-up and review Each lesson begins with a review of previous material and connects that material to the present lesson. Quick review activities prompt students' memory. Warm-up activities at the beginning of class introduce the new lesson. These activities may take many forms, but they are quick, focused, and connected to the new material to be introduced. A warm-up also helps teachers ascertain what students already know about the topic and what they are able to say.

Presentation During this stage of the lesson, the teacher presents new information, but it should not be a one-way delivery. Rather, it is a dynamic process of student input and interaction – a give-and-take between the teacher and students as well as students and students. The teacher may give examples rather than rules, model rather than tell, and relate the material to students' experiences.

Practice It is important that students have enough time to practice. A comfortable classroom environment needs to be created so that students are not afraid to take risks. The practice needs to be varied and interesting. There should be a progression from guided to independent practice. In the *Ventures* grammar lessons, for example, practice begins with mechanical aspects such as form, moves to a focus on meaning, and ends with communicative interactions.

Comprehension check Asking, "Do you understand?" is not enough to ascertain whether students are following the lesson. The teacher must ask concrete questions and have students demonstrate that they understand. In this stage, students are asked to repeat information in their own words. Students are also invited to come to the board or to interact with other students in some way.

Application A teacher must provide opportunities for students to practice newly-acquired language in realistic situations. These situations could be in class or out of class. The important point is that students use what they have learned in new ways. In the grammar lessons, for example, the Communicate section asks students to role-play, interview, share information, or ask questions.

Evaluation An ongoing part of the lesson is to determine whether students are meeting the lesson objectives. This can be done formally at the end of a unit by giving the unit test and having students complete the self-assessment, but it can also be done informally toward the end of the lesson. Each lesson in the Teacher's Edition ends with a review and verification of understanding of the lesson objectives. Any in-class assignment or task can serve as an evaluation tool as long as it assesses the objectives. Having students complete Add Ventures worksheets or Workbook pages can also serve as an informal evaluation to gauge where students may be having difficulty.

The following chart presents the most common order of stages and suggests how long each stage could take within a one-hour class period.

Stages of the lesson	Approximate time range
Warm-up and review	5–10 minutes
Presentation	10–20 minutes
Practice	15–20 minutes
Comprehension check	5–10 minutes
Application	15–20 minutes
Evaluation	10–15 minutes

The Teacher's Edition includes:

- Interleaved Student's Book pages with answers
- Lesson objectives and step-by-step teaching instructions
- Expansion activities, extra teaching tips, and culture notes
- Activities to encourage learner persistence and community building
- Tests, games, self-assessments, and projects
- Ideas for multilevel classroom management
- Class audio listening scripts
- An assessment CD-ROM with test audio and customizable tests.

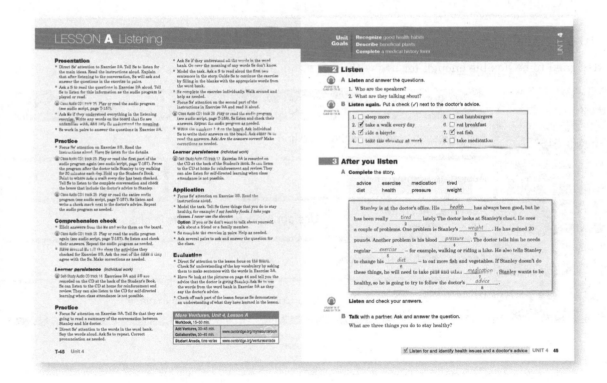

End-of-unit activities

Ventures provides several resources to help wrap up a unit:

The **Self-assessment** referenced at the end of Lesson F and available in the Online Teacher's Resource Room www.cambridge.org/myresourceroom as well as in the back of the Student's Book can be used in several ways:

- To identify any needs for additional practice before the unit test.
- For portfolio assessment. Print out copies for each student and keep completed self-assessments in a folder.
- For pre- and post-assessment. Print out two self-assessments for each student. Have students complete one before beginning and another after finishing the unit.

The **Projects** are another useful tool and a fun way to wrap up a unit. They are in the back of the Teacher's Edition and can be found on the Online Teacher's Resource Room.

The **Unit Tests** are a third end-of-unit activity. They are available at the back of this book. In addition, customizable unit tests can be found on the Assessment Audio CD / CD-ROM included in the back of this book.

Class time guidelines

Ventures is designed to be flexible enough for use with one-, two-, and three-hour classes.

Component	One-hour class	Two-hour class	Three-hour class
Student's Book	Follow lesson plan in Teacher's Edition		
Workbook	Assign as homework		Use in class
Add Ventures	Assign appropriate worksheets as homework	Use appropriate worksheets in class	
Student Arcade	Assign for lab or homework		
Online Teacher's Resource Room		Use Collaborative Activities in class	

Gretchen Bitterlin has been an ESL teacher and an ESL department chair. She is currently the ESL coordinator for the Continuing Education Program at San Diego Community College District. Under Gretchen's leadership, the ESL program has developed several products – for example, an ESL oral interview placement test and writing rubrics for assessing writing for level exit – now used by other agencies. She is a co-author of *English for Adult Competency*, has been an item writer for CASAS tests, and chaired the task force that developed the TESOL *Adult Education Program Standards*. She is a recipient of her district's award, Outstanding Contract Faculty. Gretchen holds an MA in TESOL from the University of Arizona.

Dennis Johnson had his first language-teaching experience as a Peace Corps volunteer in South Korea. Following that teaching experience, he became an in-country ESL trainer. After returning to the United States, he became an ESL trainer and began teaching credit and non-credit ESL at City College of San Francisco. As ESL site coordinator, he has provided guidance to faculty in selecting textbooks. He is the author of *Get Up and Go* and co-author of *The Immigrant Experience*. Dennis is the demonstration teacher on the *Ventures Professional Development DVD*. Dennis holds an MA in music from Stanford University.

Donna Price began her ESL career teaching EFL in Madagascar. She is currently associate professor of ESL and vocational ESL / technology resource instructor for the Continuing Education Program, San Diego Community College District. She has served as an author and a trainer for CALPRO, the California Adult Literacy Professional Development Project, co-authoring training modules on contextualizing and integrating workforce skills into the ESL classroom. She is a recipient of the TESOL Newbury House Award for Excellence in Teaching, and she is author of *Skills for Success*. Donna holds an MA in linguistics from San Diego State University.

Sylvia Ramirez started as an instructional aide in ESL. Since then she has been a part-time teacher, a full-time teacher, and a program coordinator. As program coordinator at Mira Costa College, she provided leadership in establishing Managed Enrollment, Student Learning Outcomes, and Transitioning Adults to Academic and Career Preparation. Her more than forty years in adult ESL includes multilevel ESL, vocational ESL, family literacy, and distance learning. She has also provided technical assistance to local ESL programs for the California State Department of Education. In 2011 she received the Hayward Award in education. Her MA is in education / counseling from Point Loma University, and she has certificates in TESOL and in online teaching.

K. Lynn Savage first taught English in Japan. She began teaching ESL at City College of San Francisco in 1974, where she has taught all levels of non-credit ESL and has served as vocational ESL resource teacher. She has trained teachers for adult education programs around the country as well as abroad. She chaired the committee that developed *ESL Model Standards for Adult Education Programs* (California, 1992) and is the author, co-author, and editor of many ESL materials including *Crossroads Café, Teacher Training through Video, Parenting for Academic Success, Building Life Skills, Picture Stories, May I Help You?*, and *English That Works*. Lynn holds an MA in TESOL from Teachers College, Columbia University.

Welcome

1 Meet your classmates

A Look at the pictures. What do you see?

B What are the people doing?

1.

2.

My Goal: _____

Steps to reach my goal:

1. _____
2. _____
3. _____

Lesson objectives

- Ask and answer questions about personal information
- Introduce a partner to the class

Warm-up

- Before class. Write today's lesson focus on the board.
  Welcome unit:
  Ask and answer questions
  Introduce your partner to the class
- Begin class. Books closed. Say: *Welcome to English class.*
- Introduce yourself to the class. Write your name on the board. Point to it. Tell Ss your name and ask them to repeat it. Tell Ss where you are from and anything else of interest you would like to add, for example: *I have a pet turtle.* or *I like to read.*
- Ask Ss to introduce themselves briefly to the class. Encourage them to say their names, where they are from, and anything else they wish to add.

> ▼ **Teaching tip**
> If any Ss feel uncomfortable or unable to add extra information to their introduction, don't force them. Ss can share more information later as they become more familiar with the teacher and one another.

Presentation

- Books open. Set the scene. Hold up the Student's Book. Show Ss the three pictures on page 2. Ask Ss: *What do you see?* Elicit and write on the board any vocabulary that Ss know, such as: *classroom, students, poster, teacher.*
- Direct Ss' attention to Exercise **1B**. Read the question aloud. Hold up the Student's Book. Point to the teacher. Ask: *What is she doing?* Elicit an appropriate answer, for example: *She is talking.* or *She's giving a lecture.* Point to the Ss. Ask: *What are they doing?* Elicit an appropriate answer, for example: *They're listening.*
- Ss in pairs. Tell Ss to continue the exercise by pointing to people in the picture and asking questions about what they are doing. Walk around and help as needed.
- Ask several pairs to ask and answer the questions for the rest of the class.

> ▼ **Teaching tip**
> It might be helpful to review the different forms of present continuous questions in Exercise **1B**. Write *he, she,* and *they* on the board. Ask Ss to tell you the question forms using these pronouns. Write the questions on the board: *What is he doing? What is she doing? What are they doing?*

Expansion activity (whole group)

- Point to people in the picture and ask more questions, or encourage Ss to think of more questions to ask about the picture.
- Call on Ss individually or put Ss in pairs to ask and answer additional questions, such as: *Who are they? Where are they? What are they studying? Where are they from? What will they do after class?*

Comprehension check

- Hold up the Student's Book. Ask Ss *Yes / No* questions about people's actions in the picture. Encourage Ss not to answer with single-word answers *Yes* or *No,* but to use the short forms, such as: *Yes, she is. No, she isn't. Yes, they are. No, they aren't.*

  Point to the teacher. Ask: *Is she walking?* (No, she isn't.) Point to the Ss writing their goals. Ask: *Are they talking?* (No, they aren't.)

Expansion activity (whole group)

- Direct Ss' attention to the Career Map. Tell Ss that the map shows a visual image of the different components of career exploration. Ask Ss to discuss their educational and career path goals in pairs. Ss share their partner's answers with the class.

Learner persistence (group work)

- If possible, take your Ss to the school library. Explain how to use the library. This will make Ss feel more comfortable, and it will show them a place for independent learning.

Welcome

Warm-up

- Write on the board: *Goals*. Point to the word. Say it aloud. Ask Ss to repeat. Ask: *What are "goals"?* Elicit an appropriate response, such as: *"Goals" are things you want to do in the future*.
- Tell Ss one of your goals for the future, for example: *I want to learn another language*. Write *want to* and *need to* on the board. Tell Ss that we often use these words when talking about goals. *Want to* tells the goal. *Need to* tells the steps to take to reach the goal. Say: *I want to learn another language. What do I need to do?* Elicit an appropriate response, for example: *You need to go to language classes or visit another country*.
- Ask Ss to give examples of their goals using the words *want to* and *need to*.

Practice

- Direct Ss' attention to Exercise **2A**. Tell Ss they are going to hear a conversation between Silvia and her classmate.
- ⊙ Class Audio CD1 track 2 Play or read the audio program (see audio script, page T-155). Ask Ss if they understood all or most of the words in the conversation. If Ss have questions about particular words, write them on the board.
- Tell Ss to listen to the conversation again and write the correct verbs in the blanks. Ss complete the exercise individually as they listen.
- Direct Ss' attention to the second part of Exercise **2A**. Read the instructions aloud. Play or read the audio program. Ss listen and check their answers. Repeat the audio program as needed.

  Write the numbers *1–6* on the board. Ask individual Ss to come to the board to write their answers.

Learner persistence *(individual work)*

- ⊙ Self-Study Audio CD track 2 Exercise **2A** is recorded on the CD at the back of the Student's Book. Ss can listen to the CD at home for reinforcement and review. They can also listen to the CD for self-directed learning when class attendance is not possible.
- Focus Ss' attention on Exercise **2B**. Read the instructions aloud.
- Model the task. Ask a S to read aloud the example sentences about Vinh below the chart and to complete the sentence that begins: *Second, he needs to . . .*

- Ss complete the exercise in pairs. Help as needed.
- Ask two Ss to talk to the class about Vinh's and Sofiya's goals.

Application

- Direct Ss' attention to Exercise **2C**. Read the instructions aloud.
- Model the task. Think of a goal that you have. Ask a S to ask you the example questions. Answer the questions for the class, for example: *I want to learn Japanese. First, I need to take a Japanese class. Second, I need to study hard. Third, I need to practice speaking Japanese with students from Japan*.
- Hold up the Student's Book. Point to the chart. Tell Ss to take notes on their partner's answers. Guide them to write the answers in short form in the chart. Remind them that short form means not using complete sentences.
- Ss complete the activity in pairs. Help as needed.
- Ask several pairs to ask and answer the questions for the class.

  Option Draw a chart on the board. Ask one S to ask a partner questions. Write the answers in the chart.

Community building *(whole class)*

- Call out the names of two Ss. Ask them to say one thing they learned about each other that both Ss feel comfortable in sharing. Continue with as many Ss as time allows.

Evaluation

- Direct Ss' attention to the lesson focus on the board.
- Write on the board *past, present continuous, present,* and *future*. Ask Ss to give you examples of sentences in each of these verb forms.
- Ask several Ss in the class to tell you a goal using *want to*. Have them use *need to* to tell you one step they will take toward achieving this goal.
- Check off each part of the lesson focus as Ss demonstrate an understanding of what they have learned in the lesson.

2 Goals

A **Listen.** Silvia is talking about her goals with a classmate. Write the three steps that Silvia needs to take to reach her goals.

Main goal: She ___*wants to open*___ her own beauty salon someday.
1. want / open

Steps to take to reach the goal:

First, she ___*needs to go*___ to beauty school for two years. Second, she
2. need / go

___*needs to take*___ an exam to get her license. Third, she ___*needs to work*___ in a
3. need / take   4. need / work

salon to get experience. She ___*hopes to become*___ a business owner in five years
5. hope / become

because she ___*doesn't want to work*___ for anyone else.
6. not want / work

Listen again. Check your answers.

B **Work** with a partner. Talk about Vinh and Sofiya.

Name	Wants to . . .	Needs to . . .
Vinh	open a restaurant	1. learn to cook 2. take business classes 3. work in a restaurant
Sofiya	get a GED	1. improve her English 2. go to night school 3. take the GED test

Vinh wants to open a restaurant. First, he needs to learn how to cook. Second, he needs to . . .

C **Talk** with a partner. Complete the chart. Ask and answer questions about goals.

I want to . . .	I need to . . .		
(Answers will vary.)	1.	2.	3.

A What do you want to do?
B I want to . . .

A What steps do you need to take?
B First, I need to . . .

Share information with your classmates.

3 Verb tense review (present and present continuous)

STUDENT TK 3
CLASS CD1 TK 3

A Listen to each sentence. Check (✓) the correct column.

	Present	Present continuous			Present	Present continuous
1.	✓			6.	✓	
2.	✓			7.	✓	
3.		✓		8.		✓
4.		✓		9.	✓	
5.		✓		10.		✓

Listen again. Check your answers.

B Read. Complete the story. Use the present or present continuous.

Oksana Petrova _____*is*_____ from Russia. She _____*is living*_____ in
       1. be   2. live

Philadelphia right now. She _____*works*_____ at an elementary school. She
                                  3. work

_____*has*_____ a job as a teacher's assistant. She _____*is working*_____ at the
    4. have   5. work

school right now. She _____*is helping*_____ the students with math at the moment.
                              6. help

Oksana _____*wants*_____ to become a teacher in the U.S. She
                   7. want

_____*studies*_____ English every evening. She _____*plans*_____ to take
    8. study   9. plan

elementary education classes at the community college next year. She

_____*is saving*_____ her money right now, because college classes are very
    10. save

expensive. She also _____*is looking*_____ for another part-time job. She
                          11. look

_____*needs*_____ to pay her bills every month.
    12. need

STUDENT TK 4
CLASS CD1 TK 4

Listen and check your answers.

C Talk with a partner. Ask and answer questions.

Every day	Every week	Right now	At the moment
What do you do every day?	What do you do every week?	What are you doing right now?	What are you studying at the moment?
Do you go to school every day?	Do you do homework every week?	Are you working right now?	Are you living in an apartment at the moment?

Lesson objectives

- Review present and present continuous verb forms
- Read and talk about goals
- Review past and future verb forms

Warm-up and review

- Before class. Write today's lesson focus on the board.

  Welcome unit:
  Review verb forms
  Read and talk about goals

- Write *present* and *present continuous* on the board. Ask Ss when we use the present tense. Elicit answers, such as: *For things we do regularly / always / every day.* Write Ss' answers on the board.

- Ask Ss when we use the present continuous tense. Elicit answer: *For things we are doing right now / at this minute.* Write Ss' answers on the board.

- Describe yourself in the present tense. For example: *I am a teacher. I have two books.* Ask volunteer Ss to describe themselves in the present tense.

- Write Ss' answers on the board, and describe this action in the present continuous. Say: *I am writing on the board.* Ensure Ss understand the difference between the two tenses.

Presentation

- Books open. Direct Ss' attention to Exercise **3A**. Read the instructions aloud.

- Class Audio CD1 track 3 Model the task. On the board, draw a chart similar to the one in Exercise **3A**. Play or read the audio program for number 1 (see audio script, page T-155). Pause the audio program after the first sentence. Point to the chart on the board. Ask: *Which column should I check?* (Present.)

- Hold up the Student's Book. Point to the check mark in the *Present* column in number 1. Say: *Listen and check the correct column for the rest of the sentences.*

- Class Audio CD1 track 3 Play or read the rest of the audio program (see audio script, page T-155). Ss listen and complete the exercise individually.

- Focus Ss' attention on the second part of Exercise **3A**. Read the instruction aloud.

- Class Audio CD1 track 3 Play or read the audio program again (see audio script, page T-155). Ss listen and check their answers.

- Class Audio CD1 track 3 Play or read the audio program (see audio script, page T-155). Pause the program after each sentence. Ask: *Which column did you check?*

Learner persistence (individual work)

- Self-Study Audio CD track 3 Exercise **3A** is recorded on the CD at the back of the Student's Book. Ss can listen to the CD at home for reinforcement and review. They can also listen for self-directed learning when class attendance is not possible.

Practice

- Direct Ss' attention to Exercise **3B**. Read the instructions aloud.

- Model the task. Ask a S to read the first sentence aloud.

- Ss complete the exercise individually. Help as needed.

- Direct Ss' attention to the second part of the instructions for Exercise **3B**.

- Class Audio CD1 track 4 Play or read the audio program (see audio script, page T-155). Ss listen and check their answers.

  Option Write the numbers *1–12* on the board. Ask Ss to come to the board to write their answers.

Learner persistence (individual work)

- Self-Study Audio CD track 4 Exercise **3B** is recorded on the CD at the back of the Student's Book. Ss can listen to the CD at home for reinforcement and review. They can also listen for self-directed learning when class attendance is not possible.

Application

- Focus Ss' attention on Exercise **3C**. Read the instructions aloud.

- Model the task. Ask for a volunteer to answer the questions.

- Ss complete the exercise in pairs. Make sure that Ss use the correct tense when responding.

Warm-up and review

- Write *past* and *future* on the board. Ask Ss when we use the past tense. Elicit answers, such as: *For things we did in the past / last year / last week*. Write Ss' answers on the board.

- Ask Ss when we use the future tense. Elicit answers, such as: *For things we are planning to do in the future / tomorrow / next year*. Write Ss' answers on the board.

- Describe something you did in the past, for example: *I traveled to Mexico last year*. Tell Ss to write two sentences about themselves in the past tense. Ss share their sentences with a partner.

- Describe a goal you have using the future tense, for example: *I will learn to play the violin*. Tell Ss to write two goals for themselves in the future tense. Ss share their sentences with a new partner.

Presentation

- Books open. Direct Ss' attention to Exercise **4A**. Read the instructions aloud.

- Class Audio CD1 track 5 Model the task. On the board, draw a chart similar to the one in Exercise **4A**. Play or read the audio program for number 1 (see audio script, page T-155). Pause the audio program after the first sentence. Point to the chart on the board. Ask: *Which column should I check?* (Past.)

- Hold up the Student's Book. Point to the check mark in the *Past* column in number 1. Say: *Listen and check the correct column for the rest of the sentences.*

- Class Audio CD1 track 5 Play or read the rest of the audio program (see audio script, page T-155). Ss listen and complete the exercise individually.

- Class Audio CD1 track 5 Play or read the audio program (see audio script, page T-155). Pause the program after each sentence. Ask Ss: *Which column did you check?*

- Direct Ss' attention to Exercise **4B**. Read the instruction aloud. Read the time phrases in the box aloud. Ask Ss to repeat. Ensure Ss understand the time phrases.

- Class Audio CD1 track 5 Play or read the audio program (see audio script, page T-155). Ss listen and circle the time phrases they hear. Ask Ss: *Which time phrases did you hear?*

- Ss then write the time phrases in the correct columns. Check answers with the class.

Learner persistence (individual work)

- Self-Study Audio CD track 5 Exercises **4A** and **4B** are recorded on the CD at the back of the Student's Book. Ss can listen to the CD at home for reinforcement and review. They can also listen to the CD for self-directed learning when class attendance is not possible.

Practice

- Direct Ss' attention to Exercise **4C**. Read the instructions aloud.

- Model the task. Ask a S to read the first sentence aloud.

- Ss complete the exercise individually. Help as needed. Check answers with the class.

Comprehension check

- Class Audio CD1 track 6 Play or read the audio program (see audio script, page T-155). Ss listen and check their answers

- Ask Ss to read the questions and answers in pairs. Ask other Ss if the answers are correct. Make corrections as needed.

Learner persistence (individual work)

- Self-Study Audio CD track 6 Exercise **4C** is recorded on the CD at the back of the Student's Book. Ss can listen to the CD at home for reinforcement and review. They can also listen to the CD for self-directed learning when class attendance is not possible.

Application

- Focus Ss' attention on exercise **4D**. Read the instructions aloud.

- Model the task. Ask two Ss to read the questions in Exercise **4D**.

- Ss read and answer the questions in pairs. Ask Ss to share information they learned about their classmates.

Evaluation

- Direct Ss attention to the lesson focus on the board.

- Write on the board *past* and *future*. Ask Ss to give you examples of sentences in each of those verb forms.

- Check off each part of the lesson focus as Ss demonstrate an understanding of what they have learned in the lesson.

4 Verb tense review (past and future)

STUDENT TK 5
CLASS CD1 TK 5

A **Listen** to each sentence. Check (✓) the correct column.

	Past	Future		Past	Future
1.	✓		6.	✓	
2.	✓		7.		✓
3.	✓		8.	✓	
4.		✓	9.		✓
5.		✓	10.		✓

STUDENT TK 5
CLASS CD1 TK 5

B **Listen again.** Circle the time phrases you hear. Then write them in the correct column.

(in 2005)   last night   (last year)   (next month)   (next year)   soon

Past	Future
in 2005	next month
last year	next year

C **Write.** Complete the sentences. Use the past or future.

1. **A** When ___did___ you ___move___ to this city?
(move)

   B I ___moved___ here in 2011.
(move)

2. **A** How long ___will___ you ___stay___ here?
(stay)

   B Maybe I ___will___ ___stay___ here for one more year.
(stay)

3. **A** Where ___did___ you ___live___ before you moved here?
(live)

   B I ___lived___ in Taiwan.
(live)

4. **A** How long ___will___ you ___study___ English in the future?
(study)

   B I ___will___ ___study___ English for two more years.
(study)

Listen and check your answers.

STUDENT TK 6
CLASS CD1 TK 6

D **Talk** with your classmates. Ask and answer the questions.

1. When did you move to this city?
2. How long will you stay here?
3. Where did you live before you moved here?
4. How long will you study English?

LESSON A
Listening

1 Before you listen

A What do you see?

B What is happening?

C What's the story?

...ctives
...nts to the topic
...students know about the topic
...it by talking about the pictures
...vocabulary
...ening skills

...-up and review

...re class. Write today's lesson focus on the board.

...sson A:
...Different personality types
Describe personality types and personal interests

- Begin class. Books closed. Point to *personality types* in the lesson focus. Say the words aloud. Ask Ss to repeat. Ask: *What are some examples of different personality types?* If Ss don't know, give them some examples, such as: *friendly, shy, outgoing, nervous, quiet,* etc. On the board, write these words and any other examples that Ss brainstorm.

- Point to each word on the board. Say it aloud. Ask Ss to repeat. Make sure that all Ss understand the meaning of each word.

- Ask: *What's your personality type? Are you _____?* (Point to each word on the board in turn.) Ss can say *Yes* or *No* in response.

> **Teaching tip**
> Explain the difference between *going out* and *outgoing*. Tell Ss that *going out* is a verb, that means to do something outside the house and *outgoing* is an adjective that describes a person who is very friendly and not shy.

Presentation

- Books open. Set the scene. Direct Ss' attention to the pictures on page 6. Ask the question from Exercise **1A**: *What do you see?* Elicit and write on the board any vocabulary that Ss know, such as: *club, Fernando, Danny, band, dancing, people.*

- Point to each of the words on the board. Say the word aloud and ask Ss to repeat. Hold up the Student's Book and point to the parts of the pictures that correspond to the words.

- Direct Ss' attention to the question in Exercise **1B**. Read it aloud. Ask individual Ss to describe what is happening in the picture. Elicit appropriate responses, such as: *Fernando is dancing. Danny is at home.*

Practice

- Direct Ss' attention to Exercise **1C**. Ask a S to read the question aloud. Tell Ss that as a class they are going to tell a story about Fernando and Danny.

- Model the task. Ask individual Ss to tell you sentences about Danny and Fernando. Write Ss' sentences on the board. Create a story with Ss' ideas, for example: *Fernando is outgoing. He's dancing at a nightclub. Danny is shy. He's at home.*, etc. Elicit as many ideas as possible. Tell Ss that this is a speaking and listening exercise and they are not expected to write the story.

- When the story is finished, ask Ss to read the sentences aloud. Correct Ss' pronunciation.

- Erase key words in the story on the board – for example, all the verbs. Ask Ss to try to tell the story by including the missing words.

- Gradually, erase more words until the story is written in skeletal form on the board. Ask if any Ss can remember the missing sentences.

- Finally, erase all the words. Ask pairs to retell the story using their own words. Help as needed.

- Ask Ss to tell you a summary. Explain that in a summary, Ss will say only the most important parts of the story, not the unimportant details. Let Ss know that they will see an example of a summary on the second page of this lesson.

- Write *summary* on the board. Point to the word and say it aloud. Explain that writing a summary is an important skill that Ss will practice many times in the Student's Book.

Expansion activity (student pairs)

- Tell Ss to make up a phone conversation that Fernando and Danny are having the day after the scene in the opening pictures.

- Model the activity. Ask Ss to come up with the beginning of the conversation as a class. Write the beginning of the conversation on the board.

- Ss finish the conversation in pairs.

- Ask several Ss to role-play the conversation for the class.

> **Teaching tip**
> Explain to Ss that each unit is set up in a similar way. Lesson A begins with Ss' talking about a story that is shown in pictures. Then Ss listen to a conversation between the characters in the pictures. Later, Ss practice new vocabulary learned from the story and read a summary of the important events in the pictures.

Presentation

- Direct Ss' attention to Exercise **2A**. Tell Ss that they are going to hear a conversation between Danny and Fernando, the young men who are pictured on page 6. Explain that after listening to the conversation, Ss will ask and answer the questions in the exercise in pairs.
- Ask a S to read aloud the questions in Exercise **2A**. Tell Ss to listen for this information as the audio program is played or read.

Practice

- Class Audio CD1 track 7 Play or read the audio program (see audio script, page T-155). Ask Ss if they understood all or most of the words in the conversation. If Ss have questions about particular words, write the words on the board. Tell Ss to listen to the conversation again to try to guess the meaning of the new words from context.
- Ss ask and answer the questions in Exercise **2A** in pairs. Repeat the audio program as needed.
- Check answers. Ask Ss the two questions in Exercise **2A**. Elicit appropriate responses.
- Direct Ss' attention to Exercise **2B**. Read the instructions aloud. Model the task. Hold up the Student's Book. Ask: *Who is tired this morning?* (Fernando) Point to the check mark under Fernando. Say: *Check the correct name for each description.*
- Class Audio CD1 track 7 Play or read the audio program (see audio script, page T-155). Ss complete the exercise individually as they listen.

Comprehension check

- Draw on the board the chart from Exercise **2B**.
- Ask several Ss to come to the board to check the boxes in the chart, indicating their answers.
- Class Audio CD1 track 7 Play or read the audio program again (see audio script, page T-155). Ss listen and check their answers.

Learner persistence (individual work)

- Self-Study Audio CD track 7 Exercises **2A** and **2B** are recorded on the CD at the back of the Student's Book. Ss can listen to the CD at home for reinforcement and review. They can also listen to the CD for self-directed learning when class attendance is not possible.

Practice

- Focus Ss' attention on Exercise **3A**. Read the instructions aloud. Tell Ss that the story in this exercise is a summary of the conversation in Exercises **2A** and **2B**.

- Direct Ss' attention to the words or phra[ses in the] bank. Say each word or phrase aloud. Ask Ss [to repeat.] Correct pronunciation as needed.
- Ask Ss if they know the meaning of each word i[n the] word bank. Explain any new words.
- Model Exercise **3A**. Ask a S to read aloud the first [two] sentences in the story.
- Ss complete the exercise individually. Help as needed.
- Class Audio CD1 track 8 Play or read the audio program (see audio script, page T-155). Ss listen and check their answers. Repeat the audio program as needed.
- Write the numbers *1–8* on the board. Ask individual Ss to come to the board to write their answers.

Learner persistence (individual work)

- Self-Study Audio CD track 8 Exercise **3A** is recorded on the CD at the back of the Student's Book. Ss can listen to the CD at home for reinforcement and review. They can also listen for self-directed learning when class attendance is not possible.

Application

- Focus Ss' attention on Exercise **3B**. Read the instructions aloud.
- Model the task. Ask a S the two questions in the exercise. Have Ss listen to the answers.
- Ss complete the exercise in pairs. Help as needed.

Evaluation

- Direct Ss' attention to the lesson focus on the board. Ask individual Ss to tell you about Fernando's and Danny's likes and dislikes and to think of words to describe their personalities. Ask other Ss to tell you about their own personal interests and personality types.
- Check off each part of the lesson focus as Ss demonstrate an understanding of what they have learned in the lesson.

More Ventures, Unit 1, Lesson A	
Workbook, 20–30 min.	
Add Ventures, 30–45 min. **Collaborative,** 30–45 min.	www.cambridge.org/myresourceroom
Student Arcade, time varies	www.cambridge.org/venturesarcade

Unit Goals	Identify personality types
	Describe likes and interests
	Interpret personal ads

2 Listen

STUDENT TK 7
CLASS CD1 TK 7

A **Listen** and answer the questions.

1. Who are the speakers?   2. What are they talking about?

STUDENT TK 7
CLASS CD1 TK 7

B **Listen again.** Put a check (✓) under the correct name.

	Fernando	Danny
1. is tired this morning	✓	
2. likes staying home		✓
3. worked on his car		✓
4. Is outgoing	✓	
5. went out with his girlfriend	✓	
6. wants a girlfriend		✓

3 After you listen

A **Read.** Complete the story.

alone	dislikes	going out	party animal
dance club	enjoys	outgoing	shy

> Fernando and Danny are talking about their weekend. Fernando is a very friendly and ___*outgoing*___ person. He ___*enjoys*___ dancing. Last night, he went to a
> $\quad\quad$ 1 $\quad\quad\quad\quad\quad\quad\quad\quad$ 2
> ___*dance club*___ and stayed until late. Danny thinks Fernando is a _*party animal*_ .
> $\quad$ 3 $\quad\quad\quad\quad\quad\quad\quad\quad\quad\quad\quad\quad\quad\quad\quad\quad\quad\quad\quad\quad\quad\quad$ 4
>
> Danny is different from Fernando. He is ___*shy*___ and quiet. He ___*dislikes*___
> $\quad\quad\quad\quad\quad\quad\quad\quad\quad\quad\quad\quad\quad\quad\quad$ 5 $\quad\quad\quad\quad\quad\quad\quad\quad\quad\quad$ 6
> dancing. Danny was home ___*alone*___ the whole weekend. He likes staying at
> $\quad\quad\quad\quad\quad\quad\quad\quad\quad\quad\quad\quad\quad$ 7
> home more than ___*going out*___ . He wants a girlfriend who likes staying home, too.
> $\quad\quad\quad\quad\quad\quad\quad\quad$ 8

STUDENT TK 8
CLASS CD1 TK 8

Listen and check your answers.

B **Talk** with a partner. Ask and answer the questions.

1. What are some things you enjoy doing on the weekend?

2. Are you outgoing or shy? Give some examples.

☑ Listen for activities and adjectives that describe personalities   **UNIT 1**   **7**

LESSON **B** Verbs + gerunds

1 Grammar focus: questions and statements

Yes/No questions	Short answers
Do you **enjoy dancing**?	Yes, I **do**.
Does he **like staying** home?	No, he **doesn't**.

Statements	Negatives
I **love dancing**.	He **doesn't like dancing**.
He **hates staying** home.	I **don't mind staying** home.

Gerunds often follow these verbs:
dislike	hate	love
enjoy	like	mind

Turn to page 141 for a complete grammar chart and explanation.

Turn to page 141 for a complete grammar chart and explanation.

USEFUL LANGUAGE

Do you mind? = Does it bother you?
I don't mind. = It doesn't bother me.
* Don't say ~~I mind~~.

2 Practice

A Write. Complete the sentences. Use gerunds.

be	get	listen	play
do	go	pay	shop

1. Does Katrina like _____*shopping*_____ for clothes online?
2. My brother enjoys _____*playing*_____ soccer.
3. Mrs. Tanaka doesn't mind _____*getting*_____ up early.
4. I love _____*listening*_____ to the birds in the morning.
5. Do you mind _____*going*_____ to the movies by yourself?
6. Do you enjoy _____*being*_____ alone?
7. Most people don't enjoy _____*paying*_____ bills every month.
8. Winston dislikes _____*doing*_____ English homework.

Listen and check your answers.

CLASS CD1 TK 9

Lesson objectives
- Introduce verbs + gerunds
- Practice questions and statements
- Practice talking about likes and dislikes

Warm-up and review

Before class. Write today's lesson focus on the board.

Lesson B:
Verbs + gerunds
Likes and dislikes

- Books open. Begin class. Direct Ss' attention to the pictures on page 6. Ask questions about Fernando and Danny, such as: *Who is outgoing?* (Fernando.) *Who likes dancing?* (Fernando.) *Who is shy?* (Danny.) *Who likes staying home?* (Danny.)

- Divide the board into two columns with *Danny* and *Fernando* as headings. Ask Ss to brainstorm descriptions of the two young men. Write Ss' descriptions in the appropriate column, for example: Fernando: *outgoing, friendly, enjoys dancing*; Danny: *shy, likes staying home, wants a girlfriend.*

Presentation

Focus on meaning / personalize

- Books closed. Divide the board into two columns with *Enjoy doing* and *Dislike doing* as headings. Write one example in each column that is true for yourself, for example: Enjoy: *going to movies*; Dislike: *cleaning the house.* Say: *I enjoy going to movies. I dislike cleaning the house.*

- Explain that Ss will do a pantomime activity. Write *I enjoy ____*, and *I dislike ____.* on the board. Demonstrate one thing you enjoy by smiling and pantomiming the action, for example, *driving.* Have Ss guess the gerund (*driving*). After Ss guess correctly, say: *I enjoy driving.* Ask a S volunteer to pantomime an activity he or she likes and one he or she dislikes, and have the class guess the activities. After Ss guess correctly, reinforce the gerund by saying the complete sentence, for example: *Jian Yu enjoys playing volleyball.*

Focus on form

- Books open. Point to the gerunds in the two columns on the board. Say: *These are gerunds. Gerunds look like verbs. They are made up of the base form of a verb + -ing.* Gerunds often follow verbs that talk about preferences.

- Direct Ss' attention to the charts in Exercise **1**. Explain that gerunds are used in the same way as nouns, for example, as an object of a sentence. Point out *dancing* and *staying* as examples.

- Direct Ss' attention to the Yes / No questions and Short answers charts. Read each one aloud. Ask Ss to repeat. Direct Ss' attention to the Statements and Negatives charts. Read each one aloud. Ask Ss to repeat.

- Direct Ss' attention to the list of verbs that are often followed by gerunds. Read each verb. Ask Ss to repeat. Ask Ss to give you examples of gerunds with the verbs *hate, like, love,* and *mind.*

▼**Useful language**

Have Ss look at the Useful language box, and point out that the verb *mind* is only used in questions and negative statements. Tell Ss that not all verbs can be followed by gerunds.

Practice

- Focus Ss' attention on Exercise **2A**. Read the instructions aloud.

- Direct Ss' attention to the word bank. Say each verb. Ask Ss to repeat. Remind Ss that gerunds are formed by adding *-ing* to the base form of a verb.

- Model the task. Ask a S to read the first question aloud.

- Ss complete the exercise individually. Help as needed.

- Class Audio CD1 track 9 Play or read the complete audio program (see audio script, page T-155). Ss listen and check their answers.

LESSON B Verbs + gerunds

Presentation

- Direct Ss' attention to the pictures in Exercise **2B**. Ask Ss to look at picture 1. Ask: *What's happening?* Elicit an appropriate response, such as: *Liz and Fred are working in the garden.* Ask about each of the other pictures in turn. Elicit responses, such as: Picture 2, *Karl is taking out the garbage. He's not happy.*
- Read the instructions aloud. Model the task. Ask two Ss to read aloud the first example conversation. Check that they understand that they should use the cues under each picture. Ask two other Ss to read aloud the second example conversation.
- Ss complete the exercise in pairs. Help as needed.
- Have several pairs ask and answer the questions for the rest of the class.

Practice

- Read aloud the second part of the instructions for Exercise **2B**.
- Ask a S to read aloud the example sentence.
- Ss complete the exercise individually. Help as needed.
- Write the numbers *1–6* on the board. Ask Ss to come to the board to write their sentences.
- Ask different Ss to read the sentences aloud. Other Ss can correct them as needed.

Expansion activity *(student pairs)*

- Direct Ss' attention to the pictures and cues in Exercise **2B**. Have Ss ask their partners questions using these cues.
- Model the activity. Write on the board: *Do you _____?* *Yes, I do. / No, I don't.*
- Ask a S: *Do you love working in the garden?* Elicit a *Yes* or *No* response.
- Ss complete the exercise in pairs. Help as needed.
- Ask several pairs to ask and answer the questions for the rest of the class.

Application

- Direct Ss' attention to Exercise **3A** and read the instructions aloud.
- Model the task. Ask two Ss to read the example conversation aloud.

▼ Useful language

Read the Useful language box aloud. Ask Ss to repeat the example questions after you. Model the language. Say to a S: *I like reading magazines. What about you?* Elicit an appropriate response, such as: *I do, too. So do I.* or *I don't like reading magazines at all.* Say: *I don't like being alone. How about you?* Elicit an appropriate response, such as: *I don't either. Neither do I. I don't mind it. I like being alone.*

- Ss complete the exercise in small groups. Help as needed.
- Direct Ss' attention to Exercise **3B**. Read the instructions aloud.
- Model the task. Ask Ss what they learned about the people in their group in Exercise **3A**, for example: *Li likes surfing the Internet.*
- Continue the exercise by asking Ss to share information they learned about their classmates.

Evaluation

- Direct Ss' attention to the lesson focus on the board.
- Write on the board: *dislike, like, enjoy, love, hate,* and *mind.* Go around the room. Ask each S in turn to make a sentence about his or her likes or dislikes using the verbs on the board and a gerund.
- Check off each part of the lesson focus as Ss demonstrate an understanding of what they have learned in the lesson.

More Ventures, Unit 1, Lesson B	
Workbook, 20–30 min.	
Add Ventures, 30–45 min. **Collaborative,** 30–45 min.	www.cambridge.org/myresourceroom
Student Arcade, time varies	www.cambridge.org/venturesarcade

B Talk with a partner. Ask and answer questions about the pictures. Use gerunds.

> **A** Do Liz and Fred love working in the garden?
> **B** Yes, they do. They love working in the garden.

> **A** Does Karl enjoy taking out the garbage?
> **B** No, he doesn't. He doesn't enjoy taking out the garbage.

Liz and Fred

1. love / work in the garden

Karl

2. enjoy / take out the garbage

Ramon

3. like / go to the beach

Kim

4. dislike / stand in line

Nasim

5. mind / work out

Marissa and Ethan

6. hate / eat vegetables

Write a sentence about each picture.

Liz and Fred love working in the garden.
(Answers will vary.)

3 Communicate

A Work in a small group. Ask and answer questions about the activities.

> **A** Tam, do you like being alone?
> **B** I don't mind it. What about you?

- be alone
- dance
- learn languages

- surf the Internet
- play sports
- read magazines

- talk on the phone
- exercise
- clean the house

USEFUL LANGUAGE

Say *What about you?* OR *How about you?* to ask the same question someone asked you.

B Share information about your classmates.

LESSON C Comparisons

1 Grammar focus: *more than, less than, as much as*

Statements

I enjoy walking **more than** driving.
She likes cooking **less than** eating.
They enjoy singing **as much as** dancing.

Turn to page 147 for a complete grammar chart and explanation.

2 Practice

A Write. Complete the sentences. Use *more than, less than,* or *as much as.*

1. Sally enjoys cooking
   _____*more than*_____ washing
   dishes.

2. Sally likes washing dishes
   _____*less than*_____ cooking.

3. Alfredo loves listening to music
   _____*as much as*_____ playing an
   instrument.

4. Alfredo enjoys playing an instrument
   _____*as much as*_____ listening to
   music.

5. Pam likes working
   _____*less than*_____ going
   to school.

6. Pam enjoys going to school
   _____*more than*_____ working.

7. Marta enjoys painting
   _____*more than*_____ jogging.

8. Marta likes jogging
   _____*less than*_____ painting.

Listen and check your answers.

CLASS CD1 TK 10

Lesson objectives
- Introduce *more than, less than, as much as*
- Practice statements with comparisons

Warm-up and review
- Before class. Write today's lesson focus on the board.
  Lesson C:
  Comparing likes and dislikes
  More than, less than, as much as
- Books closed. Begin class. Write the following sentences on the board:
  I'm <u>cooking</u> dinner for my family tonight.
  I enjoy <u>cooking</u> dinner for my family.
  Ask Ss to look at the underlined words. Ask: *Which one is a gerund?* (the second one) *Why?* (The first one is a part of the verb *am cooking*. The second one is a gerund serving as a noun after the verb *enjoy*.)
- Write on the board: *dislike, enjoy, hate, like, love*. Ask individual Ss to make statements about their likes or dislikes using the verbs on the board and a gerund. Next, have individual Ss ask and answer questions using the same verbs and gerunds.

Presentation

Focus on meaning / personalize
- Books closed. Direct Ss' attention to the lesson focus on the board. Read it aloud. Demonstrate the meaning of *comparing*. Hold up two books of different sizes. Say: *This book is bigger than this book.*
- Write the following heading on the board: *Fun outdoor activities*. Elicit five or six outdoor activities, such as *walking in the park* and *playing soccer*, and write them on the board. Underline the *-ing* in each activity, and remind Ss that these are gerunds.
- Write on the board: *1 = don't like, 2 = like a little, 3 = like quite a lot, 4 = like very much*. Say that you are going to rate the activities on the board according to how much you enjoy them. Read each activity on the board and then rate it. Write the rating to the right of each activity.

- Summarize the information by pointing to the numbers and making three comparative sentences, such as: *I like playing soccer more than swimming. I enjoy jogging less than playing tennis. I like going on picnics as much as fishing.*
- Write the three sentences on the board, underlining *more than, less than,* and *as much as*. Explain that we use *more than, less than,* and *as much as* to compare nouns. Remind Ss that gerunds are often used as nouns.
- Books open. Direct Ss' attention to the Statements chart in Exercise **1**. Read each statement aloud. Have Ss repeat. For each sentence, ask Ss to identify the two activities being compared using the gerund form.

Practice

Focus on form
- Direct Ss' attention to the first picture in Exercise **2A**. Ask: *What is Sally doing?* (She's cooking.) *Does she look like she enjoys cooking?* (Yes.) Direct Ss' attention to the second picture. Ask: *What is Sally doing now?* (She's washing dishes.) *Does it look like she enjoys washing dishes?* (No.) Ask a S to read the example sentence.
- Continue asking questions about the other pictures.
- Read the instructions for Exercise **2A** aloud. Ss complete the exercise individually. Walk around and help as needed.

Comprehension check
- Read aloud the second part of the instructions for Exercise **2A**.
- Class Audio CD1 track 10 Play or read the audio program (see audio script, page T-155). Ss listen and check their answers.
- Ask four Ss to read the completed sentence pairs aloud.

LESSON C Comparisons

Presentation

- Books open. Direct Ss' attention to the pictures on page 6. Ask: *What does Fernando like doing?* (dancing, going to parties, talking to friends, etc.) Tell Ss that they are going to look at a bar graph that shows Fernando's interests.

- Write *bar graph* on the board. Point to the words and say them aloud. Direct Ss' attention to the bar graph in Exercise **2B**. Explain that this is an example of a bar graph. Hold up the Student's Book. Point to the numbers on the left side of the graph. Tell Ss that these numbers indicate how many hours per weekend Fernando does the activities listed below the graph.

- Focus Ss' attention on the activities at the bottom of the graph. Point to the bar above *socializing*. Say: *Fernando likes socializing a lot. He spends 8 hours per weekend socializing.* Point to the bar above *reading*. Say: *Fernando doesn't like reading very much. He spends only 1 hour per weekend reading. He likes reading less than socializing. He likes socializing more than reading.*

- Continue asking about the other activities. For example, *How many hours does he spend working out?*

- Read the instructions aloud. Model the task. Ask two Ss to read the example conversation to the class. Hold up the Student's Book. Point to the graph to show how *more than* is illustrated by the height of the bars.

▼ **Useful language**
Read the Useful language box aloud. Ask Ss to repeat the word *socializing*. Ask Ss who they socialize with outside of class. Check Ss' understanding by making sure that they answer the question appropriately.

Practice

- Ss complete Exercise **2B** in pairs. Walk around and help as needed.

- Ask several pairs to make sentences about Fernando's weekend activities. Have the second speaker in the pair say other expressions that mean *That's right*, such as: *I agree with you.* or *You're right.*

- Read aloud the instructions in the second part of Exercise **2B**. Ask a S to read the example sentence aloud.

- Ss complete the exercise individually. Help as needed.

- Ask individual Ss to write their sentences on the board. Ask other Ss to read each sentence aloud.

Expansion activity (individual work)

- Ask Ss to write additional sentences about the bar graph. Model the activity. Show Ss how they can switch the words around and use *less than* instead of *more than* and vice versa. For example, in number 1, the sentence could be *Fernando likes reading less than socializing*.

- Ss write the sentences individually. Help as needed.

- Ask several Ss to say their sentences aloud. Ask the class: *Is that sentence correct?*

Expansion activity (student pairs)

- Ask Ss to make a bar graph about Danny's weekend activities. Ss can guess how much Danny likes the same activities that are shown in Fernando's bar graph.

- Ask several Ss to draw their graphs on the board. Ask other Ss to make sentences about Danny's preferences using the bar graphs on the board.

Application

- Direct Ss' attention to Exercise **3A**. Read the instructions aloud.

- Model the task. Ask two Ss to read aloud the example question and answer. Be sure that Ss understand the question. Explain that *Which do you like more, playing sports or socializing?* means *Do you like playing sports more than socializing?*

- Ss complete the exercise in small groups. Help as needed.

- Ask several pairs to ask and answer the questions for the rest of the class.

- Direct Ss' attention to Exercise **3B**. Read the instructions aloud.

- Model the task. Ask Ss what they learned about people in their group, for example: *Li likes socializing more than working out.*

- Continue the exercise by asking Ss to share information they learned about their classmates.

Evaluation

- Direct Ss' attention to the lesson focus on the board. Ask Ss to make sentences using *more than*, *less than*, and *as much as*.

- Check off each part of the lesson focus as Ss demonstrate an understanding of what they have learned in the lesson.

More Ventures, Unit 1, Lesson C	
Workbook, 20–30 min.	
Add Ventures, 30–45 min.	www.cambridge.org/myresourceroom
Collaborative, 30–45 min.	
Student Arcade, time varies	www.cambridge.org/venturesarcade

B **Work** with a partner. Talk about the bar graph. Use *more than*, *less than*, and *as much as*.

Fernando's Weekend Activities

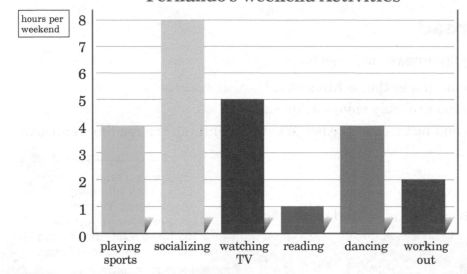

hours per weekend

A Fernando likes socializing more than reading.
B That's right.

1. socializing / reading
2. playing sports / dancing
3. socializing / working out
4. watching TV / socializing
5. reading / playing sports
6. working out / reading

Write sentences about Fernando's weekend activities.

Fernando enjoys socializing more than reading.
(Answers will vary.)

3 Communicate

A **Work** in a small group. Ask and answer questions about the activities in Exercise 2B.

Which do you like more, playing sports or socializing?

I like socializing more than playing sports.

B **Share** information about your classmates.

Amelia likes socializing more than playing sports.

☑ Use *more than*, *less than*, and *as much as* to compare   **UNIT 1**   **11**

LESSON **D** Reading

1 Before you read

Look at the reading tip. Answer the questions.

1. What jobs do the people in the pictures have?
2. What kind of person probably enjoys doing each job?
3. Look at the title and pictures to predict. What do you think the reading is about?

2 Read

Read the magazine article. Listen and read again.

STUDENT TK 9
CLASS CD1 TK 11

> Before you read, look at the title and the pictures. Predict, or guess, what you are going to read about. This will help you to read faster.

Your *Personality* and Your Job

What is the perfect job for you? It depends a lot on your personality. People think, act, and feel in different ways, and there are interesting jobs for every kind of person. Three common personality types are outgoing, intellectual, and creative.

Outgoing people enjoy meeting others and helping them. They are good talkers. They are friendly, and they get along well with other people. They often become nurses, counselors, teachers, or social workers.

Intellectual people like thinking about problems and finding answers to hard questions. They often enjoy reading and playing games like chess. Many intellectual people like working alone more than working in a group. They may become scientists, computer programmers, or writers.

Creative people enjoy making things. They like to imagine things that are new and different. Many of them become artists such as painters, dancers, or musicians. Architects, designers, and photographers are other examples of creative jobs.

Before you choose a career, think about your personality type. If you want to be happy in your work, choose the right job for your personality.

Warm-up and review

- Before class. Write today's lesson focus on the board.
  Lesson D:
  Use title and pictures to predict
  Use clues to guess meaning
- Begin class. Books closed. Write *jobs* on the board. Draw a circle around it to create a word web. Ask Ss to brainstorm different types of jobs. Write the jobs on the board around the circle, for example: *teacher*, *doctor*, *nurse*, *firefighter*, *cook*, etc.
- Point to each job on the board. Ask: *What kind of person enjoys being a nurse?* Elicit appropriate responses. For example, for *nurse* they might say: *A person who likes helping others.*

Presentation

- Books open. Direct Ss' attention to Exercise **1** and read the instructions aloud.
- Direct Ss' attention to the first question in Exercise **1**. Ask a S to read it aloud. Elicit appropriate responses from Ss, such as: *She is a nurse.* (top picture); *He works with computers.* (middle picture); *She is an artist.* (last picture).
- Ask another S to read question number 2. Elicit appropriate responses about the kind of person who probably enjoys doing each job.
- Focus Ss' attention on question number 3. Direct Ss' attention to the title of the magazine article. Ask a S to read it aloud. Elicit appropriate responses to question number 3.
- Read the tip box aloud. Make sure that Ss understand the word *predict*.

Practice

- Read the instructions for Exercise **2** aloud. Ask Ss to read the article silently before they listen to the audio program.
- Class Audio CD1 track 11 Play or read the audio program and ask Ss to read along (see audio script, page T-156). Repeat the audio program as needed.
- While Ss are listening to and reading the article, ask them to write in their notebooks any words they don't understand. When the audio program is finished, ask Ss to write the new vocabulary words on the board.

- Point to each word on the board. Say it aloud and have Ss repeat. Give brief explanations of the words, or ask Ss to explain the words if they are familiar with them. If Ss prefer to look up the new words in their dictionaries, allow them to do so.

▼ **Teaching tip**

If Ss come from the same language background, ask them to help each other translate unfamiliar words into their own language. This encourages a sense of community and ownership in the learning process.

- Encourage Ss to find the meaning of each new word from the context of the article. For example, if a S writes *intellectual* on the board, show how the meaning of the word is in the article: *Intellectual people like thinking about problems and finding answers to hard questions.* Give examples of famous intellectuals such as Albert Einstein, or ask Ss to name intellectuals from their cultures or countries.

Learner persistence (individual work)

- Self-Study Audio CD track 9 Exercise **2** is recorded on the CD at the back of the Student's Book. Ss can listen to the CD at home for reinforcement and review. They can also listen for self-directed learning when class attendance is not possible.

Community building (whole group)

- Invite someone from your school, such as an administrator or another teacher, to come to the class and give a short talk about his or her job duties and whether or not the job fits his or her personality.

Expansion activity (small groups)

- Draw three columns on the board. Write the headings *Outgoing*, *Intellectual*, and *Creative* above the columns.
- Ask Ss to form groups of three or four Ss. Have Ss brainstorm a list of different jobs and categorize the jobs according to the three personality types. If Ss need help beginning the activity, have them start with some examples from the article.
- When Ss are finished, ask one S from each group to come to the board to write examples of jobs under each category. Ask the class if they agree with the categorization of the jobs on the board.

Comprehension check

- Direct Ss' attention to Exercise **3A**. Read the instructions aloud.
- Ask four Ss to read the questions aloud, one at a time. Make sure that all Ss understand the questions.
- Ss in pairs. Ask Ss to ask and answer the questions with a partner. Tell them that they can refer to the magazine article on page 12.
- Ask several pairs to ask and answer the comprehension questions for the rest of the class.
- Focus Ss' attention on Exercise **3B**. Read aloud the instructions in numbers 1 and 2. Model the task. Hold up the Student's Book. Show where the word *personality* appears in the reading. Ss complete the task individually. Walk around and help as needed.
- Ask Ss to compare their underlined and circled words and phrases with a partner. Make sure that Ss have found all the words and phrases in Exercise **3B**.

Practice

- Direct Ss' attention to number 3 in Exercise **3B**. Ask a S to read the instructions aloud.
- Write *clue* on the board. Say it aloud and ask Ss to repeat. Tell Ss that a clue is a word or set of words that helps you guess the meaning of something.
- Model the task. Hold up the Student's Book. Point to the word *personality* in the first paragraph of the article. Read aloud the first part of the sentence following the word *personality: People think, act, and feel in different ways.* Tell Ss that this clue helps them understand the meaning of the word *personality*.
- Ss complete the exercise individually. Walk around and help as needed.
- When Ss are finished, ask individual Ss to read aloud the clues they found to help them understand the meanings of the words in this exercise. Ask the rest of the class if they agree with these Ss. If they disagree, ask them to correct the words.
- Focus Ss' attention on number 4 in Exercise **3B**. Ask a S to read the instructions aloud.
- Model the task. Ask Ss what a definition for *personality* could be. Tell Ss to use the clues they wrote in number 3 of Exercise **3B** to help them with this exercise.

- Ss complete the exercise individually. Walk around and help as needed.
- Write the numbers *1–6* on the board. Ask Ss to come to the board to write the letters of their responses. Ask other Ss if the answers are correct. Make corrections as needed.

Application

- Focus Ss' attention on Exercise **3C**. Read the instructions aloud.
- Ask a S to read aloud the questions.
- Ss complete the exercise in pairs. Walk around and help as needed.
- Ask several pairs to ask and answer the questions for the rest of the class.

Evaluation

- Direct Ss' attention to the lesson focus written on the board.
- Write on the board the words from number 1 in Exercise **3B**. Ask Ss to make sentences about the magazine article using these words. Ask other Ss to make sentences about themselves using the words on the board.
- Check off each part of the lesson focus as Ss demonstrate an understanding of what they have learned in the lesson.

Learner persistence (individual, pairs)

- You may wish to assign Extended Reading Worksheets from the *Online Teacher's Resource Room* for Ss to complete outside of class. The purpose of these worksheets is to encourage Ss to read for pleasure in English outside of the English class. The worksheets can also be assigned as extended reading in class.

More Ventures, Unit 1, Lesson D	
Workbook, 20–30 min.	
Add Ventures, 30–45 min.	
Collaborative, 30–45 min.	www.cambridge.org/myresourceroom
Extended Reading and worksheet, 45–60 min.	
Student Arcade, time varies	www.cambridge.org/venturesarcade

3 After you read

A Check your understanding.

1. What do outgoing people enjoy doing? What jobs are good for them?
2. What do intellectual people like doing? What jobs are good for them?
3. What do creative people enjoy doing? What jobs are good for them?
4. Why is it important for you to know your personality type?

B Build your vocabulary.

1. Find these words in the reading, and underline them.

artists	intellectual	personality
creative	outgoing	type

2. Find these phrases in the reading, and circle them.

enjoy meeting others	think, act, and feel in different ways
like to imagine things that are new and different	painters, dancers, or musicians
like thinking about problems	every kind of person

3. Look at the phrases in Exercise B2. They are clues to help you guess the meaning of these words. Write the phrases under the words.

1. personality
   think, act, and feel in different ways
2. type
   every kind of person
3. outgoing
   enjoy meeting others
4. intellectual
   like thinking about problems
5. creative
   like to imagine things that are new and different
6. artists
   painters, dancers, or musicians

4. Match the words and the definitions.

1. personality __e__
2. type __a__
3. outgoing __f__
4. intellectual __c__
5. creative __b__
6. artist __d__

a. a kind of person or thing
b. good at making things that are new and different
c. enjoys thinking and finding answers
d. a person who paints, dances, writes, or draws
e. the natural way a person thinks, feels, and acts
f. friendly

C Talk with a partner. Ask and answer the questions.

1. What personality type are you? Why do you think so?
2. What is a good job for you?

LESSON E Writing

1 Before you write

A **Work** in a small group. Think of adjectives that describe someone at work. Write them on the lines.

artistic	hard-working	honest	*(Answers will vary.)* _____
creative	highly-trained	patient	_____ _____
friendly	helpful	reliable	_____ _____

B **Talk** with a partner. Look at the pictures. Answer the questions.

1. What are these people doing? What are their jobs?
2. What are some adjectives that can describe these people?

a.

b.

c.

d.

e.

f.

...p and review

...e class. Write today's lesson focus on the board.

...son E:

...scuss and write about personality types and jobs

...Use descriptive adjectives

- Begin class. Books closed. Review vocabulary and grammar from the unit. Ask questions about the magazine article that Ss read in Lesson D: *What type of people enjoy meeting others and helping them?* (outgoing people.) *What type of people like thinking about problems and finding answers to hard questions?* (intellectual people.) *What type of people enjoy making things?* (creative people.)

Presentation

- Books open. Direct Ss' attention to Exercise **1A** and read the instructions aloud. Explain that adjectives are words that describe people or things.
- Read the instructions for **1A**. Direct Ss' attention to the words in columns. Say each word aloud. Ask Ss to repeat.
- Ask Ss if they know the meaning of each word. Explain any new words.
- Have Ss work in small groups of three or four to complete **1A**. Encourage Ss to use dictionaries to find adjectives. Walk around and help as needed.
- When Ss are finished, ask individual Ss to come to the board to write their adjectives. Explain the meaning of any new words.
- Ask individual Ss which adjective they think best describes them.

Comprehension check

- Direct Ss' attention to the words in **1A**. Ask a few individual Ss which profession would be the best fit for their personality and why. Ensure Ss use one of the adjectives that were generated in **1A**.

▼**Teaching tip**
Don't spend a lot of time trying to define adjectives. Some may be difficult to define. Instead, have Ss from similar language backgrounds use their first language to define words so that the class can move on.

Expansion activity *(student pairs)*

- Write these questions on the board:
  1. *Which do you like more, taking photographs or cooking?*
  2. *Which do you enjoy more, teaching or drawing plans?*
  3. *Which do you dislike more, building things or putting things together? Why?*
- Ss in pairs. Direct Ss to the pictures of different jobs in Exercise **1B**. Tell Ss to ask their partner the questions on the board. Encourage Ss to use adjectives in their answers, for example: *I like taking photographs more than cooking because a photographer has a more exciting life.* If Ss are not interested in these jobs or activities, have them tell their partner about a different job they would like to have.
- Direct Ss' attention to the big picture on page 6. Remind Ss about Danny and Fernando. Ask: *Which job do you think Danny would like? What about Fernando?* Tell Ss to choose from the jobs in Exercise **1B** or to make up different jobs that Danny and Fernando might like more.

Practice

- Read the instructions for **1B**. Tell Ss to discuss the questions in pairs. Help as needed.
- Have pairs ask and answer the questions for the rest of the class. Ask Ss if they agree with the adjectives Ss suggest for each profession.

▼**Teaching tip**
Encourage Ss to use graphic organizers such as the one in Exercise **1A** to organize their thoughts before writing. Explain how a list will help them to think about different ideas they can use in their writing.

Expansion activity *(small groups)*

- **Materials needed** Highlighter and enough copies of the classified ad section of your local newspaper to distribute to groups of three or four Ss.
- Tell Ss that a classified ad often describes the type of person wanted for a job.
- Give each group a highlighter. Ask Ss to highlight adjectives that they find in the ads, for example: *hardworking, responsible, friendly,* etc.
- Ask a representative of each group to come to the board to write some of the adjectives they found in the ads.

LESSON E Writing

Presentation

- Direct Ss' attention to Exercise 1C.
- Ask: *Who wrote this paragraph?* (Marcos.) *When did he write it?* (September 9th.)
- Ask Ss to read the paragraph silently. Tell them to underline any words they don't understand.
- Ask Ss to write the new words on the board. Point to each word. Say it aloud. Ask Ss to repeat.
- Remind Ss of the strategies they learned in Exercise 3B in Lesson D for clues to help them guess the meaning of a word. For example, if a S writes *warm* on the board, point to the phrase *warm and helpful.* Ask: *What do you think "warm" means in this case?* Elicit an appropriate response, such as: *It means that you are friendly and nice.*

▼ **Teaching tip**

If Ss are unfamiliar with the word *fits*, have them read the last sentence of the paragraph: *I think a nurse is a good job for her because it fits her personality.* Compare this meaning of *fits* with the example of shoes or clothes fitting properly. In this case the job fits Leona because she is a helpful person.

Practice

- Direct Ss' attention to the second part of Exercise 1C. Read the instructions aloud.
- Model the task. Ask a S the first question. Elicit an appropriate response, for example: *Leona's job fits her personality.*
- Ss complete the exercise in pairs. Help as needed.
- Ask several pairs to ask and answer the questions for the rest of the class.

▼ **Culture tip**

Tell Ss about common ways to look for jobs in the United States. Explain that job seekers often look online or in classified ads of their local newspaper. Discuss how jobs are categorized by job type.

Application

- Direct Ss' attention to Exercise 2 and read the instructions aloud.
- Ss complete the exercise individually. Help as needed.

Learner persistence (individual work)

- If you have Ss who have difficulty writing, sit w them and help them while the other Ss are writin Encourage them to use the adjective chart from Exercise 1A as a guide for the adjectives they can us

Comprehension check

- Direct Ss' attention to Exercise 3A and read the instructions aloud. Ask a S to read the three checklist sentences to the class.
- Model the task. Direct Ss' attention to the example paragraph in Exercise 1C. Ask Ss to identify all the checklist items in this paragraph.
- Ss complete the exercise individually. Help as needed. If any S checked *No* for one or more of the checklist items, ask the S to revise his or her paragraph to include the missing detail(s). Read the S's paragraph to make sure that all the checklist items have been included.

Evaluation

- Focus Ss' attention on Exercise 3B and read the instructions aloud. This exercise asks Ss to work together to peer-correct their writing. Ask a S to read numbers 1 and 2 aloud.
- Ss complete the exercise in pairs. Reading aloud enables the writer to review his or her own writing. Reading to a partner allows the writer to understand the need to write clearly for an audience.
- Ask several volunteers to read their paragraphs to the class. Ask other Ss to ask questions.
- Direct Ss' attention to the lesson focus on the board. Books closed. Write the jobs in the pictures in Exercise 1B on the board. Ask Ss to describe the jobs using descriptive adjectives, for example: *An architect is creative. A teacher is outgoing.*, etc.
- Check off each part of the lesson focus as Ss demonstrate an understanding of what they have learned in the lesson.

More Ventures, Unit 1, Lesson E	
Workbook, 20–30 min.	
Add Ventures, 30–45 min.	www.cambridge.org/myresourceroom
Collaborative, 30–45 min.	

Lesson objec
- Discuss and wri
- Practice using the paragraph.

Warm-up
- Before
  Less
  Di
  U

Marcos
September 9

The Right Job

My sister, Leona, has the right job for her personality. She's a nurse. She works in a big hospital in the Philippines. Leona is a very outgoing person. She's very friendly with all her patients, and she enjoys talking to everybody in the hospital. She is warm and helpful. I think a nurse is a good job for her because it fits her personality.

Work with a partner. Answer the questions.

1. What does the first sentence say about Leona?
2. What is Leona's job?
3. Where does she work?
4. Leona is an outgoing person. Which sentences explain this?
5. Which adjectives describe Leona?
6. Is a nurse a good job for Leona? Why?

2 Write

Write a paragraph about the right job for someone you know. Describe the person and what he/she likes or enjoys. Use a topic sentence and supporting sentences. Use Exercises 1B and 1C to help you.

> A good paragraph is organized. Use a clear topic sentence and supporting sentences.

3 After you write

A Check your writing.

	Yes	No
1. I included a job and a personality type.	☐	☐
2. I described the person and what he/she likes or enjoys.	☐	☐
3. I used a topic sentence and supporting sentences.	☐	☐

B Share your writing with a partner.

1. Take turns. Read your paragraph to a partner.
2. Comment on your partner's paragraph. Ask your partner a question about the paragraph. Tell your partner one thing you learned.

LESSON F Another view

1 Life-skills reading

USEFUL LANGUAGE

DM = divorced male
N/S = nonsmoker
SF = single female
SM = single male

Fun-loving DM (46, 5'11", salt-and-pepper hair, N/S) enjoys taking motorcycle trips, camping outdoors, and spending time at the ocean. Seeking outgoing SF (40–50) for bike trips and fun.

Warm, kind, intelligent SM (27, 5'8") enjoys playing guitar, cooking, taking pictures. Seeking gentle SF (25–30) for musical evenings at home.

Caring SF (30, 5'5") loves playing tennis. Seeking good-looking, honest, active SM (28–35) with a good heart to share life together.

A **Read** the questions. Look at the Web page. Fill in the answer.

1. How tall is the man on the motorcycle?
   - Ⓐ under 5 feet
   - Ⓑ 5 feet 2 inches
   - ● 5 feet 11 inches
   - Ⓓ over 6 feet

2. What word describes the younger man?
   - Ⓐ friendly
   - Ⓑ fun-loving
   - Ⓒ honest
   - ● kind

3. What does the woman enjoy doing?
   - Ⓐ playing guitar
   - ● playing tennis
   - Ⓒ taking motorcycle trips
   - Ⓓ none of the above

4. Which ad talks about evenings at home?
   - Ⓐ the first ad
   - ● the second ad
   - Ⓒ the third ad
   - Ⓓ all of the above

B **Talk** with your classmates. Ask and answer the questions.

Is the Internet a good place to find a new friend? Why or why not?

- Practice reading an Internet Web page of personal ads
- Use *must* for logical conclusions
- Complete the self-assessment

Warm-up and review

- Before class. Write today's lesson focus on the board.
  Lesson F:
  Read and talk about personal ads
  Review vocabulary and grammar from Unit 1
  Complete the self-assessment
- Begin class. Books closed. Write *personal ads* on the board. Point to the words. Say them aloud. Ask Ss to repeat. Ask: *What are personal ads?* Elicit an appropriate response, or explain that these are ads that people use to find a boyfriend or girlfriend.
- Ask Ss if they have these types of personal ads in their home countries. If they do, ask where people can read them. After Ss respond, tell them that in the United States they can find these ads online or in a local weekly newspaper.
- Write *Web page* on the board. Point to the words and say them aloud. Ask Ss to repeat. Ask Ss if they know what a Web page is. If any Ss say *Yes*, ask them to tell the class what it is, for example: *It's a page on the Internet. It gives people information.* Ask Ss to give examples of different types of Web pages. Elicit appropriate responses, such as: *personal Web pages, Web pages for shopping.*
- Say: *We are going to look at a Web page that has personal ads.*

▼ **Teaching tip**
If possible, bring in a local weekly newspaper and show Ss an example of personal ads.

Presentation

- Books open. Direct Ss' attention to the pictures in Exercise 1. Ask: *What do you see?* Elicit descriptions of the three photos, such as: *I see a man on a motorcycle, a man playing the guitar, and a woman playing tennis.*

▼ **Useful language**
Read the Useful language box aloud. Explain that these abbreviations are used to describe people in the ads. Go over each abbreviation with the class.

- Direct Ss' attention to the descriptions of the people in the ads. Ask three Ss to read the ads aloud. While they are reading, ask the other Ss to underline any words that they don't understand. Ask Ss to write these new words on the board.

- Point to each word in turn. Say it aloud. Encourage the class to figure out the meaning of the words by using clues in the pictures and the text.
- Remind Ss of the reading strategies they learned in Lesson D for figuring out the meanings of new words from context.
- To help guide Ss, write these brief definitions on the board:
  seeking = looking for
  caring = warm, affectionate
  honest = tells the truth

Practice

- Direct Ss' attention to Exercise **1A** and read the instructions aloud. This exercise helps prepare Ss for standardized-type tests they may have to take. Be sure that Ss understand the task. Have Ss individually scan for and fill in the answers.
- Check answers with the class. Ask Ss to read the questions and their answers aloud.

Application

- Direct Ss' attention to Exercise **1B** and read the instructions aloud. Ask a S to read the questions to the class.
- Ss ask each other the questions in small groups. Walk around and help as needed.
- Open up the discussion to the entire class. Debate the pros and cons of finding a new friend on the Internet.

Community building *(whole group)*

- Be sure to warn Ss that it can be dangerous to meet with someone in person after writing to him or her online. Let Ss know that sometimes people lie about their identity when they are placing or responding to a personal ad online and that the Internet may not be the best place to meet people.
- Consider asking your class to brainstorm safe ways to meet new people. Have a discussion to compare how to meet people in the United States with how to meet people in Ss' home countries.

Warm up and Review

- Books closed. Ask Ss: *What's a gerund?* Elicit answers, such as: *Gerunds look like verbs. They are made up of the base form of a verb + "-ing."* Gerunds often follow verbs that talk about preferences.

- Ask individual Ss questions about their preferences using the verbs *dislike, enjoy, hate, like, love,* and *mind.* For example: *Do you dislike taking out the trash? Do you enjoy cooking? Do you like playing soccer?*

Presentation

- Books closed. Write the following sentences on the board:

  John is a cook.
  He <u>must</u> enjoy cooking.

- Read each statement aloud. Ask Ss to repeat.

- Explain that the modal *must* can be used to show that a speaker is mostly certain about something. The modal *must* shows that a person is making a logical conclusion or guess. In this example, we can guess that John enjoys cooking because he chose to cook for a living.

- Direct Ss attention to the verb *enjoy.* Tell Ss that *must* is always followed by verbs in the simple form.

Practice

- Books open. Direct Ss' attention to the chart in Exercise **2A**. Write the following sentences on the board:

  Julia works until 11:00 pm every night.
  She <u>must have</u> a difficult job.
  She <u>must not eat</u> dinner at home.

- Explain to Ss that we can conclude Julia's job is difficult because it causes her to work late. We can also guess that she doesn't eat dinner at home often since she is still at work at dinnertime.

- Focus Ss' attention on the instructions in **2A**. Read the instructions aloud. Ask individual Ss to read the example sentences for speakers B, C, and D to the class.

- Have Ss follow the instructions in **2A** in small groups. Walk around and help as needed.

- Review each situation in the box. Ask Ss for examples of logical conclusions they can make about each situation. Ask other Ss if the answers are correct. Make corrections as needed.

Comprehension Check

- Focus Ss' attention on the instructions in **2B**. Read the instructions aloud. Ask a pair of Ss to model the example dialog.

- Have Ss follow the instructions in **2B** in pairs. Walk around and help.

- Ask a few pairs to model examples of their dialog to the class.

Expansion Activity *(whole group)*

- Ask Ss to think of a question they would like to ask other Ss and to write it in their notebooks, for example: *What do you enjoy doing on Sundays?*

- Ask Ss to stand up and form two lines so that all of the Ss are facing each other.

- Tell Ss that they are going to ask the person facing them their question. Then they will answer that person's question to them using the structure *You must _____.* or *You must not _____.*

- After a few minutes, say: *Change!* Everyone moves down one person, and asks their question again.

- Continue the game until Ss have asked everyone in the class a question.

Evaluation

- Before asking students to turn to the self-assessment on page 136, do a quick review of the unit. Have Ss turn to Lesson A. Ask the class to talk about what they remember about this lesson. Prompt Ss, if necessary, with questions, for example: *What are the conversations about on this page? What vocabulary is in the pictures?* Continue in this manner to review each lesson quickly.

- **Self-assessment** Read aloud the instructions for Exercise **3**. Ask Ss to turn to the self-assessment page to complete the unit self-assessment. The self-assessments are also on the *Online Teacher's Resource Room.* If you prefer to collect the assessments and save them as part of each S's portfolio assessment, print out the unit self-assessment from the *Resource Room,* ask students to complete it, and collect and save it.

- If Ss are ready, administer the unit test on pages T-165–T-166 of this Teacher's Edition (or on the Assessment Audio CD / CD-ROM). The audio and audio script for the tests are on the Assessment Audio CD / CD-ROM.

More Ventures, Unit 1, Lesson F	
Workbook, 20–30 min.	
Add Ventures, 30–45 min.	www.cambridge.org/myresourceroom
Collaborative, 30–45 min.	
Student Arcade, time varies	www.cambridge.org/venturesarcade

2 Grammar connections: *must* for logical conclusions

| Julia works until 11:00 p.m. every night. | → She **must have** a difficult job.
→ She **must not eat** dinner at home. |

A **Work** in a small group. Choose a situation and make conclusions. Take turns.

> A David's phone bill is usually over $200 a month.
> B He must talk on the phone a lot.
> C He must send a lot of texts, too.
> D He must not have a free Internet phone service.

1. David's phone bill is usually over $200 a month.
2. Susan gets up at 10:30 a.m. every morning.
3. Brenda buys a new car every year.
4. Sally spends a lot of time at the library.
5. Carlos goes to the gym five times a week.
6. George and Linda never cook at home.
7. Ivan doesn't have a computer.
8. Shawn and Olivia go to dance clubs a lot.

B **Talk** with a partner. Say something interesting about yourself. Your partner makes conclusions about you.

> A I went to 20 concerts last year.
> B You **must love** music.
> A Yes, I do. I love it!

3 Wrap up

Complete the **Self-assessment** on page 136.

LESSON **A**
Listening

1 **Before you listen**

A What do you see?

B What is happening?

C What's the story?

1.

March 15

Bella

Alex

DICTIONARY

2.

April 15

concentrate

To do

Lesson objectives
- Introduce students to the topic
- Find out what students know about the topic
- Preview the unit by talking about the pictures
- Practice key vocabulary
- Practice listening skills

Warm-up and review
- Before class. Write today's lesson focus on the board.
  Lesson A:
  Study problems and solutions
- Begin class. Books closed. Write *How long do you study at home?* on the board. Elicit appropriate responses, such as: *one hour, two hours,* etc.
- Focus Ss' attention on the words *study problems* in the lesson focus. Ask Ss to give examples of problems they have with studying and write them on the board, for example: *no time to study, don't understand the lesson, no place to study, have difficulty concentrating, need a dictionary, feel disorganized,* etc.
- Ask: *Do you have any study problems?* Elicit appropriate responses, such as: *I don't have time to study. No one in my house can help me study.,* etc.

Learner persistence *(whole group)*
- If many of your Ss say that they have no one to help them study at home, try to arrange for a volunteer tutor to come to your school to help Ss outside the class. If you cannot get a volunteer tutor, ask Ss to exchange phone numbers with classmates. Encourage them to call each other if they have a question about the lesson.

Presentation
- Books open. Set the scene. Ask Ss to look at the two pictures on page 18. Ask the question from Exercise 1A: *What do you see?* Elicit and write on the board as much vocabulary about the pictures as possible: *library, computers, students, books,* etc. Hold up the Student's Book and point to the parts of the picture that correspond to the words.
- Ask individual Ss to look at the two pictures and talk about the differences: *There are five students in Picture 1; there are seven students in Picture 2; Bella is standing in Picture 1; she is sitting in Picture 2. Alex looks worried in Picture 1; he looks calm in Picture 2; the table is messy in Picture 1 and neat in Picture 2; they are talking in Picture 1 and studying in Picture 2,* etc.

- Direct Ss' attention to the question in **1B**. Read it aloud. Focus on Picture 1. Hold up the Student's Book. Point to the calendar. Ask: *What's the date?* (March 15th.) Ask Ss to describe what is happening on this date in the picture.
- Focus on Picture 2. Hold up the Student's Book. Point to the calendar. Ask: *What's the date?* (April 15th.) Ask Ss to describe what is happening on this date in the picture.

Practice
- Direct Ss' attention to Exercise **1C**. Read the question. Tell Ss that as a class, they are going to tell a story about Alex and Bella.
- Model the task. Ask individual Ss to tell you sentences about Alex and Bella. Write Ss' sentences on the board. Create a story with Ss' ideas, for example: *On March 15th, Alex was worried. He had a lot of homework. He talked to his friend, Bella. She helped him develop new study skills.,* etc.

▼ **Teaching tip**
Encourage Ss to be creative. At this point, there is no single correct story.

Community building *(student pairs)*
- Ask Ss to work in pairs to create a story about the pictures. Try to pair Ss of different ability levels. In this way, a more advanced S can help a less English-proficient S with the exercise.

Expansion activity *(student pairs)*
- Tell Ss to work in pairs to create a conversation between Bella and Alex. Tell Ss that they will be talking about study problems. Encourage Ss to use some of the study problems written on the board during the Warm-up. Ask Ss to include solutions for those problems in their conversations.
- Ask for volunteers to role-play their conversations for the class. Elicit the following study skills from the conversations and write them on the board: *make a list, be an active listener, write vocabulary words on index cards.*

Warm-up and review

- Direct Ss' attention to the first picture on page 18. Hold up the Student's Book and point to Alex. Ask: *How does Alex feel?* Elicit appropriate responses and write them on the board: *He feels sad, frustrated, unhappy*, etc. If the word *discouraged* doesn't come up, write it on the board. Point to it and say it aloud. Ask Ss to repeat the word. Say: *Alex is discouraged. He has too many things to do for homework.*

- Focus Ss' attention on Alex in the second picture. Ask: *How does Alex feel in this picture?* Elicit: *He feels happy and relaxed.* Ask: *Why does he feel relaxed?* Elicit an appropriate response, such as: *He is more organized. Bella helped him develop study skills.*

- Direct Ss' attention to Alex's checked off to-do list in the second picture. Explain that this is a *to-do list*. Write the phrase, say it, and have Ss repeat. Tell Ss a *to-do list* helps people organize what they need to do.

Learner persistence (whole group)

- Encourage Ss to make to-do lists in English class when doing homework or studying for a test. Point out that learning how to prioritize tasks that they need to do outside the class is a valuable skill.

Practice

- Direct Ss' attention to Exercise **2A**. Read the instructions and questions aloud.

- Class Audio CD1 track 12 Play or read the audio program (see audio script, page T-156). Ss listen and write the answers in their books. Repeat the audio program as needed.

- Make sure that Ss understand all the words in the listening exercise. For example, write these words and phrases on the board: *write a paper, concentrate, main ideas*.

- Ask Ss if they know what the words on the board mean. If Ss don't know, explain that *writing a paper* is something you do for homework, such as writing an essay or a report; *to concentrate* means to think hard about something; and *main ideas* are the most important ideas in a paragraph, paper, article, or book.

- Direct Ss' attention to Exercise **2B**. Read the instructions aloud.

- Class Audio CD1 track 12 Play or read the audio program (see audio script, page T-156). Ss listen and check off Alex's study problems.

Comprehension check

- Ask Ss to also listen for Bella's advice for each study problem and write it to the right.

- Class Audio CD1 track 12 Play or read the audio program (see audio script, page T-156). Ss listen and check their answers. Repeat the audio program as needed.

Learner persistence (individual work)

- Self-Study Audio CD track 10 Exercises **2A** and **2B** are recorded on the CD at the back of the Student's Book. Ss can listen to the CD at home for reinforcement and review. They can also listen to the CD for self-directed learning when class attendance is not possible.

Practice

- Direct Ss' attention to Exercise **3A**. Read the instructions aloud. Tell Ss that the story in this exercise is a summary of the conversation in Exercises **2A** and **2B**.

- Focus Ss' attention on the words in the word bank. Say each word or phrase aloud. Ask Ss to repeat. Explain any words that are new to Ss.

- Model the task. Ask a S to read the first sentence aloud. Tell Ss to continue the exercise by filling in the blanks with the words from the word bank.

- Ss complete the exercise individually. Help as needed.

- Class Audio CD1 track 13 Play or read the audio program (see audio script, page T-156). Ss listen and check their answers. Repeat the audio program as needed.

Learner persistence (individual work)

- Self-Study Audio CD track 11 Exercise **3A** is recorded on the CD at the back of the Student's Book. Ss can listen to the CD at home for reinforcement and review. They can also listen for self-directed learning when class attendance is not possible.

Application

- Direct Ss' attention to Exercise **3B**. Read the instructions aloud.

- Ss complete the exercise in pairs. Help as needed.

- Ask Ss to share their answers with the class. Write any new study problems on the board. List the solutions as well.

Evaluation

- Direct Ss' attention to the lesson focus on the board. Ask individual Ss to tell you about Alex's study problems and how Bella helped him find a solution.

- Check off the lesson focus as Ss demonstrate an understanding of what they have learned in the lesson.

More Ventures, Unit 2, Lesson A	
Workbook, 15–30 min.	
Add Ventures, 30–45 min.	www.cambridge.org/myresourceroom
Collaborative, 30–45 min.	
Student Arcade, time varies	www.cambridge.org/venturesarcade

Unit Goals | **Identify** learning strategies
Relate learning strategies to study problems
Recognize test-taking strategies

2 Listen

STUDENT TK 10
CLASS CD1 TK 12

A **Listen** and answer the questions.

1. Who are the speakers? 2. What are they talking about?

STUDENT TK 10
CLASS CD1 TK 12

B **Listen again.** Put a check (✓) next to Alex's study problems. Then write Bella's advice.

Study problems	Bella's advice
1. ☑ too many things to do	*make a to-do list; do important things first*
2. ☐ always late for school	
3. ☑ can't concentrate	*be more active when reading*
4. ☐ can't pronounce English words	
5. ☑ can't remember vocabulary	*write important words on index cards and study them*

3 After you listen

A **Read.** Complete the story.

active   boring   concentrate   discouraged   index cards   list   paper

> Alex has been at the library for a long time, and he is ___*discouraged*___ . He has
> many things to do. He needs to study for a test and write a ___*paper*___ . He
> needs to finish reading a book, but he can't ___*concentrate*___ . He says the book is
> ___*boring*___ .
>
> Alex's friend Bella gives him some study advice. First, she tells Alex to make
> a ___*list*___ of all the things he needs to do. Next, she says he has to be a
> more ___*active*___ reader. Finally, she tells him to write vocabulary words on
> ___*index cards*___ and study them when he has free time. With Bella's help, Alex plans
> to study smarter, not harder.

STUDENT TK 11
CLASS CD1 TK 13

Listen and check your answers.

B **Talk** with a partner. Ask and answer the questions.

1. What study problems do you have? 2. What can you do to study better?

LESSON B Present perfect

1 Grammar focus: *how long, for, since*

Questions

How long has Alex **lived** here?
How long have you **known** Alex?

Answers

He **has lived** here **for** two years.
I **have known** him **since** January.

Past participles

Regular verbs	Irregular verbs
live → lived	be → been
wait → waited	have → had
work → worked	know → known
	speak → spoken
	teach → taught

Time phrases

for two hours	since 6:00 p.m.
for one year	since February
for five months	since last year

Turn to page 143 for a complete grammar chart and explanation.
Turn to page 146 for a list of irregular verbs.

2 Practice

A Write. Complete the sentences. Use the present perfect.

1. **A** How long ____*has*____ Manya ____*been*____ in the computer lab?
   (be)
   B Since six o'clock.

2. **A** How long ____*has*____ Avi ____*known*____ Bella?
   (know)
   B For four months.

3. **A** How long ____*has*____ Kayla ____*worked*____ at the library?
   (work)
   B Since September.

4. **A** How long ____*has*____ Mrs. Bateson ____*taught*____ at the adult school?
   (teach)
   B For 20 years.

5. **A** How long ____*have*____ you ____*lived*____ in Canada?
   (live)
   B For one year.

6. **A** How long ____*has*____ Omar ____*had*____ two jobs?
   (have)
   B Since last year.

CLASS CD1 TK 14

Listen and check your answers. Then practice with a partner.

Lesson objectives

- Introduce the present perfect
- Practice questions with *How long*
- Introduce past participles and time phrases

Warm-up and review

Before class. Write today's lesson focus on the board.

Lesson B:
The present perfect
Questions with How long
Answers with since and for

- Begin class. Books open. Direct Ss' attention to the pictures on page 18. Ask Ss: *What are Alex's problems?* (too many things to do; can't concentrate.) *What does Bella suggest?* (make a to-do list; write vocabulary words on index cards.) *What happened one month later?* (Alex has better study habits; studies smarter, not harder.)

Presentation

Focus on meaning / personalize

- Books closed. Direct Ss' attention to the lesson focus on the board. Point to *How long* in the lesson focus. Explain that Ss are going to learn to describe periods of time to answer questions with *How long*.
- Ask: *What time did class start today?* Write the correct answer on the board, such as: *9:00.* Say: *(9:00) is the time that class started today.* Say and write: *We have been in this class since (9:00) today.* Explain that *since* is used to describe a point of time that continues to now (the present).
- Ask: *How many minutes have we been in class?* Elicit answers, such as: *30 minutes.* Say and write: *We have been in this class for (30 minutes).* Explain that *for* is used to describe a period of time from start to end.

Focus on form

- Books open. Direct Ss' attention to the Questions and Answers charts in Exercise 1. Read the questions and answers aloud. Ask Ss to repeat.
- Write on the board and say: *Past participle.* Tell Ss that verbs in English have four parts – the base form, simple past, present participle, and past participle. Explain that you will focus on three of them – the base form, the simple past form, and the past participle form.

- Write on the board:

Base form	Simple past	Past participle
be	was / were	been
study	studied	studied

- Point to each one and say it aloud. Have Ss make present (base) and simple past sentences using *be* / *good student*, for example: *He is a good student. He was a good student.*
- Tell Ss the present perfect is formed by *have* or *has* + past participle. Say: *You have been / studied in this class for (30 minutes) today.* Explain that the present perfect is used to talk about actions that started in the past and continue to now.
- Direct Ss' attention to the past participles chart in Exercise 1. Read each one aloud. Ask Ss to repeat. Tell Ss that a list of irregular verbs is on page 146.
- Direct Ss' attention to the time phrases beginning with *for* and *since*. Read each one aloud. Ask Ss to repeat.

Practice

- Focus Ss' attention on Exercise 2A. Read the instructions aloud.
- Read the example aloud and make sure Ss understand the task. Ss complete the exercise individually. Help as needed.

Comprehension check

- Direct Ss' attention to the second part of the instructions for Exercise 2A.
- Class Audio CD1 track 14 Play or read the complete audio program (see audio script, page T-156). Ss listen and check their answers.
- Ss practice the questions and answers with a partner.

LESSON B Present perfect

Presentation

- Books closed. Draw a horizontal line on the board with arrows at each end. Tell Ss that it is a time line. Write *time line* on the board. Say it aloud and ask Ss to repeat. Tell Ss that a time line is a line that shows important dates and events.
- Model the concept. Write some important dates (month and year) on the time line that reflect your life, for example: the date you moved to the city you live in now, the date you got the job you have now, etc.
- Write *How long have you _____?* on the board. Point to the words. Tell Ss to ask you questions using the time line on the board, such as: *How long have you lived in _____?*
- Respond to Ss' questions by pointing to the corresponding dates on the board, for example: *Since 2006. / For _____ years.* Be sure to respond using both *for* and *since* to model the two time phrases.

Practice

- Books open. Direct Ss' attention to the time line in Exercise **2B**. Ask Ss: *What do you see?* Elicit an appropriate response, for example: *This is a time line of Alex's life.*
- Focus Ss' attention on the title of the time line. Ask a S to read it aloud. Explain that *recent history* means events that happened a short time ago.
- Read the instructions aloud. Model the task. Ask two Ss to read the example question and answer.
- Ss complete the exercise in pairs. Help as needed.
- Ask several pairs to ask and answer the questions for the rest of the class. Listen to make sure that Ss are using the correct form of the verb for the past participle.
- Read aloud the second part of the instructions for Exercise **2B**.
- Model the task. Ask a S to read the example aloud. Ask Ss for today's date and write it on the board. Complete the sentence about Alex using the date on the board. Be sure Ss understand how to quantify Alex's history to the present.
- Ss complete the exercise individually. Help as needed.
- Ask individual Ss to write their sentences on the board. Ask other Ss to read the sentences aloud.

Application

- Direct Ss' attention to Exercise **3A** and read the instructions aloud.
- Model the task. Ask two Ss to read the example conversation aloud.

- Ss complete the exercise in small groups. Help as needed.
- Direct Ss' attention to Exercise **3B**. Read the instructions aloud.
- Model the task. Ask Ss what they learned about a person in their group in Exercise **3A**. Ask Ss to make sentences about this person, for example: (Student's name) *has studied English since 2010.*
- Continue the exercise by asking Ss to share information they learned about their classmates.

Expansion activity (individual work, student pairs)

- Ask Ss to make a time line of important events in their lives. Have them include only those events that they wish to talk about with a partner.
- When Ss are finished, have pairs use *How long* to ask questions about each other's time lines: *How long have you lived here? How long have you studied English in this class?* etc.
- Ask Ss to exchange their time lines. First Ss change *I* ➔ *you* to discuss their partner's time line. Then, ask Ss to share their partner's information with the class changing *I* ➔ *he* or *she.*

Evaluation

- Direct Ss' attention to the lesson focus written on the board.
- Write *How long* on the board. Have Ss ask questions using *How long.* Ask other Ss to answer the questions using *for* and *since.*
- Check off each part of the lesson focus as Ss demonstrate an understanding of what they have learned in the lesson.

More Ventures, Unit 2, Lesson B	
Workbook, 15–30 min.	
Add Ventures, 30–45 min. **Collaborative,** 30–45 min.	www.cambridge.org/myresourceroom
Student Arcade, time varies	www.cambridge.org/venturesarcade

B Talk with a partner. Ask and answer questions about Alex. Use *since*.

A How long has Alex been in the United States?
B Since January 2012.

Alex's Recent History

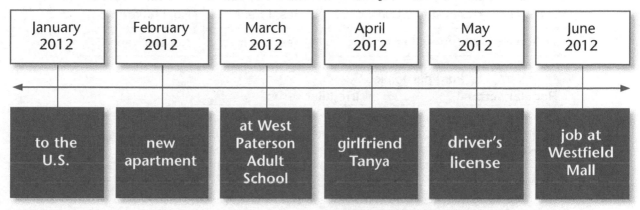

January 2012	February 2012	March 2012	April 2012	May 2012	June 2012
to the U.S.	new apartment	at West Paterson Adult School	girlfriend Tanya	driver's license	job at Westfield Mall

1. be in the U.S.
2. live in his new apartment
3. study at West Paterson Adult School
4. know his girlfriend Tanya
5. have a driver's license
6. work at Westfield Mall

Write today's date. Then write sentences about Alex. Use *for*.

Today is July 23, 2015.

Alex has been in the U.S. for three years and six months.
(Answers will vary.)

3 Communicate

A Work in a small group. Ask and answer questions with *how long*.

A How long have you studied English?
B For three years.
A That's interesting. How long have you lived in this country?
B Since 1998.
A Wow!

> **USEFUL** LANGUAGE
>
> To express interest or surprise, you can say:
> *That's interesting.*
> *Really?*
> *Wow!*

1. study / English
2. live / in this country
3. be / at this school
4. work / in this country
5. have / your job
6. know / our teacher
7. be / married
8. lived / in your present home

B Share information about your classmates.

☑ Use the present perfect with *how long*, *for*, and *since*

LESSON C Present perfect

1 Grammar focus: questions with *ever*; short answers

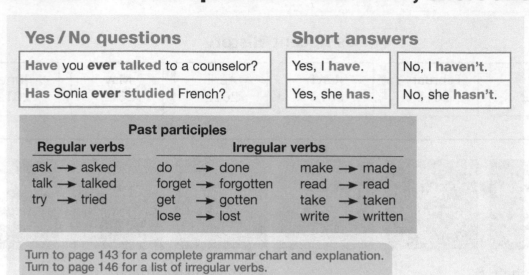

Yes / No questions

| Have you **ever talked** to a counselor? |
| Has Sonia **ever studied** French? |

Short answers

| Yes, I **have**. | No, I **haven't**. |
| Yes, she **has**. | No, she **hasn't**. |

Past participles

Regular verbs	Irregular verbs	
ask → asked	do → done	make → made
talk → talked	forget → forgotten	read → read
try → tried	get → gotten	take → taken
	lose → lost	write → written

Turn to page 143 for a complete grammar chart and explanation.
Turn to page 146 for a list of irregular verbs.

2 Practice

A Write. Complete the sentences. Use *ever*.

> Check your past participle verb form. Use the chart on page 146.

1. A _____Has Laura ever talked_____ to her school counselor?
       (Laura / talk)

    B No, she hasn't.

2. A _____Have you ever forgotten_____ your teacher's name?
       (you / forget)

    B Yes, I have.

3. A _____Has Joseph ever read_____ a book in English?
       (Joseph / read)

    B No, he hasn't. But he wants to.

4. A _____Have Mary and Paula ever been_____ late to school?
       (Mary and Paula / be)

    B No, they haven't.

5. A _____Have you ever tried_____ to speak English with your neighbors?
       (you / try)

    B Yes, I have.

6. A _____Has Tomas ever taken_____ the wrong bus to school?
       (Tomas / take)

    B No, he hasn't.

 Listen and check your answers. Then practice with a partner.

CLASS CD1 TK 15

Lesson objectives

- Introduce present perfect questions with *ever*
- Practice present perfect short answers

Warm-up and review

Before class: Write today's lesson focus on the board.

Lesson C:
Present perfect questions with <u>ever</u>
Present perfect short answers

- Books open. Begin class. Ask Ss to quickly look over Lesson B, Exercise 3, Communicate. Have Ss underline the present perfect and circle the time phrases *(since / for)* in the box. Ask: *How do you form the present perfect?* (have / has + past participle.) *When do you use the present perfect?* (to talk about actions that started in the past and continue to now.).

- Have Ss ask you questions using *How long*. Answer the questions. Then have them ask other questions using *How long*. Encourage Ss to respond using long and short answers. Make corrections as needed.

Presentation

Focus on meaning / personalize

- Books closed. Direct Ss' attention to the lesson focus on the board. Read it aloud. Ask students what activities they like to do. Elicit six activities and write them on the board, for example: *play soccer, walk on the beach, travel to San Francisco, go to the park, go dancing, go for a drive.*

- Write on the board: *ever = at any time in the past.* Say: *I have never played soccer. But I have gone to San Francisco.* Ask Ss *Have you ever* questions about the activities on the board. Elicit a few *Yes / No* answers.

- Explain that we use *ever* in *Yes / No* questions with the present perfect to ask about things a person may have done at any time before now.

Focus on form

- Books open. Direct Ss' attention to the Questions and Short answers charts in Exercise 1. Ask one S to read the first question and answer. Then write both on the board. Ask Ss to identify the present perfect *(have talked)*. Do the same for the second question and answer *(have studied)*.

- Review the correct form of *have* with pronouns. Say and write: *I, you, he, she, it, we, you,* and *they* on the board. Ss choose *has* or *have* for each pronoun. Write the correct answers next to each pronoun on the board.

- Write individual Ss' names next to each of the activities on the board. Ask each student one of the questions below if they have done the activity listed. Once the student has answered, tell the class to turn that sentence into a third person pronoun. For example, *Has (S's name) played soccer?* (Yes, she / he has. No, she / he hasn't.) Ask additional Ss questions and then ask the class about two Ss and the same activity. For example, *Have (S's name and S's name) gone dancing?* (Yes, they have. No, they haven't.)

Practice

- Direct Ss' attention to Exercise 2A. Read the instructions aloud.

- Model the task. Ask two Ss to read aloud the example question and answer. Point out the words under the blanks. Be sure Ss understand that they are to use these words in their questions.

- Ss complete the exercise individually. Walk around and help as needed.

Comprehension check

- Read aloud the second part of the instructions in Exercise 2A.

- Class Audio CD1 track 15 Play or read the audio program (see audio script, page T-156). Ss listen and check their answers.

- Ss practice saying the questions and answers with a partner. Walk around and listen to Ss' pronunciation. Correct as needed.

Expansion activity *(Individual work, whole group)*

- Help Ss create a verb book. Draw a vertical line down the board to make two columns. Title the left column *Base verb.* Title the right column *Past participle.*

- Ask Ss for a verb to write in the left column, such as *live.* Elicit what you should write in the right column: *lived.* Continue with other verbs.

- Ask Ss to copy the two columns into their notebooks. Have Ss add to the columns each time they see a new verb. From time to time throughout the course, write the two columns on the board and ask Ss to add verbs that they have learned. Encourage them to share these new verbs with classmates.

Presentation

- Books closed. Write on the board: *Good study habits.* Say the words aloud. Ask Ss to repeat. Have Ss define what *a habit* is. Elicit an appropriate response, such as: *an action you do all the time.*
- Tell Ss that good study habits are things you do often to learn and understand something more easily. Ask Ss to brainstorm good study habits. Write Ss' ideas on the board, such as: *study every night, write new words on index cards,* etc.
- Books open. Focus Ss' attention on Exercise **2B**. Read the instructions aloud.
- Have Ss look at the list of good study habits. Ask a S to read the list aloud. If Ss don't remember what a *to-do list* is, explain that it is a list of things that a person plans to do. Ask Ss if they make to-do lists. If a S says *Yes,* ask what kinds of things he or she writes on the list. Write the examples on the board, or make up a to-do list with the class, such as: *go to the grocery store, do the laundry, do English homework.*
- Model the task. Ask two Ss to read the example conversation aloud.
- Ss complete the exercise in pairs. Help as needed.

Practice

- Read aloud the instructions in the second part of Exercise **2B**. Ask a S to read the example sentence aloud. Tell Ss to write sentences about their partner.
- Ss complete the exercise individually. Help as needed.
- Tell Ss to show their partner the sentences they wrote and to ask their partner if the information is correct and if the sentences are written correctly. Ss should work in pairs to correct each other's sentences.
- Ask Ss to read aloud a sentence about their partners to the rest of the class.
- When Ss are finished, ask: *Do you think these are good study habits? Why or why not?*

Application

- Direct Ss' attention to Exercise **3A**. Read the instructions aloud.
- Model the task. Ask two Ss to read aloud the example question and answer.
- Review the word *concentrating.* Write it on the board. Ask Ss if they remember what it means. Elicit an appropriate response, such as: *It means to focus and think hard about something.*
- Ss complete the exercise in small groups. Help as needed.

- Direct Ss' attention to Exercise **3B**. Read the instructions aloud.
- Model the task. Ask two Ss to read aloud the example sentences.
- Continue the exercise by asking Ss to share information they learned about their classmates and the advice they gave them.

Expansion activity (student pairs)

- Role-play. Ask Ss to practice role-playing the activity of a S asking a school counselor for advice. Write an example of a conversation on the board, such as:

Student:	*I'm having problems in school.*
Counselor:	*What kinds of problems are you having?*
Student:	*I have trouble concentrating.*
Counselor:	*Have you ever tried studying in a quiet place?*
Student:	*That's a good idea. I'll try that.*

- Ask two Ss to read aloud the example conversation.
- Have Ss work in pairs to write and practice their own conversation.
- Ask several pairs to act out their conversations for the rest of the class. Tell Ss that they can use the examples of study problems in Exercise **3A** for their conversations.

Learner persistence (whole group)

- The expansion activity can be used to give Ss with real study problems ideas about how to gain better study habits and be more successful in English class.

Evaluation

- Direct Ss' attention to the lesson focus on the board. Ask as many Ss as possible to ask a question using *ever.* Encourage Ss to ask one another about study problems.
- Check off each part of the lesson focus as Ss demonstrate an understanding of what they have learned in the lesson.

More Ventures, Unit 2, Lesson C	
Workbook, 15–30 min.	
Add Ventures, 30–45 min. **Collaborative,** 30–45 min.	www.cambridge.org/myresourceroom
Student Arcade, time varies	www.cambridge.org/venturesarcade

B **Talk** with a partner. Ask and answer questions about study habits.

A Have you ever made a to-do list?
B No, never.
A Have you ever asked questions in class?
B Yes, I have.

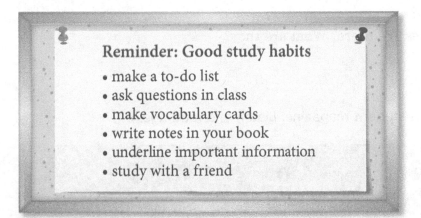

Reminder: Good study habits

- make a to-do list
- ask questions in class
- make vocabulary cards
- write notes in your book
- underline important information
- study with a friend

Write sentences about your partner.

Omar has never made a to-do list. He has asked questions in class.
(Answers will vary.)

USEFUL LANGUAGE

has never = hasn't ever

3 Communicate

A **Work** in a small group. Ask and answer questions about study problems. Complete the chart.

A Have you ever had trouble concentrating?
B Yes, I have.

Study problems	Name: _____	Name: _____
have trouble concentrating	Yes	
forget to study for a test	(Answers will vary.)	
lose your textbook		
do the wrong homework		
be late to school		
(your idea)		

B **Share** information about your classmates. Give advice.

Ana has had trouble concentrating.

She should do her homework in a quiet place.

☑ Use the present perfect to ask and answer *Yes / No* questions with *ever* **UNIT 2** **23**

LESSON D Reading

1 Before you read

Look at the title and strategies. Answer the questions.

1. What is the reading about?
2. What are *strategies*?
3. How many strategies are there? What are they?

2 Read

STUDENT TK 12
CLASS CD1 TK 16

Read the article from a student magazine. Listen and read again.

Strategies for Learning English

Have you ever felt discouraged because it's hard to speak and understand English? Don't give up! Here are three strategies to help you learn faster and remember more.

Strategy #1 Set goals.

Have you ever <u>set</u> goals for learning English? When you set goals, you decide what you want to learn. After you determine your purpose for learning, you can make a <u>plan</u> to help you reach your goals. Maybe your goal is to learn more vocabulary. There are many ways to do this. For example, you can read in English for 15 minutes every day. You can also learn one new word every day.

Strategy #2 Look for opportunities to practice English.

Talk to everyone. Speak with people in the store, at work, and in the park. Don't worry about making mistakes. And don't forget to ask questions. For example, if your teacher uses a word you don't understand, ask a question like "What does that word mean?"

Strategy #3 <u>Guess</u>.

Don't try to translate every word. When you read, concentrate on <u>clues</u> such as <u>pictures</u> or other words in the sentence to help you understand. You can also make guesses when you are talking to people. For example, look at their faces and hand <u>gestures</u> – the way they move their hands – to help you guess the meaning.

Set goals, look for opportunities to <u>practice</u>, and guess. Do these things every day, and you will learn more English!

In a reading, *for example* means *details will follow*.

Lesson objectives

- Introduce and read "Strategies for Learning English"
- Identify examples that support statements
- Identify parts of speech to define words

Warm-up and review

- Before class. Write today's lesson focus on the board.
  Lesson D:
  Identify examples that support statements
  Identify parts of speech to define words
- Begin class. Books closed. Point to *Strategies* on the board. Say the word aloud. Ask Ss to repeat. Ask what the word means. Help Ss understand that strategies are ideas about ways to reach a goal.
- Ask: *Have you ever thought of good strategies for waking up on time for an early morning class? What are some of these strategies?* Elicit appropriate responses, such as: *set an alarm, ask a friend to call on the phone, ask a relative to wake you up, keep curtains open for the sun to come into the room.*

Presentation

- Books open. Direct Ss' attention to Exercise **1** and read the instructions aloud.
- Ask a S to read the three questions to the class.
- Have Ss skim the article for answers to the questions. Remind Ss that "to skim" means to read something quickly. Discuss the answers. Ask Ss to tell you where the answers are found in the reading.

Practice

- Read the instructions for Exercise **2** aloud. Ask Ss to read the article silently before they listen to the audio program.
- Class Audio CD1 track 16 Play or read the audio program and ask Ss to read along silently (see audio script, page T-156). Repeat the audio program as needed.
- While Ss are listening and reading the article, ask them to write any words in their notebooks that they don't understand. When the audio program is finished, ask Ss to write the new vocabulary words on the board.
- Point to each word on the board. Say it aloud. Ask Ss to repeat. Give a brief explanation of each word, or ask Ss to explain the word if some of them are familiar with it.
- Encourage Ss to find the meanings of the new words from context. For example: If a S writes *goals* on the board, show where the meaning of the word is in the article: . . . *you decide what you want to learn. . . . make a plan. . . .* Ask Ss to give examples of goals that they have in their lives, such as: *I want to get a better job.*

Read the tip box aloud. Ask Ss to find places in the article where *for example* is used. Have Ss locate the details that follow this phrase.

Learner persistence *(individual work)*

- Self-Study Audio CD track 12 Exercise **2** is recorded on the CD at the back of the Student's Book. Ss can listen to the CD at home for reinforcement and review. They can also listen for self-directed learning when class attendance is not possible.

Expansion activity *(whole group)*

- Write this grid on the board.

Name	What strategy do you use for learning English?

- Ask Ss to copy this grid onto a piece of paper. Tell Ss to talk to five classmates and to write down their names and answers to the question in the chart.
- Call on several Ss to share what they learned about their classmates.

Expansion activity *(student pairs)*

- Books closed. Ask Ss to try to recall the strategies for learning English from the article in Exercise **2**.
- Tell Ss to work in pairs and write down the three strategies they read about in the article. Then encourage them to give each other examples of each of the strategies.
- Walk around and listen to Ss as they discuss the strategies. This type of retelling exercise can show you how much Ss have comprehended after doing a reading exercise.

Comprehension check

- Books open. Direct Ss' attention to Exercise **3A**. Read the instructions aloud.
- Ask individual Ss to read the questions aloud, one at a time. Make sure that all Ss understand the questions.
- Ss in pairs. Ask Ss to ask and answer the questions with a partner. Tell them that they can refer to the magazine article on page 24.
- Discuss the answers to the questions with the class. Ask where in the reading the answers are found.

Practice

- Focus Ss' attention on Exercise **3B**. Read the instructions aloud. Be sure that Ss understand the three steps in this exercise.
- Model the task. Point to the word *set* in the chart. Ask Ss to find the word in the reading on page 24. Have a S read the sentence with this word. Tell Ss to underline the word *set* in the article. Ask a S to say whether *set* is a noun or a verb in this sentence and to read the definition that matches the part of speech in the chart.
- Ss complete the exercise individually. Walk around and help as needed.
- Ask Ss to compare their answers with a partner. Ask if Ss have any answers that differ from those of their partner. If there are differences, ask the class to say what they think the correct answer is. Ask Ss to explain their reasons for choosing the parts of speech and definitions they chose.

▼ **Teaching tip**
It might be helpful to discuss the different parts of speech with the class. Write *Noun* and *Verb* on the board. Ask Ss to give examples of these words. Write them on the board under the appropriate heading. Ask Ss to look at the examples and to give a definition of each of these words. Write the definitions on the board, for example: *A noun is a person, place, or thing (man, town, class); a verb is an action or a feeling word (set, like, be).*

Learner persistence *(individual work)*

- Encourage each S to use a dictionary to check the meanings of words and the parts of speech. A learner's dictionary is helpful. Encouraging the use of a dictionary to increase vocabulary is a good way to support each S's independent learning.

Application

- Focus Ss' attention on Exercise **3C**. Read the instructions aloud.
- Ask a S to read aloud the three questions in Exercise **3C**.
- Ss complete the exercise in pairs. Walk around and help as needed.
- Ask several pairs to ask and answer the questions for the rest of the class.

Evaluation

- Direct Ss' attention to the lesson focus on the board.
- Books closed. Write the words from Exercise **3B** on the board. Ask Ss to make sentences about the magazine article using these words.
- Check off each part of the lesson focus as Ss demonstrate an understanding of what they have learned in the lesson.

Learner persistence *(individuals, pairs)*

- You may wish to assign Extended Reading Worksheets from the *Online Teacher's Resource Room* for Ss to complete outside of class. The purpose of these worksheets is to encourage Ss to read for pleasure outside of the English class. The worksheets can also be assigned as extended reading in class.

More Ventures, Unit 2, Lesson D	
Workbook, 20–30 min.	
Add Ventures, 30–45 min.	
Collaborative, 30–45 min.	www.cambridge.org/myresourceroom
Extended Reading and worksheet, 45–60 min.	
Student Arcade, time varies	www.cambridge.org/venturesarcade

3 After you read

A Check your understanding.

1. What are goals?
2. What is an example of setting goals?
3. What is an example of looking for opportunities to practice English?
4. You ask someone in line at a supermarket, "What time is it?" What strategy are you using?
5. If you read a story without using a dictionary, what clues help you guess?

B Build your vocabulary.

1. Look at the chart. Find the vocabulary words in the article. Underline them.
2. Use the context to decide the part of speech of each word – *noun* or *verb*. Write it in the chart.
3. Circle the best definition to match the part of speech.

Vocabulary	Part of speech	Definition
1. set	*verb*	a. a group of related things, such as dishes b. to choose or decide on something, such as a goal
2. plan	*noun*	a. something you have decided to do b. to decide about something you want to do
3. practice	*verb*	a. an activity you do to improve your ability b. to do something regularly to improve your ability
4. guess	*verb*	a. an answer that you think is right, but you're not sure b. to give an answer that you think is right
5. clues	*noun*	a. information you use to guess or solve problems b. to give someone useful information
6. pictures	*noun*	a. paintings, drawings, or photographs b. to paint, draw, or photograph something
7. gestures	*noun*	a. hand movements that have a special meaning b. to tell something by moving your hands

C Talk with a partner. Ask and answer the questions.

1. Have you ever set goals for learning English?
   What were they?
2. How do you practice something new?
   Give an example.
3. When you speak, what gestures do you use?

LESSON E Writing

1 Before you write

A **Work** in a small group. Complete the chart with examples of strategies for learning English. Use the reading on page 24 and your own ideas.

Strategy	Examples from reading	Your examples
Set goals.	Read for 15 minutes in English every day.	Write in English every day for five minutes.
Practice English.	(Answers will vary.)	
Guess.		

B **Read** the paragraph.

My Strategies for Learning English

There are two strategies I'm going to use to help me learn English. My first strategy is to learn more English vocabulary. There are many ways I will do this. For example, I'm going to learn one new English word every day. I'm also going to write my new words in a notebook. Another strategy I will use is looking for places to practice my English. For example, I'm going to talk to more English speakers at the store and at work. I can't wait to try these new strategies because I want to speak, read, and write English better.

Use examples to support your ideas.

Work with a partner. Answer the questions.

1. What is the writer's first strategy? *learn more English vocabulary*
2. What examples does the writer give of the first strategy? *learn new word every day; write new words in notebook*
3. What is the writer's second strategy? *look for places to practice English*
4. What example does the writer give of the second strategy? *talk to people at the store and work*
5. The writer says, "I can't wait to try these new strategies." What does that mean? *He/she wants to try them soon.*
6. Do you think these strategies could help you? *(Answers will vary.)*

Warm-up and review

- Before class. Write today's lesson focus on the board.
  Lesson E:
  Read and write about strategies for learning English
  Use the present perfect
- Begin class. Books closed. Review vocabulary and grammar from the unit. Ask: *What have you learned about good strategies for learning English?* Elicit appropriate responses, such as: *set goals, practice outside of the class, ask questions, make guesses,* etc.
- Review the use of *Have you ever.* Ask individual Ss: *Have you ever set a goal for learning English? Have you ever talked to someone in the supermarket in English? Have you ever had trouble understanding English on TV? Have you ever made a joke in English?,* etc. Make sure that Ss respond using short answers in the present perfect (*Yes, I have. / No, I haven't.*)

Presentation

- Direct Ss' attention to Exercise **1A** and read the instructions aloud.
- Model the task. Ask a S to read aloud the example in the chart. Tell Ss that they will write other examples for each strategy in the chart.
- Ss complete the task in small groups. Walk around and help as needed.
- Copy the blank chart on the board. Have individual Ss come to the board to write their examples.
- Ask other Ss if they agree with the examples on the board. Ask different Ss to give other examples that could be added to the chart.

Practice

- Focus Ss' attention on Exercise **1B**. Read the instructions aloud.
- Ss read the paragraph silently. Ask them to underline any words in the paragraph that are unfamiliar.
- Have Ss tell you the words they underlined. Write them on the board. Go over the meaning of each word.

Learner persistence (individual work)

- Refer to the reading. Ask Ss if they keep a notebook for new vocabulary words. Encourage Ss to keep a notebook of new words and to review the words often. A part of every class could be devoted to asking Ss to share new words they have discovered.

Read the tip box aloud. Explain that in this case *support your ideas* means to help show what your ideas mean. Ask Ss to underline the examples in the paragraph. Explain how the examples support the main ideas in the paragraph. Ask Ss to underline the topic sentence and conclusion in the model paragraph.

Comprehension check

- Focus Ss' attention on the second part of the instructions in Exercise **1B** and read it aloud.
- Ask individual Ss to read the questions to the class. Make sure that Ss understand them.
- Ss work in pairs to ask and answer the questions. Walk around and help as needed.
- Ask several pairs to ask and answer the questions for the rest of the class.

Expansion activity (individual work)

- Ask Ss to think about something they would like to learn. Give examples of a hobby, a sport, or another language. Ask Ss to start by setting a goal for learning the new skill; then have them give examples of strategies for reaching this goal. Give an example for yourself. Write it on the board:
  Goal: *Learn to knit*
  Strategies to reach this goal: *Go to a knitting class; ask a friend to teach me; start by knitting something simple.*
- When Ss are finished, ask for volunteers to describe their goals and strategies for learning something new. Ask if any Ss are pursuing new skills at this time. Ask those Ss to describe how they are learning the new skill.

Learner persistence (individual work)

- If you have any Ss who are having problems with study skills, try to arrange a time to talk with each of these Ss after the class. Help these Ss to set goals for themselves. Brainstorm ways that these Ss can improve their English by using the strategies that are described in the unit.

LESSON E Writing

Presentation

- Direct Ss' attention to Exercise 1C and read the instructions aloud.
- Ask Ss to think about the strategies they have learned in this unit and have wanted to try. Have them think about other strategies they have heard, read about, or seen. Make a list on the board of Ss' suggestions.

Practice

- Ask individual Ss to read the five questions in Exercise 1C aloud. Make sure Ss understand them.
- Ss complete the task individually. Walk around and help as needed.
- Ask a few Ss to tell you their answers.

Application

- Direct Ss' attention to Exercise 2 and read the instructions aloud.
- Ss complete the paragraph individually. Walk around and help as needed.

▼ **Teaching tip**
If Ss are unsure of how to begin their paragraphs, ask for suggestions and write them on the board. Alternately, offer the following topic sentence and first supporting sentence as a way for Ss to begin writing: *My goal is to learn more English. I have heard about several strategies to reach this goal. For example, . . .*

Community building (small groups)

- If some Ss find writing very challenging, form small groups of Ss of differing abilities. Ask Ss to work together to write their paragraph as a group.

Comprehension check

- Direct Ss' attention to Exercise 3A. Read the instructions aloud.
- Ss complete the task individually. Walk around and help as needed.
- If Ss check *No* for any of the statements, encourage them to revise their paragraphs so that all the checklist items in Exercise 3A are included.

Evaluation

- Read the instructions for Exercise 3B aloud. Read the sentences to the class. Make sure that Ss understand the task.
- Ss complete the exercise to peer-correct their writing. Reading aloud enables the writer to review his or her own writing. Reading to a partner allows the writer to understand the need to write clearly for an audience.
- Ask several Ss what they have learned from the paragraph their partner wrote.

▼ **Teaching tip**
If Ss don't understand the verb *comment*, explain that it means to talk or give your opinion about something. Explain that *comment* can be both a noun and a verb. Give examples of each.

- Direct Ss' attention to the lesson focus on the board. Then refer Ss to the paragraph in Exercise 1B on page 26. Ask: *What strategies does this person use for learning English?* Elicit appropriate responses, for example: *This person likes setting goals such as learning a new English word every day and looking for places to practice English outside of class.*
- Have Ss recall what they have learned. Ask: *What did you learn to do in this writing lesson?* Elicit appropriate responses, for example: *We learned how to use strategies for planning a paragraph. We learned why strategies are important for learning English.*
- Check off each part of the lesson focus as Ss demonstrate an understanding of what they have learned in the lesson.

Community building (individual, whole group)

- Encourage your class to set goals as individuals and as a group. What do Ss want to learn most in the class? Write examples on the board. Do an informal needs assessment by looking at Ss' examples. Try to incorporate Ss' wants and needs for learning English into your lessons.

More Ventures, Unit 2, Lesson E	
Workbook, 15–30 min.	
Add Ventures, 30–45 min.	www.cambridge.org/myresourceroom
Collaborative, 30–45 min.	

C **Write** a plan for a paragraph about strategies for learning English. Answer the questions.

1. What is one strategy you want to try?	*(Answers will vary.)*
2. What is one example of this strategy?	
3. What is another strategy you want to try?	
4. What is one example of this strategy?	
5. Why do you want to try these strategies?	

2 Write

Write a paragraph about strategies for learning English. Include a topic sentence that focuses on strategies. Write about two strategies and give one or two examples for each one. Use Exercises 1B and 1C to help you.

3 After you write

A **Check** your writing.

	Yes	No
1. I included a topic sentence that focuses on strategies.	☐	☐
2. I wrote about two strategies I want to try.	☐	☐
3. I gave two examples for each strategy.	☐	☐

B **Share** your writing with a partner.

1. Take turns. Read your paragraph to a partner.
2. Comment on your partner's paragraph. Ask your partner a question about the paragraph. Tell your partner one thing you learned.

LESSON F Another view

1 Life-skills reading

Tips for Taking Tests

1 Read the instructions carefully. Ask the teacher if you don't understand them.

2 Skim the whole test before you begin. This will help you decide how to use your time.

3 Answer the easiest questions first.

4 Don't spend a lot of time on one question. Go back to it later if you have time.

5 Don't worry if other classmates finish before you. Pay attention to your own test.

6 Leave time to check your answers. Make sure you have answered every question.

7 Don't look at another student's paper. Be responsible for your own work.

> **CULTURE NOTE**
>
> During a test, don't look at another student's paper, ask another student for help, or help another student. These are types of cheating.

A Read the questions. Look at the tips. Fill in the answer.

1. Which tip says to read the whole test quickly before you answer any questions?
   - Ⓐ Tip 1
   - Ⓒ Tip 6
   - ● Tip 2
   - Ⓓ Tip 7

2. Which tip tells you to answer the questions you know first?
   - Ⓐ Tip 1
   - ● Tip 3
   - Ⓑ Tip 2
   - Ⓓ Tip 4

3. Which tip tells you to skip the questions you don't know and go back to them later?
   - Ⓐ Tip 3
   - Ⓒ Tip 5
   - ● Tip 4
   - Ⓓ Tip 6

4. Which tip says you should answer every question?
   - Ⓐ Tip 1
   - Ⓒ Tip 4
   - Ⓑ Tip 3
   - ● Tip 6

B Talk with a partner. Ask and answer the questions.

1. Have you ever tried any of these tips? Did they help you?
2. Do you have any other tips for taking tests? What are they?

Lesson objectives
- Read "7 Tips for Taking Tests"
- Contrast simple past and present perfect
- Complete the self-assessment

Warm-up and review

- Before class. Write today's lesson focus on the board.

  Lesson F:
  Tips for taking tests
  Review vocabulary and grammar from Unit 2
  Complete the self-assessment

- Begin class. Books closed. Focus Ss' attention on *Tips for taking tests* in the lesson focus. Say the words aloud. Ask Ss to repeat.

- Ask Ss what *tips* are. If they don't know, explain that they are helpful hints or pieces of information that help you do something better.

▼ Teaching tip
Ss may confuse this word with *tips* that are left in a restaurant. It might be helpful to go over the two meanings of the word.

- Ask Ss to brainstorm tips for doing well on tests. Write their ideas on the board. Elicit appropriate responses, such as: *go to bed on time the night before the test, eat a good breakfast on the day of the test, read the instructions carefully.*

Community building *(whole group)*

- Ask Ss if they have followed any of the tips on the board before taking a test. Ask if the tips helped them. If any Ss in your class have difficulty with test-taking, encourage them to get tips about taking tests from other Ss in the class or from the lesson they are about to study in the book.

Presentation

- Books open. Direct Ss' attention to the reading in Exercise 1. Ask Ss: *What is the title of the reading?* ("7 Tips for Taking Tests"). Have Ss read the tips silently. Tell Ss to underline any words that they don't understand. Ask Ss to write these words on the board.

- When Ss are finished, point to the words on the board in turn. Say them aloud. Ask Ss to repeat. Then explain the meanings of the words.

▼ Teaching tip
Remind Ss of the reading strategies they learned in the last unit for figuring out the meanings of new words from context.

▼ Culture note
Read the culture note aloud. Explain that cheating on a test can have severe consequences, such as a grade of 0. Explain that if Ss don't complete their tests individually, teachers have no idea of what Ss have learned in the class. Explain that cheating is very serious and is not permitted.

Practice

- Direct Ss' attention to Exercise **1A** and read the instructions aloud. This task helps prepare Ss for standardized-type tests they may have to take. Be sure Ss understand the task. Have Ss individually scan for and fill in the answers.

Comprehension check

- Check answers with the class. Ask Ss to read the questions and their answers aloud. Ask Ss: *Is that answer correct?* Make any necessary corrections.

Application

- Focus Ss' attention on Exercise **1B** and read the instructions aloud. Ask a S to read the questions to the class.

- Ss work in pairs to ask each other the questions. Walk around and help as needed.

- After pairs have discussed the questions, open up the discussion to the whole class.

Learner persistence *(whole group)*

- Write on the board any innovative tips that Ss talk about in response to question number 2 in Exercise **1B**. Encourage Ss to write down the tips to use in the future.

- Make a poster of test tips and learning strategies to display in the classroom.

Warm-up and review

- Books closed. Ask Ss: *When do you use the present perfect?* Elicit answers, such as: *To talk about actions that started in the past and continue to now.* Ask Ss questions with *How long* and *ever.* Ask Ss to repeat other Ss' answers changing the pronoun *I* into *he* or *she*.

Presentation

- Books open. Direct Ss' attention to the chart in Exercise 2A. Read aloud the first sentence: *She studied Spanish in 2011.* Ask Ss what the sentence conveys. Elicit answers, such as: *The sentence refers to a specific time (2011) when she studied Spanish.* Read aloud the second sentence: *She has studied Spanish for 10 years.* Ask Ss what the sentence conveys. Elicit answers such as: *The sentence describes an action (studying) that started ten years ago and continues to the present.*

- Contrast the two sentences. Explain that we use simple past for an activity that happened and ended at a specific time in the past. Explain that the present perfect describes an activity that began in the past and continues to the present.

- Write these two questions on the board:
  When did you move to the United States?
  How long have you lived in the United States?

- Underline the verb chunk *did you move* in the first question and point out that the verb chunk is in the simple past. Underline the verb phrase *have you lived* in the second sentence and point out that the verb phrase is in the present perfect. Ensure Ss understand the difference between the two verb tenses. Ask a few Ss the questions, and write their answers on the board. Urge Ss to use *for* and *since* to answer the second question.

Practice

- Direct Ss' attention to the instructions in 2A. Read the instructions aloud. Ensure Ss understand the activity. Ask a pair of Ss to read the dialog aloud.

- Ss complete the exercise in pairs. Walk around and help as needed. Encourage Ss to make a list of the reasons why they are choosing a particular tutor.

- Direct Ss' attention to the instructions in 2B. Read the instructions aloud. Model the activity. Read the two sentence lead-ins. Ask several pairs to share the reasons why they chose Rita or Dao. Ensure Ss use the present perfect and simple past correctly in their answers.

Evaluation

- Before asking students to turn to the self-assessment on page 136, do a quick review of the unit. Have Ss turn to Lesson A. Ask the class to talk about what they remember about this lesson. Prompt Ss, if necessary, with questions, for example: *What are the conversations about on this page? What vocabulary is in the pictures?* Continue in this manner to review each lesson quickly.

- **Self-assessment** Read the instructions for Exercise 3. Ask Ss to turn to the self-assessment page and complete the unit self-assessment. The self-assessments are also on the *Online Teacher's Resource Room*. If you prefer to collect the assessments and save them as part of each S's portfolio assessment, print out the unit self-assessment from the *Resource Room*, ask students to complete it, and collect and save it.

- If Ss are ready, administer the unit test on pages T-167–T-168 of this Teacher's Edition (or on the Assessment Audio CD / CD-ROM).

More Ventures, Unit 2, Lesson F	
Workbook, 15–30 min.	
Add Ventures, 30–45 min.	www.cambridge.org/myresourceroom
Collaborative, 30–45 min.	
Student Arcade, time varies	www.cambridge.org/venturesarcade

2 **Grammar connections:** simple past and present perfect

Use the *simple past* for an activity that happened at a specific time in the past.	Use the *present perfect* for an activity that began in the past and continues to the present.
She **studied** Spanish in 2011.	She **has studied** Spanish for ten years.

A **Talk** with a partner. You need an English tutor. Look at the chart and compare the two tutors. Use the simple past and present perfect to talk about the tutors' experience. With your partner, choose the tutor you think is best.

A   Rita would be a good tutor. She studied Spanish for four years, and she took French classes. She has also studied Arabic since 2010.

B   Maybe, but she hasn't had any tutoring experience. Dao has tutored English since 2011. He also . . .

Rita Lawrence

1950 – 1970	live in Phoenix, AZ
1970 – 1974	study Spanish in college
1974	graduate from college with B average, degree in education
1974 – 1980	teach English in Mexico
1981	get married to English teacher
1982 – 2006	stay home with children
2006 – 2009	study French at night school
2006 – now	teach at an elementary school
2010 – now	study Arabic online
2011 – now	volunteer at a hospital translating Spanish to English

Dao Lin

1985 – 1999	live in Shanghai, China
1999	move to Chicago, IL
1999 – 2003	learn English in high school
2003 – 2007	study English and computer science in college
2007	graduate from college with A average, degree in computer science
2007	travel around U.S. for four months
2007 – 2009	work for travel agency
2010 – now	work as a computer technician
2011 – now	tutor English at a high school
2012 – now	live with aunt and uncle, who only speak Chinese

B **Share** your decision with the class.

We chose Rita because . . .

We chose Dao because . . .

3 **Wrap up**

Complete the **Self-assessment** on page 136.

☑ Scan a tip sheet to identify test-taking strategies; contrast simple past and present perfect   **UNIT 2   29**

Review

1 Listening

Listen. Put a check (✓) under the correct name.

CLASS CD1 TK 17

	Vladimir	Marisol
1. asks the teacher questions		✓
2. asks another student questions	✓	
3. writes vocabulary on index cards	✓	
4. talks to co-workers		✓
5. is shy	✓	
6. is outgoing		✓

Talk with a partner. Check your answers.

2 Grammar

A **Write.** Complete the story. Use the correct words.

Homework Problems

Jameela ___has had___ a lot of problems with her son, Faisal, for
  1. has / has had
the past two months. He doesn't enjoy ___studying___ science. He
  2. studying / study
___has gotten___ bad grades on his tests. The teacher said that Faisal
  3. get / has gotten
___hasn't done___ his homework since December. Faisal said he hates
  4. doesn't do / hasn't done
___doing___ his science homework because he doesn't understand it.
  5. do / doing
Jameela ___has worked___ overtime at her job for the past two months, so she
  6. works / has worked
___hasn't been___ able to help him. What should Jameela and her son do?
  7. hasn't been / won't be

B **Write.** Look at the answers. Write the questions.

1. **A** How long *has Jameela had problems with her son* ?
   B Jameela has had problems with her son for the past two months.

2. **A** *Has Faisal* ever *gotten bad grades on his tests* ?
   B Yes, he has. Faisal has gotten bad grades on his tests for the past two months.

3. **A** How long *has Jameela worked overtime* ?
   B Jameela has worked overtime for the past two months.

Talk with a partner. Ask and answer the questions.

Lesson objectives
- Review vocabulary and grammar from Units 1 and 2
- Introduce stressing content words

UNITS 1&2

Warm-up and review

- Before class. Write today's lesson focus on the board.
  Review unit:
  Review vocabulary, pronunciation, and grammar from Units 1 and 2
  Stress content words

- Begin class. Books closed. Review language for personality types and study problems. Ask individual Ss:

  Do you enjoy going out? Do you like staying home?
  Do you like cooking more than washing dishes?
  What are some examples of personality types? (outgoing, intellectual, creative)
  Have you ever had study problems? What are they?
  What are some good study habits?
  Have you ever made a to-do list?

Presentation

- Books open. Direct Ss' attention to Exercise 1 and read the instructions aloud. Tell Ss that they will hear a conversation between Vladimir (a male student) and Marisol (a female student).

- Class Audio CD1 track 17 Model the task. Play or read only the first part of the conversation on the audio program (see audio script, page T-156). Pause the program after Marisol and Vladimir have each spoken once. Direct Ss' attention to the first item in the chart (*asks the teacher questions*). Ask: *Who does this – Vladimir or Marisol?* (Marisol.) Tell Ss to check the box under *Marisol.*

- Read aloud the remaining items in the chart. Say: *Who does these things – Vladimir or Marisol? Listen and put a check mark next to the correct speaker.*

- Class Audio CD1 track 17 Play or read the complete audio program (see audio script, page T-156). Ss listen and check the boxes. Repeat the audio program as needed.

- Read aloud the second part of the instructions for Exercise 1. Ss complete the exercise in pairs.

Expansion activity (whole group)

- Do a *Find Someone Who* activity using the study strategies in the chart in Exercise 1. Tell Ss to add to the Student's Book a column to the right side of the chart, writing the heading *Students in my class.*

- Tell Ss that they need to find other Ss in the class who use the study strategies in the chart. Write on the board: *Do you _____?* and *Are you _____?*

- Ask Ss to think of questions to ask other Ss about the strategies in the chart. Write the questions on the board, for example: *Do you ask the teacher questions? Do you ask another student questions? Do you put vocabulary on index cards? Do you talk to co-workers in English? Are you shy? Are you outgoing?*

- Model the activity. Ask a S: *Do you ask the teacher questions?* If the S says *Yes*, write that S's name in the same row as the activity in the added chart column. If the S says *No*, ask other Ss until you find a S who says *Yes.*

- Encourage Ss to walk around the room to ask the questions of as many Ss as possible.

- When Ss are finished, ask the class who answered *Yes* to each of the questions.

Practice

- Direct Ss' attention to Exercise 2A. Ask Ss: *What is the title of this story?* ("Homework Problems")

- Read aloud the instructions in Exercise 2A. Read the first sentence and ask Ss to repeat. Tell Ss to continue reading the story and filling in the blanks. Explain that Ss must choose the correct words under the blanks. This exercise does not ask Ss to change the word forms.

- Ss complete the exercise individually. Help as needed.

- Write the numbers *1–7* on the board. Ask Ss to come to the board to write the answers. Tell them to write only the words that are missing from the blanks, not the entire sentences.

- Ask Ss to read the completed story silently to get the main idea. When Ss have finished reading, ask: *What is the story about?* (Faisal's homework problems.)

- Read the story aloud using Ss' answers. Make corrections on the board.

▼ **Teaching tip**
Remind Ss to look for clues that will help them determine which form of the verb to use in the sentences. Remind them that *for* and *since* are used with the present perfect; therefore, if these words are used in the sentences, Ss should choose the present perfect form of the verb.

- Direct Ss' attention to Exercise 2B. Read the instructions aloud. Ask two Ss to read aloud the example question and answer.

- Ss work individually to write the questions. Help as needed.

- Check answers with the class. Ask for volunteers to read their questions. Correct as needed.

- Read aloud the second part of the instructions for Exercise 2B.

- Ss work in pairs to ask and answer the questions. Help with pronunciation.

Review

Warm-up and review

- Write on the board: *I like speaking English with my friends.* Say the sentence, giving each word the same amount of time and the same stress. Point to each word as you say it. The sentence will sound unnatural and robotic. Explain that this is what stress sounds like and that in English, not all words are stressed. Say the sentence again naturally, stressing only the underlined words. Explain that this is natural English stress. Point to only the stressed words as you say the sentence naturally. Ask Ss to repeat the sentence.

Presentation

- Direct Ss' attention to Exercise **3A**. Read the instructions aloud. Tell Ss to listen for the underlined content words in each sentence.

- 🎧 Class Audio CD1 track 18 Play or read the complete audio program (see audio script, page T-157). Repeat the program as needed.
- Direct Ss' attention to the second part of the instructions in Exercise **3A**, and read it aloud.
- 🎧 Class Audio CD1 track 18 Play or read the complete audio program (see audio script, page T-157). Ss listen and repeat the sentences. Stop or repeat the audio program as needed.
- Direct Ss' attention to Exercise **3B**. Read the instructions aloud.
- 🎧 Class Audio CD1 track 19 Model the task. Play or read the first sentence in the audio program (see audio script, page T-157). Ask Ss to repeat the sentence and look at the underlined words in the example in the exercise. Make sure Ss can recognize which words are being stressed.
- Write the second sentence on the board. Play or read the second sentence in the audio program and ask students to identify the content words. Underline the words in the sentence.
- 🎧 Class Audio CD1 track 19 Play or read the complete audio program (see audio script, page T-157). Ss listen, repeat the sentences, and underline the stressed words. Stop or repeat the audio program as needed.

Practice

- Read aloud the second part of the instructions for Exercise **3B**. Model the task. Write the third sentence from Exercise **3B** on the board. Ask a volunteer to come to the board and read the sentence aloud. Ask the S to underline the stressed content words in the sentence.
- Ask another S to come to the board and read the sentence again. Ask if the second S agrees with the words that the first S underlined.
- Ss complete the task in pairs. Help as needed.
- Read each sentence aloud with the correct stress. Ask Ss to repeat.

Comprehension check

- Direct Ss' attention to Exercise **3C** and read the instructions aloud.
- Ss complete the exercise individually.
- Read the paragraph in a natural way, and ask Ss to listen and check their underlined content words against what they hear.
- Read aloud the second part of the instructions in Exercise **3C**.
- Ss complete the exercise in pairs. Make sure that Ss are stressing the correct words.

Evaluation

- Direct Ss' attention to the lesson focus on the board.
- Ask individual Ss questions using the grammar points in the lesson focus. For example: *Do you like dancing? Do you enjoy studying English as much as working? How long have you lived here? Have you ever been to Canada?*
- Write the questions on the board. Ask Ss to read the questions aloud, using the correct word stress for content words.
- Check off each part of the lesson focus as Ss demonstrate an understanding of what they have learned in the lesson.

3 **Pronunciation:** stressing content words

CLASS CD1 TK 18

A **Listen** to the stressed content words in each sentence. Content words include main verbs, nouns, adverbs, adjectives, and question words.

1. She <u>loves</u> <u>playing</u> <u>cards</u> with <u>friends</u>.
2. He <u>hates</u> <u>working</u> in the <u>garden</u>.
3. Do you <u>like</u> <u>being</u> <u>alone</u>?
4. She <u>enjoys</u> <u>cooking</u> less than <u>eating</u>.
5. I <u>like</u> <u>living</u> in the <u>city</u>.
6. <u>How</u> <u>long</u> has Shen <u>studied</u> <u>English</u>?
7. He's been <u>here</u> for <u>six</u> <u>months</u>.
8. Have you <u>ever</u> <u>studied</u> <u>Korean</u>?

Listen again and repeat. Stress the content words.

CLASS CD1 TK 19

B **Listen and repeat.** Then underline the content words.

1. <u>What</u> is the <u>perfect</u> <u>job</u> for you?
2. The <u>perfect</u> <u>job</u> <u>depends</u> on your <u>personality</u>.
3. Have you <u>ever</u> <u>felt</u> <u>discouraged</u>?
4. Have you <u>ever</u> <u>set</u> <u>goals</u> for <u>learning</u> <u>English</u>?
5. <u>What</u> does that <u>word</u> <u>mean</u>?
6. <u>Intellectual</u> <u>people</u> <u>often</u> <u>enjoy</u> <u>working</u> <u>alone</u>.

Read your sentences to a partner. Compare your answers.

C **Read** the paragraph. Underline the content words.

My <u>sister</u> has the <u>right</u> <u>job</u> for her <u>personality</u>. She's a <u>nurse</u>. She <u>works</u> in a <u>big</u> <u>hospital</u> in the <u>Philippines</u>. She is a very <u>outgoing</u> <u>person</u>. She's very <u>friendly</u> with all her <u>patients</u>, and she <u>enjoys</u> <u>talking</u> to <u>people</u> in the <u>hospital</u>. She is <u>warm</u> and <u>helpful</u>. I <u>think</u> a <u>nurse</u> is a <u>good</u> <u>job</u> for her because it <u>fits</u> her <u>personality</u>.

Talk with a partner. Compare your answers. Read the paragraph to your partner. Stress the content words.

LESSON A
Listening

1 Before you listen

A What do you see?

B What is happening?

C What's the story?

Warm-up and review
- Before class. Write today's lesson focus on the board.
  Lesson A:
  Neighborhood problems
- Begin class. Books closed. Direct Ss' attention to the lesson focus. Point to *neighborhood*. Ask: *What is a neighborhood? How long have you lived in your neighborhood? Are there stores in your neighborhood? Do you know your neighbors? Have you ever asked your neighbors for help? Have you ever offered to help a neighbor?*
- Elicit answers and discuss.

Presentation
- Books open. Set the scene. Direct Ss' attention to the pictures on page 32. Ask the question from Exercise **1A**: *What do you see?* Elicit and write on the board as much vocabulary about the picture as possible, such as: *Ana, Maria, telephone, smoke alarm, magazine, husband, battery.*
- If Ss are unfamiliar with any words that are illustrated in the picture, teach the new words by holding up the Student's Book and pointing to the corresponding pictures.
- Direct Ss' attention to the question in Exercise **1B**. Read the question aloud.
- Have Ss work in pairs. Tell Ss to explain to their partners what is happening in the pictures. Walk around and help as needed.
- When Ss have finished, ask the whole group to tell you what is happening in the pictures. Write Ss' ideas on the board, for example: *Ana has a problem. Her smoke alarm is beeping. Maria is talking on the phone.*

Practice
- Direct Ss' attention to the question in Exercise **1C**. Have Ss find a different partner.
- Ask Ss to brainstorm question words in English. Write them on the board (*what, who, why, when, where, how*). Have Ss use these words to ask the class questions about the pictures. For example: *What is Ana doing? Where is she? Who is she talking to?*

- Ask pairs of Ss to write questions about the pictures. One partner writes questions about the first picture. The other writes questions about the second picture. Ss ask each other the questions and write down each other's answers. Encourage pairs to use the answers to write a story about the pictures.
- Walk around and help partners as they write their stories.
- When Ss have finished, ask several pairs to tell their stories to the class.

▼**Teaching tip**
Encourage Ss to be creative. At this point, there is no single correct story.

Expansion activity *(student pairs)*
- Ask pairs of Ss to imagine and then write the telephone conversation that the two women are having. Have Ss practice the conversation together.
- Have several pairs role-play their conversations for the rest of the class.

Community building *(whole group)*
- Ask Ss if they have ever been in a situation such as the one shown in the pictures. Have Ss tell who they can call for help if they have such a problem.
- Have a discussion about neighbors. Do Ss have neighbors who can help them in an emergency situation? Encourage Ss to get to know one another better in class so that they can help when anyone has a problem in the class or at home.

▼**Culture tip**
You may want to share with Ss the idea that in North America, many communities have a welcoming committee. The committee includes people in the community who visit new neighbors and welcome them, often with a gift or food and an offer to help them learn about the neighborhood and meet new people.

LESSON A Listening

Presentation

- Direct Ss' attention to Exercise **2A**. Read the instructions aloud.
- Ask a S to read the questions in Exercise **2A** aloud.
- Class Audio CD1 track 20 Play or read the audio program (see audio script, page T-157). If Ss have questions about particular words, write the unfamiliar words on the board. Quickly explain the meaning of each new word.
- Ask Ss the questions in Exercise **2A**. Elicit appropriate responses.

Practice

- Focus Ss' attention on Exercise **2B**. Read the instructions aloud.
- Class Audio CD1 track 20 Model the task. Play or read the first part of the audio program (see audio script, page T-157). Pause the program after Ana says she's been "super busy." Hold up the Student's Book. Point to where *been busy* has been checked. Tell Ss to listen to the complete conversation and check the boxes that show Ana's problems. Be sure that Ss understand the words in the box.
- Class Audio CD1 track 20 Play or read the entire audio program (see audio script, page T-157). Ss listen and write a check next to Ana's problems. Repeat the program as needed.

Comprehension check

- Elicit answers from the Ss and write them on the board.
- Class Audio CD1 track 20 Play or read the audio program again (see audio script, page T-157). Ss listen and check their answers. Repeat the program as needed.

Learner persistence (individual work)

- Self-Study Audio CD track 13 Exercises **2A** and **2B** are recorded on the CD at the back of the Student's Book. Ss can listen to the CD at home for reinforcement and review. They can also listen to the CD for self-directed learning when class attendance is not possible.

Practice

- Focus Ss' attention on Exercise **3A**. Read the instructions aloud. Tell Ss that the story in this exercise is a summary of what happened to Ana. Review the meaning of *summary* (a summary contains the most important parts of a story).
- Direct Ss' attention to the words in the word bank. Say the words aloud. Ask Ss to repeat.
- Ask Ss if they understand all the words in the word bank. Go over the meaning of any words that Ss don't know.
- Model the task. Ask a S to read aloud the first two sentences in the story. Tell Ss to complete the story by filling in the blanks with appropriate words from the word bank.

- Ss complete the exercise individually. Help as needed.
- Class Audio CD1 track 21 Play or read the audio program (see audio script, page T-157). Ss listen and check their answers. Repeat the program as needed.
- Write the numbers *1–8* on the board. Ask individual Ss to come to the board to write their answers.

Learner persistence (individual work)

- Self-Study Audio CD track 14 Exercise **3A** is recorded on the CD at the back of the Student's Book. Ss can listen to the CD at home for reinforcement and review. They can also listen for self-directed learning when class attendance is not possible.

▼ Useful language

Read the Useful language box aloud. Ask Ss to give you examples of *lending* and *borrowing* by using items in the classroom. For example, ask a S to borrow a pencil from another S. Point to the S who is lending the pencil. Say that this S is *lending* the pencil. Point to the first S. Say that this S is *borrowing* the pencil. Then ask a S to stand up. Take a book and give it to the S. Say: *I am lending you this book. Please give it back to me tomorrow*. Point to the S. Say: *He / She is borrowing the book. He / She will give it back to me tomorrow*.

Application

- Focus Ss' attention on Exercise **3B**. Read the instructions aloud.
- Model the task. Ask two Ss to read the questions aloud. Make sure Ss understand the questions.
- Ss complete the exercise in pairs. Help as needed.
- Ask several pairs to ask and answer the questions for the rest of the class.

Evaluation

- Direct Ss' attention to the lesson focus on the board. Ask Ss to look at the pictures on page 32 and tell you the story of what happened to Ana. Encourage as many Ss as possible to tell you one sentence about what happened in the story.
- Check off each part of the lesson focus as Ss demonstrate an understanding of what they have learned in the lesson.

More Ventures, Unit 3, Lesson A	
Workbook, 15–30 min.	
Add Ventures, 30–45 min.	www.cambridge.org/myresourceroom
Collaborative, 30–45 min.	
Student Arcade, time varies	www.cambridge.org/venturesarcade

Describe a housing problem
Read an article in a newsletter about Neighborhood Watch
Write a letter of complaint

2 Listen

A Listen and answer the questions.

STUDENT TK 13
CLASS CD1 TK 20

1. Who are the speakers?   2. What are they talking about?

B Listen again. Put a check (✓) next to Ana's problems.

STUDENT TK 13
CLASS CD1 TK 20

1. ☑ been busy   4. ☐ car alarm broken
2. ☐ children sick   5. ☑ smoke alarm needs battery
3. ☑ ceiling is too high   6. ☐ neighbors are noisy

3 After you listen

A Read. Complete the story.

| appreciates | come over | favor | noisy |
| borrow | complain | noise | owe |

Ana and Maria are neighbors. Ana calls Maria because she needs a ___*favor*___.
                                                                              1
The smoke alarm in Ana's kitchen is beeping. She needs to change the battery, but

the ceiling in her kitchen is too high. Ana asks to ___*borrow*___ Maria's ladder.
                                                          2

Maria says her husband, Daniel, will ___*come over*___ with a ladder and help Ana.
                                            3
Ana says, "I ___*owe*___ you one." This means she ___*appreciates*___ Maria and
              4   5
Daniel's help, and she will do a favor for them in the future.

Next, Maria tells Ana about their ___*noisy*___ neighbors. The neighbors had a
                                        6
party on Saturday night. Because of the ___*noise*___, Maria and Daniel couldn't
                                              7
sleep. Ana tells Maria that she should ___*complain*___ to the apartment manager.
                                             8

Listen and check your answers.

STUDENT TK 14
CLASS CD1 TK 21

B Talk with a partner. Ask and answer the questions.

1. Have you ever borrowed something from a neighbor?
   What did you borrow?

2. Have you ever lent something to a neighbor?
   What did you lend?

> **USEFUL LANGUAGE**
>
> When you *lend* something *to* someone, you give it for a short time. When you *borrow* something *from* someone, you receive it.

LESSON B Phrases and clauses with *because*

1 Grammar focus: *because of* phrases and *because* clauses

because of + noun phrase	*because* + clause
Ana can't reach the smoke alarm **because of** the high ceiling.	Ana can't reach the smoke alarm **because** the ceiling is too high.
Because of the high ceiling, Ana can't reach the smoke alarm.	**Because** the ceiling is too high, Ana can't reach the smoke alarm.

Turn to page 147 for a grammar explanation.

> **USEFUL** LANGUAGE
>
> When you read aloud, pause when you see a comma.
> *Because of the high ceiling,* (pause)
> *Ana can't reach the smoke alarm.*

2 Practice

A Write. Complete the sentences. Use *because* or *because of*.

A Nice Surprise

Lei wanted to bake a cake ___*because*___ it was her
                                    1

neighbor Margy's birthday. Lei needed to go to the store

___*because*___ she didn't have any flour. However, her
        2

car had a flat tire. ___*Because of*___ this problem, she couldn't drive to the store. She
                            3

couldn't walk to the store ___*because of*___ the distance. It was more than a mile away.
                                    4

Lei had a clever idea. She went to Margy and asked to borrow a cup of flour. Margy

was happy to help ___*because*___ she had a lot of flour and she was a good neighbor.
                            5

Two hours later, Lei returned to Margy's house with a beautiful cake. When Margy

opened the door, Lei shouted, "Happy birthday!" Margy was very surprised and happy.

___*Because of*___ the nice surprise, Margy had a wonderful birthday!
        6

Listen and check your answers.

CLASS CD1 TK 22

Warm-up and review

Before class: Write today's lesson focus on the board.

Lesson B:
Clauses with <u>because</u> and phrases with <u>because of</u>

- Books open. Begin class. Direct Ss' attention to the pictures on page 32. Ask the following questions:

  Is Ana worried? (Yes, she is.)

  Why is Ana worried? (because her smoke alarm is going off.)

  What is Ana doing? (calling Maria.)

  Why is Ana calling Maria? (because she wants to borrow Maria's ladder.)

  Why couldn't Maria and Daniel sleep last night? (because their neighbors were noisy.)

Presentation

Focus on meaning / personalize

- Books closed. Direct Ss to the lesson focus on the board. Read it aloud.
- Say: *I want to take a trip to Europe, but I can't. Why do you think I can't go to Europe now?* Elicit three or four reasons. Write the reasons in two columns on the board – one for clauses (*because I have to work*) and one for phrases (*because of my job*). Elicit from a S volunteer something he or she wants to do but can't. Have other Ss give possible reasons why he or she can't do that thing. Write the reasons in the appropriate columns on the board.
- Choose one of the reasons, and write two sentences on the board. (*I can't take a trip because I have to work. I can't take a trip because of my job.*) Ask: *Is the meaning of these two sentences the same or different?* (the same.) Underline the clause (*because I have to work*), and circle the phrase (*because of my job*). Point out that these are two different ways to give a reason or an explanation.

Focus on form

- Books open. Direct Ss' attention to the charts in Exercise **1**.
- Read aloud the first sentence under "*because +* clause." Ask Ss to repeat. Ask: *What is the subject after "because"?* (the ceiling.) *What is the verb?* (is.) Explain that a *clause* is a group of words with a subject and a verb.
- Read aloud the first sentence under "*because of +* noun phrase." Ask Ss to repeat. Explain that a *noun phrase* is a group of words with a noun and no verb. Elicit the noun phrase (the high ceiling). Ask: *Do we use "because of" with a subject and a verb?* (No.) *Do we use "because of" with a noun phrase only?* (Yes.)

- Read and have Ss repeat the second sentence in each chart. Point to the commas in both sentences. Ask: *Why do you think there is a comma in these sentences?* (because the clause and phrase come first)

Expansion activity *(student pairs)*

- Write on the board: *Why do you want to learn English? Because . . . / Because of . . .*
- Model the activity. Ask a S the question on the board. Point to *because*. Encourage the S to give a response beginning with this word, such as: *Because I want to speak better*. Point to *because of*. Encourage the S to give a response beginning with these words, such as: *Because of my job*.
- Ask pairs to ask each other the question. Encourage Ss to answer using the two forms on the board.

Practice

- Direct Ss' attention to the picture in Exercise **2A**. Ask: *What do you see?* Elicit an appropriate response: *a birthday cake and a bag of flour*.
- Have a S read the title of the story. Ask: *What do you think this story is about?* Elicit an appropriate response, such as: *It's about a surprise birthday party. / It's about baking a cake for a birthday party.*
- Read the instructions aloud for Exercise **2A**. Ss complete the exercise individually. Help as needed.

Comprehension check

- Focus Ss' attention on the second part of the instructions in Exercise **2A** and read it aloud.
- 🔊 Class Audio CD1 track 22 Play or read the audio program (see audio script, page T-157). Ss listen and check their answers. Repeat the audio program as needed.
- If any Ss are confused about the answers, refer them to the grammar chart in Exercise **1**. Ask them to underline the subject and verb in the sentence if the answer is *because*, or the noun phrase if the answer is *because of*.

Presentation

- Books closed. Write *problems* on the board. Remind Ss about the problem Ana had in the pictures on page 32. Ask Ss to brainstorm some problems they could have at home or at school. Write the problems on the board, for example: *I didn't study last night. I was late for class.* Have Ss give reasons for these problems: *I didn't have my books. My car broke down.*
- Ask Ss to make sentences using these problems and reasons using *because* or *because of.*

Practice

- Books open. Direct Ss' attention to the picture in Exercise **2B**. Ask Ss what they see. Elicit appropriate responses, such as: *an apartment building, rain, a flat tire, a party, an empty refrigerator.*
- Read the instructions aloud. Model the task. Ask two Ss to read the example question and answer to the class.
- Tell Ss to read the problems and reasons silently and to underline any unfamiliar words.
- Write the new words on the board. Explain the meanings, or ask other Ss if they are able to explain the words to the class.
- Ss complete the exercise in pairs. Walk around and help as needed.

▼**Teaching tip**

It might be helpful to point out that all the questions except for numbers 3 and 5 have the same form as the example question, *Why couldn't you _____?* Explain that numbers 3 and 5 have different subjects and will change accordingly, for example: *Why couldn't the neighbors lock the door?* and *Why couldn't the children play outside?* Also explain that in speaking, people use a short answer to a *why* question. Short answers include only the *because* clause or *because of* phrase. In writing, people tend to write the complete sentence.

- Ask several pairs to say their conversations for the rest of the class.
- Focus Ss' attention on the second part of the instructions for Exercise **2B**, and read it aloud.
- Ask a S to read the example sentence aloud.

- Ss complete the exercise individually. Walk around and help as needed.
- Ask several Ss to write their sentences on the board. Ask other Ss to read them aloud. Work with the class to make corrections on the board as needed.

Application

- Focus Ss' attention on Exercise **3A**. Read the instructions aloud.
- Model the task. Ask two Ss to read the example conversation aloud. Encourage Ss to use short answers, as shown in the examples.
- Hold up the Student's Book. Show Ss how to take notes of their classmates' answers in the chart.
- Ss complete the exercise in small groups. Walk around and help as needed.
- Direct Ss' attention to Exercise **3B**. Model the task. Talk about the S in the example. Say: *Shakir came to this country because his children live here. He lives in this neighborhood because he is close to his job. He lives in this neighborhood because of his job.*

Evaluation

- Direct Ss' attention to the lesson focus on the board.
- Ask Ss questions with *why* to elicit answers with *because* and *because of.* Ask about the story in the lesson: *Why did Lei want to bake a cake?* (Because of Margy's birthday. Because she wanted to give the cake to Margy.) *Why did Lei need to go to the store?* (Because she needed some flour.) *Why couldn't she drive to the store?* (Because she had a flat tire. Because of her flat tire.) *Why was Margy surprised and happy?* (Because of Lei's birthday cake. Because Lei baked her a cake.) Review all appropriate responses.
- Check off each part of the lesson focus as Ss demonstrate an understanding of what they have learned in the lesson.

More Ventures, Unit 3, Lesson B	
Workbook, 15–30 min.	
Add Ventures, 30–45 min.	www.cambridge.org/myresourceroom
Collaborative, 30–45 min.	
Student Arcade, time varies	www.cambridge.org/venturesarcade

B **Talk** with a partner. Ask and answer questions about the problems.

> **A** Why couldn't you sleep last night?
> **B** Because of my noisy neighbors.

Problem	Reason
1. You couldn't sleep last night.	noisy neighbors
2. You couldn't make a cake.	didn't have any eggs
3. The neighbors couldn't lock the door.	lock was broken
4. You couldn't change the alarm battery.	didn't have a ladder
5. The children couldn't play outside.	the rain
6. You couldn't come to school.	car had a flat tire

Write a sentence about each problem.

I couldn't sleep last night because of my noisy neighbors.
(Answers will vary.)

3 Communicate

A **Work** in a small group. Ask and answer questions. Complete the chart.

> **A** Why did you come to this country, Shakir?
> **B** Because of my children. They live here.
> **A** Why do you live in your neighborhood?
> **B** Because it's close to my job.

Name	Why did you come to this country?	Why do you live in your neighborhood?
Shakir	children live here	close to job
(Answers will vary.)		

B **Share** information about your classmates.

☑ Use *because* and *because of* to give reasons   **UNIT 3**   **35**

LESSON C Adverbs of degree

1 Grammar focus: *too* and *enough*

too + adjective

The ceiling is **too high**.
It's **too high** to reach.

Adjective + *enough*

The ladder is **tall enough**.
It's **tall enough** to reach the ceiling.

not + adjective + *enough*

The woman is **not tall enough**.
She is **not tall enough** to reach the ceiling.

Adjectives

big	expensive	far
close	experienced	high

Use the shorter sentence when the listener knows what you are talking about. Example: *The ladder is tall enough.*

Turn to page 147 for a grammar explanation.

2 Practice

A Write. Complete the sentences. Use *too* or *enough*.

Too Far to Visit

My neighbors – the Mansours – have four children. Their house isn't big ___enough___ . Mr. and Mrs. Mansour think it's
1

___too___ expensive to live in the city. Their rent is
2

___too___ high. Last weekend, the Mansours bought a
3

house outside the city. It has four bedrooms. It's big

___enough___ for the whole family. However, the new house is
4

___too___ far from Mr. Mansour's job, so he's going to look for a new job.
5

Mr. Mansour is an experienced engineer. He's

experienced ___enough___ to find a new job.
6

I will miss the Mansours. I probably can't

visit them. Their new house isn't close

___enough___ for me to visit.
7

 Listen and check your answers.

CLASS CD1 TK 23

Warm-up and review

Before class: Write today's lesson focus on the board.
Lesson C:
Enough and *too* with adjectives

• Books open. Begin class. Direct Ss' attention to the pictures on page 32. Ask: *Why can't Ana reach the smoke alarm?* (because the ceiling is too high / because of the high ceiling.) Ask other questions to elicit answers with *because* and *because of*, such as: *Why do I need a jacket?* (because it is cold / because of the cold weather.)

Presentation

Focus on meaning / personalize

• Books closed. Direct Ss' attention to the lesson focus on the board. Read it aloud. Books closed.

• Make a rough drawing of three houses on the board. In the first house, draw a square inside the house and label it "bedroom"; in the second house draw two bedrooms; and in the third house, draw 10 bedrooms. Number them as follows: *1*. One-bedroom house. *2*. Three-bedroom house. *3*. Ten-bedroom house. Describe the three houses, for example: *Number 1, This house has one bedroom.*

• Draw a family with a mother, father, and two children. Point to house 1. Ask: *How many bedrooms?* (1) *How many children?* (2) Say: *It isn't big enough. It's too small.* Point to house 3. Ask: *How many bedrooms?* (10) *How many children?* (2) Say: *It's too big.* Point to house 2. Ask: *How many bedrooms?* (3) *How many children?* (2) Say: *It's big enough.*

• Write the following on the board:
  1. too big
  2. big enough
  3. not big enough

• Ask: *Does "too" mean more than the right amount or less than the right amount?* (more than the right amount) *Does "enough" mean the right amount or more than the right amount?* (the right amount.)

Focus on form

• Books open. Explain and write on the board:
  too + *adjective = more than the right amount of something*
  adjective + *enough* = *the right amount of something*
  not + *adjective* + *enough (negative) = less than the right amount*

• Direct Ss' attention to the chart in Exercise **1**. Read aloud the sentences in the chart under "Adjective + *enough*." Ask Ss to repeat. Ask: *Can I reach the ceiling with the ladder?* (Yes.) Say: *The ladder is tall enough.* Write the sentence on the board. Point to the sentence and ask: *Does "enough" come before or after the adjective?* (after.). Point to house 2 on the board. Say: *This house is big enough.* Ask Ss to repeat.

• Direct Ss' attention to the adjectives in the grammar chart. Read each adjective aloud. Ask Ss to repeat. Check that Ss understand the meaning of the adjectives.

Practice

• Direct Ss' attention to the first picture in Exercise **2A**. Ask: What's the problem? Elicit: *The house is too small. The house is not big enough.*

• Focus Ss' attention on the second picture in the story. Ask: *What do you see?* Elicit an appropriate response, such as: *Now the house is big enough.*

• Read the instructions for Exercise **2A** aloud. Ask a S to read the first sentence to the class. Read the second sentence aloud, and pause at the blank. Have Ss finish the sentence. Elicit: *enough.* Ask Ss to complete the exercise by writing *enough* or *too* in the blanks.

• Ss complete the exercise individually. Walk around and help as needed. Ask Ss to underline any words they don't know. Write the new words on the board. Encourage Ss to guess the meaning of each of the new words from context.

Comprehension check

• Read aloud the second part of the instructions for Exercise **2A**.

• Class Audio CD1 track 23 Check answers with the class. Play or read the audio program (see audio script, page T-157). Ss listen and check their answers.

• Ask Ss to work in pairs to read to each other the completed story in Exercise **2A**. Walk around and listen to Ss' pronunciation. Correct pronunciation as needed.

• Write any words on the board that Ss have difficulty pronouncing.

LESSON C Adverbs of degree

Presentation

- Ask Ss: *How's the weather today?* Elicit an appropriate response about the current weather conditions. Ask: *Is it hot enough to go swimming today?* (Elicit a *Yes* or *No* response.) Ask: *Is it cold enough to go skiing?* (Elicit a *Yes* or *No* response.)
- Direct Ss' attention to the first picture in Exercise **2B**. Ask: *How's the weather?* (It's cold. / It's snowing.) Ask: *What can you see?* (a swimming pool) Ask: *Is it hot enough to go swimming?* (No, it isn't.)

Practice

- Read the instructions for Exercise **2B** aloud. Model the task. Point to Picture 1. Ask two Ss to read the example conversation aloud. Focus Ss' attention on Picture 2. Ask two different Ss to read the second example conversation to the class.

> **Teaching tip**
> Be sure Ss understand that the words under the pictures are cues to help Ss make sentences with *enough* and *too*. Then point out the ways of expressing agreement in the examples: *I agree. Yes, you're right.*

- Ss complete the exercise in pairs. Walk around and help as needed.
- If Ss are not familiar with the verb *lift* in numbers 5 and 6, demonstrate the meaning by lifting a chair in your classroom. If you can lift it, say: *I'm strong enough to lift the chair.* Pretend to lift something heavy in the classroom. Say: *I'm not strong enough to lift this.*
- Direct Ss' attention to the second part of the instructions in Exercise **2B**.
- Ask a S to read the example sentences aloud.
- Ss complete the exercise individually. Walk around and help as needed.
- Write the numbers *1–6* on the board. Ask individual Ss to come to the board to write their sentences. Have different Ss read them aloud. Ask: *Are the sentences correct?* Correct the sentences as needed.

Expansion activity (small groups)

- **Materials needed** Bring apartment or house rental ads from local newspapers or from online sources to class.
- Make enough copies to give to small groups of four or five Ss.
- Have Ss look through the ads to make sentences with *too*, *enough*, and *not . . . enough*.

- Model the activity. Find an apartment that has a high rent. Write on the board: *This apartment is too expensive. It is not cheap enough.*
- Encourage Ss to use different adjectives to describe the places for rent, such as: *too far from home, not close enough to work, too big, not small enough*, etc.
- Ask a representative from each group to read some sentences that the group wrote.

Application

- Direct Ss' attention to Exercise **3** and read the instructions aloud. Make sure Ss know what the word *opinion* means. Explain that it means saying what you believe to be true.

> ▼**Useful language**
> Read the Useful language box aloud. Ask Ss to repeat each of these phrases after you: *I agree. I disagree. I don't agree.* Tell a S your opinion about something, such as: *It's too cold to swim today.* Encourage Ss to respond to your opinion by saying *I agree. or I disagree.* Encourage Ss to use these expressions as they talk about their opinions in Exercise **3**.

- Ask two Ss to read aloud the example opinion and response statement. Brainstorm some additional topics about age, for example: *to have a baby, to drive, to vote, to have a credit card, to retire, to get a senior citizens' discount.* Write the topics on the board.
- Ss complete the exercise in small groups. Walk around and help as needed.
- Ask several Ss to share their opinions with the rest of the class. Ask other Ss if they agree or disagree.

Evaluation

- Direct Ss' attention to the lesson focus on the board. Ask Ss to summarize the story about the Mansours and to give examples from the story using *too* and *enough*.
- Check off the lesson focus as Ss demonstrate an understanding of what they have learned in the lesson.

More Ventures, Unit 3, Lesson C	
Workbook, 15–30 min.	
Add Ventures, 30–45 min. **Collaborative,** 30–45 min.	www.cambridge.org/myresourceroom
Student Arcade, time varies	www.cambridge.org/venturesarcade

B **Work** with a partner. Talk about the pictures. Use *too*, *enough*, and *not . . . enough*.

A Can they swim today?
B I don't think so. It's too cold to swim today.
A Yeah, you're right. It really isn't warm enough.

A Can she swim today?
B Yes, it's hot enough to swim.

1. cold / swim / warm

2. hot / swim

3. young / drive / old

4. old / drive

5. weak / lift the TV / strong

6. strong / lift the TV

Write sentences about each picture.

It's too cold to swim.

It isn't warm enough to swim.
(Answers will vary.)

3 **Communicate**

Work in a small group. Talk about what you are *too young*, *too old*, *young enough*, or *old enough* to do. Give your opinions.

I'm too young to get married.

I agree. Young people should wait to get married.

USEFUL LANGUAGE
I agree. = My opinion is the same as yours.
I disagree. / I don't agree. = My opinion is different from yours.

LESSON D Reading

1 Before you read

Look at the title and the picture. Answer the questions.

1. Have you ever heard of Neighborhood Watch? What is it?
2. Is there a Neighborhood Watch in your area?

2 Read

Read the article from a neighborhood newsletter.
Listen and read again.

STUDENT TK 15
CLASS CD1 TK 24

> The first sentence of a paragraph usually tells the main idea. The other sentences give details. Facts and examples are types of details.

Neighborhood Watch Success Story

by Latisha Holmes, President, Rolling Hills Neighborhood Watch

People often ask me about the role of Neighborhood Watch. My answer is *Because of Neighborhood Watch, our neighborhood is safer and nicer.* Members of Neighborhood Watch help each other and look after the neighborhood. For example, we look after our neighbors' houses when they aren't home. We help elderly neighbors with yard work. Once a month, we get together to paint over graffiti.

Last Wednesday, the Neighborhood Watch team had another success story. Around 8:30 p.m., members of our Neighborhood Watch were out on a walk. Near the Corner Café, they noticed two men next to George Garcia's car. George lives on Rolling Hills Drive. The men were trying to break into the car. Suddenly, the car alarm went off. The men ran away and got into a car down the street. But they weren't quick enough. Our Neighborhood Watch members wrote down the car's license plate number and called the police. Later that night, the police arrested the two men.

I would like to congratulate our Neighborhood Watch team on their good work. Because so many people participate in Neighborhood Watch, Rolling Hills is a safer neighborhood today.

For information about Neighborhood Watch, please call 773-555-1234.

Lesson objectives

- Introduce and read "Neighborhood Watch Success Story"
- Practice using new topic-related words
- Practice using two-word verbs
- Understand the main idea and details

Warm-up and review

- Before class. Write today's lesson focus on the board.
  Lesson D:
  Read and understand "Neighborhood Watch Success Story"
  Practice new vocabulary
  Practice using two-word verbs
  Understand the main idea and details
- Begin class. Books closed. Write on the board: *neighbors*. Ask Ss: *Do you know your neighbors well? Did you know your neighbors well in your own country? How are neighbors in your country different from neighbors here?* (Elicit appropriate responses.)
- Ask Ss how neighbors can help one another. Write Ss' responses on the board, for example: *Neighbors can get your mail for you when you are away. They can lend you something you need.*

Presentation

- Books open. Direct Ss' attention to Exercise 1 and read the instructions aloud.
- Ask a S to read the two questions aloud. Make sure that Ss understand the meaning of the words in the title of the story: Ask Ss if they have ever heard of *Neighborhood Watch.* Have Ss skim the newsletter to tell you what a Neighborhood Watch is.

Practice

- Read the instructions for Exercise 2 aloud. Ss read the article silently.
- Ask Ss to underline any words they don't know. Write the new words on the board. Encourage Ss to guess the meaning of each new word from context.

Read the tip box aloud. Ask a S to read aloud the first sentence of the article. Ask: *What is the main idea of the article?* (the role of Neighborhood Watch) Ask another S to give examples of details in the first paragraph that support the main idea (neighbors help each other and watch out for each other by watching neighbors' houses when they aren't home, by helping elderly neighbors with yard work, by painting over graffiti, etc.) Make sure that Ss understand that facts and examples are types of details. Explain that facts are statements that are true. Ask a S to find a fact in the article, such as: *George on Rolling Hills Drive.*

Class Audio CD1 track 24 Play or read the audio program and ask Ss to read along silently (see audio script, page T-157). Repeat the audio program as needed.

Learner persistence (individual work)

Self-Study Audio CD track 15 Exercise **2** is recorded on the CD at the back of the Student's Book. Ss can listen to the CD at home for reinforcement and review. They can also listen for self-directed learning when class attendance is not possible.

Expansion activity (whole group)

- Books closed. Point to the new vocabulary words from Exercise **2** that you elicited from Ss and wrote on the board. Say each word aloud. Ask Ss to repeat.
- Have Ss retell the story in Exercise **2**, using the words on the board as a guide.
- Ask as many Ss as possible to say something about the article. Listen closely to make sure that Ss have understood the article.
- Ask Ss: *Would you want to join the Neighborhood Watch? Why?*

Comprehension check

- Read the instructions for Exercise **3A** aloud.
- Ask individual Ss to read the questions. Make sure Ss understand all the questions.
- Ss work in pairs to ask and answer the questions. Help as needed.
- Ask individual Ss the questions. Ask different Ss to correct the responses as needed.

Presentation

- Focus Ss' attention on Exercise **3B**. Explain that vocabulary can be built just as a house is built, piece by piece.
- Focus Ss' attention on number 1 in Exercise **3B**. Ask a S to read aloud the dictionary entry for *get*.
- Go over the basic components of the dictionary entry for *get*. Ask Ss to tell you the different parts of the entry, for example: the pronunciation, the different verb forms, and the definition.
- Guide Ss to see that the second part of the entry is the definition for the two-word verb *get together*. Explain that a two-word verb has a completely different meaning from the meaning of the verb on its own.

▼ Teaching tip

This might be a good opportunity to suggest that Ss get a good learner's dictionary to use in and outside of class to help build their vocabulary in English. Do dictionary skills work with Ss when class time allows.

- Ask Ss to find the sentence with the phrase *get together* in the reading (the last sentence of the first paragraph) and to read the sentence aloud.

Practice

- Focus Ss' attention on number 2 in Exercise **3B**. Read the instructions aloud.
- Model the task. Show Ss how *get* is matched with *together* to form the two-word verb *get together*.
- Ss complete the exercise individually. Help as needed.
- Write the numbers *1–6* on the board. Ask individual Ss to write their answers on the board.
- When the two-word verbs are written on the board correctly, point to each one in turn. Say the verb. Ask Ss to repeat.

- Focus Ss' attention on number 3 in Exercise **3B**. Read the instructions aloud.
- Model the task. Ask a S to read the first example to the class.
- Ss complete the exercise individually. Help as needed.
- Ask Ss to tell you each two-word verb to check the answers in the chart.

Application

- Focus Ss' attention on number 4 in Exercise **3B**. Read the instructions aloud. Ask a S to read the example sentence to the class.
- Ss complete the exercise individually. Help as needed.
- Ask six Ss to read the completed sentences aloud. Ask the class: *Are the sentences correct?*
- Focus Ss' attention on Exercise **3C**. Read the instructions aloud.
- Ask two Ss to read the questions to the class.
- Ss complete the exercise in pairs. Help as needed.

Evaluation

- Direct Ss' attention to the lesson focus on the board. Ask Ss: *What is a Neighborhood Watch?* (a group of neighbors that helps to keep a neighborhood safe) Write on the board the two-word verbs from number 2 of Exercise **3B**. Ask individual Ss to write sentences about the article using these two-word verbs.
- Check off each part of the lesson focus as Ss demonstrate an understanding of what they have learned in the lesson.

Learner persistence (individual, pairs)

- You may wish to assign Extended Reading Worksheets from the *Online Teacher's Resource Room* for Ss to complete outside of class. The purpose of these worksheets is to encourage Ss to read for pleasure in English outside of the English class. The worksheets can also be assigned as extended reading in class.

More Ventures, Unit 3, Lesson D	
Workbook, 20–30 min.	
Add Ventures, 30–45 min.	
Collaborative, 30–45 min.	www.cambridge.org/myresourceroom
Extended Reading and worksheet, 45–60 min.	
Student Arcade, time varies	www.cambridge.org/venturesarcade

3 After you read

A Check your understanding.

1. What is the main idea of the first paragraph?
2. What are three examples of the role of Neighborhood Watch?
3. Does the second paragraph give facts or examples?
4. What did the Neighborhood Watch team see? What did they do?

B Build your vocabulary.

1. Read the dictionary entry for the word *get*. Find the definition of *get together*.

> **get** /get/ [T] **getting**, *past* **got**, *past part* **gotten** to take (something)
>   into your possession
>   **get together** *v/adv* [I/T] to meet; to have a meeting or party

2. *Get together* is a two-word verb. Look at the article in Exercise 2. Match the two-word verbs.

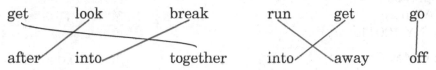

get   look   break   run   get   go

after   into   together   into   away   off

3. Write each verb in Exercise B2 next to its definition.

1. to meet	*get together*
2. to enter (a car legally)	*get into*
3. to enter (a car illegally)	*break into*
4. to make a sudden, loud noise	*go off*
5. to escape; to leave a place very fast	*run away*
6. to take care of	*look after*

4. Complete the sentences with the verbs in Exercise B3.

a. Let's _____*get together*_____ for coffee tomorrow, OK?

b. Somebody tried to _____*break into*_____ my neighbor's house.

c. I saw the girl next door _____*get into*_____ a car and drive away.

d. My cats always _____*run away*_____ when the door is open.

e. My neighbor's car alarm _____*goes off*_____ at 3:00 a.m. every morning.

f. All the people on my street _____*look after*_____ each other's houses.

C Talk with a partner. Ask and answer the questions.

1. Do you enjoy getting together with friends? What do you do?
2. Do you and your neighbors look after each other? How?

☑ Identify the main idea, facts, and examples in a text;
find the meaning of two-word verbs **UNIT 3 39**

LESSON E Writing

1 Before you write

A **Talk** with a partner. Answer the questions.

1. Have you ever complained to your landlord or apartment manager?
2. What was the problem?
3. How did you complain – in person, by telephone, or in writing?
4. What happened?

B **Read** the letter of complaint.

LUIS RAMOS

January 14, 2013

Acme Properties
100 25th Avenue
New York, NY 10011

To Whom It May Concern:

My name is Luis Ramos. I live at 156 South
Flower Street, Apartment 3. I am writing
because my neighbors in Apartment 9 are too
noisy. I asked them to be quiet, but they still
have loud parties almost every night. Because
of the noise, my children can't sleep.

Can you please tell them to be quiet? I hope
you will take care of this as soon as possible.

Thank you in advance.

Sincerely,

Luis Ramos

> **CULTURE NOTE**
>
> When you don't know the
> name of the person you
> are writing to, use
> *To Whom It May Concern.*

Work with a partner. Answer the questions.

1. What is the date of the letter?
2. Who is the letter to?
3. Does the writer know the person's name?
4. Who wrote the letter?
5. What is the problem?
6. What does the writer want Acme Properties to do?

Lesson objectives
- Read and write a letter of complaint
- Support the main idea with examples
- Use *To Whom It May Concern*

Warm-up and review
- Before class. Write today's lesson focus on the board.
  Lesson E:
  Read and write a letter of complaint
  Support the main idea with examples
- Begin class. Books closed. Point to *complaint* in the lesson focus. Say it aloud. Ask Ss to repeat. Ask: *What is a complaint?* Elicit an appropriate response, such as: *A complaint is something a person says when they are annoyed or unhappy with someone or something.*
- Write *complain* on the board. Explain that this is a verb and that *complaint* is a noun. Ask Ss to give examples of sentences with *complain* and *complaint* in them. Write the sentences on the board, for example: *I complained about my noisy neighbors. I made a complaint about my noisy neighbors.*
- Tell Ss to imagine that they are having problems in the apartment building in which they live. Ask them what some of their complaints could be. Write Ss' responses on the board, such as: *noisy neighbors*, *broken appliances*, *leaking pipes*.
- Ask Ss if they have any real complaints about the places where they live. Listen to Ss if they are willing to tell the class their complaints.
- Ask: *What can you do if you have any complaints about where you live?* If Ss don't know, say: *You can talk to the apartment manager. You can write the manager a letter of complaint. You can talk with your neighbors. You can discuss solutions with your teacher and classmates.*

Learner persistence *(whole group)*
- Housing problems can be a reason for Ss' not being able to attend class. If Ss are having trouble with their housing situation, it may be that they have not understood their rights and obligations as a tenant or neighbor. This could be a good time to help Ss with the language they need to explain problems in person and in a letter. Use the problems Ss may offer as the basis of role plays or decision-making activities.

Presentation
- Tell Ss that in this lesson they are going to read and write a letter of complaint.
- Books open. Direct Ss' attention to Exercise **1A** and read the instructions aloud.
- Write on the board: *landlord* and *in writing*. Point to each one in turn and say it aloud. Ask Ss to repeat. Explain that a landlord is the owner of a house or an apartment building that is rented out. Ask Ss if they have a landlord. Tell Ss that *in writing* means that you write about something – in this case a letter of complaint to the landlord or apartment manager.

- Ask four Ss to read the questions aloud. Model the task. Answer according to a true or made-up experience you have had, for example: *I complained to my landlord when I first saw the carpets in the apartment I rented. They were very dirty. I talked to the apartment manager about the problem. He got the carpets cleaned before I moved in.*
- Ss complete the exercise in pairs. Help as needed.

▼**Culture tip**
Tell Ss that it is helpful to keep a copy of a letter of complaint after sending the original letter. This copy acts as proof that you complained about something in case you don't get a response and need to complain about the problem again.

- Direct Ss' attention to Exercise **1B**. Have Ss read the letter silently.
- Tell Ss to underline any new words that they don't know. Write these words on the board. Pronounce each word in turn. Encourage Ss to guess the meaning of each new word from context or to use their dictionaries to find out the meaning of each of the words.

▼**Culture note**
Point out the use of the colon after the expression *To Whom It May Concern*. Explain that this is a formal, polite way of opening a business letter when you don't know the name of the person you are writing to. Mention, however, that it is good to address a business letter to the person in charge. Remind Ss that there are other ways to begin a letter and ask for some examples (*Dear _____:* or *Dear _____,*). Review key parts of a business letter, including the date, address, body, and closing.

Comprehension check
- Direct Ss' attention to the second part of Exercise **1B** and read the instructions aloud. Ask several Ss to read the questions to the class. Make sure that all Ss understand the questions.
- Ss complete the exercise in pairs. Help as needed.
- Ask several pairs to ask and answer the questions for the rest of the class.

LESSON **E** Writing

Practice

- Books open. Direct Ss' attention to Exercise **1C** and read the instructions aloud.
- Focus Ss' attention on the words in the word bank. Say each word aloud and ask Ss to repeat.
- Model the task. Ask a S to read aloud the salutation and the first three sentences of the letter. Tell Ss to complete the exercise by filling in each of the blanks with the appropriate word from the word bank.
- Ss complete the exercise individually. Walk around and help as needed.
- Write the numbers *1–6* on the board. Ask individual Ss to come to the board to write their answers. Tell Ss to write only the words from the blanks, not the entire sentences.
- Ask different Ss to read aloud sentences from the letter, filling in the blanks with the words on the board. Ask: *Are the answers correct?* Ask other Ss to correct the errors as needed.

> Read the tip box aloud. Ask Ss to look at the letter in Exercise **1C** to find the problem (*the pipes under the kitchen sink are leaking*), the examples (*the water bill will be high, and the water is bad for the kitchen floor*), and a request to fix the problem (*Can you please come as soon as possible?*).

- Focus Ss' attention on Exercise **1D**. Read the instructions aloud.
- Ss complete the exercise in small groups. Walk around and help as needed.
- Ask Ss to tell the class the list of housing problems they brainstormed for Exercise **1D**. Write Ss' examples on the board.

Community building *(whole group)*

- If any Ss are having real housing problems, encourage them to write about their problem in class so that you can review the letter and help them send it to the right person.

Application

- Focus Ss' attention on Exercise **2**. Read the instructions aloud.
- Ss complete the task individually. Walk around and help as needed.

Comprehension check

- Direct Ss' attention to Exercise **3A** and read the instructions aloud. This exercise asks Ss to develop skills to review and edit their own writing.
- Ss complete the exercise individually. Walk around and help as needed.
- Ask Ss if they checked *No* for any of the three boxes. If they did, encourage them to revise their letter so that the missing item or items are included.

Evaluation

- Focus Ss' attention on Exercise **3B**. Read the instructions aloud. This exercise asks Ss to work together to peer-correct their writing. Reading aloud enables the writer to review his or her own writing. Reading to a partner allows the writer to understand the need to write clearly for an audience.
- Listen to Ss as they ask their partner questions about their letters and talk about one thing they learned.
- When Ss are finished, ask several Ss to comment on what they learned from their partners' letters.
- Direct Ss' attention to the lesson focus on the board.
- Check off each part of the lesson focus as Ss demonstrate an understanding of what they have learned in the lesson.

More Ventures, Unit 3, Lesson E	
Workbook, 15–30 min.	
Add Ventures, 30–45 min.	www.cambridge.org/myresourceroom
Collaborative, 30–45 min.	

C Complete the letter of complaint.

| advance | because | because of | sincerely | soon | very |

To Whom It May Concern:

My name is Alina Krasinski. I live at 156 South Flower Street, Apartment 6. I am writing __because__ the pipes under my kitchen
1
sink are leaking. __Because of__ the leak, my water bill will be
2
__very__ high next month. The water is also bad for the kitchen
3
floor. Can you please come as __soon__ as possible to fix the leak?
4

Thank you in __advance__.
5
__Sincerely__,
6
Alina Krasinski

A letter of complaint should include:
• the problem
• examples
• a request to fix the problem

D Talk with your classmates. What housing problems do people complain about?

2 Write

Write a letter of complaint. Use *To Whom It May Concern* or the person's name. Include the problem, an example, and a request to fix the problem. Use the letters in Exercises 1B and 1C to help you.

3 After you write

A Check your writing.

	Yes	No
1. I used *To Whom It May Concern* or the person's name.	☐	☐
2. I included the problem and an example.	☐	☐
3. I included a request to fix the problem.	☐	☐

B Share your writing with a partner.

1. Take turns. Read your letter to a partner.
2. Comment on your partner's letter. Ask your partner a question about the letter. Tell your partner one thing you learned.

LESSON F Another view

1 Life-skills reading

Community Center Volunteers Needed

HOME   ABOUT US   CONTACT US

Organization:	Oak Park Community Center
Volunteers needed:	10
Date:	Open
Time:	9:00 a.m. – 10:00 p.m.
Estimated time:	4 hours per day
Location:	15 Franklin Street Dallas, TX 75231
Description:	1. Volunteers to provide food and drinks to visitors 2. Volunteers for theater to greet people, answer questions, assist with seating 3. Volunteers for Arts Program to assist teachers with classes
Requirements:	Reliable; teamwork skills; good customer service Prefer 18 years old and over

A Read the questions. Look at the ad. Fill in the answer.

1. How many volunteers does the center need?
   - Ⓐ four
   - Ⓑ five
   - ● ten
   - Ⓓ twenty

2. What can a volunteer do at this center?
   - Ⓐ greet people
   - Ⓑ help the art teachers
   - Ⓒ serve food
   - ● all of the above

3. How long do volunteers need to work?
   - Ⓐ one hour a day
   - ● four hours a day
   - Ⓒ eight hours a day
   - Ⓓ nine hours a day

4. Which statement is true?
   - Ⓐ Volunteers must be artists.
   - Ⓑ Volunteers must be experienced cooks.
   - Ⓒ Volunteers must be over 21 years old.
   - ● Volunteers must be team players.

B Talk with your classmates. Ask and answer the questions.

1. Have you ever volunteered in your community?
2. If yes, what did you do?

Lesson objectives
- Read an Internet Web site for community volunteers
- Use *be able to* for ability
- Complete the self-assessment

Warm-up and review

- Before class. Write today's lesson focus on the board.
  Lesson F:
  Read and talk about volunteering
  Review vocabulary and grammar from Unit 3
  Complete the self-assessment
- Before class. Books closed. Write *Web site* on the board. Point to the words. Say them aloud. Ask Ss to repeat. Ask Ss if they know what a Web site is. Elicit appropriate responses, such as: *A Web site offers information on the Internet.*
- Ask Ss how much they use the computer at home and at school. Ask what kinds of Web sites they like to look at. Write the types of Web sites on the board, for example: school Web sites, ESL Web sites, news Web sites.
- Tell Ss that they are going to look at an example of an ad on a Web site.

Presentation

- Books open. Direct Ss' attention to the reading in Exercise **1**. Ask Ss: *What kind of ad is this?* (an ad for community center volunteers) Ask: *What is the name of the organization?* (Oak Park Community Center.)
- Have Ss underline any words in the ad that they don't know. Write the new words on the board. Encourage Ss to guess the meaning of each of the new words from context, for example: *assist* with seating means *help* with seating.

> **▼ Culture tip**
> It might be helpful to explain that many Americans choose to spend their free time working without pay, or volunteering, in the community. Also explain that a community center is a place where people can get together for a variety of events that are often offered for free, such as concerts, lectures, sports, and games. Many communities have these centers. They are especially popular with young children and senior citizens.

Practice

- Read the instructions for Exercise **1A** aloud. This exercise helps prepare Ss for standardized-type tests they may have to take. Make sure Ss understand the exercise. Have Ss individually scan for and fill in the answers.

Comprehension check

- Go over the answers to Exercise **1A** with the class. Make sure that Ss followed the instructions and filled in their answers.
- Make any necessary corrections.

Application

- Read the instructions for Exercise **1B** aloud. Ask two Ss to read the questions to the class.
- Ss complete the exercise in small groups. Walk around and help as needed.
- Ask several Ss to share something that they learned from other Ss in the class.

Expansion activity (small groups)

- **Materials needed** Bring in ads for volunteers from the local newspaper and online sources.
- Make or bring enough copies for each small group of four or five Ss.
- Give each group a copy of the ads. Write these questions on the board:
  1. What are the job duties of the volunteers?
  2. Which organization is looking for volunteers?
  3. What kind of person are they looking for?
  4. How many hours a week will the person work?
  5. Will the person have to participate in training?
- Underline *job duties.* Say the words aloud. Ask Ss to repeat. Explain that job duties are the tasks that people do when they are volunteering.
- Tell Ss to look through the ads to find one ad that they think seems interesting. One person looks at the ad. The other Ss in the group ask that person one of the questions on the board. Tell Ss to change roles so that everyone has a chance to answer a question.
- Ss complete the activity in small groups. Walk around and help as needed.

Warm-up and review

- Books closed. Ask Ss: *Who can touch the ceiling?* Elicit answers such as: *I can't.* or *I can't touch the ceiling.* Ask Ss: *Why can't you touch the ceiling?* Guide Ss to reply using *because, because of, enough,* or *too.* (Because it's too high. / I'm not tall enough.)
- Tell Ss there is another verb they can use instead of *can.* Write *be able to* on the board. Explain that *can* and *be able to* both express ability. However, *be able to* can be conjugated into present, past, or future; while *can* has present (*can*) and past (*could*) forms but no future form.

Presentation

- Books open. Direct Ss' attention to the chart in Exercise **2A**. Read aloud the first sentence: *I'm able to drive.* Ask Ss what the sentence conveys. Elicit answers such as: *He or she can drive a car.* Read aloud the second sentence: *Isabel isn't able to drive.* Ask Ss what the sentence conveys. Elicit answers such as: *Isabel can't drive a car.*
- Underline the contractions *I'm* and *isn't.* Show Ss that the *be* in *be able to* is conjugated, but *able* remains in the simple form.

Practice

- Direct Ss' attention to the instructions in **2A**. Read the instructions aloud. Ensure Ss understand the activity. Ask a pair of Ss to read the dialog aloud.
- Split the class into small groups. Pass out pennies to each group. Ss play the game. Walk around and help as needed.

- Direct Ss' attention to the instructions in **2B**. Read the instructions aloud. Ask a S to read the example sentences. Ss complete the exercise in pairs. Encourage each S to share a sentence about a person in their group.

Evaluation

- Before asking students to turn to the self-assessment on page 137, do a quick review of the unit. Have Ss turn to Lesson A. Ask the class to talk about what they remember about this lesson. Prompt Ss, if necessary, with questions, for example: *What are the conversations about on this page? What vocabulary is in the pictures?* Continue in this manner to review each lesson quickly.
- **Self-assessment** Read the instructions for Exercise **3**. Ask Ss to turn to the self-assessment page and complete the unit self-assessment. The self-assessments are also on the *Online Teacher's Resource Room.* If you prefer to collect the assessments and save them as part of each S's portfolio assessment, print out the unit self-assessment from the *Resource Room*, ask students to complete it, and collect and save it.
- If Ss are ready, administer the unit test on pages T-169–T-170 of this Teacher's Edition (or on the Assessment Audio CD / CD-ROM).

More Ventures, Unit 3, Lesson F	
Workbook, 20–30 min.	
Add Ventures, 30–45 min.	www.cambridge.org/myresourceroom
Collaborative, 30–45 min.	

2 Grammar connections: *be able to*

Use *be able to* for ability.

I'm **able to drive**.	Isabel **isn't able to drive**.

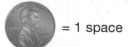 = 1 space

 = 2 spaces

A **Work** in a small group. Play the game. Write your name on a small piece of paper. Flip a coin to move your paper. Then tell your group about the topic in the square. Use *be able to* in your answer. Take turns.

> **A** This says, "A food you are able to make in less than 15 minutes." OK. I'm able to make cookies in less than 15 minutes.
> **B** My space says, "Something you aren't able to lift." I'm not able to lift my nephew! He's ten years old and very heavy!

Start here →	A food you are able to make in less than 15 minutes →	Something you aren't able to lift →	Someone you know who isn't able to drive
A sport you aren't able to do well ←	Someone you know who is able to play a musical instrument ←	Something you aren't able to do while you're talking ←	An animal that isn't able to swim
A non-food item you are able to buy at a supermarket →	Something you are able to do with one hand →	A language you are able to speak well →	Someone you know who isn't able to sing well
Finish! ←	Something you are able to do in a swimming pool ←	Something you aren't able to cook ←	A sport you are able to do well

B **Share** information about your classmates.

> Katia is able to make cookies in less than 15 minutes.

> Carlos isn't able to lift his nephew.

3 Wrap up

Complete the **Self-assessment** on page 137.

☑ Interpret an ad for volunteers; use *be able to* for ability **UNIT 3** **43**

LESSON A
Listening

1 Before you listen

A What do you see?

B What is happening?

C What's the story?

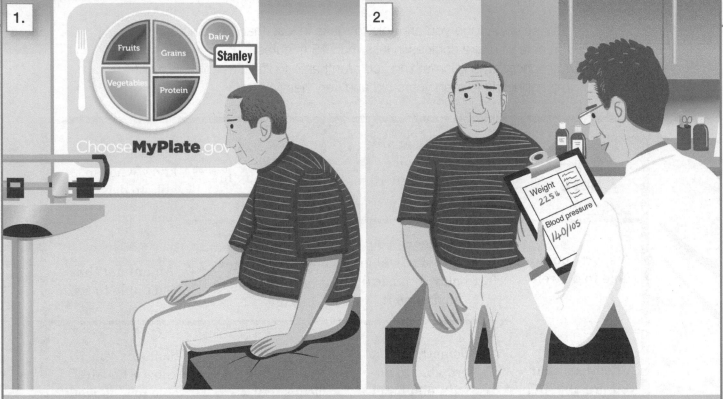

Lesson objectives
- Introduce students to the topic
- Find out what students know about the topic
- Preview the unit by talking about the pictures
- Practice key vocabulary
- Practice listening skills

UNIT
4

Warm-up and review

- Before class. Write today's lesson focus on the board.
  Lesson A:
  Healthy habits and routines
- Begin class. Books closed. Point to *healthy habits* in the lesson focus. Ask Ss what the words *habit* and *routine* mean. Elicit answers, such as: *Something you do regularly and often, usually without thinking about it.* Ask Ss to brainstorm some healthy habits and routines. Write Ss' ideas on the board, for example: *exercising, cooking, eating healthy food.*
- Draw a food chart on the board. Divide the chart into five columns. Label the columns:
  1. Milk, yogurt, cheese
  2. Meat, fish, poultry, beans, eggs, nuts
  3. Vegetables
  4. Fruit
  5. Bread, cereal, rice, pasta
- Ask Ss to give you examples of food they eat from each group and write them in the correct column. Ask Ss which foods they think are the most and least healthy.
- Draw a plate on the board. You can find pictures of the food plate on *myplate.gov*. Help Ss place the food from the chart on the board in the correct section of the food plate. Discuss healthy eating habits with the class.

▼ **Teaching tip**
When discussing personal choices such as these, be sure to be sensitive to the cultural and economic choices your Ss may make regarding food.

Presentation

- Books open. Set the scene. Direct Ss' attention to the pictures on page 44. Ask the question in Exercise 1A: *What do you see?* Elicit and write on the board as much vocabulary about the pictures as possible: *doctor's office, doctor, patient, food plate.* Explain unfamiliar words.
- Direct Ss' attention to the question in Exercise 1B and read the question aloud.
- Ss in pairs. Tell Ss to explain to their partner what is happening in the picture. Walk around and listen to Ss as they are speaking.
- Write Ss' ideas on the board.

Practice

- Direct Ss' attention to the question in Exercise 1C. Tell Ss to find a different partner.
- Ask Ss to write a role play between the doctor and Stanley.
- Ask several pairs to perform their role play for the class.

▼ **Teaching tip**
Encourage Ss to avoid reading their lines in a role play. One way is to have Ss read a line silently to themselves, then look up and say the line. This encourages fluency and confidence in speaking.

Expansion activity

- Ask Ss to brainstorm question words in English. Write them on the board: *what, who, why, when, where, how.*
- Encourage Ss to construct questions about the story in the pictures using the question words on the board. Write Ss' questions as they tell them to you, for example:
  What is the doctor doing?
  Why did Stanly go to the doctor?
- Ask Ss to use the questions on the board to write a story about Stanley. Ss work individually or in pairs. Have Ss include what happens to Stanley after he leaves the doctor's office.
- Collect the stories and make a storyboard, displaying it for the class to read.

Community building (whole group)

- Ask Ss if they have gone to a doctor who speaks only English. Encourage Ss to describe any difficulty they have had in explaining their health problems to the doctor. Brainstorm ways that Ss can feel more comfortable about talking to medical personnel in English. Examples may include: asking an English-speaking friend or family member to come with you; asking for an interpreter once at the hospital or clinic; looking for words in a dictionary before you go to your appointment; writing out questions to ask the doctor in your own language and asking someone to write them in English, then bringing the questions with you to show the doctor; asking the doctor to write answers to your questions and later showing them to someone who can translate them for you.

Presentation

- Direct Ss' attention to Exercise **2A**. Tell Ss to listen for the main ideas. Read the instructions aloud. Explain that after listening to the conversation, Ss will ask and answer the questions in the exercise in pairs.
- Ask a S to read the questions in Exercise **2A** aloud. Tell Ss to listen for this information as the audio program is played or read.
- Class Audio CD1 track 25 Play or read the audio program (see audio script, page T-157).
- Ask Ss if they understood everything in the listening exercise. Write any words on the board that Ss are unfamiliar with, and help Ss understand the meaning.
- Ss work in pairs to answer the questions in Exercise **2A**.

Practice

- Focus Ss' attention on Exercise **2B**. Read the instructions aloud. Have Ss listen for the details.
- Class Audio CD1 track 25 Play or read the first part of the audio program again (see audio script, page T-157). Pause the program after the doctor tells Stanley to try walking for 30 minutes each day. Hold up the Student's Book. Point to where *take a walk every day* has been checked. Tell Ss to listen to the complete conversation and check the boxes that include the doctor's advice to Stanley.
- Class Audio CD1 track 25 Play or read the entire audio program (see audio script, page T-157). Ss listen and write a check mark next to the doctor's advice. Repeat the audio program as needed.

Comprehension check

- Elicit answers from the Ss and write them on the board.
- Class Audio CD1 track 25 Play or read the audio program again (see audio script, page T-157). Ss listen and check their answers. Repeat the audio program as needed.
- Have several Ss tell the class the activities they checked for Exercise **2B**. Ask the rest of the class if they agree with the Ss. Make corrections as needed.

Learner persistence (individual work)

- Self-Study Audio CD track 16 Exercises **2A** and **2B** are recorded on the CD at the back of the Student's Book. Ss can listen to the CD at home for reinforcement and review. They can also listen to the CD for self-directed learning when class attendance is not possible.

Practice

- Focus Ss' attention on Exercise **3A**. Tell Ss that they are going to read a summary of the conversation between Stanley and his doctor.
- Direct Ss' attention to the words in the word bank. Say the words aloud. Ask Ss to repeat. Correct pronunciation as needed.

- Ask Ss if they understand all the words in the word bank. Go over the meaning of any words Ss don't know.
- Model the task. Ask a S to read aloud the first two sentences in the story. Guide Ss to continue the exercise by filling in the blanks with the appropriate words from the word bank.
- Ss complete the exercise individually. Walk around and help as needed.
- Focus Ss' attention on the second part of the instructions in Exercise **3A** and read it aloud.
- Class Audio CD1 track 26 Play or read the audio program (see audio script, page T-158). Ss listen and check their answers. Repeat the audio program as needed.
- Write the numbers *1–8* on the board. Ask individual Ss to write their answers on the board. Ask other Ss to read the answers. Ask: *Are the answers correct?* Make corrections as needed.

Learner persistence (individual work)

- Self-Study Audio CD track 17 Exercise **3A** is recorded on the CD at the back of the Student's Book. Ss can listen to the CD at home for reinforcement and review. They can also listen for self-directed learning when class attendance is not possible.

Application

- Focus Ss' attention on Exercise **3B**. Read the instructions aloud.
- Model the task. Tell Ss three things that you do to stay healthy, for example: *I eat healthy foods. I take yoga classes. I never use the elevator.*

  Option If you or Ss don't want to talk about yourself, talk about a friend or a family member.
- Ss complete the exercise in pairs. Help as needed.
- Ask several pairs to ask and answer the question for the class.

Evaluation

- Direct Ss' attention to the lesson focus on the board. Check Ss' understanding of the key vocabulary by asking them to make sentences with the words in Exercise **3A**.
- Have Ss look at the pictures on page 44 and tell you the advice that the doctor is giving Stanley. Ask Ss to use the words from the word bank in Exercise **3A** as they say the doctor's advice.
- Check off each part of the lesson focus as Ss demonstrate an understanding of what they have learned in the lesson.

More Ventures, Unit 4, Lesson A	
Workbook, 15–30 min.	
Add Ventures, 30–45 min.	www.cambridge.org/myresourceroom
Collaborative, 30–45 min.	
Student Arcade, time varies	www.cambridge.org/venturesarcade

<table>
<tr><td>Unit
Goals</td><td>Recognize good health habits
Describe beneficial plants
Complete a medical history form</td></tr>
</table>

2 Listen

STUDENT TK 16
CLASS CD1 TK 25

A Listen and answer the questions.

1. Who are the speakers?
2. What are they talking about?

STUDENT TK 16
CLASS CD1 TK 25

B Listen again. Put a check (✓) next to the doctor's advice.

1. ☐ sleep more   5. ☐ eat hamburgers
2. ☑ take a walk every day   6. ☐ eat breakfast
3. ☑ ride a bicycle   7. ☑ eat fish
4. ☐ take the elevator at work 8. ☐ take medication

3 After you listen

A Complete the story.

| advice | exercise | medication | tired |
| diet | health | pressure | weight |

Stanley is at the doctor's office. His ___health___ has always been good, but he

has been really ___tired___ lately. The doctor looks at Stanley's chart. He sees
                    2

a couple of problems. One problem is Stanley's ___weight___. He has gained 20
                                                3

pounds. Another problem is his blood ___pressure___. The doctor tells him he needs
                                       4

regular ___exercise___ – for example, walking or riding a bike. He also tells Stanley
          5

to change his ___diet___ – to eat more fish and vegetables. If Stanley doesn't do
                6

these things, he will need to take pills and other ___medication___. Stanley wants to be
                                                    7

healthy, so he is going to try to follow the doctor's ___advice___.
                                                       8

STUDENT TK 17
CLASS CD1 TK 26

Listen and check your answers.

B Talk with a partner. Ask and answer the question.

What are three things you do to stay healthy?

☑ Listen for and identify health issues and a doctor's advice   **UNIT 4   45**

LESSON B Present perfect

1 Grammar focus: *recently* and *lately*

Questions	Statements
Have you **gained** weight **recently**?	I **have gained** weight **recently**.
Has Sheila **gone** to the gym **lately**?	Sheila **hasn't gone** to the gym **lately**.

Past participles

Regular verbs				Irregular verbs			
check	→ checked	start	→ started	eat	→ eaten	lose	→ lost
exercise	→ exercised	visit	→ visited	give	→ given	see	→ seen
gain	→ gained	weigh	→ weighed	go	→ gone	sleep	→ slept

Turn to page 143 for a complete grammar chart and explanation.
Turn to page 146 for a list of irregular verbs.

2 Practice

A Write. Complete the sentences. Use the present perfect.

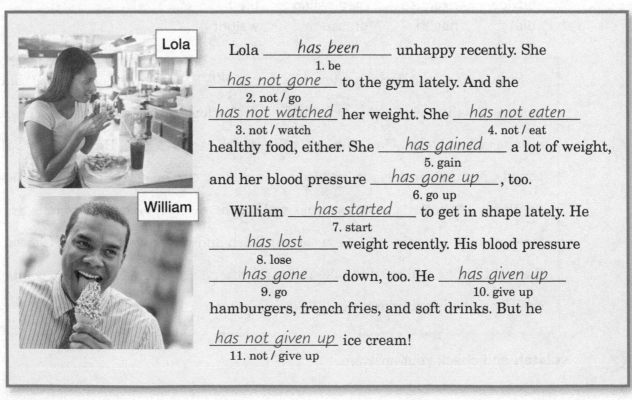

Lola _____*has been*_____ unhappy recently. She
1. be
_____*has not gone*_____ to the gym lately. And she
2. not / go
*has not watched* her weight. She _____*has not eaten*_____
3. not / watch   4. not / eat
healthy food, either. She _____*has gained*_____ a lot of weight,
5. gain
and her blood pressure _____*has gone up*_____, too.
6. go up
William _____*has started*_____ to get in shape lately. He
7. start
_____*has lost*_____ weight recently. His blood pressure
8. lose
_____*has gone*_____ down, too. He _____*has given up*_____
9. go   10. give up
hamburgers, french fries, and soft drinks. But he

*has not given up* ice cream!
11. not / give up

Listen and check your answers.

CLASS CD1 TK 27

Lesson objectives

- Introduce *recently* and *lately*
- Practice questions and statements in the present perfect
- Practice past participles with regular and irregular verbs

Warm-up and review

Before class: Write today's lesson focus on the board.
Lesson B:
Present perfect
Use of recently and lately

- Books closed. Begin class. Ask Ss when to use the present perfect. Elicit the answer: *To talk about actions that started in the past and continue to now.* Remind Ss that we use past participles with present perfect verbs.
- Write on the board, in a list, the base form of the past participles in Unit 2, Lesson C: *ask, talk, try, do, forget, get, lose, make, read, take,* and *write.* Elicit and write the past participles next to the base forms on the board: *asked, talked, tried, done, forgotten, got, lost, made, read, taken, written.*
- Review present perfect *Yes / No* questions and answers. Write on the board: *Have you ever _____?* Ask S volunteers to make questions, such as: *Have you ever talked to a doctor in English? Have you ever forgotten an appointment? Have you ever taken your blood pressure?* Ask other S volunteers to answer with *Yes, I have. / No, I haven't.*

Presentation

Focus on meaning / personalize

- Books closed. Direct Ss' attention to the lesson focus on the board. Read it aloud.
- Explain that we use the present perfect to talk about things we have done in the recent past and will continue doing in the future. Explain that, for this reason, the present perfect always has some connection to now (the present).
- Ask: *What do "recently" and "lately" mean? Do they mean "in the recent past" (a short time ago) or "in the distant past" (a long time ago)?* Ensure Ss understand that both terms refer to things that happened a short time ago.
- Tell Ss something you have done recently. For example: *I've gone to the gym recently. I've read two books recently.* Then ask Ss questions about things they have done recently. For example: *Have you been to a movie recently? Have you watched TV lately? Have you gone back to your home country recently?* After each answer, ask: *When?* The answer will confirm whether or not Ss understand what *recently* means.
- Tell Ss that present perfect can be used with other time phrases as long as they are recent, for example: *today* or *this week.*

Focus on form

- Books open. Direct Ss' attention to the charts in Exercise 1. Read aloud the questions and statements. Ask Ss to repeat. Elicit and have Ss underline the present perfect (*have gained / has gone*) (*have gained / hasn't gone*). Point out that to form the negative, we put the word *not* between *has* or *have* and the main verb (*has not gone*).
- Direct Ss' attention to the past participles. Say the base form of each verb and elicit the past participle. After each response, say the past participle again and ask Ss to repeat.

Practice

- Direct Ss' attention to the first picture in Exercise 2A. Ask: *What do you see? What is the woman eating?* Elicit appropriate responses and write them on the board.
- Direct Ss' attention to the second picture. Ask: *What do you see? What is the man eating?* Elicit appropriate responses.
- Draw a plate divided into four sections with a fifth section to the right that is not connected on the board, and have Ss tell you where the food in the pictures goes in the plate. Ask Ss if they think the people in the pictures are eating healthy food.

Comprehension check

- Read aloud the instructions for Exercise 2A.
- Model the task. Ask a S to read the example sentence aloud. Tell Ss to continue the exercise by filling in the blanks with the appropriate form of the verbs.
- Ss complete the exercise individually. Help as needed.
- Focus Ss' attention on the second part of the instructions in Exercise 2A, and read it aloud.
- Class Audio CD1 track 27 Play or read the audio program (see audio script, page T-158). Ss listen and check their answers. Repeat the audio program as needed.
- Write the numbers *1–11* on the board. Ask several Ss to come to the board to write their answers. Tell them to write only the words that are missing.

Practice

- Books open. Direct Ss' attention to Exercise 2B.
- Read the instructions aloud. Model the task. Ask two pairs to read aloud the example questions and answers. Be sure Ss understand how to use the words and the pictures to cue the questions and answers.
- Ss complete the exercise in pairs. Help as needed.
- Focus Ss' attention on the second part of the instructions for Exercise 2B.
- Ask a S to read the example sentence aloud. Model a negative statement. Ask a S to describe Roberto in Picture 2, for example: *Roberto hasn't given up desserts recently.*
- Ss complete the exercise individually. Help as needed.
- Ask several Ss to write their sentences on the board. Ask other Ss to read them aloud.

Expansion activity *(student pairs)*

- Divide the class into two teams. Ask one person from each team to come to the board. Say a verb, such as: *check.* Each person has to write the past participle of that verb on the board (*checked*). Use the verbs written in the grammar charts on pages 22 and 46 in the Student's Book.
- Give a point to the S who writes the correct past participle the most quickly. Tally the points. The team with the most points wins the game.

Application

- Focus Ss' attention on Exercise 3A. Read the instructions aloud.
- Model the task. Ask two pairs of Ss to read the example questions and answers aloud. Draw the chart in Exercise 3A on the board. Ask for a S volunteer. Write his or her name at the top of the chart. Ask the student two or three of the questions in the chart. Write a check mark in the correct column of the chart.

▼ **Teaching tip**
Remind Ss that *How about you?* and *What about you?* are ways of asking someone the same question the person asked you. Encourage Ss to respond and keep the conversation going before moving to the next question in the chart.

- Ss complete the exercise in pairs. Help as needed.
- Direct Ss' attention to Exercise 3B. Read the instructions aloud.
- Ask Ss to share information about their partners with the class.

Community building *(whole group)*

- Ask Ss if they can recommend good doctors or dentists to the class. Have Ss bring in the names and addresses of medical people, clinics, or hospitals they would recommend. Include the languages spoken by these professionals if other than English. Compile a list and distribute to the class. Be sure Ss understand that they should always check the qualifications of doctors and dentists, even those recommended by friends. Librarians at public libraries often are willing to help.

Learner persistence *(whole group)*

- If any Ss have a hard time remembering the past participle form of the verbs, encourage them to write the base form of the verbs on one side of an index card and the past participle form on the other side. Tell Ss to test themselves on the verbs at home alone. Consider giving Ss a quiz on past participles to encourage them to study at home.

Evaluation

- Direct Ss' attention to the lesson focus on the board. Focus Ss' attention on the pictures on page 44.
- Have Ss ask questions about Stanley using the guideline: *Has Stanley _____ lately? Has Stanley _____ recently?* Make sure Ss use the correct form of the past participle, for example: *Has Stanley exercised recently? Has he eaten well lately?*
- Say the different verbs from the grammar chart on page 46. Ask Ss to tell you their corresponding past participles.
- Check off each part of the lesson focus as Ss demonstrate an understanding of what they have learned in the lesson.

More Ventures, Unit 4, Lesson B	
Workbook, 15–30 min.	
Add Ventures, 30–45 min.	www.cambridge.org/myresourceroom
Collaborative, 30–45 min.	
Student Arcade, time varies	www.cambridge.org/venturesarcade

B **Talk** with a partner. Ask and answer questions. Use the present perfect with *recently* and *lately*.

> **A** Has Elisa lost weight recently?
> **B** Yes, she has.

> **A** Has Roberto given up desserts lately?
> **B** No, he hasn't.

1. Elisa / lose weight

2. Roberto / give up desserts

3. Joy / start taking vitamins

4. Ahmet / gain weight

5. Martin and Julie / start exercising a lot

6. Lee / sleep much

Write a sentence about each picture. Use the present perfect with *recently* and *lately*.

Elisa has lost weight recently.
(Answers will vary.)

3 Communicate

A **Work** with a partner. Ask and answer questions. Complete the chart.

> **A** Have you eaten a lot of fish lately?
> **B** Yes, I have. How about you?

> **A** Have you had a cold lately?
> **B** No, I haven't. What about you?

Partner's name: _____	Yes	No
1. eat a lot of fish	(Answers will vary.)	
2. have a cold		
3. check your blood pressure		
4. see a doctor		
5. go to the gym		
6. visit a dentist		

B **Share** information about your partner.

LESSON C *Used to*

1 Grammar focus: statements and questions

Statements	*Yes / No* questions	Short answers
I **used to** eat a lot of fatty foods.	**Did** you **use to** eat a lot of fatty foods?	Yes, I did.
She **didn't use to** go to bed late.	**Did** she **use to** go to bed late?	No, she didn't.

Turn to page 144 for a complete grammar chart and explanation.

2 Practice

A **Write.** Complete the sentences. Use *use to* or *used to*.

1. **A** Did he _____use to_____ stay up all night?
   B Yes, he did, but he goes to bed early now.

2. **A** How often do you eat meat?
   B I _____used to_____ eat meat every night, but now I usually have fish.

3. **A** Did you _____use to_____ drive to work?
   B Yes, I did, but now I ride my bike.

4. **A** What do you usually do after work?
   B We _____used to_____ go straight home, but now we take dance classes twice a week.

5. **A** Do you exercise every day?
   B I _____used to_____ exercise every day, but now I exercise only on weekends.

Listen and check your answers. Then practice with a partner.

CLASS CD1 TK 28

Lesson objectives
- Introduce *used to*
- Practice questions and statements with *used to*

Warm-up and review

Before class: Write today's lesson focus on the board. *Lesson C:*
used to

- Books open. Begin class. Review the present perfect with *recently* and *lately*. Direct Ss' attention to the pictures on page 44. Write on the board: *Have you _____ recently?* Have Ss use the question form on the board to make questions that the doctor might have asked Stanley, for example: *Have you exercised lately? Have you gained weight recently?* Write the questions on the board.

Presentation

Focus on meaning / personalize

- Books closed. Direct Ss' attention to the lesson focus on the board. Read it aloud. Books closed.
- Divide the board into three columns with *Name, Before*, and *Now* as headings. Say: *Stanley used to exercise a lot, but now he just works.* Write *exercise a lot* under *Before* and *just works* under *Now*. Give an example from your own life, such as: *I used to cook a lot, but now I eat out most of the time.* Write *cook a lot* under *Before*. Write *eat out* under *Now*. For example:

Name	*Before*	*Now*
Stanley	*exercise a lot*	*just works*
Teacher	*cook a lot*	*eat out*
Akira	*eat sushi*	*eat hamburgers*

- Have Ss share things they used to do in their home countries that they don't do now, and write them in the appropriate column. Ask Ss to repeat other Ss' answers changing the *I* pronoun to *he* or *she*. For example: *He used to eat a lot of fruit, but now he mostly eats junk food.*
- Ask: *Do I cook a lot now?* (No.) *Did I cook a lot before?* (Yes.) *Does "used to" mean I do the activity now, or does it mean I did the activity in the past, and I don't do it anymore?* (in the past)

Focus on form

- Books open. Direct Ss' attention to the charts in Exercise 1. Read aloud the two statements, then the *Yes / No* questions and short answers. Ask Ss to repeat.
- Have Ss underline the different forms of *used to* in the statements and questions. Ask: *What is the verb tense in the statement?* (past tense.)
- Direct Ss' attention to the questions. Elicit how to make the statement a question. (*used to* changes to *Did _____ use to . . . ?*) Remind Ss that this is the same as the question form for other verbs in the past tense. Write on the board as an example: *<u>Did</u> you <u>walk</u> to the store?* NOT *<u>Did</u> you <u>walked</u> to the store?*

Practice

- Direct Ss' attention to the pictures in Exercise 2A.
- Ask: *What do you see in each picture?* Elicit an appropriate response, such as: *A man is asleep. It's 10:00.* Say: *These are pictures of things people do now. They didn't use to do these things.*
- Read the instructions aloud. Model the task. Ask two Ss to read the example question and answer to the class.
- Ss complete the exercise individually. Walk around and help as needed.
- Ask volunteers to write their answers on the board. Ask the class to correct any mistakes. Be sure Ss understand when to write *use* and *used*.

Comprehension check

- Read the second part of the instructions for Exercise 2A aloud.
- Class Audio CD1 track 28 Play or read the audio program (see audio script, page T-158). Ss listen and check their answers.
- Ask Ss to read the questions and answers in pairs. Ask other Ss if the answers are correct. Make corrections as needed.

Presentation

- Books closed. Write on the board: *when I was a child* and *now*. Tell the class about the things you used to do when you were a child and the things you do now, for example: *I used to play with dolls. Now I play with my children. I used to play with cars. Now I drive a car.*

▼ **Teaching tip**
If you don't wish to talk about yourself, make up sentences about a fictional person or talk about a famous person.

- Ask Ss to give you examples of what they used to do as children and what they do now.

Practice

- Books open. Focus Ss' attention on the pictures in Exercise **2B**. Point to the first picture. Tell Ss that this is what Michael used to look like when he was younger. Point to the second picture. Tell Ss that this is what Michael looks like now.
- Read the instructions aloud. Model the task. Ask a S to read aloud the example sentences to the class. Show Ss the sentences in the chart that correspond to the example.
- Ss complete the exercise in pairs. Walk around and help as needed.
- Ask individual Ss to make sentences with the descriptions in Exercise **2B**. After each description, ask the class: *Are those sentences correct?* Ask volunteers to make corrections as needed.
- Direct Ss' attention to the second part of Exercise **2B**. Read the instructions aloud. Model the exercise. Ask a S to read the example sentences to the class.
- Ss complete the exercise individually. Walk around and help as needed.

Community building (small groups)

- If possible, bring to class an old picture of the town or city where your school is located. Ask: *How has the town changed? What did it use to be like?* Discuss and write Ss' answers on the board.

Expansion activity (whole group)

- Ask Ss if they can bring a picture of themselves as a baby or as a child to the next class. Bring a picture of yourself to class to use as an example. Describe the picture using *used to*, for example: *I used to have short hair. I used to live in Michigan.*

Application

- Direct Ss' attention to Exercise **3A** and read the instructions aloud. Remind Ss what the words *healthy habits* mean. Explain that healthy habits are things you do often to stay healthy, such as exercising and eating foods that are good for you.
- Ask volunteers to read and complete the example sentences aloud.
- Ss complete the exercise in small groups. Walk around and help as needed.
- Ask several Ss to share with the class what they learned about a classmate's past and current healthy habits.

Evaluation

- Direct Ss' attention to the lesson focus on the board. Ask Ss to look at the pictures in Exercise **2A** and make sentences about the people with *used to*. Have Ss look at the pictures of Michael in Exercise **2B** and make questions with *used to*.
- Check off each part of the lesson focus as Ss demonstrate an understanding of what they have learned in the lesson.

More Ventures, Unit 4, Lesson C	
Workbook, 15–30 min.	
Add Ventures, 30–45 min. **Collaborative,** 30–45 min.	www.cambridge.org/myresourceroom
Student Arcade, time varies	www.cambridge.org/venturesarcade

B Work with a partner. Talk about Michael as a young man and Michael today.

> Michael used to play sports, but he doesn't anymore. Now he watches sports on TV.

When Michael was young	Michael now
1. play sports	watch sports on TV
2. skip breakfast	eat three meals a day
3. take vitamins	not take vitamins
4. drink coffee	drink tea
5. sleep late	get up early
6. eat fruit between meals	eat candy and chips between meals
7. work out every afternoon	take a nap every afternoon

Write sentences about Michael.

When Michael was young, he used to play sports. Now he watches sports on TV. (Answers will vary.)

3 Communicate

A Work in a small group. Complete the sentences. Talk about your health habits.

1. When I was a child, I used to . . . , but now I . . .
2. In my country, I used to . . . , but now I . . .
3. When I was a teenager, I used to . . . , but now I . . .
4. When I first came to this country, I used to . . . , but now I . . .
5. When I had more time, I used to . . . , but now I . . .

B Share information about your classmates.

LESSON **D** Reading

1 Before you read

Look at the reading tip. Then read the first and last paragraphs. Answer the questions.

1. Which two plants is the reading about?
2. How long have people used them?

USEFUL LANGUAGE

Use *beneficial* to describe something that's good for you.

2 Read

Read the magazine article. Listen and read again.

STUDENT TK 18
CLASS CD1 TK 29

The first paragraph of a reading is the **introduction**. It tells you the topic. The last paragraph is the **conclusion**. It often repeats the topic with different words.

Two Beneficial Plants

Since the beginning of history, people in every culture have used plants to stay healthy and to prevent sickness. Garlic and chamomile are two beneficial plants.

Garlic is a plant in the onion family. The green stem and the leaves of the garlic plant grow above the ground. The root – the part under the ground – is a bulb with sections called cloves. They look like the pieces of an orange. The bulb is the part that people have traditionally used for medicine. They have used it for insect bites, cuts, earaches, and coughs. Today, some people also use it to treat high blood pressure and high cholesterol.

Chamomile is a small, pretty plant with flowers that bloom from late summer to early fall. The flowers have white petals and a yellow center. Many people use dried chamomile flowers to

make tea. Some people give the tea to babies with upset stomachs. They also drink chamomile tea to feel better when they have a cold or the flu, poor digestion, or trouble falling asleep.

For thousands of years, people everywhere have grown garlic, chamomile, and other herbal medicines in their gardens. Today, you can buy them in health-food stores. You can get them in dried, powdered, or pill form.

- Introduce and read "Two Beneficial Plants"
- Identify topic from first and last paragraphs
- Recognize word families

Warm-up and review

- Before class. Write today's lesson focus on the board.

  Lesson D:
  Read and understand "Two Beneficial Plants"
  Identify topic from first and last paragraphs
  Recognize word families

- Begin class. Books closed. Focus Ss' attention on the words *Beneficial Plants* in the lesson focus. Say the words aloud. Ask Ss to repeat. Tell Ss that *benefical* means *helpful.*

- Ask Ss to brainstorm different beneficial plants. Write the names of the plants on the board, for example: *ginger, garlic, green tea.*

- Have a brief discussion about how the plants on the board can be used for good health, for example: *If you have a sore throat, you can drink green tea with lemon and honey in it.*

Presentation

- Books open. Direct Ss' attention to Exercise **1** and read the instructions aloud.

- Ask a S to read the two questions aloud. Have Ss skim the article to find the answers to the questions. Elicit the correct responses.

> Read the tip box aloud. Ask a S to read aloud the first paragraph of the article. Tell Ss that this is the introduction. Guide Ss to identify the topic (garlic and chamomile are two beneficial plants). Have a different S read the last paragraph aloud. Tell Ss that this is the conclusion to the article.

Practice

- Focus Ss' attention on the pictures in Exercise **2**. Ask Ss what they can see (*garlic and chamomile*).

- Read the instructions for Exercise **2** aloud. Ss read the article silently.

- Ask Ss to underline any words that are unfamiliar. Write the new words on the board. Encourage Ss to guess the meaning of each new word from context. For example: *stem* and *root*. Ask Ss to read the first paragraph in the article and guess the meanings of the words. Elicit an appropriate answer, such as: *The stem grows above the ground, and the root grows under the ground.* Draw a labeled picture on the board as illustration.

- Class Audio CD1 track 29 Play or read the audio program and ask Ss to read along silently (see audio script, page T-158). Repeat the audio program as needed.

Learner persistence (individual work)

- Self-Study Audio CD track 18 Exercise **2** is recorded on the CD at the back of the Student's Book. Ss can listen to the CD at home for reinforcement and review. They can also listen for self-directed learning when class attendance is not possible.

Expansion activity (student pairs)

- ~~Materials needed~~ Index cards.

- Twenty Questions game. Write the following vocabulary words on the board: *garlic, chamomile, beneficial, stem, root, cough, blood pressure, herbal medicines, health-food stores.* Make sure Ss understand the meaning of each of these words.

- Write each word on an index card and shuffle the cards.

- Model the activity. Pick one of the index cards and look at the vocabulary word. Tell the class that they must ask you *Yes* or *No* questions to guess the vocabulary word. Encourage them to ask questions, such as: *Is it a noun? Is it an adjective? Is it a plant?*

- Answer Ss' questions about your word. Keep track of the number of questions Ss have asked by keeping a tally on the board. Ss cannot ask more than 20 questions. The person who guesses the word is the next S to come to the front of the room and choose an index card.

- Continue the game until all the vocabulary words have been reviewed.

Comprehension check

- Read the instructions for Exercise **3A** aloud.
- Ask the questions. Elicit correct responses.

Presentation

- Focus Ss' attention on Exercise **3B**. Read the instructions aloud. Ask a S to read the questions in number 1. Go over the answers with the class. Make sure that Ss can understand the words in the dictionary entry.
- Ss may not be familiar with the word *antonym*. Explain that it is a word that means the opposite of another word. Give an example, such as: *"Good" is an antonym of "bad."*
- Write on the board: *digestion, indigestion, digest, digestive*. Say the words aloud. Ask Ss to repeat. Have Ss identify the part of speech for each form of the word (*noun, noun, verb, adjective*).

▼ **Teaching tip**
Review the parts of speech and help Ss find words in the reading that illustrate nouns, verbs, and adjectives. Encourage Ss to look for word families as a way to increase their vocabulary.

Practice

- Focus Ss' attention on number 2 in Exercise **3B**. Read the instructions aloud.
- Model the task. Ask a S to read the examples to the class.
- Ss complete the exercise individually. Walk around and help as needed.
- Draw the chart on the board. Ask Ss to come to the board to fill in the blanks.
- Point to each word written in the chart. Ask: *Is the word correct?* Ask different Ss to correct the word form as needed.
- Focus Ss' attention on number 3 in Exercise **3B**. Read the instructions aloud.
- Model the task. Ask a S to read the first example aloud. Ss complete the exercise individually. Walk around and help as needed.
- Write letters *a–e* on the board. Ask individual Ss to come to the board to write their answers to number 3. Tell Ss to write only the words missing from the blanks, not the entire sentences.
- Ask other Ss to read aloud the completed sentences. Point to the answers written on the board. Ask: *Are these words correct?* Make corrections as needed.

Application

- Focus Ss' attention on Exercise **3C**. Read the instructions aloud.
- Ask three Ss to read the questions to the class.
- Ss complete the exercise in pairs. Walk around and help as needed.
- Ask Ss to share what they learned about their partners.

Expansion activity (whole group)

- Write on the board: *home remedies*. Explain that home remedies are ways to treat sickness that come from the advice of family and friends instead of a doctor. Ask Ss to tell the kinds of home remedies that are common in their home countries. Ask if Ss are more comfortable using home remedies or going to a doctor when they or their family members are sick.

Evaluation

- Direct Ss' attention to the lesson focus on the board. Books closed. Ask Ss to retell the information they learned from the article about beneficial plants. Ask a S to say one sentence about the article, the next S to continue, and so forth.
- Write some of the words from Exercise **3B** number 2 on the board. Ask Ss to identify the part of speech and to make a sentence using the word.
- Ask Ss what kind of information about a word they can find in a dictionary. Elicit: *the part of speech, the definition, antonyms, other forms of the word*.
- Check off each part of the lesson focus as Ss demonstrate an understanding of what they have learned in the lesson.

Learner persistence (individual, pairs)

- You may wish to assign Extended Reading Worksheets from the *Online Teacher's Resource Room* for Ss to complete outside of class. The purpose of these worksheets is to encourage Ss to read for pleasure in English outside of the English class. The worksheets can also be assigned as extended reading in class.

More Ventures, Unit 4, Lesson D	
Workbook, 15–30 min.	
Add Ventures, 30–45 min.	
Collaborative, 30–45 min.	www.cambridge.org/myresourceroom
Extended Reading and worksheet, 45–60 min.	
Student Arcade, time varies	www.cambridge.org/venturesarcade

3 After you read

A Check your understanding.

1. What is the reading about?
2. What is the word for the sections of the garlic bulb?
3. What do people use garlic for?
4. What does the chamomile plant look like?
5. What can you make from chamomile?
6. What do people use chamomile for?
7. Which plant could you use for high blood pressure?

B Build your vocabulary.

1. Read the dictionary entry for *digestion*. What part of speech is it? What does it mean? What is the antonym? What is the verb? What is the adjective?

> **digestion** /n/ the ability of the body to change food so the body
> can use it; antonym: **indigestion**; **digest** /v/ – **digestive** /adj/

2. Use a dictionary. Fill in the chart with the missing forms.

Noun	Verb	Adjective
digestion	digest	digestive
prevention	prevent	preventable
sickness		sick
treatment	treat	treatable
herbs		herbal

3. Complete the sentences. Write the correct form of the word from Exercise B2.

a. You shouldn't swim right after you eat. You should wait to __digest__ your food.

b. Chamomile, basil, oregano, and thyme are examples of __herbs__.

c. Some people can't drink milk. It makes them __sick__.

d. Some people drink orange juice to __prevent__ a cold or the flu. They don't want to get sick.

e. A hot bath is a good __treatment__ for sore muscles.

C Talk with a partner. Ask and answer the questions.

1. How can you prevent a sore throat? A cold? Weight gain?
2. In your opinion, what is the best treatment for a headache? A stomachache? An earache?
3. What herbs do you like to cook with? What's your favorite herb?

☑ Identify the topic of a text by reading the first and last paragraphs;
recognize word families

LESSON E Writing

1 Before you write

A Talk with a partner. Answer the questions.

1. Do you or your family members ever use beneficial plants?
2. Which ones do you use?
3. What do you use them for?

Aloe vera

B Read the paragraph.

Licorice

Licorice is a popular herb in my native country, Greece. The plant has feathery leaves and purple flowers. It tastes sweet. My mother used to use licorice to make a medicine for my grandmother's arthritis. Mother grew the licorice plant in our backyard. She used to cut the licorice roots into pieces and put them inside a warm, wet cloth. Then she put the cloth on my grandmother's shoulders and knees. The licorice helped with the pain. Today, I use licorice when I have sore muscles.

> The first sentence of a paragraph is called the *topic sentence*. It names the topic and gives basic information about it.
>
> *Licorice* (topic) *is a popular herb in my native country, Greece.* (basic information)

Work with a partner. Put the information from the paragraph in order.

 _4_ how the writer's mother used the plant

 _1_ where the plant grows

 _5_ how the plant helped

 _3_ how the plant tastes

 _2_ how the plant looks

 _6_ how the writer uses the plant today

Lesson objectives

- Write a descriptive paragraph about a plant
- Write topic sentences

Warm-up and review

- Before class. Write today's lesson focus on the board.

  Lesson E:
  Write a descriptive paragraph about a plant
  Use a topic sentence

- Begin class. Books closed. Ask Ss what they do to: *cure a cold*, *help a sore throat*, *treat insect bites*, *reduce indigestion*. Write the answers on the board.

- Ask Ss if they ever use plants or herbs to help with their health problems. Write on the board the names of the plants and the problems they cure.

▼ **Culture tip**

It might be interesting to tell Ss that some Americans take vitamins and supplements to stay healthy. Bring in flyers or ads from local health-food stores. Ask Ss to find supplements in the ads that are made from beneficial plants. Ask Ss if they think it's a good idea to take any of these supplements.

Presentation

- Books open. Direct Ss' attention to the picture in Exercise 1A. Ask Ss what they can see. Write the words *aloe vera* on the board. Say the word aloud and have Ss repeat. Ask Ss if they know this plant.

- If any S knows about the aloe vera plant, have the S give a few facts about it.

- Read the questions aloud. Have Ss discuss the questions in pairs. Walk around and help as needed.

- Ask several pairs to share any interesting information they talked about with the class.

- Direct Ss' attention to Exercise 1B and read the instructions aloud.

- Focus Ss' attention on the title of the paragraph. Say the word aloud. Ask Ss to repeat. Ask if Ss are familiar with this herb. Focus Ss' attention on the picture of licorice. Tell Ss that this is a picture of the licorice plant. Ask Ss if they have ever eaten licorice.

- Ss read the paragraph silently. Ask Ss to read the paragraph once and then again. When they read it the second time, ask them to underline any words they are unfamiliar with. Write the new vocabulary words on the board.

▼ **Culture tip**

Tell Ss that licorice is a popular candy flavor in some countries. Ask Ss if licorice is popular as a candy flavor in countries they know.

Practice

- Direct Ss' attention to the second part of Exercise 1B. Read the instructions aloud. Explain that *in order* means *first, second, third, and so forth*.

- Model the task. Ask a S to read the example phrase aloud. Ask Ss to find and read aloud the sentence in the paragraph that states where the plant grows. Point out that it is the first piece of information. Ask a S to find the second piece of information in the paragraph. When you are certain that Ss understand the task, have them complete the exercise individually. Help as needed.

- Write the numbers *1–6* on the board. Assign a number 1–6 to individual Ss. Ask Ss to come to the board to write the phrases from Exercise 1B that correspond to their numbers. Ask the class if they agree with the sequence on the board. Have Ss correct the sequence as needed.

Read the tip box aloud. Ask Ss to look at the second paragraph in the article "Two Beneficial Plants" in Lesson D, on page 50. Have them tell what the topic of the second paragraph is *(garlic)*. Ask Ss to identify the topic of the third paragraph of the article *(chamomile)*.

Presentation

- Direct Ss' attention to Exercise 1C and read the instructions aloud.
- Focus Ss' attention on the plan for the paragraph about a beneficial plant. Ask individual Ss to read the questions aloud. Ensure Ss understand all of the vocabulary in the questions.
- Explain that the purpose of the chart is to help Ss think of information to use in the paragraphs that they will be writing in Exercise 2.
- Write the names of beneficial plants you've already discussed on the board, such as *licorice* and *aloe vera*. Ask Ss to think of other beneficial plants. Write four to five additional suggestions on the board (*ginger*, *garlic*, *chamomile*, and *Echinacea*).

Practice

- Ask Ss to choose one of the plants on the board. Tell Ss they will write about this plant in the chart in Exercise 1C.
- Encourage Ss to use a dictionary, encyclopedia or online resource to find out information about the plant they have chosen. Ss can use these resources to answer the questions in the chart.

Application

- Focus Ss' attention on Exercise 2. Read the instructions aloud.
- Ss complete the task individually. Walk around and help as needed. Ensure Ss are using the paragraph plans they created in 1C.

Comprehension check

- Direct Ss' attention to Exercise 3A and read the instructions aloud. This exercise asks Ss to develop skills to review and edit their own writing.
- Model the task. Focus Ss' attention on the example paragraph in Exercise 1B. Ask Ss to find the items in the checklist and underline them. (*The herb is licorice. It is described in the second and third sentences. Its uses are explained in the rest of the sentences*).

- Ss complete the exercise individually. Help as needed.
- Ask Ss if anyone checked "No" for any of the three boxes. If anyone did, encourage that S to change the paragraph so that the missing items are included.

Evaluation

- Focus Ss' attention on Exercise 3B and read the instructions aloud. This exercise asks Ss to work together to peer-correct their writing. Reading aloud enables the writer to review his or her own writing. Reading to a partner allows the writer to understand the need to write clearly for an audience.
- Listen to Ss as they ask their partners questions about their paragraph and talk about one thing they learned.
- Direct Ss' attention to the lesson focus on the board. Have Ss look at the pictures of the plants on pages 50 and 52. Ask Ss to come to the board to write a topic sentence for a paragraph about one of the plants.
- Check off each part of the lesson focus as Ss demonstrate an understanding of what they have learned in the lesson.

More Ventures, Unit 4, Lesson E	
Workbook, 15–30 min.	
Add Ventures, 30–45 min.	www.cambridge.org/myresourceroom
Collaborative, 30–45 min.	

C **Write** a plan for a paragraph about a beneficial plant. Answer the questions.

What's the name of the beneficial plant?	*(Answers will vary.)*
What do people use it for?	
Where does the plant grow?	
What does the plant look like?	
Can you eat the plant? What does it taste like?	
What does the plant smell like?	
What does the plant feel like?	

2 Write

Write a paragraph about a plant that people use as medicine. Name the herb and give basic information about it in the topic sentence. Describe the plant and how people use it. Use Exercises 1B and 1C to help you.

3 After you write

A **Check** your writing.

	Yes	No
1. In my topic sentence, I named the plant and gave basic information about it.	☐	☐
2. I described the plant.	☐	☐
3. I explained how people use the plant.	☐	☐

B **Share** your writing with a partner.

1. Take turns. Read your paragraph to a partner.
2. Comment on your partner's paragraph. Ask your partner a question about the paragraph. Tell your partner one thing you learned.

LESSON F Another view

Medical History Form

1. Chief complaint: Describe the problem and approximately when it began.

Problem	Date problem began

2. Have you ever had any of the following?

☐ allergies	☐ back pain	☐ frequent headaches	☐ high blood pressure
☐ arthritis	☐ chest pains	☐ heart attack	☐ high cholesterol
☐ asthma	☐ diabetes	☐ heart disease	☐ tuberculosis

3. Are you pregnant?   Yes   No

4. Are you currently taking medications?   Yes   No

5. If yes, list all medications, including vitamins and herbal supplements.

_____

6. List any major illness, injury, or surgery that you have had in the past year.

_____

The above information is correct to the best of my knowledge.

7. Signature: _____   8. Date: _____

A Read the questions. Look at the form. Fill in the answer.

1. Where do you write the reason for this doctor visit?

    ● (A) number 1   (C) number 4
    (B) number 3   (D) number 5

2. Where do you write the names of the medicines you take?

    (A) number 2   ● number 5
    (B) number 4   (D) number 7

3. Where do you write that you had back surgery last year?

    (A) number 1   (C) number 5
    (B) number 2   ● number 6

4. Where do you write when the problem began?

    ● (A) number 1   (C) number 5
    (B) number 3   (D) number 6

B Work with a partner. First, complete the form about yourself or someone you know. Then ask questions about your partner's form. Are the medical histories similar?

Lesson objectives
- Read and discuss a medical history form
- Use reported commands
- Complete the self-assessment

Warm-up and review
- Before class. Write today's lesson focus on the board.

  Lesson F:
  Read a medical history form
  Review topic vocabulary
  Complete the self-assessment

- Begin class. Books open. Direct Ss' attention to the pictures on page 44 at the beginning of the unit. Ask Ss questions to review unit vocabulary and grammar, for example: *Why is Stanley at the doctor's office?* (Because he is overweight, and his blood pressure is too high.) *Has Stanley exercised recently?* (No, he hasn't.) *Has he eaten healthy food lately?* (No, he hasn't.) *Did he use to exercise a lot?* (Yes, he did.) *Did he use to eat healthier food?* (Yes, he did.)

- Direct Ss' attention to the words *Medical History Form* in the lesson focus. Say the words aloud. Explain that this is a form that you have to fill out when you go to see the doctor.

- Ask Ss what type of information the patient has to write on the form. Write Ss' responses on the board, such as: *name, health problems, names of medications that the patient is taking.*

Presentation
- Direct Ss' attention to the form in Exercise 1. Ask Ss if they have had to fill out one of these forms at the doctor's office. Ask them if they have had trouble filling out the form. If any Ss say *Yes*, have them say what was difficult for them to understand about the form.

- Ask Ss to skim the form and answer the following questions: *Where do you write that you have had high blood pressure in the past?* (in question 2) *Where do you write if you are pregnant or not?* (in question 3) *Why do you have to sign the form?* (to say that the information you wrote is true and correct)

- Ss may have trouble pronouncing some of the health problems listed in question number 2 on the form. Say the words aloud. Ask Ss to repeat.

- Make sure Ss understand the meaning of the words on the form. Go over the definitions of any new words with the class.

Practice
- Read aloud the instructions for Exercise **1A**. This task helps prepare Ss for standardized-type tests they may have to take. Make sure Ss understand the task. Have Ss individually scan for and fill in the answers.

Comprehension check
- Correct the answers to Exercise **1A** with the class.
- Discuss any questions Ss have about the form.

Application
- Read aloud the instructions for Exercise **1B**. Tell Ss that they can write about an invented health problem or a real one. They can also write about someone they know if they prefer not to write about themselves.

- Ss complete the exercise individually. Walk around and help as needed.

- Ss in pairs. Encourage Ss to ask each other questions about the health problems they answered on the form.

- Write some questions on the board as guidelines, for example: *How long have you had _____? How long have you taken _____?*

Expansion activity (whole group)
- **Materials needed** Copies of a medical history form from a local doctor's office.

- If Ss want extra practice filling out forms, ask them to fill out the form as an in-class activity. Write any words that Ss are unfamiliar with on the board. Go over the meaning of each word with the class.

Warm up and review

- Books open. Direct Ss' attention to the story on page 45. Ask Ss what Stanley's doctor suggested he do to be more healthy. Elicit answers such as: *Eat more fish and vegetables. Get regular exercise, such as walking or riding a bike.*

- Write the following sentences on the board:

  Stanley's doctor <u>told him to eat</u> more vegetables.
  Stanley's doctor <u>told him to get</u> more exercise.

- Point to the underlined words in the sentences. Write *tell _____ to _____* on the board. Tell Ss we can use this structure to explain what someone has suggested we do. Stanley's doctor suggested he do several things, and we can express these with a form of the structure *tell _____ to _____*.

Presentation

- Books open. Direct Ss' attention to the chart in Exercise **2A**. Ask Ss what a *command* is. Elicit answers, such as: *Something that someone tells you to do.*

- Read aloud the first command: *Park over there.* Read aloud the parallel reported command: *The policewoman told me to park over there.* Ask Ss to compare the two sentences. Tell Ss that the first sentence is a command and that the second sentence is someone talking about the command.

- Ask a S to read aloud the second command: *"Don't talk during tests."* Ask another S to read aloud the parallel reported command: *The teacher told us not to talk during tests.* Ask Ss to compare the two sentences. Ask Ss what is the difference between the two reported commands. Point out that the negative form of the reported command structure is *tell _____ **not** to _____*.

Practice

- Direct Ss' attention to the instructions in **2A**. Read the instructions aloud. Ensure Ss understand they need to complete the chart with the commands they imagine a teacher and a police officer might say. Ask Ss to complete the chart in pairs. Walk around and help as needed.

- Direct Ss' attention to the instructions in **2B**. Read the instructions aloud. Tell Ss they will pretend one of the people in the list gave them a command. Their partner needs to guess who that person is. Ss complete the exercise in pairs.

- Ask Ss to perform their dialogs in front of the class.

Evaluation

- Before asking students to turn to the self-assessment on page 137, do a quick review of the unit. Have Ss turn to Lesson A. Ask the class to talk about what they remember about this lesson. Prompt Ss, if necessary, with questions, for example: *What are the conversations about on this page? What vocabulary is in the pictures?* Continue in this manner to review each lesson quickly.

- **Self-assessment** Read the instructions for Exercise **3**. Ask Ss to turn to the self-assessment page and complete the unit self-assessment. The self-assessments are also on the *Online Teacher's Resource Room*. If you prefer to collect the assessments and save them as part of each S's portfolio assessment, print out the unit self-assessment from the *Resource Room*, ask students to complete it, and collect and save it.

- If Ss are ready, administer the unit test on pages T-171–T-172 of this Teacher's Edition (or on the Assessment Audio CD / CD-ROM).

More Ventures, Unit 4, Lesson F	
Workbook, 15–30 min.	
Add Ventures, 30–45 min.	www.cambridge.org/myresourceroom
Collaborative, 30–45 min.	

2 Grammar connections: reported *commands*

Commands	Reported commands
"**Park** over there."	The policewoman **told me to park** over there.
"**Don't talk** during tests."	The teacher **told us not to talk** during tests.

A **Work** with a partner. Complete the chart with commands the people might give.

	Commands	Reported commands
A teacher	Affirmative: "_Listen carefully____._"	Affirmative: _He told us to listen carefully_.
	Negative: "_Don't (Answers will vary.)_	Negative: _____.
A police officer	Affirmative: "_____."	Affirmative: _____.
	Negative: "_____."	Negative: _____.

B **Talk** with a partner. Use a reported command to say what a person in the list below might say. Your partner guesses who said it. Take turns.

a dentist	an eye doctor	a parent	a soccer coach
a doctor	a manager	a police officer	a teacher

A This person told me to wear my glasses every day.
B An eye doctor!
A Yes! That's right!

3 Wrap up

Complete **the Self-assessment** on page 137.

Review

CLASS CD1 TK 30

Listen. Put a check (✓) under the correct name(s).

	Jenny	Sara
1. used to have time to call friends	✓	
2. used to work 50 hours a week		✓
3. used to exercise more		✓
4. used to cook healthy food	✓	
5. used to take care of herself	✓	✓
6. used to take the stairs at work	✓	

Talk with a partner. Check your answers.

2 Grammar

A Write. Complete the story. Use the correct words.

A Happy Ending

Last year, Frank went to his doctor ___*because of*___ his health. His doctor

1. because / because of
told him that his blood pressure was ___*too*___ high. Frank got very

2. enough / too
nervous because he didn't ___*use to*___ have health problems.

3. use to / used to
Frank ___*has started*___ to get in shape lately. He ___*used to*___ take the

4. started / has started　　　　　5. use to / used to
elevator at work, but now he takes the stairs. He ___*has had*___ a lot more

6. has / has had
energy lately. The hardest thing he ___*has given up*___ recently is his favorite

7. has given up / gives up
food – ice cream!

B Write. Look at the answers. Write the questions.

1. **A** ___*Has*___ Frank ___*started to get in shape*___ lately?
   B Yes, he has. Frank has started to get in shape.

2. **A** ___*Did*___ Frank ___*go to the doctor last year*___?
   B Yes, he did. Frank went to the doctor last year because of his health.

3. **A** ___*Did*___ Frank ___*use to take the elevator at work*___?
   B Yes, he did. Frank used to take the elevator at work.

Talk with a partner. Ask and answer the questions.

Lesson objectives
- Review vocabulary and grammar from Units 3 and 4
- Introduce voiced and voiceless *th* sounds

Warm-up and review

- Before class. Write today's lesson focus on the board.
  Review unit:
  Review vocabulary, pronunciation, and grammar from Units 3 and 4
- Begin class. Books closed. Review the present perfect with *recently* and *lately*. Ask several Ss questions using this form:
  Have you exercised recently?
  Have you spoken English outside of class lately?, etc.
  (Elicit *Yes, I have. / No, I haven't.*)
- Ask Ss questions with *used to*, for example:
  Did you use to exercise more?
  Did you use to study English in your country?, etc.
  (Elicit *Yes, I did. / No, I didn't.*)
- Ask Ss questions with *because* or *because of*, for example:
  Why did you come to this country?
  Why are you studying English?
  (Elicit short sentences that begin with *Because . . .* or *Because of . . .*)
- Ask Ss questions with *enough* or *too*, for example:
  What are you too old to do?
  What are you old enough to do?
  (Elicit answers that utilize both forms.)

Presentation

- Books open. Direct Ss' attention to Exercise **1** and read the instructions aloud. Tell Ss that they will hear a conversation between two friends, Jenny and Sara.
- Class Audio CD1 track 30 Model the task. Play or read only the first part of the conversation on the audio program (see audio script, page T-158). Pause the program after *That's too bad.*
- Direct Ss' attention to number 1 in the chart: *used to have time to call friends.* Ask: *Who use to have time to call friends – Jenny or Sara?* (Jenny) Tell Ss to check the box under *Jenny.*
- Ask individual Ss to read aloud the remaining phrases with *used to.* Say: *Now listen and check the correct boxes in the chart.*
- Class Audio CD1 track 30 Play or read the complete audio program (see audio script, page T-158). Ss listen and check the boxes. Repeat the audio program as needed.

Comprehension check

- Read aloud the second part of the instructions in Exercise **1**.
- Ss complete the exercise in pairs. Help as needed.
- Ask Ss to make sentences about Jenny and Sara using the information in the chart.

Practice

- Review *because, because of, enough, too, used to,* and *present perfect.* Write the words on the board. Have Ss say or write sentences with each to confirm their understanding of the key grammar points.
- Direct Ss' attention to Exercise **2A**. Ask: *What is the title of this story?* ("A Happy Ending") Have Ss tell what they think the story will be about. Ask: *What could have a happy ending?* Elicit any appropriate answer, such as: *a job interview.* Ask Ss to explain what the happy ending would be.
- Have Ss read the story silently to get the main idea. When Ss have finished reading, ask: *What is the story about?* (Frank's health.)
- Read the instructions for Exercise **2A** aloud. Ask a S to read aloud the first sentence in the story and explain the choice of word to complete the sentence. Explain that Ss must choose the correct words under the blanks. This exercise does not ask Ss to change the word forms.
- Ss complete the exercise individually. Help as needed.

▼ **Teaching tip**
In multilevel classes, create small groups of heterogeneous ability. Encourage the Ss who have little difficulty with this grammar review to help those Ss who find it more challenging. Have Ss turn to the lessons in the book to work together to review the grammar presentation and exercises.

- Write the numbers *1–7* on the board. Ask Ss to come to the board to write the answers. Have them write only the words that are missing from the blanks, not the entire sentences.
- Read the story aloud using Ss' answers. Correct as needed.
- Direct Ss' attention to Exercise **2B**. This exercise reviews question formation by asking questions related to the reading "A Happy Ending."
- Read the instructions aloud. Model the task. Focus Ss' attention on Speaker B's answer in number 1. Ask: *What question can you ask to have this answer?* Give other examples if needed.
- Ss work individually to write the questions. Help as needed.
- Check answers with the class. Ask for volunteers to read their questions.
- Read aloud the second part of the instructions for Exercise **2B**.
- Pairs ask and answer the questions. Help as needed.

Review

Presentation

- Write on the board: *voiced and voiceless th sounds*. Explain that there are two ways to pronounce *th*: voiced *th* as in the word *this* and voiceless *th* as in the word *month*. The position of the tongue for both sounds is between and touching the top of the front teeth. However, with voiced sounds, air passes over the tongue.

▼ **Teaching tip**

These pronunciation exercises enable Ss to become aware of certain sound features in English. They are not presented as an exhaustive study of pronunciation. Many Ss are not sensitive to the different sounds of *th* in English, since this sound does not exist in their first language. They may hear this sound as a *d* or *z* sound, for example.

- Direct Ss' attention to Exercise **3A**. Read the instructions aloud.
- 🔊 Class Audio CD1 track 31 Play or read the complete audio program (see audio script, page T-158).
- Repeat the audio program. Pause after each phrase to allow Ss time to repeat. Play the audio program as many times as needed.

Expansion activity (individual work)

- Books closed. To reinforce the sound-symbol correspondence, ask Ss to write the phrases for Exercise **3A** as you dictate them.
- Have Ss underline the *th* in the phrases they wrote.

Practice

- Direct Ss' attention to Exercise **3B**. Read the instructions aloud.
- 🔊 Class Audio CD1 track 32 Model the task. Play or read the first few lines in the first dialog in the audio program (see audio script, page T-158). Ask Ss to underline the *th* sounds in the sentences.
- Have Ss write the words on the board. Correct as needed.
- Tell Ss to pay attention to the words with the *th* sounds as they listen and repeat. Play or read the audio program, stopping as needed for Ss to repeat the sentences.
- 🔊 Class Audio CD1 track 32 Play or read the complete audio program again (see audio script, page T-158).
- Read aloud the second part of the instructions for Exercise **3B**.
- Ss complete the task in pairs. Walk around and listen to Ss' pronunciation. Help Ss to pronounce the voiced and voiceless *th* sounds correctly.

Application

- Direct Ss' attention to Exercise **3C**. Read the instructions aloud.
- Ss complete the exercise in pairs. Walk around and listen to Ss' pronunciation. Write any words on the board that Ss had trouble pronouncing. Point to the words. Say them aloud. Ask Ss to repeat.

Expansion activity (whole group)

- Books closed. Draw a chart on the board. Write *voiced* above one column and *voiceless* above the other. Write numbers *1–8* on the side of the chart. Ask Ss to write numbers *1–8* on a piece of paper and write *voiced* or *voiceless* as you read the following words: *1. thank you* (voiceless), *2. mouth* (voiceless), *3. mother* (voiced), *4. that* (voiced), *5. healthy* (voiceless), *6. this* (voiced), *7. thirteen* (voiceless), *8. think* (voiceless).
- Have Ss come to the board and check the correct column for each word. Ask Ss to ensure one another's answers are correct. Repeat each word several times as a group.

▼ **Teaching tip**

Be sensitive to your Ss' personalities, as some Ss may be embarrassed to pronounce words incorrectly in class. Creating a supportive environment can help reduce embarrassment.

Evaluation

- Focus Ss' attention on Exercise **3D**. Read the instructions aloud.
- Model the task. Ask a S to read the example question to the class. Point out *this morning* in the sentence as the phrase that comes from exercise **3A**.
- Walk around and listen to Ss' pronunciation as they ask and answer the questions.
- Ask four Ss to write their questions on the board. Check the questions for accuracy.
- Ask four different Ss to read the questions aloud. Ask the rest of the class if they heard and understood the *th* words. If Ss have trouble with these words, read them aloud and ask the class to repeat.
- Check off each part of the lesson focus as Ss demonstrate an understanding of what they have learned in the lesson.

3 **Pronunciation:** voiced and voiceless *th* sounds

CLASS CD1 TK 31

A **Listen** to the *th* sounds in these phrases.

1. **th**is morning
2. sore **th**roat
3. **Th**at's too bad!
4. heal**th** problems

5. **th**e neighbors
6. on Sou**th** Street
7. **th**ey are
8. **th**is month

9. asked **th**em
10. **th**ree times
11. How are **th**ings?
12. **th**anks

Listen again and repeat.

CLASS CD1 TK 32

B **Listen and repeat.** Then underline the words with the voiced and voiceless *th* sounds.

1. A Where's Tommy <u>this</u> morning?
   B He's sick. He has a sore <u>throat</u>.
   A <u>That's</u> too bad!
   B He often has <u>health</u> problems.
   A I'm sorry to hear that.

2. A <u>The</u> neighbors on <u>South</u> Street are really noisy.
   B Yes, <u>they</u> are.
   A <u>This</u> <u>month</u>, I've asked <u>them</u> <u>three</u> times to be quiet.
   B Let's write <u>them</u> a letter.
   A <u>That's</u> a good idea.

Talk with a partner. Compare your answers.

C **Talk** with a partner. Practice the conversations. Pay attention to the words with the *th* sounds.

1. A What can your friends do to be more healthy?
   B Well, they can exercise more this month.
   A That's a good idea.
   B And they can eat healthy meals three times a day.

2. A How are things?
   B Not great. I have three tests this week.
   A Oh, I think you'll do fine.
   B Thanks.

D **Write** four questions. Use the words in Exercise 3A. Ask your partner.

Have you eaten this morning?

1. *(Answers will vary.)* _____
2. _____
3. _____
4. _____

LESSON A
Listening

1 Before you listen

A What do you see?
B What is happening?
C What's the story?

Warm-up and review

- Before class. Write today's lesson focus on the board.
  Lesson A:
  Community events
- Begin class. Books closed. Direct Ss' attention to the lesson focus. Point to *community events*. Say the words aloud. Ask Ss to repeat. Tell Ss that community events are activities for and organized by people living in the same area. Ask Ss to brainstorm some places where community events might take place. Write their ideas on the board, for example: *the park, the library, museums, town hall, community centers*, etc.
- Tell Ss that there are often free community events that people can attend. Ask Ss what kinds of events there are in their community. If they do not know, write examples on the board, such as: *concerts, festivals, story hour, puppet shows, exercise classes, lectures.*

Community building *(whole group)*

- **Materials needed** A local newspaper that lists community events.
- Ask Ss if they have ever attended any free community events. If Ss are unaware of these events, show them where they can find the events advertised in the paper. Make copies of that section of the newspaper, and hand it out in class. Ask Ss which events they might be interested in attending. If possible, organize class participation in community events.

Presentation

- Books open. Set the scene. Direct Ss' attention to the pictures on page 58. Ask the question in Exercise **1A**: *What do you see?* Elicit and write on the board as much vocabulary about the pictures as possible, such as: *newspapers, living room, sofa, library, band shell, a family.*
- Direct Ss' attention to the question in Exercise **1B**.
- Ss in pairs. Tell Ss to describe what is happening in the pictures. Help as needed.
- When Ss have finished, ask the class to tell you what is happening. Write Ss' ideas on the board, for example: *Mei and Wen are at home. They are reading newspapers. They are looking at community events in the papers.*

Practice

- Direct Ss' attention to the question in Exercise **1C**. Ask Ss to form small groups of three.
- Ask Ss to make up a conversation between Mei, Wen, and Chen. Tell Ss that they will perform their conversation as a role-play activity for the rest of the class.
- Model the activity. Write the names of the characters in list form on the board: *Mei, Wen, Chen.*
- Ask: *How do you think the conversation will begin?* Write a S's response on the board, for example:
  Mei: What do you want to do this weekend?
- Ask another S to think of Wen's response to this question, for example:
  Wen: Let's look in the newspaper for ideas.
- Ask a different S to think of what Chen might say at this point in the conversation, for example:
  Chen: I want to go to the park!
- Ss continue making up the conversation among the three members of the family. Tell Ss that this is a speaking exercise and they don't have to write anything down. If they wish, Ss can write notes so that they will be able to remember the sequence of the conversation. Help as needed.

▼**Teaching tip**
Encourage Ss to be creative. At this point, there is no single correct story.

- Ask as many groups as possible to perform their role play for the rest of the class.
- When Ss have finished, tell them to think of the most important points in the story and brainstorm sentences for a summary. Write their ideas on the board.
- Point out to Ss that writing a summary is an important academic skill that they will have to do on a regular basis as they continue to study English in the future.

Community building *(whole group)*

- Encourage Ss to attend free events in the community. Tell Ss that this is an excellent way for them to be exposed to English and to practice English with others. If you are teaching in a program with grades, consider giving Ss extra credit for going to a community event and then telling the class about it.

Presentation

- Books open. Direct Ss' attention to Exercise **2A**. Read the instructions aloud.
- Ask a S to read the questions in Exercise **2A** aloud. Tell Ss to listen for this information and take notes as the audio program is played or read.
- Class Audio CD1 track 33 Play or read the audio program (see audio script, page T-158). Repeat the audio program as needed.
- Ask Ss if they understood everything. Write any unfamiliar words on the board.
- Elicit answers to the questions in **2A**.

Practice

- Focus Ss' attention on Exercise **2B**. Read the instructions aloud.
- Class Audio CD1 track 33 Model the task. Play or read the first part of the audio program again (see audio script, page T-158). Pause the program after Wen says that the Museum of Art opens at 10:00 a.m. Hold up the Student's Book. Point to where *c* is written for the first statement. Say: *The art exhibit opens at 10:00.*
- Tell Ss to listen to the complete conversation and write the appropriate letters in the blanks.
- Play or read the entire audio program (see audio script, page T-158). Ss listen and match the events. Repeat the audio program as needed.

Comprehension check

- Elicit answers from the Ss and write them on the board.
- Class Audio CD1 track 33 Play or read the audio program again (see audio script, page T-158). Ss listen and check their answers. Repeat the audio program as needed.

Learner persistence (individual work)

- Self-Study Audio CD track 19 Exercises **2A** and **2B** are recorded on the CD at the back of the Student's Book. Ss can listen to the CD at home for reinforcement and review. They can also listen to the CD for self-directed learning when class attendance is not possible.

Practice

- Focus Ss' attention on Exercise **3A**. Tell Ss that the story in this exercise is a summary of the conversation in Exercise **2A** and **2B**.
- Focus Ss' attention on the words in the word bank. Say each word aloud. Ask Ss to repeat. Correct Ss' pronunciation as needed.
- Ask Ss if they understand all the words in the word bank. Go over the meaning of any words that Ss don't know.

- Model the task. Ask a S to read aloud the first two sentences of the story.
- Ss complete the exercise individually. Walk around and help as needed.
- Direct Ss' attention to the second part of the instructions in Exercise **3A**.
- Class Audio CD1 track 34 Play or read the audio program (see audio script, page T-158). Ss listen and check their answers. Repeat the audio program as needed.
- Write the numbers *1–8* on the board. Ask individual Ss to come to the board to write their answers. Ask other Ss to read the sentences using the words on the board in the blanks. Ask: *Are the answers correct?* Make corrections on the board as needed.

Learner persistence (individual work)

- Self-Study Audio CD track 20 Exercise **3A** is recorded on the CD at the back of the Student's Book. Ss can listen to the CD at home for reinforcement and review. They can also listen for self-directed learning when class attendance is not possible.

Application

- Focus Ss' attention on Exercise **3B**. Read the instructions aloud.
- Ss complete the exercise in pairs. Walk around and help as needed.
- Ask Ss to share information they have learned about their classmates.

Evaluation

- Direct Ss' attention to the lesson focus on the board. Check Ss' understanding of the key vocabulary by asking them to use the words in Exercise **3A** to make sentences about Mei and Wen's weekend plans.
- Ask Ss to look at the pictures on page 58 to tell you the story of Mei and Wen's weekend plans. Encourage Ss to tell you one sentence about what happened in the story.
- Check off each part of the lesson focus as Ss demonstrate an understanding of what they have learned in the lesson.

More Ventures, Unit 5, Lesson A	
Workbook, 15–30 min.	
Add Ventures, 30–45 min.	www.cambridge.org/myresourceroom
Collaborative, 30–45 min.	
Student Arcade, time varies	www.cambridge.org/venturesarcade

Unit Goals | **Describe** events in the community
Identify positive and negative words from context clues
Interpret announcements

UNIT 5

2 Listen

STUDENT TK 19
CLASS CD1 TK 33

A **Listen** and answer the questions.

1. Who are the speakers?
2. What are they talking about?

STUDENT TK 19
CLASS CD1 TK 33

B **Listen again.** Read and match the events. You may use an event more than once.

1. It opens at 10:00. __c__
2. It starts at 10:30. __d__
3. It starts at 11:00. __b__
4. The family will do this first. __d__
5. The family will do this if the weather is nice. __a__

a. outdoor concert
b. garden tour
c. art exhibit
d. storytelling

3 After you listen

A **Read.** Complete the story.

| admission | concert | exhibit | storytelling |
| afford | events | options | tour |

It is Thursday. Wen and Mei are talking about their plans for the weekend.

They can't _____afford_____ to spend a lot of money on entertainment. They decide
         1

to check the newspaper for free community ___events___ on Sunday. They have
                                             2

many ___options___. There's an outdoor ___concert___ in the park, a walking
         3   4

___tour___ of the gardens, a modern art ___exhibit___ at the art museum, and
   5   6

storytelling for children at the library. All these events have free ___admission___.
                                                                         7

   The problem is that all these things are happening on Sunday at the same time.

Mei and Wen decide to take their son to the ___storytelling___ first. Then, if the weather
                                                8

is nice, they will go to the concert. Later, they might go to the art museum.

Listen and check your answers.

STUDENT TK 20
CLASS CD1 TK 34

B **Talk** with a partner. Ask and answer the question.

What kind of entertainment do you enjoy on the weekend?

☑ Listen for and identify community events and times   **UNIT 5**   **59**

LESSON B Verbs + infinitives

1 Grammar focus: questions and answers

Questions	Answers	
Where do you **plan to go**?	I **plan to go** to the park.	infinitive = *to* + base form of verb
Do you **plan to go** to the park?	Yes, I do. No, I don't.	

Verbs infinitives often follow

agree	decide	hope	need	promise	want
(can / can't) afford	expect	intend	plan	refuse	would like

Turn to page 142 for a complete grammar chart and explanation.

2 Practice

A Write. Complete the sentences.

1. **A** How much do you ___expect to pay___ for the concert?
      (expect / pay)
   B No more than $25.

2. **A** What have you ___decided to do___ for your birthday?
      (decided / do)
   B I'm going to an exhibit at the art museum.

3. **A** Can you ___afford to buy___ a ticket for the show?
      (afford / buy)
   B Not really. I need to start saving money.

4. **A** What did you ___agree to do___ next weekend?
      (agree / do)
   B We agreed to go to the park.

5. **A** How does Tom ___intend to get___ to the park?
      (intend / get)
   B He's going to ride his bike.

6. **A** Have you ever ___refused to go___ on a trip with your family?
      (refused / go)
   B No, I haven't.

7. **A** Did they ___promise to visit___ their relatives this weekend?
      (promise / visit)
   B Yes, they did.

> **USEFUL** LANGUAGE
>
> *afford to do something = have enough money to do it*

Listen and check your answers. Then practice with a partner.

CLASS CD1 TK 35

60 UNIT 5

Warm-up and review

Before class: Write today's lesson focus on the board.

Lesson B:
Verbs + infinitives
Questions and answers about future plans

- Books open. Begin class. Direct Ss' attention to the picture on page 58. Ask: *Do you remember some of the things Mei and Wen might do this weekend?* (They might go to the library, attend a concert, go to a museum, take a garden tour.)

Presentation

Focus on meaning / personalize

- Books closed. Direct Ss' attention to the lesson focus on the board. Read it aloud. Give an example of what you plan to do after class, such as: *I plan to meet a friend after class.*
- Draw a four-column chart on the board. Write *I plan to* in the first row of column 2 and *after class* in the first row of column 4. Say: *I plan to meet my friend after class.* Write *meet my friend* in the first row of column 3.
- Then ask Ss: *What about you? What do you plan to do after class?* Elicit Ss' plans, such as: *buy groceries, go to the library, pick up children,* and *go home* and write them on the board in column 2. It is not necessary for Ss to answer in full sentences at this stage. Write Ss' names in column 1.
- Write: *I plan to _____.* on the board. Ask Ss: *Is this about now, the past, or the future?* (the future). Write on the board: *I plan to meet a friend after class.* Underline the verb *plan* and circle the infinitive *to meet.*

Focus on form

- Books open. Direct Ss' attention to the Questions and Answers charts in Exercise 1. Read each question and answer aloud. Ask Ss to repeat.
- Direct Ss' attention to the box next to the charts, and explain that infinitives consist of *to* + the base form of a verb. Point to *plan* on the board. Say: *This is the main verb.* Point to the circled *to meet.* Say: *This is the infinitive.*

- Direct Ss' attention to the box below the grammar focus. Say that infinitives often follow certain verbs. Read each verb aloud and ask Ss to repeat. Give examples for each verb, such as: *I refuse to drink soda. I intend to go to college after I learn English well.*
- Explain that the main verb, not the infinitive, shows the verb tense, and that it agrees with the subject. Write on the board: *Last night, Sue decided to make some soup.* Ask Ss: *What is the main verb?* (decided.) *What is the infinitive?* (to make.) *Is this the present or the past?* (past.)

Practice

- Direct Ss' attention to Exercise 2A.
- Read the instructions aloud. Model the task. Ask two Ss to read aloud the first question and answer. Be sure Ss understand that they should fill in the blanks with the correct forms of the verbs that appear below the blanks.
- Ss complete the exercise individually. Help as needed.

Comprehension check

- Direct Ss' attention to the second part of the instructions in Exercise 2A.
- Class Audio CD1 track 35 Play or read the audio program (see audio script, pages T-158–T-159). Ss listen and check their answers. Repeat the audio as needed.
- Write the numbers *1–7* on the board. Ask individual Ss to come to the board to write the words that they wrote in the blanks. Ask other Ss to read aloud the complete questions and answers.
- Have Ss work in pairs to practice asking and answering the questions.

LESSON B Verbs + infinitives

Presentation

- Books closed. Draw a calendar on the board that includes your weekday (Monday through Friday) plans. Your calendar should be similar to the one in Exercise **2B** in the Student's Book. Write some activities on the calendar, for example:

Monday	Tuesday	Wednesday
Write a class quiz	Have lunch with my friend	Go to the gym

Thursday	Friday
Go shopping	Go to a restaurant for dinner

- Point to the different days of the week on the calendar and ask questions, such as: *What do I intend to do on Monday? What do I hope to do on Friday? What do I need to do on Thursday? What do I plan to do on Wednesday?* Elicit appropriate responses.

Practice

- Books open. Direct Ss' attention to Exercise **2B**. Read the instructions aloud.
- Focus Ss' attention on the word bank. Say each verb. Ask Ss to repeat. Make sure that Ss understand the meanings of all the verbs in the word bank.
- Model the task. Ask two Ss to read aloud the example question and answer.
- Ss complete the exercise in pairs. Walk around and help as needed.
- Ask several pairs to say their questions and answers for the rest of the class.
- Direct Ss' attention to the second part of the instructions for Exercise **2B**. Read it aloud.
- Ask a S to read the example sentence to the class.
- Ss complete the exercise individually. Walk around and help as needed.
- Ask several Ss to write their sentences on the board. Ask other Ss to read them aloud. Make corrections with the class if needed.

Application

- Direct Ss' attention to Exercise **3A**. Read the instructions aloud.
- Model the task. Ask a S to read the example sentence to the class.
- Hold up the Student's Book. Show Ss the chart. Tell Ss to use the verbs and time expressions from the chart.
- Ss complete the exercise in small groups. Help as needed.
- Direct Ss' attention to Exercise **3B**. Read the instructions aloud.
- Ask as many Ss as possible to share information about their classmates.

Expansion activity (whole group)

- Books closed. Divide the class into two teams. Have one person from each team come to the board. Give these two Ss a verb and a future time phrase from the chart in Exercise **3A**. Have them write a sentence on the board with that verb plus an infinitive.
- Model the activity. Ask a volunteer to come to the board. Say: *plan / next year*. The S should write a sentence on the board with *plan* + an infinitive, such as: *I plan to get a job next year*.
- Start the game. Give a point to the S who writes a correct sentence the most quickly on the board. Tally the points. The team with the most points wins.

Evaluation

- Direct Ss' attention to the lesson focus on the board. Focus Ss' attention on the pictures on page 58. Read a few verbs from the grammar chart on page 60. Ask Ss to make sentences about the pictures using the verbs.
- Check off each part of the lesson focus as Ss demonstrate an understanding of what they have learned in the lesson.

More Ventures, Unit 5, Lesson B	
Workbook, 15–30 min.	
Add Ventures, 30–45 min.	www.cambridge.org/myresourceroom
Collaborative, 30–45 min.	
Student Arcade, time varies	www.cambridge.org/venturesarcade

B **Talk** with a partner. Ask and answer questions about Sharon's plans. Look at her calendar. Use the verbs in the box and an infinitive.

> **A** What does Sharon plan to do on Tuesday?
> **B** She plans to go to a concert with Linda.

expect	hope	intend	need	plan	want

May

Sunday	Monday	Tuesday	Wednesday	Thursday	Friday	Saturday
		1	2	3	4	5
		12:30 p.m. Go with Linda to a concert.	5:30 p.m. Meet Joe at the gym.	9:00 a.m. See the dentist. 3:00 p.m. See the new art exhibit.	7:30 a.m. Go to work with John. 6:00 p.m. Have dinner with Andrew???	Sit on the beach all day!

Write sentences about Sharon's plans.

On Tuesday, Sharon plans to go to a concert with Linda.

3 Communicate

A **Work** in a small group. Choose one item from each column. Answer questions about your plans.

> **A** What do you expect to do tomorrow?
> **B** I plan to meet my friends for lunch tomorrow.

expect		tomorrow
hope		next week
intend		next month
need	(infinitive of any verb)	next year
plan		two years from now
want		three years from now
would like		five years from now

B **Share** information about your classmates.

LESSON C Present perfect

1 Grammar focus: *already* and *yet*

Yes/No questions

Have you **bought** the tickets **yet**?
Has she **already** seen the movie?

Short answers

Yes, I **have**.	No, I **haven't**.
Yes, she **has**.	No, she **hasn't**.

Affirmative statements

I've **already** bought the tickets.
She's **already** seen the movie.

Negative statements

I **haven't bought** the tickets **yet**.
She **hasn't seen** the movie **yet**.

Past participles: Irregular verbs

begin	→	begun	get	→	gotten	put	→	put
bring	→	brought	go	→	gone	read	→	read
buy	→	bought	make	→	made	set	→	set
do	→	done	pay	→	paid			

Turn to page 143 for a complete grammar chart and explanation.
Turn to page 146 for a list of irregular verbs.

2 Practice

A Write. Complete the sentences. Use *already* or *yet*.

1. It's 11:00 p.m. The salsa concert has _____*already*_____ ended.

2. It's 8:00 a.m. The science museum opens at 9:00. It hasn't opened _____*yet*_____.

3. It's July 5th. The Independence Day parade has _____*already*_____ finished.

4. It's the beginning of August. School begins in September. School activities haven't begun _____*yet*_____.

5. It's 2:00 a.m. The dance club stays open until 3:00. It hasn't closed _____*yet*_____.

6. It's Friday evening. The weekend has _____*already*_____ started.

7. It's 7:45 p.m. The movie starts at 8:00. We haven't missed the movie _____*yet*_____.

8. It's Monday. I've _____*already*_____ bought tickets for next Sunday's soccer game.

Listen and check your answers.

CLASS CD1 TK 36

Lesson objectives
- Introduce the present perfect with *already* and *yet*
- Practice questions and answers with *already* and *yet*
- Practice past participles of irregular verbs

Warm-up and review

Before class: Write today's lesson focus on the board.

Lesson C:
<u>*already*</u> *and* <u>*yet*</u> *in present perfect questions*
and statements
Past participles of irregular verbs

- Books closed. Begin class. Write on the board in list form: *eat, work, give, go, talk, study, lose, see, sleep.* Ask Ss to tell you the past participles of each of these verbs. Write the past participles next to the verbs: *eaten, worked, given, gone, talked, studied, lost, seen, slept.*
- Review present perfect *Yes / No* questions with *recently* or *lately.*
- Brainstorm a list of things Ss like to do, such as: *watch TV, go to a movie, play computer games, walk on the beach.* Ss work in pairs to make *Yes / No* questions with the present perfect and *recently* or *lately,* such as: *Have you gone to a movie recently?*

Presentation

Focus on meaning / personalize

- Books closed. Direct Ss' attention to the lesson focus on the board. Read it aloud. Write two example sentences on the board using *yet* and *already,* such as: *We haven't studied Unit 6 in our book* <u>*yet*</u>. *We've* <u>*already*</u> *studied Unit 4.*
- Divide the board into three columns with *Name*; *Yes, has [already] seen*; and *No, hasn't seen [yet]* as headings.
- Write on the board the name of a movie that is currently showing in your area or the name of a popular TV show. Point to the name and ask: *Have you seen (movie name) / watched (TV show name) yet?* Elicit: *Yes, I have. / No, I haven't.* Ask another S: *Has (name of first S) seen this movie yet?* Elicit: *Yes, she has. / No, she hasn't.* After each response, model the complete sentence and write it on the board, for example:

José has already seen this movie.
Maria hasn't seen it yet.

Name	Yes, has seen [already]	No, hasn't seen [yet]
José	X	
Maria		X

- Direct Ss' attention to columns 2 and 3 on the board. Ask them to try to guess when we use *already* (to talk about things that we have done) and *yet* (to talk about things we have not done but will possibly do in the future). Explain that, as with the other present perfect sentences Ss have studied, we use the present perfect to talk about something as it relates to the present.

Focus on form

- Books open. Direct Ss' attention to Questions and Short answers charts in Exercise **1**. Read aloud the two questions and short answers. Ask Ss to repeat. Next, read the Affirmative and Negative statements charts. Ask Ss to repeat.

Practice

- Direct Ss' attention to Exercise **2A**. Read the instructions aloud.
- Model the task. Ask a S to read the example sentence to the class. Ss complete the exercise individually. Help as needed.

Comprehension check

- Read aloud the second part of the instructions for Exercise **2A**.
- Class Audio CD1 track 36 Play or read the audio program (see audio script, page T-159). Ss listen and check their answers.
- Write the numbers *1–8* on the board. Ask individual Ss to come to the board to write the words from the blanks. Ask different Ss to read the sentences aloud using the answers on the board. Make corrections on the board as needed.
- Ask pairs to read the sentences in Exercise **2A** to each other.

▼ **Teaching tip**
Point out that in questions, *already* can also be placed at the end of the sentence. Some people find this a common placement for this adverb. You may want to write a few examples on the board, such as: *Has she bought the tickets already? Have you seen that movie already?*

LESSON C Present perfect

Presentation

- Books open. Focus Ss' attention on the pictures in Exercise **2B**. Tell Ss that Jaime is talking to his wife, Andrea, about their school's fund-raiser.

> ▼ **Culture note**
> Read the culture note aloud. Say *fund-raiser.* Have Ss repeat. Ask Ss if they have participated in fund-raisers at their children's schools or elsewhere. If any Ss say *Yes,* ask them to describe the fund-raiser. Give examples of different types of fund-raisers, such as car washes, yard sales, and silent auctions.

Practice

- Focus Ss' attention on Exercise **2B**. Read the instructions aloud. Direct Ss' attention to the to-do list. Tell Ss that writing a to-do list is a good way to get organized. Remind Ss that in Unit 2, Alex organized his workload for school. Here, Jaime and Andrea are organizing their work for the school fund-raiser. Point out that the check marks indicate tasks that each has already completed.
- Read the title aloud. Ask: *What does Jaime have to do before the fund-raiser?* Elicit the unchecked items on his list. Ask: *What does Andrea have to do before the fund-raiser?* Elicit the unchecked items on her list.
- Make sure that Ss understand all the words in the to-do list.
- Ask two Ss to read the example conversation aloud.
- Ss complete the exercise in pairs. Walk around and help as needed.
- Direct Ss' attention to the second part of the instructions for Exercise **2B** and read it aloud. Ask two Ss to read the example sentences to the class.
- Ss complete the exercise individually. Walk around and help as needed.
- Ask Ss to compare their sentences. Tell Ss whose sentences are not the same to write them on the board. Ask the class to comment on the sentences and make corrections as needed.

Expansion activity *(whole group)*

- Books closed. Divide the class into two teams. Ask one person from each team to come to the front of the room. Tell the Ss a verb, such as *begin,* from the *Irregular verbs* chart on page 62. The Ss have to try to write the correct past participle of the verb on the board. The S who writes the past participle correctly and the most quickly earns a point. Then another S from each team comes to the board.

- Continue asking Ss all the verbs in the grammar chart.
- Tally the points at the end of the game. The team with the most points wins.

Application

- Direct Ss' attention to Exercise **3A**. Read the instructions aloud.
- Focus Ss' attention on the chart in the exercise. Ask individual Ss to read the activities aloud.
- Model the task. Ask two Ss to read aloud the example questions and answers. Tell Ss to check the correct box in the chart according to their partner's answers.
- Ss complete the activity in pairs. Help as needed. Make sure that Ss are asking the questions correctly.
- Direct Ss' attention to the instructions for Exercise **3B**.
- Ask as many Ss as possible to share information about their classmates with the class.

Learner persistence *(whole group)*

- Reviewing material as a class helps reinforce information for Ss who have been in class and keeps Ss who have missed lessons from falling behind. Encourage Ss to look through the first four units of the Student's Book and to ask questions about anything they do not remember or still do not understand. Take time to review whenever possible.

Evaluation

- Direct Ss' attention to the lesson focus on the board. Ask Ss to look at the pictures on page 58 and to make sentences using *already* and *yet,* such as: *Mei and Wen haven't decided what to do yet.*
- Encourage Ss to make sentences about Mei and Wen using the verbs in the *Irregular verbs* chart on page 62, for example: *Mei and Wen haven't gone out yet.*
- Check off each part of the lesson focus as Ss demonstrate an understanding of what they have learned in the lesson.

More Ventures, Unit 5, Lesson C	
Workbook, 15–30 min.	
Add Ventures, 30–45 min. **Collaborative,** 30–45 min.	www.cambridge.org/myresourceroom
Student Arcade, time varies	www.cambridge.org/venturesarcade

B **Talk** with a partner. Jaime and Andrea are helping at their school's fund-raiser. Ask and answer questions about them. Use *yet*.

A Has Jaime bought refreshments yet?
B Yes, he has.
A Has Andrea set up the tables yet?
B No, she hasn't.

Things to do before the fund-raiser

Jaime

✓ buy refreshments
✓ borrow more chairs
  call the chair-rental store
  get name tags
  pick up the DJ

Andrea

  set up the tables
✓ organize the volunteers
✓ make the food
  bring the music CDs
✓ put up the decorations

Write sentences about Jaime and Andrea. Use *already* and *yet*.

Jaime has already bought refreshments.

Andrea hasn't set up the tables yet.

3 Communicate

A **Work** with a partner. Ask and answer questions. Complete the chart.

A Have you done your homework yet?
B Yes, I have.
A Have you already paid your bills?
B No, I haven't.

Activities	Yes	No
1. do your homework	☐	☐
2. pay your bills	☐	☐
3. go to a baseball game in this country	☐	☐
4. read the newspaper today	☐	☐
5. (your question)	☐	☐
6. (your question)	☐	☐

B **Share** information about your classmates.

☑ Use present perfect with *already* and *yet*

LESSON **D** Reading

1 Before you read

Talk with your classmates. Answer the questions.

1. Do you like salsa music?

2. Have you ever gone to an outdoor concert? Where? When?

2 Read

STUDENT TK 21
CLASS CD1 TK 37

Read the concert review. Listen and read again.

When you see a new word, try to guess if the meaning is positive or negative. *The volume was **excessive**.* *I had to wear my earplugs.* You can guess that *excessive* has a negative meaning.

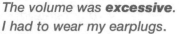

If you missed the outdoor concert at Century Park last Saturday evening, you missed a great night of salsa music and dancing – and the admission was free!

The performers were the popular band Salsa Starz. Bandleader Ernesto Sanchez led the five-piece group and two dancers. Sanchez is a <u>versatile</u> musician.

He sang and played maracas and guitar. The other musicians were also <u>superb</u>. The group's excellent playing and great energy <u>galvanized</u> the crowd. No one sat down during the entire show!

However, the evening had some problems. At first, the sound level of the music was <u>excessive</u>. I had to wear earplugs.

Then, the level was too low. The change in sound was <u>irritating</u>. In addition, the stage was plain and <u>unremarkable</u>. I expected to see lights and lots of color at the performance. The weather was another problem. The night started out clear. By 10:00 p.m., some <u>ominous</u> black clouds moved in, and soon it started to rain. The band intended to play until 11:00, but the show ended early because of the rain.

Century Park has free concerts every Saturday evening in July and August. If you haven't attended one of these concerts yet, plan to go next weekend. But take an umbrella!

Warm-up and review

- Before class. Write today's lesson focus on the board.
  Lesson D:
  Read and understand "Salsa Starz at Century Park," a review of a concert
  Learn new vocabulary: positive and negative adjectives
- Begin class. Books closed. Focus Ss' attention on the words *review of a concert* in the lesson focus.
- Say the words aloud. Ask Ss to repeat. Ask: *What is a review? Where would you find a review? Why would you read a review?* Elicit appropriate responses or explain that a review gives the reviewer's opinion about a place, a book, a play, a movie, or an event. Reviews are often found in newspapers and magazines.
- Find out if any Ss have ever been to a concert. If they have, ask the Ss to tell the class about the concert. Write on the board any positive or negative words Ss use.

  Option Talk about a concert that you have seen or heard about. Write on the board any positive or negative words you use.

Presentation

- Books open. Direct Ss' attention to Exercise 1. Read the instructions aloud.
- Ask a S to read the first question to the class. Ask Ss to raise their hands if they like salsa music. If any Ss are unfamiliar with salsa music, ask if anyone can describe the music to the class; talk briefly about the rhythm and instruments.
- Ask a S to read aloud the questions in number 2 in Exercise 1. Tell Ss to ask a partner each of the questions.
- Walk around and listen to Ss' answers. Write any words on the board that Ss have difficulty pronouncing. Say each word aloud while pointing to it. Ask Ss to repeat.
- Ask Ss if anyone answered *Yes* to the questions in number 2. Ask a few Ss to describe their experiences at outdoor concerts.

Read aloud the first sentence in the tip box. Ask a S to read the example sentences to the class. Ask Ss: *Is it positive or negative if the writer had to wear earplugs at the concert?* (negative) Read aloud the last sentence in the tip box. Say the word *excessive*. Ask Ss to repeat. Have Ss guess what they think the word means. Explain that *excessive* means there is too much of something.

Practice

- Focus Ss' attention on the picture in Exercise 2. Ask Ss what they see and elicit some of the instruments: *drums, saxophone, trumpet.*
- Ask a S to read aloud the title of the article. Ask Ss what they think the article will be about. Elicit appropriate responses.
- Read the instructions for Exercise 2 to the class. Have Ss read the article silently.
- Ask Ss to come to the board to write any words they are unfamiliar with. Encourage Ss to guess the meanings of the new words from context. For example: *"Versatile" means to be able to do many things, such as sing, and play the maracas and the guitar.* Point to each new word in turn. Say it and ask Ss to repeat.

▼**Teaching tip**
Write *Starz* on the board. Explain that this is an intentional misspelling of the word *Stars* and that it is used to draw attention to the name of the group.

🔊 Class Audio CD1 track 37 Play or read the audio program and ask Ss to read along silently (see audio script, page T-159). Repeat the audio program as needed.

Learner persistence *(individual work)*

🔊 Self-Study Audio CD track 21 Exercise 2 is recorded on the CD at the back of the Student's Book. Ss can listen to the CD at home for reinforcement and review. They can also listen for self-directed learning when class attendance is not possible.

Community building *(whole group)*

- Ask Ss to talk about the kind of music they enjoy. Focus on the rhythms, the words, the instruments, and famous musicians. If you feel it is appropriate and if Ss are able, ask them to bring in samples of their favorite music to share with the class.
- Encourage Ss to talk about the music and share their opinions. Write positive and negative words on the board that Ss' use or could use.

Comprehension check

- Read aloud the instructions for Exercise **3A**.
- Point out the use of stars in many reviews to describe how much or how little the reviewer liked a performance, a restaurant, a movie, etc.
- Make sure that Ss understand the questions. Ask Ss the questions. Encourage Ss to read aloud the sentences in the review to support their answers.

Presentation

- Focus Ss' attention on Exercise **3B**. Read the instructions aloud. Ask a S to read the questions in number 1.
- Model the exercise. Read aloud the sentence with *versatile* in it and the sentence after it. Tell Ss that *versatile* means to be able to do many different things. Ask: *Is this a positive or negative word?* Elicit: *It's positive because it means Ernesto Sanchez could do many things. He led the group, sang, and played two instruments.*
- Ss complete the exercise in pairs. Help as needed.
- Go over the answers with the class. Say each word in the chart in Exercise **3B**. Have Ss repeat. Ask Ss in turn: *Do you think _____ is a positive or negative word? Why do you think so?*

▼**Teaching tip**
To help Ss pronounce the words in Exercise **3B** number 1, it might be helpful to write the words on the board and underline the stressed syllable in each word, for example: *superb.* Explain that the underlined syllables are stressed. Say each word again, pointing to the stressed syllable as you say it, and have Ss repeat.

Practice

- Focus Ss' attention on Exercise **3B** number 2. Read the instructions aloud.
- Model the task. Ask Ss to look at the concert review to find a positive word, such as: *excellent.* Have Ss find a negative word, such as: *plain.*
- Ss work in small groups to complete the exercise. Help as needed.
- Draw a vertical line on the board, making two columns. Write *Positive* and *Negative* as headings for the columns. Ask Ss to come to the board and write in the appropriate column the words they found. Ask other Ss if they agree with the way the words on the board are categorized.

Application

- Direct Ss' attention to Exercise **3C**. Read the instructions aloud.
- Ss complete the exercise in pairs. Help as needed.
- Ask Ss to share the information they learned from their partner with the rest of the class.

Expansion activity (small groups)

- **Materials needed** One copy of a review of a concert, movie, or play from a local newspaper for each small group of four or five Ss.

  Option If there are several reviews in your local paper, consider giving each group a different review in order to make the sharing of the reviews more interesting.
- Write on the board: *What is the review about? Is the review positive or negative? What are some words that tell you if the reviewer liked the event or not?*
- Ss answer the questions about their review in small groups. Help as needed. Encourage Ss to underline the positive and negative words in their reviews.

Evaluation

- Books closed. Direct Ss' attention to the lesson focus on the board. Ask Ss to retell the information they learned in the concert review about Salsa Starz. Ask a S to say one sentence about the article, the next S to continue, and so forth.
- Write some of the words on the board from Exercise **3B** question 2. Ask individual Ss to say if the words are positive or negative. Have different Ss recall what these words described in the article.
- Check off each part of the lesson focus as Ss demonstrate an understanding of what they have learned in the lesson.

Learner persistence (individual, pairs)

- You may wish to assign Extended Reading Worksheets from the *Online Teacher's Resource Room* for Ss to complete outside of class. The purpose of these worksheets is to encourage Ss to read for pleasure in English outside of the English class. The worksheets can also be assigned as extended reading in class.

More Ventures, Unit 5, Lesson D	
Workbook, 15–30 min.	
Add Ventures, 30–45 min.	
Collaborative, 30–45 min.	www.cambridge.org/myresourceroom
Extended Reading and worksheet, 45–60 min.	
Student Arcade, time varies	www.cambridge.org/venturesarcade

3 After you read

A **Check** your understanding.

1. Where did Salsa Starz perform?
2. What were two positive things about the concert?
3. What were three negative things?
4. Did the audience like the concert? How do you know?
5. How do you think the reviewer rated the overall performance? Find the words in the reading to support your opinion.

| **** excellent | *** very good | ** OK | * bad |

B **Build** your vocabulary.

1. Find these words in the reading, and underline them. Which words are positive? Which words are negative? What clues helped you guess?

Word	Positive	Negative	Clue
1. versatile	✔	☐	*He sang and played maracas and guitar.*
2. superb	✔	☐	*excellent playing*
3. galvanized	✔	☐	*energy; no one sat down*
4. excessive	☐	✔	*I had to wear earplugs.*
5. irritating	☐	✔	*Then, the level was too low.*
6. unremarkable	☐	✔	*plain*
7. ominous	☐	✔	*black clouds*

2. Work with your classmates. Write four more words in the reading that have a positive or negative meaning. Write *P* next to positive words. Write *N* next to negative words.

a. *(Answers will vary.)*   c. _____

b. _____   d. _____

C **Talk** with a partner.

1. Tell your partner about a superb restaurant.
2. Tell about a versatile artist.
3. Tell about an irritating experience.
4. Tell about an unremarkable TV program.

LESSON E Writing

1 Before you write

A **Talk** with your classmates.

1. Do you use e-mail? How often?
2. What do you use it for?

B **Read** the e-mail.

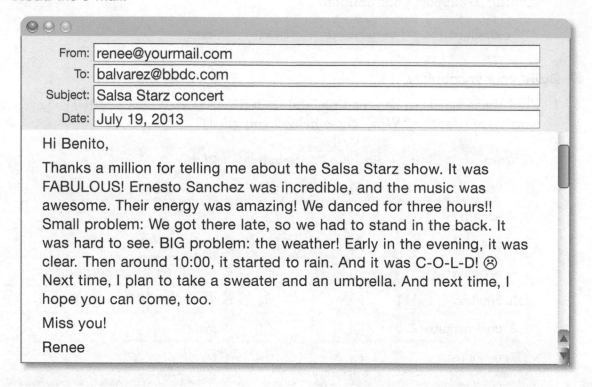

From: renee@yourmail.com
To: balvarez@bbdc.com
Subject: Salsa Starz concert
Date: July 19, 2013

Hi Benito,

Thanks a million for telling me about the Salsa Starz show. It was FABULOUS! Ernesto Sanchez was incredible, and the music was awesome. Their energy was amazing! We danced for three hours!! Small problem: We got there late, so we had to stand in the back. It was hard to see. BIG problem: the weather! Early in the evening, it was clear. Then around 10:00, it started to rain. And it was C-O-L-D! ☹ Next time, I plan to take a sweater and an umbrella. And next time, I hope you can come, too.

Miss you!

Renee

Work with a partner. Complete the diagram with positive and negative information about the concert.

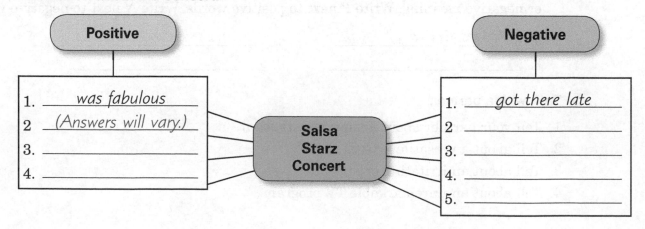

Positive

1. _was fabulous_
2 _(Answers will vary.)_
3. _____
4. _____

Salsa Starz Concert

Negative

1. _got there late_
2 _____
3. _____
4. _____
5. _____

C **Write** the name of a concert, a movie, or a performance you have seen in the middle of the diagram. Complete the diagram with positive and negative information.

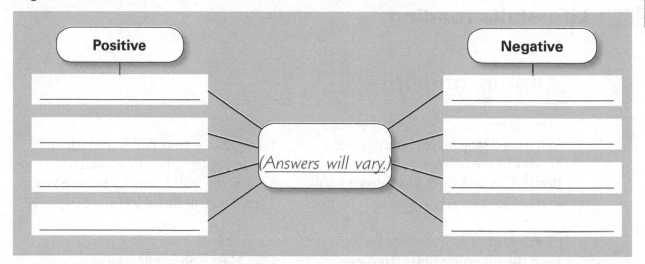

Positive

Negative

(Answers will vary.)

Share your information with a partner.

2 Write

Write an e-mail about a concert, a movie, or a performance you have seen. Name the event in your first sentence. Use positive and negative words to describe the event. Use an informal writing style in the e-mail. Use Exercises 1B and 1C to help you.

The style of a friendly e-mail is informal.
- Some sentences are not complete.
  Miss you!
  BIG problem: the weather!
- Writers use capital letters and symbols to express their feelings.
  It was FABULOUS!
  It was C-O-L-D! ☹

3 After you write

A **Check** your writing.

	Yes	No
1. I named the event in my first sentence.	☐	☐
2. I used positive and negative words to describe the event.	☐	☐
3. I used an informal writing style in my e-mail.	☐	☐

B **Share** your writing with a partner.

1. Take turns. Read your e-mail to a partner.
2. Comment on your partner's e-mail. Ask your partner a question about the e-mail. Tell your partner one thing you learned.

LESSON F Another view

1 Life-skills reading

Announcements

Travel Movies

Join us at 7:00 p.m. on Saturday and Sunday to see movies on India, Japan, and Brazil. Kids welcome. Downtown Public Library. Come early – seating is limited.

Crafts Fair

Find gifts for your family and friends. Jewelry, pottery, paintings, and food from around the world. Sunday from 9:00 a.m. to 5:00 p.m. at Broadway and 5th Street.

Concerts on the Green

Hear the Riverside Brass Band every Friday this month at noon. North end of City Park, near the courthouse.

Fix a Flat

Bike Master Shop offers basic bicycle maintenance clinics this Saturday at 4:30 p.m. and Sunday at 9:00 a.m. in front of the Bike Master Shop.

A **Read** the questions. Look at the announcements. Fill in the answer.

1. At which event can you buy food?
   - (A) Concerts on the Green
   - (B) Crafts Fair ●
   - (C) Travel Movies
   - (D) all of the above

2. Which event does not happen during the day?
   - (A) Concerts on the Green
   - (B) Crafts Fair
   - (C) Fix a Flat
   - (D) Travel Movies ●

3. Which event would be good for bike riders?
   - (A) Crafts Fair
   - (B) Fix a Flat ●
   - (C) Travel Movies
   - (D) none of the above

4. Which event is at noon on Saturday?
   - (A) Concerts on the Green
   - (B) Fix a Flat
   - (C) Travel Movies
   - (D) none of the above ●

B **Talk** with a partner. Ask and answer the questions.

1. Which activity would you like to attend? Why?
2. What other activities or events do you like to attend?

Lesson objectives

- Practice reading announcements about community events
- Contrast verbs + infinitives and verbs + gerunds
- Complete the self-assessment

Warm-up and review

- Before class. Write today's lesson focus on the board.
  Lesson F:
  Read announcements about community events
  Introduce the project
  Complete the self-assessment

- Begin class. Books open. Direct Ss' attention to the pictures on page 58. Ask Ss questions to review unit vocabulary and grammar, for example: *What do Mei and Wen plan to do this weekend?* (They plan to go to some community events.) *What can't they afford to do?* (buy expensive concert tickets.) *In the first picture, have they finished dinner already?* (Yes, they have.)

- Direct Ss' attention to the words *announcements* in the lesson focus. Say the word aloud. Have Ss repeat. Tell Ss *announcements* are statements that say when and where something is going to happen. Ask Ss where they can find announcements. Elicit appropriate responses, such as: *in the newspaper, on bulletin boards.*

- Ask Ss where they can read announcements at their school. Point to any announcements in the classroom, and elicit other places where announcements are posted, such as in the school office, on bulletin boards, etc.

- Ask Ss what kind of information can be found in the announcements at their schools. Elicit appropriate responses, such as: *announcements about jobs, community events, English tutoring.*

Community building *(whole group)*

- If you have a small enough class, it might be interesting to walk around your school and read the different announcements that are posted. Ask Ss to read the announcements. Answer any questions that they have about the meaning of the announcements.

Presentation

- Direct Ss' attention to the announcements in Exercise 1.

- Divide the class into four groups. Assign one of the announcements to each group. Tell each group to read the announcement and discuss the meaning of any new words. Allow Ss to use dictionaries to look up any words they don't understand.

- Walk around and help as needed.

- Tell Ss that they are going to explain their announcement to another group without looking at the announcement as they are explaining. Ask each group to write down the name of the announcement they read and any key words that will help them remember the announcement.

- Give each S a number according to how many Ss are in each group. For example, if there are four Ss in a group, number each S from 1 to 4.

- Books closed. Have Ss get into new groups based on their numbers – 1s, 2s, 3s, and so forth. Ss tell their new groups about the announcement they read.

- Walk around and help as needed. If Ss can't remember something about their announcement, give them clues to help them recall the content.

Practice

- Read the instructions for Exercise 1A aloud. This task helps prepare Ss for standardized-type tests they may have to take. Make sure Ss understand the task. Have Ss individually scan for and fill in the answers.

Comprehension check

- Go over the answers to Exercise 1A with the class. Make sure that Ss followed the instructions and filled in the correct answers.

Application

- Direct Ss' attention to Exercise 1B and read the instructions aloud. Ask a S to read the questions to the class.

- Ss complete the exercise in pairs. Walk around and help as needed.

- Ask several pairs to share what they learned from their partner with the rest of the class.

LESSON F Another view

Warm-up and review

- Books closed. Ask Ss: *What do you hope / intend or plan to do over the coming weekend?* Ensure Ss use verbs + infinitives in their answers.
- Ask Ss to define the word *infinitive*. Elicit the answer *to* + the base form of a verb.

Presentation

- Books open. Direct Ss' attention to the chart in Exercise **2A**. Read aloud the sentence in the left column: *We intend to study tonight*. Point out that the verb *intend* requires an infinitive. Ask a S to read aloud the next sentence: *Tomas dislikes doing the laundry*. Ask Ss to describe how the middle sentence is different from the one on the left. Elicit answers, such as: *The verb "dislike" requires a gerund (doing) whereas the verb "intend" requires an infinitive.*
- Read aloud the final sentences: *I like to cook.* and *I like cooking.* Ask Ss to compare these sentences. Elicit answers, such as: *The verb "like" can be used with either infinitives or gerunds.* Explain that the verbs in the column on the right can be used with either gerunds or infinitives. Ensure Ss understand that the verbs in the left column can only be used with infinitives, those in the middle column can only be used with gerunds and those on the right can be used with either.

Practice

- Direct Ss' attention to the instructions in **2A**. Read the instructions aloud. Ensure Ss understand the activity. Ask a pair of Ss to read the dialog aloud.
- Split the class into small groups. Ask Ss to survey one another.

- Direct Ss' attention to the instructions in **2B**. Read the instructions aloud. Ask a S to read the example sentences. Ss complete the exercise in pairs. Encourage each S to share a few sentences about a person in their group.

Evaluation

- Before asking students to turn to the self-assessment on page 138, do a quick review of the unit. Have Ss turn to Lesson A. Ask the class to talk about what they remember about this lesson. Prompt Ss, if necessary, with questions, for example: *What are the conversations about on this page? What vocabulary is in the pictures?* Continue in this manner to review each lesson quickly.
- **Self-assessment** Read the instructions for Exercise **3**. Ask Ss to turn to the self-assessment page and complete the unit self-assessment. The self-assessments are also on the *Online Teacher's Resource Room*. If you prefer to collect the assessments and save them as part of each S's portfolio assessment, print out the unit self-assessment from the *Resource Room*, ask students to complete it, and collect and save it.
- If Ss are ready, administer the unit test on pages T-173–T-174 of this Teacher's Edition (or on the Assessment Audio CD / CD-ROM).
- If Ss are ready, administer the midterm test on pages T-175–T-177 of this Teacher's Edition (or on the Assessment Audio CD / CD-ROM).

More Ventures, Unit 5, Lesson F	
Workbook, 15–30 min.	
Add Ventures, 30–45 min. **Collaborative,** 30–45 min.	www.cambridge.org/myresourceroom
Student Arcade, time varies	www.cambridge.org/venturesarcade

2 **Grammar connections:** verbs + infinitives and verbs + gerunds

Verbs + infinitives	Verbs + gerunds	Verbs + infinitives or gerunds
decide need refuse intend plan want	avoid enjoy miss dislike finish suggest	continue like start hate prefer
*We **intend to study** tonight.* *We **need to go** home.*	*Tomas **dislikes exercising**.* *They **enjoy swimming**.*	*I **like to cook**.* *I **like cooking**.*

A **Work** in a small group. Ask the questions with *to do* or *doing*. Complete the survey.

> **A** What do you enjoy doing on the weekend, Viktor?
> **B** I enjoy walking in the park.
> **A** What do you intend to do after class?
> **B** I intend to study at the library.

What do you . . .	(name)	(name)	(name)
enjoy _____ on the weekend?	*(Answers will vary.)*		
intend _____ after class?			
avoid _____ at home?			
hate _____ in the morning?			
refuse _____ on the weekend?			
plan _____ at the end of the year?			
like _____ in the summer?			
miss _____ from your childhood?			

B **Share** information about your classmates.

> *Viktor enjoys walking in the park. He intends to study at the library after class. He . . .*

3 **Wrap up**

Complete the **Self-assessment** on page 138.

LESSON A
Listening

1 Before you listen

A What do you see?

B What is happening?

C What's the story?

1.

2.

3.

4.

Lesson objectives
- Introduce students to the topic
- Find out what students know about the topic
- Preview the unit by talking about the pictures
- Practice key vocabulary
- Practice listening skills

Warm-up and review

- Before class. Write today's lesson focus on the board.
  Lesson A:
  Time management

- Begin class. Books closed. Direct Ss' attention to the lesson focus. Point to *time management*. Ask Ss to guess the meaning of these words. Help Ss come to an understanding by asking: *What do you have to do on a very busy day?* List Ss' responses on the board, for example: *get children ready for school, go to work, go grocery shopping, clean the house, study for a test, do the laundry.*

- Ask Ss: *How do you manage to do everything?* Elicit appropriate answers, such as: *My children help. I sometimes miss class. I don't always manage to do everything.*

Learner persistence *(individual work)*

- By asking questions about time, you can find out if any of your Ss are struggling with managing their jobs, family, and school obligations. Time pressures can be a reason for Ss to miss class. Talk to Ss individually after class if they are having trouble managing time. Encourage Ss to exchange phone numbers so that they can call a classmate to find out about missed class work.

Presentation

- Books open. Set the scene. Direct Ss attention to the pictures on page 70. Ask the question from Exercise **1A**: *What do you see?* Elicit and write on the board vocabulary Ss know, such as: *bedroom, clock, papers, books, mother, son, notebook, to-do list, trash can.* Explain any unfamiliar words.

- Direct Ss' attention to the question in Exercise **1B**: *What is happening?* Read it aloud. Draw three vertical lines on the board, creating four columns. Write the headings *Picture 1*, *Picture 2*, *Picture 3*, and *Picture 4* above the columns. Ask Ss to say a few sentences about what is happening in each picture. Write Ss' ideas in the correct column on the board.

Practice

- Direct Ss' attention to Exercise **1C**. Tell Ss that they are going to work with a partner to write a story about what is happening in the pictures.

▼**Teaching tip**
Encourage Ss to be creative. At this point, there is no single correct story.

- Ask a S to begin the story. Then write several suggestions or paragraph-starters on the board.
- Have pairs continue to create the story. One S writes the story as partners work together.

▼**Teaching tip**
If you have a multilevel class, this would be a good time to pair Ss who feel more confident of their speaking skills with Ss who feel more comfortable with their writing skills. Encourage pairs to be supportive and to offer constructive feedback as they work together to create the story.

- Ask Ss from several pairs to read their story to the class or have Ss post their stories and then circulate and read one another's stories.

Community building

- Encourage Ss to learn from each other. As they work in pairs, have Ss keep a list of new vocabulary they learn from their classmates. Ss should be encouraged to use dictionaries in class to confirm the meaning and pronunciation of these new words.

Presentation

- Books open. Direct Ss' attention to Exercise **2A**.
- Ask a S to read the questions in Exercise **2A** aloud. Tell Ss to listen for this information as they listen.
- 🔊 Class Audio CD2 track 2 Play or read the audio program (see audio script, page T-159).
- Ask Ss if they understood everything in the listening. Write any unfamiliar words on the board and help Ss understand the meaning. Be sure that Ss understand the meaning of a *to-do list*.
- Elicit answers to the questions in Exercise **2A**.
- Ask: *What do you think Winston will write on his list?* Elicit responses and write them on the board.

Practice

- Focus Ss' attention on Exercise **2B**. Read the instructions aloud.
- Instruct Ss to first fill out Winston's to-do list. They should then number each task in order of priority.
- 🔊 Class Audio CD2 track 2 Play or read the audio program (see audio script, page T-159).
- Ss complete the exercise individually. Repeat the audio as needed. Copy the chart onto the board. Ask volunteers to write their answers in the chart.

Comprehension check

- Elicit answers and write them on the board.
- 🔊 Class Audio CD2 track 2 Play or read the audio program again (see audio script, page T-159). Ss listen and check their answers. Repeat the audio program as needed.

Learner persistence (individual work)

- 🔊 Self-Study Audio CD track 22 Exercises **2A** and **2B** are recorded on the CD at the back of the Student's Book. Ss can listen to the CD at home for reinforcement and review. They can also listen to the CD for self-directed learning when class attendance is not possible.

Practice

- Focus Ss' attention on Exercise **3A**. Read the instructions aloud. Tell Ss that the story in this exercise is a summary of what happened in the pictures on page 70.
- Direct Ss' attention to the words in the word bank. Say each word aloud. Ask Ss to repeat.
- Model the task. Ask a S to read aloud the first two sentences in the story.
- Ss complete the exercise individually. Help as needed.
- 🔊 Class Audio CD2 track 3 Play or read the audio program (see audio script, page T-159). Ss listen and check their answers. Repeat the audio program as needed.

- Write the numbers *1–7* on the board. Ask Ss to come to the board to write their answers.

Learner persistence (individual work)

- 🔊 Self-Study Audio CD track 23 Exercise **3A** is recorded on the CD at the back of the Student's Book. Ss can listen to the CD at home for reinforcement and review. They can also listen for self-directed learning when class attendance is not possible.

Expansion activity (student pairs)

- Ss in pairs. Ask partners to compare the stories they created earlier with the summary in the listening in Exercise **3A**. How are they different? How are they the same? Encourage pairs to revisit their stories and incorporate new words and new ideas.
- Have Ss continue the story and make predictions. Ask: *What do you think will happen next? What will Winston do tomorrow? Will Winston continue to follow his mother's advice?*

Application

- Focus Ss' attention on Exercise **3B**. Read the instructions aloud.
- Ss complete the exercise in pairs. Walk around and help as needed.
- Ask several pairs to ask and answer the question for the class. Write suggestions on the board for prioritizing.

Expansion activity (whole group)

- Review *too, enough, because,* and *because of* from Unit 3. Ask: *What are some examples of having too little time?* Elicit appropriate responses and write them on the board, such as: *not having enough time to finish your homework because you have to go to work.*
- Suggest ways Ss can improve their time-management skills.

Evaluation

- Direct Ss' attention to the lesson focus on the board. Ask individual Ss to look at the pictures on page 70 and make sentences using the words from Exercise **3A**.
- Check off each part of the lesson focus as Ss demonstrate an understanding of what they have learned in the lesson.

More Ventures, Unit 6, Lesson A	
Workbook, 15–30 min.	
Add Ventures, 30–45 min.	www.cambridge.org/myresourceroom
Collaborative, 30–45 min.	
Student Arcade, time varies	www.cambridge.org/venturesarcade

Unit Goals	**Identify** tips for time management
	Explain U.S. rules about time
	Describe qualities and habits of good and weak time managers

2 Listen

A **Listen** and answer the questions.

STUDENT TK 22
CLASS CD2 TK 2

1. Who are the speakers?   2. What are they talking about?

B **Listen again.** Complete Winston's to-do list. Then number the tasks in order of priority.

STUDENT TK 22
CLASS CD2 TK 2

Things to Do	Priority
• take out the trash	1
• math	3
• English essay	2
• history project	5
• practice guitar	4

3 After you listen

A **Read.** Complete the story.

chores   deadline   due   impatient   prioritize   procrastinating   tasks

Winston is listening to music in his room. His mother comes in and tells him to stop _procrastinating_. She is very ___impatient___ because he isn't taking out the
                        1   2
trash, and he isn't doing his homework.

Winston has too many things to do. His mother suggests making a to-do list. First, she tells him to list all the tasks he needs to do. Next, she tells him to ___prioritize___
                                                                                                                                                     3
– to put his ____tasks____ in order of importance. His mother says he needs to do his
                  4
homework and ____chores____ first. He decides to do his English and math homework
                     5
first because they are ____due____ the next day. He also has a history project, but
                            6
the ___deadline___ is next Tuesday. After he finishes his homework, he will practice
            7
guitar. But before he does anything else, he has to take out the trash.

Listen and check your answers.

STUDENT TK 23
CLASS CD2 TK 3

B **Talk** with a partner. Ask and answer the question.

When you have a lot of things to do, how do you decide what to do first?

LESSON B Adverb clauses

1 Grammar focus: clauses with *when*

When I **have** a lot to do, I **make** a to-do list.
When she **feels** tired, she **takes** a break.

I **make** a to-do list **when** I **have** a lot to do.
She **takes** a break **when** she **feels** tired.

Turn to page 148 for a grammar explanation.

USEFUL LANGUAGE

Use a comma when the adverb clause is at the beginning of the sentence. When you read out loud, pause after the comma.

2 Practice

A **Write.** Combine the sentences. Use *when*. Circle the adverb clause.

Tips for Managing Your Time

1. You have many things to do. Make a to-do list.
   When _you have many things to do_ , _make a to-do list_ .

2. You have a deadline. Write it on your calendar.
   When _you have a deadline_ , _write it on your calendar_ .

3. Don't let people interrupt you. You need to concentrate.
   Don't let people interrupt you when _you need to concentrate_ .

4. You want to focus on a task. Turn off the television.
   When _you want to focus on a task_ , _turn off the television_ .

5. You feel tired. Take a break.
   When _you feel tired_ , _take a break_ .

6. Give yourself a reward. You finish something difficult.
   Give yourself a reward when _you finish something difficult_ .

7. Don't procrastinate. You have a deadline.
   Don't procrastinate when _you have a deadline_ .

8. You are tired. Don't do difficult tasks.
   When _you are tired_ , _don't do difficult tasks_ .

 Listen and check your answers.

CLASS CD2 TK 4

Lesson objectives

- Introduce dependent clauses with *when*
- Ask and answer questions with *when* clauses
- Practice talking about how to manage time

Warm-up and review

Before class: Write today's lesson focus on the board.
Lesson B:
Clauses with <u>when</u>

- Books open. Begin class. Direct Ss' attention to the pictures on page 70. Ask questions about Winston and his mother, such as the following: *What chores does Winston have?* (take out the trash; do his homework.) *What advice does Winston's mother give him?* (prioritize his tasks.) *When is his math and English homework due?* (the next day.) *Why does Winston's mother think he is procrastinating?* (because he is listening to music instead of doing his homework.)

Presentation

Focus on meaning / personalize

- Books closed. Say: *When I have many things to do, I make a list. What about you? When you have many things to do, what do you do?* Elicit answers from Ss and write their responses on the board.
- Write your example sentence on the board, and underline the verbs: *When I <u>have</u> a lot to do, I <u>make</u> a list.* Ask: *What are the two actions in this sentence?* (*make* and *have*) *Do the actions happen at different times or at the same time?* (at the same time) *How do you know?* (Both verbs are in the same tense.) Explain that *when* indicates things happen at the same time and so both verbs are in the same tense.

Focus on form

- Books open. Direct Ss' attention to the sentence charts in Exercise 1. Read the first statement aloud. Ask Ss to repeat.
- Write the first statement on the board: *When I have a lot to do, I make a to-do list.* Underline the main clause (I make a to-do list). Circle the dependent clause (When I have a lot to do). Say: *This sentence has two clauses. Each is a clause because each has a subject and a verb. The main clause is "I make a to-do list." "When I have a lot to do" is a dependent clause. This dependent clause begins with the word "when."*

- Read the next statement aloud. Ask Ss to repeat. Write it on the board: *When she feels tired, she takes a break.* Tell Ss to underline the main clause and to circle the dependent clause in their books.

▼ **Useful language**

Read the Useful language box aloud, then direct Ss' attention to the charts in Exercise 1. Have Ss look at the comma placement. Ask: *Which sentences need a comma?* (the first two) *Where does the comma go?* (after the dependent clause) Elicit or explain the rule for comma placement. *(There is a comma in the sentences where the dependent clause comes at the beginning, but there is no comma when the dependent clause comes at the end.)*

Practice

- Direct Ss' attention on Exercise 2A. Read the instructions aloud.
- Model the task. Ask a S to read the example sentence aloud. Remind Ss to use a comma after the *when* clause when it is at the beginning of a sentence, not at the end.
- Ss complete the exercise individually. Help as needed.

Comprehension check

- Focus Ss' attention on the second part of the instructions in Exercise 2A, and read it aloud.
- Class Audio CD2 track 4 Play or read the audio program (see audio script, page T-159). Ss listen and check their answers. Repeat the audio as needed.
- Write the numbers *1–8* on the board. Ask several Ss to come to the board to write their combined sentences. Make corrections as needed.

LESSON B Adverb clauses

Presentation

- Direct Ss' attention to the pictures in Exercise **2B**. Have Ss look at the first picture. Ask: *What's happening?* Elicit an appropriate response, such as: *Mr. Jackson is at work. He is reading. His desk is neat.*
- Guide Ss to look at the second picture. Ask: *What's happening?* Elicit an appropriate response, such as: *Ms. Clark is also working. She is watching TV and answering the phone. Her desk is messy.*
- Say: *Mr. Jackson and Ms. Clark are teachers. They both have deadlines.* Ask: *Who is organized and who is disorganized? Who is managing time well?* Elicit appropriate answers.

Practice

- Read the instructions aloud. Then read the phrases under the pictures. Explain any unfamiliar words.
- Model the task. Ask two Ss to read the example conversation to the class. Ss complete the exercise with a partner. Walk around and help as needed.
- Read aloud the second part of the instructions for Exercise **2B**.
- Ask a S to read aloud the example sentence. Tell Ss to continue the task by writing one sentence for each action that is listed under the pictures.
- Ss complete the exercise individually. Walk around and help as needed.

Comprehension check

- Write the numbers *1–4* on the board. Ask Ss to come to the board to write their sentences.
- Have other Ss read the sentences aloud. Ask Ss if the sentences are written correctly. Make corrections on the board as needed.

Expansion activity (whole group)

- Direct Ss' attention to the pictures on page 70. Encourage Ss to use *when* clauses to make sentences about the pictures.
- Model the activity. Focus Ss' attention on the first picture. Say: *When Winston procrastinates, his mother gets angry.*

Application

- Direct Ss' attention to Exercise **3A**. Read the instructions aloud.
- Model the task. Ask three Ss to read aloud the example question and answers.
- Hold up the Student's Book. Point to the name blanks in the chart. Tell Ss to use these blanks to write the name of the Ss that they interview. Have Ss write the Ss' answers below their names.
- Ss work in small groups to complete the exercise. Help as needed.
- Direct Ss' attention to Exercise **3B**. Read the instructions aloud.
- Ask Ss to make sentences about their classmates, such as: *When* (student's name) *has a deadline, he usually procrastinates.*
- Continue the exercise by asking Ss to share with the class information they learned about their classmates.

▼**Culture tip**
Remind Ss that in North America it is important to meet deadlines. Procrastinating can have serious consequences. Missing a deadline at work can cause a person to lose his or her job. Ask Ss to talk about other situations in which they might have deadlines (applying for school, paying bills, returning library books) and what the consequences might be in missing the deadline.

Evaluation

- Direct Ss' attention to the lesson focus on the board.
- Books closed. Ask Ss to tell you tips for managing time. Encourage Ss to use *when* clauses when they say the tips, for example: *When you have a deadline, you should prioritize your tasks.*
- Check off each part of the lesson focus as Ss demonstrate an understanding of what they have learned in the lesson.

More Ventures, Unit 6, Lesson B	
Workbook, 15–30 min.	
Add Ventures, 30–45 min. **Collaborative,** 30–45 min.	www.cambridge.org/myresourceroom
Student Arcade, time varies	www.cambridge.org/venturesarcade

B **Talk** with a partner. Make sentences with *when*.

> A When Mr. Jackson has a deadline, **he doesn't answer** the phone.
> B Ms. Clark **answers every call** when she has a deadline.

Mr. Jackson

Ms. Clark

1. doesn't answer the phone	answers every call
2. closes his office door	allows people to interrupt
3. does one task at a time	does several things at once
4. does difficult tasks first	procrastinates

Write sentences about Mr. Jackson and Ms. Clark.

Mr. Jackson doesn't answer the phone when he has a deadline.
(Answers will vary.)

3 Communicate

A **Work** in a small group. Interview your classmates. Complete the chart.

> A What do you do when you have a deadline?
> B I usually procrastinate.
> C I start working right away.

What do you do when you . . .	Name: _____	Name: _____	Name: _____
have a deadline?	*procrastinate*		
have many things to do?	*(Answers will vary.)*		
finish a difficult task?			
have trouble concentrating?			
(your idea)			

B **Share** information about your classmates.

LESSON C Adverb clauses

1 Grammar focus: clauses with *before* and *after*

Before she **eats** breakfast, she **reads** the newspaper.
After I **watch** the news, I **eat** dinner.

She **reads** the newspaper **before** she **eats** breakfast.
I **eat** dinner **after** I **watch** the news.

Turn to page 148 for a grammar explanation.

USEFUL LANGUAGE

Use a comma when *before* and *after* clauses are at the beginning of a sentence. When you read out loud, pause after the comma.

2 Practice

A **Read** Bonnie's morning schedule. Write sentences with *before* and *after*.

Bonnie's Morning Schedule

6:55 take a shower	7:35 bring in the newspaper
7:15 get dressed	7:40 eat breakfast
7:30 make coffee	8:00 leave for work

take a shower / get dressed
1. After _Bonnie takes a shower_ , _she gets dressed_ .
2. _Bonnie takes a shower_ before _she gets dressed_ .

get dressed / make coffee
3. Before _Bonnie makes coffee_ , _she gets dressed_ .
4. _Bonnie makes coffee_ after _she gets dressed_ .

bring in the newspaper / eat breakfast
5. _Bonnie brings in the newspaper_ before _she eats breakfast_ .
6. _Bonnie eats breakfast_ after _she brings in the newspaper_ .

eat breakfast / leave for work
7. After _Bonnie eats breakfast_ , _she leaves for work_ .
8. Before _Bonnie leaves for work_ , _she eats breakfast_ .

Listen and check your answers.

Lesson objectives
- Introduce dependent clauses with *before* and *after*
- Ask and answer questions with *before* and *after* clauses

Warm-up and review

Before class: Write today's lesson focus on the board.
Lesson C:
Clauses with before and after

- Books closed. Begin class. Ask Ss questions, such as: *What do you do when you have homework? What do you do when you have a headache?* Write their answers on the board. Have S volunteers come to the board to underline the main clause and circle the dependent clause. Elicit corrections as needed.

Presentation

Focus on meaning / personalize

- Books closed. Direct Ss' attention to the lesson focus on the board. Read it aloud. Write on the board in a vertical time line:

Watch the news	*Come to school*	*Leave school*	*Exercise*
7:00	8:00	3:00	4:00

- Point to each one and say: *I watch the morning news at seven. I come to school at eight. I leave school at three. I exercise at four.*

- For the first two actions, say: *I watch the news before I come to school. I exercise after I leave school.* Ask: *When do we use "before" and "after" in a sentence?* (to order events) Explain that *after* introduces the second event, and *before* introduces the first event. Explain that these sentences are about daily routines, or habits, so they are in the present tense.

Focus on form

- Books open. Direct Ss to the sentence charts in Exercise 1. Write on the board the first sentence in the top chart: *Before she eats breakfast, she reads the newspaper.* Read it aloud. Ask Ss to repeat. Ask: *What is the first action?* (reads the newspaper.) Write the number *1* above *reads the newspaper.* Ask: *What is the second action?* (eats breakfast.) Write the number *2* above *eats breakfast.* Ask: *Where does "before" go? Does it go before the first action or the second action?* (the second action.)

- Write on the board: *After I watch the news, I eat dinner.* Read it aloud. Ask Ss to repeat. Ask: *What is the first action?* (watch the news.) Write the number *1* above *watch the news.* Ask: *What is the second action?* (eat dinner.) Write the number *2* above *eat dinner.* Ask: *Where does "after" go? Does it go before the first action or the second action?* (the first action.)

▼ **Useful language**

Have Ss read the Useful language box. Remind Ss that we use a comma when a dependent clause is at the beginning of a sentence, but we do not use a comma when it is at the end of a sentence. Read the two sentences on the board aloud, making sure to pause after the *before* and *after* clauses.

Practice

- Direct Ss' attention to Exercise 2A. Read the instructions aloud.

- Write on the board the two first items in Bonnie's schedule. Point out the order of the first and second activities. Ask a S to read the two example sentences aloud.

- Ss complete the exercise individually. Help as needed.

Comprehension check

- Read aloud the second part of the instructions for Exercise 2A.

- Class Audio CD2 track 5 Play or read the audio program (see audio script, page T-159). Ss listen and check their answers.

- Write the numbers *1–8* on the board. Ask several Ss to come to the board to write their combined sentences. Correct as needed.

Presentation

- Books open. Direct Ss' attention to the pictures in Exercise **2B**. Tell Ss that the pictures show the daily activities of Ken, a soap-opera star.
- Focus Ss' attention on Picture 1. Ask: *What does Ken do every day?* Elicit: *He works out.*
- Ask about each of the other pictures in turn. Elicit sentences using the phrases under the pictures. Explain any unfamiliar words.

Practice

- Read the instructions for Exercise **2B** aloud. Model the task. Ask two pairs of Ss to read the example conversations to the class.
- Ss complete the exercise in pairs. Walk around and help as needed.
- Read aloud the instructions in the second part of Exercise **2B**.
- Tell Ss to write about Ken using dependent clauses at the end of the sentence. Elicit several examples and write them on the board:

  Ken works out before he goes to the studio.
  Ken goes to the studio after he works out.

- Ss complete the exercise individually. Walk around and help as needed.
- Ask individual Ss to write their sentences on the board. Encourage Ss to write the sentences using the *before* and *after* clauses both at the beginning and at the end of the sentences.
- Ask other Ss to read aloud each of the sentences on the board. Ask: *Is this sentence correct?* Make corrections on the board as needed.

Application

- Direct Ss' attention to Exercise **3A**. Read the instructions aloud.
- Ss in small groups. Model the task. Ask two pairs of Ss in each group to read the example conversations aloud.

- Draw the chart on the board or hold up the Student's Book. Tell Ss to write the name of each member in their group in the first column. Point to the second column. Guide Ss to write the first activity that the first group member says in the second column. Then point to the third column. Have Ss write the activity that the first group member does *before* the activity in the second column. Point to the fourth column. Ask Ss to write the activity that the first group member does *after* the activity in column 2.
- Ss complete the exercise. Walk around and help as needed.
- Direct Ss' attention to Exercise **3B**. Read the instructions aloud.
- Model the task. Ask a S from each group to tell what he or she learned about a person in the group in Exercise **3A**. Ask the S to make a sentence about this person, using *before* or *after*, for example: *Esperanza watches TV before she studies.*
- Continue the exercise by asking Ss to share with the class information they learned about their classmates.

Evaluation

- Direct Ss' attention to the lesson focus on the board. Ask individual Ss to look at the pictures on page 70 and make sentences using *before* and *after* clauses, such as: *Before Winston does his homework, he needs to take out the trash.*
- Encourage Ss to say the sentences using the *before* and *after* clauses both at the beginning and at the end of the sentences.
- Check off each part of the lesson focus as Ss demonstrate an understanding of what they have learned in the lesson.

More Ventures, Unit 6, Lesson C	
Workbook, 15–30 min.	
Add Ventures, 30–45 min.	www.cambridge.org/myresourceroom
Collaborative, 30–45 min.	
Student Arcade, time varies	www.cambridge.org/venturesarcade

B **Talk** with a partner. Ask and answer questions about Ken, a soap opera star. Use *before* and *after*.

> **A** What does Ken do before he goes to the studio?
> **B** Before Ken goes to the studio, he works out.

> **A** What does Ken do after he works out?
> **B** Ken goes to the studio after he works out.

1. works out	2. goes to the studio	3. memorizes his lines
4. puts on makeup	5. performs his scene	6. goes home and rests

Write sentences about Ken's day.

Ken works out before he goes to the studio.
(Answers will vary.)

3 Communicate

A **Work** in a small group. Ask and answer questions about daily activities. Complete the chart.

> **A** What do you do every day, Emma?
> **B** I study.
> **A** What do you do before you study?
> **B** I watch TV.

> **A** What do you do after you study?
> **B** I go to bed.

Name	Everyday activity	Before activity	After activity
Emma	*study*	*watch TV*	*go to bed*
(Answers will vary.)			

B **Share** information about your classmates.

LESSON D Reading

1 Before you read

Look at the title. Answer the questions.

1. What are some rules about time in this country?
2. What are some rules about time in other countries?

2 Read

Read this article. Listen and read again.

STUDENT TK 24
CLASS CD2 TK 6

RULES about TIME

Every culture has rules about time. These rules are usually unspoken, but everybody knows them.

In some countries such as the United States, England, and Canada, punctuality is an unspoken rule. It is important to be on time, especially in business. People usually arrive a little early for business appointments. Business meetings and personal appointments often have strict beginning and ending times. When you are late, other people might think you are rude, disorganized, or irresponsible.

These countries also have cultural rules about time in social situations. For example, when an invitation for dinner says 6:00 p.m., it is impolite to arrive more than five or ten minutes late. On the other hand, when the invitation is for a party from 6:00 to 8:00 or a reception from 3:30 to 5:30, you can arrive anytime between those hours. For public events with specific starting times – movies, concerts, sports events – you should arrive a few minutes before the event begins. In fact, some theaters do not allow people to enter if they arrive after the event has started.

Other cultures have different rules about time. In Brazil, it is not unusual for guests to arrive an hour or two after a social event begins. In the Philippines, it is not uncommon for people to miss scheduled events – a class or an appointment – to meet a friend at the airport. Many Filipinos believe that relationships with people are more important than keeping a schedule.

> Dashes often signal a definition, explanation, or example. The dashes in this reading signal examples.

Lesson objectives

- Introduce and read "Rules About Time"
- Practice using new topic-related vocabulary
- Use dashes to recognize a definition, an explanation, or an example
- Identify words with prefixes meaning *not*

Warm-up and review

- Before class. Write today's lesson focus on the board.

  Lesson D:
  Read and understand "Rules About Time"
  Practice new vocabulary
  Practice using prefixes meaning <u>not</u>

- Begin class. Books closed. Focus Ss' attention on the word *Time* in the lesson focus. Write *dinnertime* on the board. Ask: *What time do you like to eat dinner? What time do you usually eat dinner? What time do people in your native country usually eat dinner?* Elicit appropriate responses and write them on the board.

- Point out that, of course, different countries and cultures have different social rules about many things, not just about dinner time. Ask Ss if they can think of other rules that they have noticed that differ among cultures, such as: *holding hands in public; bowing, shaking hands, or kissing as a greeting; expressing differing opinions in public.*

Presentation

- Books open. Direct Ss' attention to Exercise 1. Read the instructions aloud. Elicit appropriate responses, such as: *American employers expect employees to come to work on time. If employees are late too often, they could lose their jobs.*

- Compare rules about time in Ss' countries with those in North American countries.

▼ **Teaching tip**

If you have Ss from different countries in your class, give Ss partners from a culture that differs from their own. This will make their conversations more interesting.

Practice

- Read aloud the instructions for Exercise 2. Ss read the article silently.

- Class Audio CD2 track 6 Play or read the audio program and ask Ss to read along (see audio script, pages T-159–T-160). Repeat the audio program as needed.

Read the tip aloud. Write *dash* on the board. Say it and ask Ss to repeat. Draw an example of a dash on the board. Guide Ss to circle the dashes in the article. Have them underline the phrases between the dashes. Ask Ss if the words between the dashes are definitions, explanations, or examples. (*In this article they are examples.*)

- While Ss are listening to and reading the article, ask them to underline any words they don't know. When the audio program is finished, have Ss write the new vocabulary words on the board.

- Point to each word on the board. Say it aloud and ask Ss to repeat. Give a brief explanation of each word, or ask Ss who know the word to explain it. If Ss prefer to look up the new words in their dictionaries, allow them to do so.

- Encourage Ss to guess the meaning of unfamiliar words from context clues in the article. For example, if a S writes *punctuality* on the board, show the S how the meaning of the word is conveyed in the article. Explain that the sentence after *punctuality* says: *It is important to be on time.* Tell Ss that *punctuality* is the noun form of *punctual*, which means "to be on time."

Learner persistence (individual work)

- Self-Study Audio CD track 24 Exercise 2 is recorded on the CD at the back of the Student's Book. Ss can listen to the CD at home for reinforcement and review. They can also listen for self-directed learning when class attendance is not possible.

Comprehension check

- Direct Ss' attention to Exercise **3A**. Read the instructions aloud.
- Ask the class the first question. Elicit appropriate responses, such as: *"Unspoken rules" mean that no one talks about them, but everybody knows about them.*
- Ask the class the second question. Elicit appropriate responses, such as: *The author's definition of "on time" is to arrive at a scheduled time. My definition of "on time" is . . .*
- Ss in pairs. Ask Ss to ask and answer the rest of the questions with a partner.

▼**Teaching tip**

If Ss have differing ideas about what is and is not appropriate in the United States or in other English-speaking countries, this is a good time to guide Ss so that they are aware of cultural expectations.

Presentation

- Write on the board: *prefix*. Ask Ss if they know what *prefix* means. If Ss don't know, underline *pre* in the word. Explain that a prefix is a word part at the beginning of a word that gives the word a new meaning.

Practice

- Focus Ss' attention on Exercise **3B**. Read the instructions aloud for number 1.
- Model the task. Ask a S to read the example word *unspoken*. Tell Ss that this means not spoken.
- Have Ss underline the words with the prefixes *dis-*, *ir-*, and *im-* that they find in the article on page 76.
- Ss complete the exercise individually. Help as needed.
- Ask Ss to come to the board to write the words with the prefixes *dis-*, *ir-*, and *im-*.
- Have Ss focus on number 2 in Exercise **3B**. Tell pairs to discuss the meaning of the words they wrote from the prefix as well as the context.
- Direct Ss' attention to number 3 in Exercise **3B**. Ask a S to read the instructions aloud.
- Model the task. Have Ss think of other words they know, such as *unhappy* and *impatient*, that begin with the prefixes in this exercise.
- Ss complete the exercise with a partner. Help as needed. Ask Ss to write a sentence for each word in their chart. Encourage Ss to use their dictionaries if needed.

Comprehension check

- Copy the chart from Exercise **3B** onto the board. Ask Ss to come to the board to write the words from their chart in the correct column.
- Read each word aloud. Ask the class if they agree that these are real English words that use the prefixes. Invite the class to add or correct any words.

Learner persistence (individual work)

- Encourage Ss to keep a vocabulary log with prefix charts such as the one in the Student's Book.

Application

- Focus Ss' attention on Exercise **3C**. Read the instructions and questions aloud.
- Model the task. Read the first question again. Have Ss brainstorm advice to give their friend, such as: *Show your friend how to make a to-do list. Show him / her how to prioritize tasks.*
- Ss complete the exercise in pairs. Help as needed.

Evaluation

- Books closed. Direct Ss' attention to the lesson focus on the board. Ask individual Ss to retell the main points of the article, "Rules About Time."
- Books open. Focus Ss' attention on the words they wrote in the chart in Exercise **3B**. Ask Ss to make sentences with these words to show that they understand the meaning.
- Check off each part of the lesson focus as Ss demonstrate an understanding of what they have learned in the lesson.

Learner persistence (individual, pairs)

- You may wish to assign Extended Reading Worksheets from the *Online Teacher's Resource Room* for Ss to complete outside of class. The purpose of these worksheets is to encourage Ss to read for pleasure in English outside of the English class. The worksheets can also be assigned as extended reading in class.

More Ventures, Unit 6, Lesson D	
Workbook, 15–30 min.	
Add Ventures, 30–45 min.	
Collaborative, 30–45 min.	www.cambridge.org/myresourceroom
Extended Reading and worksheet, 45–60 min.	
Student Arcade, time varies	www.cambridge.org/venturesarcade

3 After you read

A Check your understanding.

1. What are "unspoken" rules?

2. How is your definition of "on time" the same or different from the author's description of the unspoken rules about time in the United States, England, and Canada?

3. What are examples of public events with specific starting times?

4. When should you arrive for the following events in the U.S.? When should you arrive for these same events in your native country?
   - a medical appointment
   - a business meeting
   - dinner at someone's house
   - a party
   - a sports event

B Build your vocabulary.

1. English has several prefixes that mean "not." Write words from the reading that begin with these prefixes.

   un- _____unspoken_____

   dis- _____disorganized_____

   ir- _____irresponsible_____

   im- _____impolite_____

2. Work with a partner. Explain the meaning of the words you wrote.

3. Work with a partner. Write more words with the prefixes. Use a dictionary if needed. Use each word in a sentence.

un-	dis-	ir-	im-
unusual	disagree	irregular	immature
unimportant	disadvantage	irresponsible	impolite
undo	disable	irrelevant	imperfect
unable	dissatisfied	irrational	immoral

C Talk with a partner. Ask and answer the questions.

1. Your friend is disorganized. What advice can you give your friend?

2. Someone is late to a job interview. Is that person irresponsible? Why or why not?

3. You are 30 minutes late for lunch with a friend. Is it impolite? Why or why not?

LESSON E Writing

1 Before you write

A **Work** in a small group. Discuss the questions. Complete the diagrams.

1. What qualities and habits does a good time manager have?

makes a to-do list

(Answers will vary.)

Good time manager

2. What qualities and habits does a weak time manager have?

procrastinates

(Answers will vary.)

Weak time manager

B **Talk** with a partner. Answer the questions.

1. What qualities and habits from each diagram do you have?

2. In general, are you a good time manager or a weak time manager? Why do you think so?

Lesson objectives

- Write about a good or a weak time manager
- Introduce concluding phrases

Warm-up and review

- Before class. Write today's lesson focus on the board.

  Lesson E:
  Write a paragraph about a good or a weak
  time manager
  Use signals before a conclusion

- Begin class. Books closed. Review vocabulary from the unit. Focus Ss' attention on the words *good time manager* and *weak time manager* in the lesson focus. Ask Ss what the difference is between a good or a weak time manager. Elicit appropriate responses, such as: *A good time manager uses his or her time well. A weak time manager wastes time and procrastinates.*

- Remind Ss about Winston and his mother from the beginning of the unit. Ask: *Was Winston a good time manager?* (No, he wasn't.) *Why not?* (He was disorganized, and he procrastinated.) *Is his mother a good time manager?* (Yes, she is.) *What advice did she give Winston about managing his time better?* (She told him to prioritize tasks in order to meet deadlines and to make a to-do list.)

Presentation

- Write on the board: *qualities.* Read it aloud and ask Ss to repeat. Tell Ss that a quality is a characteristic – something that describes a person or thing.

- Ask Ss to give you some examples of qualities that people have. Guide Ss to use adjectives to describe qualities. Elicit appropriate responses, such as: *kind, hardworking, responsible.*

- Write *habits* on the board. Ask Ss to tell you some examples of habits. Elicit appropriate responses, such as: *getting up early, getting up late, drinking coffee every morning.*

- Books open. Direct Ss' attention to Exercise 1A and read the instructions and questions aloud.

- Ss ask and answer the questions in small groups. Ss write their ideas on the blank lines next to the corresponding diagrams.

▼**Teaching tip**

Explain the difference between *qualities* and *habits.* Tell Ss to use adjectives to describe qualities and phrases with verbs to describe habits. For example, a responsible person (*quality*) gets to work on time every day (a *habit*).

Comprehension check

- Write *Good time manager* and *Weak time manager* on the board. Ask Ss to come to the board to write under the appropriate heading the qualities and habits they wrote for Exercise 1A.

- Ask different Ss to read the qualities and habits aloud. Ask the class if they agree with the descriptions on the board. Have Ss make corrections as needed.

Practice

- Direct Ss' attention to Exercise 1B. Read the instructions aloud.

- Ask two Ss to read the questions to the class. Model the task. Tell Ss about your own qualities and habits as a time manager – or use a fictional person's qualities and habits, for example: *I am a good time manager. My desk is neat and organized. I have a to-do list of tasks to do. I keep my deadlines by checking off items on my to-do list as I complete them.*

- Ss complete the exercise in pairs. Help as needed.

- Ask several Ss to share what they learned about their partner with the rest of the class.

▼**Teaching tip**

Encourage Ss to use graphic organizers such as the one in Exercise 1B to organize their thoughts before writing.

Expansion activity (small groups)

- Ask Ss to brainstorm different types of jobs. Write the jobs on the board, for example: *teacher, doctor, artist, nurse.*

- Ss in small groups. Tell Ss to write down the qualities and habits they think might be helpful for the jobs listed on the board.

- Model the activity. Point to the word *teacher* on the board. Ask: *What qualities or habits do you think are helpful for a teacher?* Elicit appropriate responses, such as: *A teacher should be organized and creative. A teacher should be punctual.*

- Ss complete the activity in small groups. Help as needed.

LESSON E Writing

Presentation

- Direct Ss' attention to Exercise **1C**. Read the instructions aloud.
- Ask a S to read the title of the paragraph to the class. Then have a S read the first sentence aloud. Elicit ideas or predictions about what the paragraph might be about.
- Ask Ss to read the paragraph silently. Tell them to underline words they don't know.
- Have Ss write the new words on the board. Point to each word. Say it and ask Ss to repeat.
- Remind Ss of the strategies they have learned for finding clues to help guess the meaning of a word. For example, if a S writes *hang up* on the board, ask the S who wrote it to tell you the situation in which the sentence was used, for example: *Lucinda was talking on the phone, and she hung up at 9:00 p.m.* Ask: *What could this phrase mean?* Elicit an appropriate response, such as: *She ended the conversation and put the phone down.*

Read the tip box aloud. Tell Ss that a *signal* is a sign that indicates something is coming next. In this case, each of the phrases signals the end of the paragraph. Say the concluding phrases and ask Ss to repeat them. Have Ss tell you the concluding phrase from the paragraph they have just read. (*In summary*)

Practice

- Direct Ss' attention to the second part of Exercise **1C**. Read the instructions aloud.
- Model the task. Focus Ss' attention on the first question, and read it to the class. Ask Ss if they remember where to find the topic sentence in a paragraph. (*It's the first sentence in the paragraph.*)
- Ss complete the exercise in pairs. Walk around and help as needed.
- Ask several pairs to ask and answer the questions for the class.

Application

- Focus Ss' attention on Exercise **2**. Read the instructions aloud.
- Ss complete the task individually. Walk around and help as needed.

Learner persistence *(individual work)*

- If you have any Ss who have difficulty writing, sit with them and help them as the other Ss are writing. Encourage Ss to use the diagram from Exercise **1A** on page 78 as a guide for the words they can use to describe a good or a weak time manager.

Comprehension check

- Direct Ss' attention to Exercise **3A**. Read the instructions aloud. This exercise asks Ss to develop skills to review and edit their own writing.
- Model the task. Focus Ss' attention on the example paragraph in Exercise **1C**. Ask Ss to identify all the checklist items in this paragraph. (*1. The first sentence tells us that the paragraph will be about Lucinda, who is not a very good time manager. 2. There are many examples of this – Lucinda gets distracted easily and procrastinates before doing her homework. She doesn't concentrate, etc. 3. The signal phrase is "In summary."*)
- Ss check their own paragraphs. Walk around and help as needed.
- Ask if any Ss checked *No* for any of the three boxes. If they did, encourage them to revise their paragraph so that the missing item or items are included.

Evaluation

- Focus Ss' attention on Exercise **3B**. Read the instructions aloud. This exercise asks Ss to work together to peer-correct their writing. Reading aloud enables the writer to review his or her own writing. Reading to a partner allows the writer to understand the need to write clearly for an audience.
- Ss complete the exercise in pairs. Walk around and help as needed.
- Listen to Ss as they ask their partner a question about the paragraph and tell their partner one thing they learned from it.
- Ask several volunteers to read their paragraph to the class. Ask other Ss to ask questions and to mention something they learned from the paragraph.
- Direct Ss' attention to the lesson focus on the board. Have Ss give examples of concluding phrases. Elicit: *In conclusion, To conclude,* and *In summary.*
- Check off each part of the lesson focus as Ss demonstrate an understanding of what they have learned in the lesson.

More Ventures, Unit 6, Lesson E	
Workbook, 15–30 min.	
Add Ventures, 30–45 min.	www.cambridge.org/myresourceroom
Collaborative, 30–45 min.	

C **Read** the paragraph.

How Lucinda Manages Her Time

Lucinda is not a very good time manager. For example, this is the way she does her homework. First, she sits down and takes out her books. Two minutes later, she decides to get a cup of coffee. She goes to the kitchen, makes coffee, and returns to her desk. Before she starts reading, she checks her e-mail. Then the phone rings. It's her best friend. They talk for 20 minutes. After they hang up, it's 9:00 p.m. – time for Lucinda's favorite TV show. She watches the show from 9:00 to 10:00. Then, she studies from 10:00 until 1:30 a.m. Of course, she is tired in the morning. In summary, Lucinda is a weak time manager because she procrastinates.

> Use one of the following phrases before your conclusion:
> *In conclusion,*
> *To conclude,*
> *In summary,*

Work with a partner. Answer the questions.

1. What is the topic sentence?
2. How many examples does the writer give about Lucinda?
3. Which phrase signals the conclusion?

2 Write

Write a paragraph about yourself or someone you know who is a good or a weak time manager. Say what kind of time manager you are writing about in the topic sentence. Include examples to support your topic sentence and a signal before your conclusion. Use Exercises 1A and 1C to help you.

3 After you write

A **Check** your writing.

	Yes	No
1. My topic sentence says what kind of time manager I am writing about.	☐	☐
2. I included examples to support my topic sentence.	☐	☐
3. I used a signal before my conclusion.	☐	☐

B **Share** your writing with a partner.

1. Take turns. Read your paragraph to a partner.
2. Comment on your partner's paragraph. Ask your partner a question about the paragraph. Tell your partner one thing you learned.

LESSON F Another view

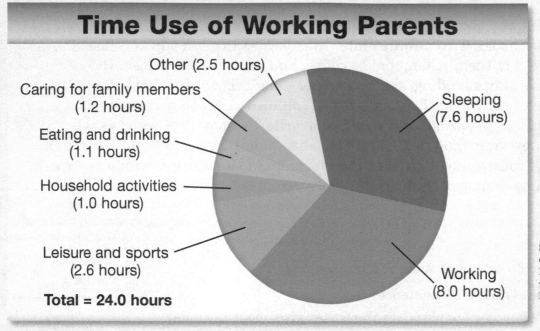

Time Use of Working Parents

Other (2.5 hours)

Caring for family members (1.2 hours)

Eating and drinking (1.1 hours)

Household activities (1.0 hours)

Leisure and sports (2.6 hours)

Total = 24.0 hours

Sleeping (7.6 hours)

Working (8.0 hours)

Source: U.S. Department of Labor, Bureau of Labor Statistics www.bls.gov/tus/charts/home.htm

A **Read** the questions. Look at the pie chart. Fill in the answer.

1. Who is the chart about?

   Ⓐ employed people with children

   Ⓑ employed people without children

   Ⓒ unemployed people with children

   Ⓓ none of the above

2. Which activity do these people spend the least time doing?

   Ⓐ caring for family members

   Ⓑ eating and drinking

   Ⓒ household activities

   Ⓓ none of the above

3. Which activity do these people spend the most time doing?

   Ⓐ eating and drinking

   Ⓑ leisure and sports

   Ⓒ working

   Ⓓ none of the above

4. Which statement is true?

   Ⓐ People spend less time working than eating, drinking, and sleeping combined.

   Ⓑ People spend more time working than eating, drinking, and sleeping combined.

   Ⓒ People spend as much time working as eating, drinking, and sleeping combined.

   Ⓓ none of the above

B **Talk** with a partner. Ask and answer the questions.

1. About how much time a day do you spend on the activities listed on the pie chart?
2. On which activities do you spend more time than the pie chart shows?
3. On which activities do you spend less time than the pie chart shows?

- Practice reading and understanding a pie chart
- Contrast *one* and *it* with *some*, *any*, and *them*
- Complete the self-assessment

Warm-up and review

- Before class. Write today's lesson focus on the board.

  Lesson F:
  Read and understand a pie chart
  Review topic vocabulary
  Complete the self-assessment

- Begin class. Books closed. Write on the board: *diagrams.* Say the word and ask Ss to repeat. Remind Ss that they worked with a diagram in Lesson E to organize their thoughts before writing a paragraph.

- Ask Ss: *What other types of diagrams have you worked with in this book?* Elicit: *a bar graph, a graphic organizer.* Write these words on the board. Remind Ss that they worked with a bar graph in Unit 1, when they were asked to compare Fernando's weekend activities. Refer Ss to page 11 in the Student's Book.

- Ask Ss where they used a graphic organizer. Remind them that they completed a graphic organizer in Unit 5, when they were asked to write positive and negative information about the Salsa Starz concert. Refer Ss to page 66.

- Tell Ss that they will practice reading and understanding a different type of diagram in this unit: a pie chart. Say the words *pie chart* and have Ss repeat.

Presentation

- Books open. Direct Ss' attention to the pie chart in Exercise 1. Tell Ss that this is an example of a pie chart. Ask Ss: *Why do you think it is called a pie chart?* Elicit an answer, such as: *Because the chart looks like a dessert called a pie.*

- Ask Ss: *What is the topic of the pie chart?* Elicit the title above the chart. Write on the board: *average.* Say the word and have Ss repeat.

- Ask Ss to define the word *average.* Allow them to use dictionaries if they wish. Elicit a definition such as: *a representative type or a typical example.*

- Ask Ss what they think the pie chart represents. Elicit: *how a typical person who works and has children spends his or her day.*

- Ask a S to read aloud the categories in the pie chart. Ask: *How many hours each day does the average working person with children sleep?* (7.6 hours.) Ask: *How many hours each day does the average working person with children work?* (8.0 hours.) Continue asking about the other sections of the chart.

▼**Teaching tip**

Lead Ss to see that learning to read and understand diagrams such as bar graphs and pie charts is a useful skill for everyday life. Ask Ss if they use these types of diagrams at work. If no one says *Yes*, explain that Ss may have jobs in the future in which they will be expected to read and use diagrams such as the ones in this book.

Practice

- Read the instructions for Exercise **1A** aloud. This task helps prepare Ss for standardized-type tests they may have to take. Make sure Ss understand the task. Have Ss individually scan for and fill in the answers.

Comprehension check

- Check answers with the class. Ask Ss to read the questions and their answers aloud. Make corrections as needed.

Application

- Direct Ss' attention to Exercise **1B** and read the instructions aloud. Ask three Ss to read the questions to the class. Make sure that all Ss understand the meaning of the questions.

- Pairs ask and answer the questions. Walk around and help as needed.

- Ask several Ss to share what they learned about their partner with the rest of the class.

LESSON **F** Another view

Warm-up and review

- Books closed. Ask Ss: What are some characteristics of a good time manager? Elicit answers, such as: *A person who prioritizes tasks and makes a to-do list.*

Presentation

- Books open. Direct Ss' attention to the chart in Exercise **2A**. Ask two Ss to read aloud the first dialog in the left column: *Do you have a bus schedule? Sure, here's one.* Underline the word *one*. Tell Ss that *one* is an indefinite pronoun. This means it refers to a non-specific noun. In this case, a person is asking someone for a schedule. It doesn't matter which schedule the person receives because there are many, and they are all the same. Therefore, we can use the indefinite pronoun *one*.

- Ask a different pair of Ss to read aloud the second dialog in the left column: *Do you have any bus schedules? Sure, there are some over there.* Point out that *some* is an indefinite pronoun and is the plural of *one*. It refers to more than one non-specific noun. In this case, a person is asking for many non-specific schedules.

- Read the second answer in the dialog: *No, we don't have any.* Write the two sentences on the board. Underline *some* and *don't have any*. Tell Ss that positive clauses use *some*, and negative clauses use *not . . . any*. Explain that *any* can follow other negative words such as *never* or *hardly*.

- Direct Ss' attention to the right side of the chart. Ask two Ss to read aloud the first dialog in the right column: *Can I see your bus schedule? Sure, here it is.* Underline the word *it*. Tell Ss that *it* is a definite pronoun. That means it refers to a specific thing. In this case, the person is referring to one specific bus schedule so we use a definite pronoun.

- Ask a different pair of Ss to read aloud the second dialog in the right column: *Can I see those bus schedules? Sure, you can take them.* Point out that *them* is also an indefinite pronoun and is the plural of *it*. It refers to more than one thing. In this case, the person is referring to a specific set of bus schedules.

Practice

- Direct Ss' attention to the instructions in **2A**. Read the instructions aloud. Be sure Ss understand the activity. Ask a pair of Ss to read the dialog in 1 aloud. Fill out the second blank as a class (*OK, **it** leaves from Gate 12.*)

- Ss complete numbers 2 and 3 in pairs. Review the correct answers with the class. Ensure Ss understand the differences between singular and plural definite and indefinite pronouns and also when to use them.

- Direct Ss' attention to the instructions in **2B**. Read the instructions aloud. Ask a S to read the example sentences. Ss complete the activity in pairs. Encourage each S to share a few sentences about a person in their group.

Evaluation

- Before asking students to turn to the self-assessment on page 138, do a quick review of the unit. Have Ss turn to Lesson A. Ask the class to talk about what they remember about this lesson. Prompt Ss, if necessary, with questions, for example: *What are the conversations about on this page? What vocabulary is in the pictures?* Continue in this manner to review each lesson quickly.

- **Self-assessment** Read the instructions for Exercise **3**. Ask Ss to turn to the self-assessment page and complete the unit self-assessment. The self-assessments are also on the *Online Teacher's Resource Room*. If you prefer to collect the assessments and save them as part of each S's portfolio assessment, print out the unit self-assessment from the *Resource Room*, ask students to complete it, and collect and save it.

- If Ss are ready, administer the unit test on pages T-178–T-179 of this Teacher's Edition (or on the Assessment Audio CD / CD-ROM).

More Ventures, Unit 6, Lesson F	
Workbook, 15–30 min.	
Add Ventures, 30–45 min.	www.cambridge.org/myresourceroom
Collaborative, 30–45 min.	

2 Grammar connections: *one / some / any* and *it / them*

	Use an indefinite pronoun (*one*, *some*, or *any*) to refer to a noun that is not specific.	Use a definite pronoun (*it* or *them*) to refer to a noun that is specific.
Singular	Do you have <u>a bus schedule</u>? Sure. Here's **one**.	Can I see <u>your bus schedule</u>? Sure. Here **it** is.
Plural	Do you have <u>any bus schedules</u>? Sure. There are **some** over there. No, we don't have **any**.	Can I see <u>those bus schedules</u>? Sure. You can take **them**.

A **Work** with a partner. Complete the sentences with *one*, *it*, *some*, *any*, or *them*.

1. **A** Which gate do the buses to Trenton leave from?

   B Which ___*one*___ do you want?

   A The 10:15 bus.

   B Let's see, the 10:15 bus? OK . . . ___*It*___ leaves from Gate 12.

2. **A** Do you have ___*any*___ bags to check?

   B No. I have two bags, but I'd like to bring ___*them*___ on the plane.

   A You're only allowed to bring on one small ___*one*___. Those are too big.

3. **A** Do you have ___*any*___ school assignments, Winston?

   B Yes, I have ___*some*___. There are three.

   A When are you going to work on ___*them*___?

   B Well, I've already finished two, and started the other. I'll finish ___*it*___ tomorrow.

B **Talk** with your classmates. Ask and answer questions. Use *it, them, one, some,* and *any* in your answers.

> Have you seen a movie this week?

> Yes, I've seen one. / No, I haven't seen one.

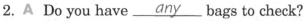

1. see / a movie / this week
2. see / the movie / *The Godfather*
3. read / any newspapers / in English?
4. read / last Sunday's / *New York Times*
5. watch / any cooking shows / on TV
6. watch / the Discovery and History Channels

3 Wrap up

Complete the **Self-assessment** on page 138.

Review

1 Listening

CLASS CD2 TK 7

Listen. Put a check (✓) under the correct name.

	Trina	Minh
1. has decided to visit his family		✓
2. is going to Las Vegas	✓	
3. hasn't bought plane tickets yet		✓
4. has already made reservations	✓	
5. won a free hotel room	✓	

Talk with a partner. Check your answers.

2 Grammar

A Write. Complete the story. Use the correct words.

A Great Time Manager

Natalia Alvarez begins work at 8:00 in the morning. It is 7:50 and she has already

_____*arrived*_____ at her job. She is a single parent, so she needs _____*to manage*_____
　　1. arrive / arrived　　　　　　　　　　　　　　　　　　　　2. manage / to manage

her time well. Every Saturday _____*before*_____ she goes shopping, she makes a
　　　　　　　　　　　　　3. before / after

list of all the food she needs. _____*After*_____ she takes her children to the park on
　　　　　　　　　　　4. When / After

Sunday, she cooks meals for the rest of the week. When she _____*comes*_____ home
　　　　　　　　　　　　　　　　　　　　　　　5. has come / comes

late, she just heats up the food she cooked on Sunday. After she helps her children with

their homework, she _____*does*_____ the laundry and goes to bed. Natalia is a
　　　　　　　　　　6. do / does

great time manager.

B Write. Look at the answers. Write the questions.

1. **A** What does Natalia do before _____*she goes shopping*_____?

   B Natalia makes a list before she goes shopping.

2. **A** What _____*does Natalia do after she goes to the park*_____?

   B She cooks meals for the rest of the week after she goes to the park.

3. **A** When _____*does she do the laundry*_____?

   B She does the laundry after she helps her children with their homework.

Talk with a partner. Ask and answer the questions.

Lesson objectives

- Review vocabulary and grammar from Units 5 and 6
- Introduce initial *st* sound

Warm-up and review

- Before class. Write today's lesson focus on the board.
  Review unit:
  Review vocabulary and grammar from Units 5 and 6
  Practice pronouncing initial st sound
- Begin class. Books closed. Ask Ss questions to review vocabulary from Units 5 and 6, for example:
  What do you usually do before you come to class?
  What do you usually do after you leave class?
  Do you plan to go shopping after class?
  Do you hope to have a vacation soon?
  Have you done your homework already?
  Do you make a to-do list when you have a lot of work?

Presentation

- Books open. Direct Ss' attention to Exercise 1 and read the instructions aloud. Tell Ss that they will hear a conversation between two friends, Trina and Minh.
- Class Audio CD2 track 7 Model the task. Play or read only the first part of the conversation on the audio program (see audio script, page T-160). Pause the program after Minh says: *I've decided to visit my family in Vietnam.*
- Direct Ss' attention to number 1 in the chart (*has decided to visit his family*). Ask: *Who has decided to visit his family?* (Minh.) Tell Ss to put a checkmark under Minh's name for number 1.
- Have four Ss read the remaining phrases in the chart. Say: *Now listen and check the correct boxes.*
- Class Audio CD2 track 7 Play or read the complete audio program (see audio script, page T-160). Ss listen and check the boxes. Repeat the audio program as needed.

Comprehension check

- Read aloud the second part of the instructions for Exercise 1.
- Ss complete the exercise in pairs. Help as needed.
- Ask several Ss to make sentences about Minh and Trina using the information in the chart. Ask individual Ss to share their sentences with the class.

▼ **Culture tip**
Explain the meaning of a vacation time-share. A time-share is a way to own vacation property in which the use and cost of running the property are shared among the different owners. These properties usually include condos, cabins, ski resorts, and hotel rooms in vacation areas. The time-share owner purchases in advance the use of the vacation spot for a number of weeks or months. Other people purchase the use of the property for different dates. The sale of the dates is usually managed by a real-estate agent. Large hotels and resorts often offer free or reduced-price vacation packages to people who are willing to listen to a sales presentation for a time-share purchase in the hotel or resort.

Practice

- Review *already*, *yet*, *before*, *after*, and *when*. Write the words on the board. Ask Ss to say or write sentences with the words to confirm their understanding of the key grammar points.

▼ **Teaching tip**
In multilevel classes, create small heterogeneous groups. Encourage the Ss who are comfortable with this grammar review to help those who are less comfortable.

- Direct Ss' attention to Exercise 2A. Ask: *What is the title of this story?* ("A Great Time Manager") Ask: *What are examples of good time management?* Elicit appropriate answers such as: *prioritizes tasks, makes to-do lists.*
- Ask Ss to read the story silently to get the main idea. When Ss have finished reading, ask: *What is the story about?*
- Read the instructions for Exercise 2A aloud. Ss choose the correct word or words to complete each sentence. This exercise does not ask Ss to change the word forms. Ask a S to read aloud the first two sentences of the story and to explain why the words they chose best complete the sentence. Tell Ss to continue reading the story and filling in the blanks.
- Ss complete the exercise individually. Help as needed.
- Write the numbers *1–6* on the board. Have Ss come to the board to write only the words, not complete sentences.
- Read the story aloud using Ss' answers. Correct the answers on the board as needed.

Comprehension check

- Direct Ss' attention to Exercise 2B. This exercise reviews question formation by asking questions related to the reading "A Great Time Manager."
- Read the instructions aloud. Model the task. Have two Ss read the example.
- Ss complete the exercise individually. Help as needed.
- Check answers with the class. Ask volunteers to read their questions. Write the correct questions on the board.
- Read aloud the second part of the instructions for Exercise 2B.
- Pairs ask and answer the questions. Help as needed.

Review

Presentation

- Write on the board: *initial st sound*. Explain that an initial sound is a sound at the beginning of a word.
- Write several words on the board that begin with *st*, such as *student* and *study*. Ask Ss to add additional words. Say each word on the board and have Ss repeat.

> ▼ **Teaching tip**
>
> These pronunciation exercises help Ss become aware of certain sound features in English. They are not presented as an exhaustive study of pronunciation. However, these exercises help raise Ss' awareness. Many Ss will not be sensitive to the pronunciation of the initial *st* sound in English if this sound does not exist in their first language. They may add a sound before the initial *st* sound. For example, they may say *ehstudent* rather than *student* or *ehstudy* rather than *study*.

- Direct Ss' attention to Exercise **3A**. Read the instructions aloud.
- 🔊 Class Audio CD2 track 8 Play or read the complete audio program (see audio script, page T-160).
- Repeat the audio program. Pause after each phrase to give Ss time to repeat. Play the audio program as many times as needed. Focus Ss' attention on the pronunciation of the letters in bold in Exercise **3A**.

Expansion activity (individual work)

- Books closed. To reinforce the sound-symbol correspondence, ask Ss to write the phrases from Exercise **3A** as you dictate them.
- Have Ss underline the initial *st* sound in the phrases they wrote.

Practice

- Direct Ss' attention to Exercise **3B**. Read the instructions aloud.
- 🔊 Class Audio CD2 track 9 Model the task. Play or read the first few lines in the first dialog on the audio program (see audio script, page T-160). Ask Ss to underline the initial *st* sound in the sentences.
- Have Ss write the words on the board. Correct as needed.
- Tell Ss to pay attention to the words with the initial *st* sound as they listen and repeat.

- 🔊 Class Audio CD2 track 9 Play or read the complete audio program again (see audio script, page T-160). Ss underline all the initial *st* sounds. Repeat the audio program as needed.
- Read aloud the second part of the instructions for Exercise **3B**.
- Ss complete the task with a partner. Walk around and listen to Ss' pronunciation. Help Ss pronounce the initial *st* sound correctly.

Application

- Direct Ss' attention to Exercise **3C**. Read the instructions aloud.
- Ss complete the exercise in pairs. Walk around and listen to Ss' pronunciation. Write any words on the board that Ss had trouble pronouncing. Point to the words. Say them aloud. Ask Ss to repeat.
- Focus Ss' attention on Exercise **3D**. Read the instructions aloud.
- Ask individual Ss to read the words aloud. Model the task. Ask a S to make up a question with the word *study* in it, for example: *Where do you study English?* Have another S answer the question, for example: *I study English at school.* Write the question and answer on the board and underline the initial *st* sound. Say the question and answer and have Ss repeat. Correct as needed.
- Ss complete the exercise individually. Walk around and help as needed.
- Tell Ss to ask their partner the questions they wrote. Walk around and listen to Ss' pronunciation as they ask and answer the questions.

Evaluation

- Direct Ss' attention to the lesson focus on the board.
- Ask individual Ss questions about Exercise **1**. For example: *Has Minh decided to visit his family? Is Trina going to go to Las Vegas? Has Trina already made reservations? Has she bought plane tickets yet? Did Trina win a free hotel room?* Make sure Ss answer the questions appropriately.
- Focus Ss' attention on the sentences in Exercise **3A**. Ask Ss to read the sentences aloud, being careful to pronounce the initial *st* sound correctly.
- Check off each part of the lesson focus as Ss demonstrate an understanding of what they have learned in the lesson.

3 **Pronunciation:** initial *st* sound

CLASS CD2 TK 8

A **Listen** to the initial *st* sound.

1. **St**udy English.
2. **St**art the computer.
3. Tell the **st**ory.
4. What **st**ate do you live in?
5. Go to the **st**ore.
6. **St**udents need to **st**udy.
7. Let's see the Salsa **St**arz.
8. **St**op procrastinating.

Listen again and repeat.

CLASS CD2 TK 9

B **Listen and repeat.** Then underline the initial *st* sound.

1. A Hi, <u>St</u>uart. I'm going to the <u>st</u>ore. What do you need?

   B Can you get me some <u>st</u>amps? It's the first of the month, and I have to pay bills.

   A Sure.

   B Thanks. I'll <u>st</u>art writing the checks now and <u>st</u>op procrastinating.

2. A Hello, <u>St</u>ephanie.

   B Hi, <u>St</u>eve. Are you <u>st</u>ill a <u>st</u>udent here?

   A Yes. I'm <u>st</u>udying appliance repair.

   B Really? Maybe you can fix my <u>st</u>ove when you're finished.

   A I hope so.

Talk with a partner. Compare your answers.

C **Talk** with a partner. Ask and answer the questions. Say the words with the initial *st* sound carefully.

1. How long have you studied at this school?
2. When you go to the store, what do you usually buy?
3. When did you move to this state?
4. When did you start working?

D **Write** five questions. Use the following words. Ask your partner the questions. Remember to pay attention to the initial *st* sound.

1. study: *(Answers will vary.)* _____
2. store: _____
3. start: _____
4. story: _____
5. student: _____

LESSON A
Listening

1 Before you listen

A What do you see?

B What is happening?

C What's the story?

Lesson objectives
- Introduce students to the topic
- Find out what students know about the topic
- Preview the unit by talking about the pictures
- Practice key vocabulary
- Practice listening skills

Warm-up and review

- Before class. Write today's lesson focus on the board.
  Lesson A:
  Saving and spending
- Begin class. Books closed. Direct Ss' attention to the lesson focus. Point to *Saving and spending*. Read the words aloud and have Ss repeat. Ask Ss what the words mean. Explain that these words are opposites. Remind Ss of the meanings of *lend* and *borrow*. Tell Ss that these words are opposites, too.
- Ask Ss to name ways of borrowing money, for example: *asking a friend, going to a bank, taking out a loan, using a credit card, buying in installments.*
- Ask Ss to name ways of saving money, such as: *opening a savings account, paying off credit cards each month, using cash to pay for items.*

Learner persistence *(individual work)*

- Ask your students questions about saving, such as: *Why is it important to save money? How much money do you save each month? What do you save money for? When do you borrow money?* By asking these questions, you can find out if Ss understand how to manage their finances. This might be a good opportunity to help Ss understand the advantages and disadvantages of buying on credit.

Presentation

- Books open. Direct Ss' attention to the pictures on page 84. Ask the question from Exercise **1A**: *What do you see?* Elicit and write on the board as much vocabulary as possible from the individual pictures: *car dealership, Big Summer Savings, customers, used cars.* Explain any unfamiliar words.

▼ **Teaching tip**
Ss may not understand the terms on the window sticker in Picture 2. If you have Ss who are familiar with cars, encourage them to explain these terms, to draw pictures on the board, or to translate these terms into languages their classmates understand. It would also be helpful to bring in auto magazines or car brochures to ask Ss to locate pictures of the items to help clarify meaning.

- Direct Ss' attention to the question in Exercise **1B**: *What is happening?* Read it aloud. Draw three vertical lines on the board, creating four columns. Write the headings *Picture 1, Picture 2, Picture 3,* and *Picture 4* above the columns. Ask Ss to say a few sentences about what is happening in each picture. Write their ideas in the corresponding column on the board.

▼ **Teaching tip**
Encourage Ss to be creative. At this point, there is no single correct story.

Practice

- Direct Ss' attention to the question in Exercise **1C**. In pairs, ask Ss to write a role play between Ken and his wife, Julie.
- Walk around and listen to Ss as they role play.
- Ask several pairs to perform their role play for the rest of the class.

▼ **Teaching tip**
In a role play, encourage Ss to avoid reading their lines. One way is to have Ss read a line silently, then look up, and say the line. This helps to encourage fluency and confidence in speaking.

▼ **Culture tip**
Write on the board and say *low-interest financing*. Explain that this means borrowing money to buy something, and paying the money back at low interest. Explain that *interest* is extra money you pay when you borrow money from a bank or another lender. Tell Ss that *low-interest* means not having to pay a lot of extra money and that *high-interest* means having to pay a lot of extra money. Point out that car dealers often offer their own financing, which is different from that of a bank rate, and that it is a good idea to compare financing before buying.

Presentation

- Books open. Direct Ss' attention to Exercise **2A**. Tell Ss to listen for the main idea. Read the instructions and questions aloud. Explain that after listening to the conversation, Ss will ask and answer questions in the exercise in pairs.
- Ask a S to read the questions in Exercise **2A** aloud. Tell Ss to listen for this information as the audio program is played or read.
- Class Audio CD2 track 10 Play or read the audio program (see audio script, page T-160).
- Ask Ss if they understood everything in the listening. Write any words on the board that Ss are unfamiliar with, and help Ss understand the meaning.

> **Teaching tip**
> There may be words in the conversation that are new to Ss. Read the audio script on page T-160 before class and write potentially difficult words on the board. You may wish to pre-teach these words before playing the audio program. You may also review these words after Ss have listened to the audio.

Practice

- Focus Ss' attention on Exercise **2B**. Read the instructions aloud. Guide Ss to listen and complete the chart.
- Class Audio CD2 track 10 Play or read the audio program (see audio script, page T-160).
- Ss complete the exercise individually. Repeat the audio program as needed. Write the numbers *1–6* on the board. Ask individual Ss to come to the board to write their answers.

Comprehension check

- Elicit answers from the Ss and write them on the board.
- Class Audio CD2 track 10 Play or read the audio program again (see audio script, page T-160). Ss listen and check their answers.

Learner persistence (individual work)

- Self-Study Audio CD track 25 Exercises **2A** and **2B** are recorded on the CD at the back of the Student's Book. Ss can listen to the CD at home for reinforcement and review. They can also listen to the CD for self-directed learning when class attendance is not possible.

Practice

- Focus Ss' attention on Exercise **3A**. Read the instructions aloud. Tell Ss that the story in this exercise is a summary of the conversation between Ken and Julie.

- Direct Ss' attention to the words in the word bank. Say each word and ask Ss to repeat. Correct Ss' pronunciation as needed and explain any unfamiliar words.
- Ss complete the exercise individually. Walk around and help as needed.
- Write the numbers *1–8* on the board. Ask individual Ss to come to the board to write their answers. Tell Ss to write only the words written on the blanks, not the entire sentences.
- Class Audio CD2 track 11 Play or read the audio program (see audio script, page T-160). Ss listen and check their answers. Repeat the audio program as needed.

Learner persistence (individual work)

- Self-Study Audio CD track 26 Exercise **3A** is recorded on the CD at the back of the Student's Book. Ss can listen to the CD at home for reinforcement and review. They can also listen for self-directed learning when class attendance is not possible.

> **Useful language**
> Read the Useful language box aloud. Write the word *credit* on the board. Ask Ss to say other phrases they know that have this word. Write the words on the board, such as: *credit card*, *credit report*, etc.

Application

- Focus Ss' attention on Exercise **3B**. Read the instructions aloud.
- Ss complete the exercise in pairs. Help as needed.
- Ask several pairs to ask and answer the questions for the class. Write responses to number 2 on the board and encourage Ss to discuss the pros and cons of buying on credit.

Evaluation

- Direct Ss' attention to the lesson focus on the board. Ask individual Ss to look at the pictures on page 84 to make sentences using the words from Exercise **3A**.
- Check off each part of the lesson focus as Ss demonstrate an understanding of what they have learned in the lesson.

More Ventures, Unit 7, Lesson A	
Workbook, 20–30 min.	
Add Ventures, 30–45 min.	www.cambridge.org/myresourceroom
Collaborative, 30–45 min.	
Student Arcade, time varies	www.cambridge.org/venturesarcade

Unit Goals	**Identify** spending habits
	Read about financial problems and solutions
	Give financial advice

2 Listen

STUDENT TK 25
CLASS CD2 TK 10

A Listen and answer the questions.

1. Who are the speakers?

2. What are they talking about?

STUDENT TK 25
CLASS CD2 TK 10

B Listen again. Complete the chart.

	How much / many?
1. cost of a new car	$27,500
2. cost of a car with tax and fees	$30,000
3. money in the savings account	less than $8,000
4. interest rate (%)	4%
5. months to pay	60 months
6. cost of a used car	$10,000

3 After you listen

A Read. Complete the story.

| afford | balance | cash | credit | debt | financing | interest | pay off |

Ken and his wife, Julie, are looking at cars. Ken wants to buy a new car that costs over $27,000. Julie thinks that they can't _____afford_____ to spend that much money.
1

The _____balance_____ in their savings account is less than $8,000. She's afraid of getting
2

into _____debt_____. But Ken says they can get _____financing_____ to help pay for the new
3   4

car. The _____interest_____ rate is low, and they can take five years to _____pay off_____ the
5   6

loan. Ken isn't worried about buying things on _____credit_____.
7

Julie disagrees. She suggests that they could buy a used car. She says her father never had a credit card. He always paid _____cash_____ for everything.
8

STUDENT TK 26
CLASS CD2 TK 11

Listen and check your answers.

B Talk with a partner. Ask and answer the questions.

1. What things do people often buy on credit?

2. Is it a good idea to buy things on credit? Why or why not?

☑ Listen for and identify numbers related to a purchase   **UNIT 7**   **85**

LESSON **B** Modals

1 Grammar focus: *could* and *should*

could for suggestions

You **could get** a smaller car and save money.

He **could keep** his money in a savings account.

should for advice

What **should** I do?

You **should open** a savings account.

Turn to page 145 for a complete grammar chart and explanation.

2 Practice

A Write. Complete the sentences. Use *could* or *should*.

1. **A** My rent is going up again. What should I do?

   B Here's my advice. You're a good tenant. I think you ____should____ talk to your landlord.

2. **A** I have to fix my credit. What should I do?

   B You ____should____ talk to a debt counselor. He can help you.

3. **A** Can you suggest a nice restaurant? It's my wife's birthday.

   B You ____could____ try Chao's – or how about Anita's?

4. **A** It's my niece's sixteenth birthday next week. What could I get her?

   B Why don't you get tickets to a concert? Or you ____could____ buy her a CD.

5. **A** That vocational school is very expensive. I can't afford it. Can you give me any advice?

   B Well, you're a good student. I think you ____should____ apply for a scholarship.

6. **A** I need a new car. Where do you suggest I look for one?

   B How about looking in the newspaper? Or you ____could____ look online.

> **USEFUL** LANGUAGE
>
> For suggestions, you can say:
>
> *Why don't you* + verb . . . ?
>
> *How about* + noun . . . ?
>
> *How about* + verb + *-ing* . . . ?

CLASS CD2 TK 12

Listen and check your answers. Then practice with a partner.

Warm-up and review

Before class: Write today's lesson focus on the board.

Lesson B:
could and *should*
Making suggestions, giving advice, and solving problems

- Books open. Begin class. Direct Ss to the pictures on page 84. Ask questions about Ken and Julie, such as: *What kind of car does Ken want to buy?* (an expensive new car.) *What kind of car does Julie want to buy?* (a cheaper used car.)

Presentation

Focus on meaning / personalize

- Books closed. Direct Ss' attention to the lesson focus on the board. Read it aloud.
- Ask Ss to think of one problem related to your school or class and write it on the board, for example: *Some students have trouble understanding people when they speak English. How can they improve their listening skills?*
- Write *could* on the board, and give a few suggestions to solve the problem, for example: *They could listen to the CD in the back of their Student's Book. They could ask native speakers to speak more slowly. They could learn five new words every day.*
- Elicit more suggestions. Write Ss' ideas on the board in note form: *listen to the CD, learn five new words every day.*
- Write the word *should* on the board and say: *We have several suggestions. Those Ss need your advice. What do you think they should do? Should they listen to the CD? Should they study more?*

Focus on form

- Books open. Direct Ss' attention to the charts in Exercise 1. Read aloud each statement and question. Ask Ss to repeat.
- Explain that modals like *could* and *should* never change form and are always followed by the base form of a verb. Explain that the word *could* is used to make a suggestion. It often highlights one of many options. Explain that *should* is used to give advice. *Should* is generally stronger than *could* and highlights one option.

Practice

- Focus Ss' attention on Exercise **2A**. Read the instructions aloud.
- Model the task. Ask two Ss to read the example question and answer to the class. Tell Ss to complete the exercise by filling in the blanks with either *could* or *should*.
- Ss complete the exercise individually. Walk around and help as needed.

Comprehension Check

- Focus Ss' attention on the second part of the instructions for Exercise **2A**. Read it aloud.
- Class Audio CD2 track 12 Play or read the complete audio program (see audio script, page T-160). Ss listen and check their answers.
- Ss practice saying the conversations with a partner. Listen to Ss' pronunciation.
- To check Ss' understanding, make general statements such as the ones below that make suggestions or give advice. Ss say *advice* or *suggestion*.

  Sophia always looks very tired. I think she should get more sleep. (advice)
  Michael wants to speak French. Maybe he could join a French club. (suggestion)
  Are you hungry? You should eat something. (advice)

LESSON B Modals

Presentation

- Direct Ss' attention to the pictures in Exercise **2B**. Ask Ss to look at Picture 1. Ask: *What's the problem?* Elicit an appropriate response, such as: *The car broke down.*
- Guide Ss to look at Picture 2. Ask: *What's the problem?* Elicit an appropriate response, such as: *The rent has gone up by $150.* Continue looking at each picture and have Ss describe the problem.

Practice

- Read the instructions aloud. Ask two Ss to read the example conversation aloud. Point out the cues for the conversation below each picture.
- Ss complete the exercise in pairs. Encourage Ss to give suggestions or advice for each problem. Walk around and help as needed.
- Read aloud the second part of the instructions for Exercise **2B**.
- Ask a S to read the example sentence aloud.
- Ss complete the exercise individually.

Comprehension check

- Write the numbers *1–6* on the board. Ask Ss to come to the board to write their sentences.
- Have other Ss read the sentences aloud. Ask Ss if the sentences are written correctly. Correct the sentences as needed.

Expansion activity (student pairs)

- Direct Ss' attention to the pictures on page 84. Tell Ss to imagine that Julie is having a conversation with one of her friends about the events taking place in the pictures.
- Ss in pairs. Tell partners that one S in the pair will be Julie and the other will be Julie's friend. Have pairs think of the conversation that Julie might be having with her friend.
- Model the activity. Ask Ss to brainstorm the first two sentences in the conversation, and write them on the board. For example:

  Julie: Ken wants to buy a new car, and it's so expensive! We can't afford to buy it.

  Friend: You could buy it on credit.

- Have pairs complete the conversation. Tell Ss that they don't have to write the entire conversation but that they can write down key words that will help them remember important parts of the conversation.
- Help as needed. Have Ss use the words from the word bank on page 85 in their conversations.
- Ask volunteers to role play their conversations.

Application

- Direct Ss' attention to Exercise **3A**. Read the instructions aloud.
- Write on the board: *spend money.* Ask Ss: *What do you spend money on?* Write their answers on the board, such as: *food, rent, gas.* Ask Ss: *What do you spend too much money on?* Write responses on the board.
- Read the sentences aloud in Exercise **3A**. Make sure Ss understand all the words in the sentences.
- Model the task. Say the first sentence. Ask the class for suggestions or advice. Write Ss' ideas on the board, for example: *Helene could shop at a cheaper supermarket.*
- Ss complete the exercise in small groups. Help as needed.
- Direct Ss' attention to Exercise **3B**. Read the instructions aloud.
- Have Ss share advice and suggestions with the class.

Expansion activity (small groups)

- **Materials needed** One copy of an advice column for each small group of Ss in your class.
- Read the problem aloud with the class. Make sure Ss understand all the words in the letter to the advice columnist.
- Ss in small groups. Tell Ss to respond to the letter in their groups. Ask them to think of suggestions and advice they could give. One person will write the group's response. Encourage Ss to use *could*, *should*, and the other phrases for suggestions and advice.
- When Ss are finished, ask one person from each group to read the letter of advice to the class.

Evaluation

- Direct Ss' attention to the lesson focus on the board.
- Books closed. Ask Ss to give examples of financial problems, such as: *I can't afford to pay my rent.* Ask different Ss to give suggestions or advice about the problems using *could* and *should*, for example: *You should talk to your landlord.*
- Check off each part of the lesson focus as Ss demonstrate an understanding of what they have learned in the lesson.

More Ventures, Unit 7, Lesson B	
Workbook, 20–30 min.	
Add Ventures, 30–45 min.	www.cambridge.org/myresourceroom
Collaborative, 30–45 min.	
Student Arcade, time varies	www.cambridge.org/venturesarcade

B Talk with a partner. Take turns. Read the problems. Make suggestions or give advice.

> **A** My car broke down.
> **B** You could take the bus, or you could ask someone for a ride.

1. "My car broke down."

2. "My rent is going up $150!"

3. "It's getting cold in here."

4. "I can't afford a new washing machine."

5. "These shoes look terrible."

6. "I don't have enough cash to pay for these groceries."

Write a suggestion or advice for each picture.

You could take the bus, or you could ask someone for a ride.
(Answers will vary.)

3 Communicate

A Work in a small group. Make suggestions or give advice.

- Helene spends too much money on food.
- Gregory spends too much money on clothes.
- Teresa spends too much money on rent.
- Youssef spends too much money on cell phone calls.

B Share your ideas with your classmates.

LESSON C Gerunds after prepositions

1 Grammar focus: questions and answers

Questions	Answers
What are you **thinking about** doing?	I'm **thinking about buying** a car.
What is she **afraid of**?	She's **afraid of losing** her job.
What are they **interested in** doing?	They're **interested in applying** for a loan.

Phrases gerunds often follow

afraid of	thank (someone) for
excited about	think about
happy about	tired of
interested in	worried about

gerund = base form
of verb + *-ing*

Turn to page 141 for a complete grammar chart and explanation.

2 Practice

A Write. Complete the sentences. Use gerunds.

1. I'm worried about ___*paying*___ interest on my credit card balance.
(pay)

2. Rob is afraid of ___*getting*___ into debt. He pays for everything with cash.
(get)

3. Have you thought about ___*opening*___ a checking account?
(open)

4. Elizabeth is happy about ___*finding*___ an apartment she can afford.
(find)

5. Elena is excited about ___*starting*___ classes at the community college.
(start)

6. I'm tired of ___*making*___ payments on my car.
(make)

7. Franco isn't interested in ___*applying*___ for a loan.
(apply)

8. Thank you for ___*lending*___ me money for school.
(lend)

9. We're thinking about ___*buying*___ a house.
(buy)

10. They were worried about ___*getting*___ a loan.
(get)

Listen and check your answers.

CLASS CD2 TK 13

Warm-up and review

Before class: Write today's lesson focus on the board.

Lesson C:
Gerunds after prepositions

- Books closed. Begin class. Ask a S volunteer to make a sentence that contains a gerund, for example: *I like getting up early*. Write it on the board and underline the gerund. Ask: *What is a gerund?* (a verb + *-ing* that is used as a noun.) Ask Ss to give examples of sentences using gerunds after *enjoy*, *like*, and *love*.

Presentation

Focus on meaning / personalize

- Books closed. Direct Ss' attention to the lesson focus on the board. Read it aloud. Write on the board: *I'm thinking about _____ ing*. Make a true statement about yourself, such as: *I'm thinking about taking a trip to (the Grand Canyon).*

- Explain that Ss will play a memory game. Point to *I'm thinking about _____ ing* on the board, and ask three S volunteers to each make a sentence about what they are thinking of doing. Then ask other S volunteers to repeat from memory what each of the three Ss said. For example: *Keiko is thinking about calling her sister in Japan. Svetlana is thinking about quitting her job.*

Focus on form

- Books open. Direct Ss' attention to the chart in Exercise 1. Read aloud each question. Ask Ss to repeat.

- Read aloud the statements in the chart. Ask Ss to repeat. Write this sentence on the board: *I'm thinking about getting a different job*. Ask:

What is the verb in the sentence? (am thinking.)
Which word is a preposition? (about.)
What follows a preposition – a noun or a verb? (a noun.)
Is "job" a noun? (Yes.)
Is "getting" a noun? (Yes.)
Is "getting" a gerund? (Yes.)
Explain that gerunds often follow prepositions.

Practice

- Direct Ss' attention to Exercise 2A. Read the instructions aloud.

- Model the task. Ask a S to read the example sentence aloud. Tell Ss to complete the exercise by filling in the blanks with the correct form of the verb that is below the blank line.

- Ss complete the exercise individually. Walk around and help as needed.

Comprehension check

- Read aloud the second part of the instructions for Exercise 2A.

- Write the numbers *1–10* on the board. Ask individual Ss to come to the board to write their answers.

- Class Audio CD2 track 13 Play or read the audio program (see audio script, page T-160). Ss listen and check their answers. Make corrections on the board as needed.

- Write the following prepositions on the board: *of, about, in, for*. Say the beginning of a sentence, stopping immediately after the verb. Ask Ss to provide the correct preposition, for example:

I'm excited _____. (about)
He is tired _____. (of)

- Say sentences like the following with correct and incorrect English. Ss indicate thumbs up if the sentence is correct English or thumbs down if the sentence is incorrect English.

I'm thinking about take a trip. (thumbs down)
Emily is interested in traveling around the world. (thumbs up)
I'm afraid of get into debt. (thumbs down)

LESSON C Gerunds after prepositions

Presentation

- Focus Ss' attention on the pictures in Exercise **2B**. Tell Ss that they will be writing a sentence about each picture.
- Direct Ss' attention to Picture 1 in Exercise **2B**. Ask Ss what they see. Elicit an appropriate response, such as: *The woman is happy. She is leaving the bank. She opened a checking account.*

▼ Culture tip
Explain the difference between a checking account and a savings account. Write the two types of accounts on the board. Explain to Ss that when you write checks, you spend the money that you have in the bank in your checking account; when you have a savings account, you save money in a bank and earn interest added to your savings.

Practice

- Read the instructions aloud.
- Model the task. Ask two Ss to read the example conversation to the class. Point to the cues below the pictures, and make sure Ss understand how to use them in their conversations.
- Ss complete the exercise in pairs. Walk around and help as needed.
- Ask several pairs to say the conversations for the rest of the class.

▼ Teaching tip
It might be helpful to emphasize that the *b* in *debt* is silent. Say the word and ask Ss to repeat.

- Read the instructions for the second part of Exercise **2B** aloud.
- Model the exercise. Ask a S to read the example sentence aloud.
- Ss complete the exercise individually. Walk around and help as needed.
- Ask individual Ss to write their sentences on the board.
- Ask different Ss to read aloud each sentence on the board. Ask: *Is this sentence correct?* Make corrections on the board as needed.

Expansion activity (small groups)

- **Materials needed** Old magazines with many pictures of people in them.
- Ss in small groups. Give each group a few magazines to look through. Have Ss find pictures of people who are happy, thinking about something, worried about something, interested in something, tired of something, or excited about something. Ask Ss to tear out pictures that fit these categories.
- Tell Ss to ask questions about the people in the pictures. Model the activity. Hold up a picture of a person who looks happy. Ask: *What's she happy about?* Elicit a response appropriate to the picture.
- Ss complete the exercise in small groups.

Application

- Direct Ss' attention to Exercise **3A**. Read the instructions aloud.
- Model the task. Ask two Ss to read the example conversation to the class.
- Divide Ss into small groups. Tell Ss to ask each other questions using the phrases in the word bank.
- Ss complete the exercise in small groups. Walk around and help as needed.
- Direct Ss' attention to Exercise **3B**. Read the instructions aloud.
- Ask Ss to share information they learned about their classmates.

Evaluation

- Direct Ss' attention to the lesson focus on the board. Have individual Ss look at the pictures on page 89 and make sentences using gerunds after prepositions.
- Check off each part of the lesson focus as Ss demonstrate an understanding of what they have learned in the lesson.

More Ventures, Unit 7, Lesson C	
Workbook, 20–30 min.	
Add Ventures, 30–45 min.	www.cambridge.org/myresourceroom
Collaborative, 30–45 min.	
Student Arcade, time varies	www.cambridge.org/venturesarcade

B Talk with a partner. Ask and answer questions.

> A What's she happy about?
> B She's happy about opening a checking account.

1. happy about / open a checking account

2. thinking about / buy a computer

3. worried about / be in debt

4. interested in / study auto mechanics

5. tired of / wait in line

6. excited about / buy a new car

Write a sentence about each picture.

She's happy about opening a checking account.
(Answers will vary.)

3 Communicate

A Work in a small group. Ask and answer questions.

| afraid of | excited about | happy about | responsible for |
| bad at | good at | interested in | tired of |

> A What are you afraid of?
> B I'm afraid of spending too much money.

B Share information about your classmates.

☑ Use gerunds after prepositions to ask and answer questions   **UNIT 7**   **89**

LESSON D Reading

1 Before you read

Look at the reading tip. Skim the magazine article. Answer the questions.

1. What problem did the people have?
2. How did they solve it?

2 Read

STUDENT TK 27
CLASS CD2 TK 14

Read the magazine article. Listen and read again.

One way to organize information is to give problems and solutions.

A Credit Card NIGHTMARE

Sun Hi and Joseph Kim got their first <u>credit card</u> a week after they got married. At first, they paid off the balance every month.

The couple's problems began after they bought a new house. They bought new furniture, a big-screen television, and two new computers. To pay for everything, they applied for more and more credit. Soon they had six different credit cards, and they were more than $18,000 in debt.

"It was a nightmare!" says Mrs. Kim. "The <u>interest rates</u> were 19 percent to 24 percent. Our <u>minimum payments</u> were over $750 a month. We both got second jobs, but it wasn't enough. I was so worried about paying off the debt, I cried all the time."

Luckily, the Kims found a solution. They met Dolores Delgado, a <u>debt counselor</u>. With her help, they looked at all of their living expenses and made a <u>family budget</u>. They combined their six credit card payments into one monthly payment with a lower interest rate. Now, their monthly budget for all living expenses is $3,400. Together they earn $3,900 a month. That leaves $500 for paying off their debt.

"We've cut up our credit cards," says Mr. Kim. "No more expensive furniture! In five years, we can pay off our debt. Now we know. Credit cards are dangerous!"

Warm-up and review

- Before class. Write today's lesson focus on the board.
  Lesson D:
  Read and understand "A Credit Card Nightmare"
  Practice new vocabulary
  Practice noun + noun combinations
- Begin class. Books closed. Direct Ss' attention to the words *credit card* in the lesson focus. Draw a vertical line on the board, creating two columns. Write *Good* and *Bad* above the columns. Ask Ss if they think buying items with a credit card is a good or a bad idea. Elicit appropriate responses. Write Ss' reasons in the corresponding column.
- Focus Ss' attention on the title on the board: "A Credit Card Nightmare." Ask Ss to define *nightmare,* or define the word for them. Have Ss guess what a credit card nightmare could be.

Presentation

- Books open. Focus Ss' attention on Exercise 1. Read the instructions aloud.

> Read the tip box aloud. Tell Ss that they are going to see an example of an article in which the author organized the information by telling the problem first and then giving a solution to the problem.

- Ask Ss if they know what the word *skim* means. If a S says *Yes,* ask him / her to explain the meaning to the class. If not, say: *To skim an article means to read it quickly and look for specific information.*
- Direct Ss' attention to the two questions in Exercise 1. Ask two Ss to read them aloud.
- Have Ss work on their own to skim the article. Then ask Ss to answer the two questions. Have Ss indicate where in the article they found the two answers.

Practice

- Read the instructions aloud for Exercise 2. Have Ss read the article silently before listening to the audio program.
- Class Audio CD2 track 14 Play or read the audio program and ask Ss to read along (see audio script, pages T-160–T-161). Repeat the audio program as needed.
- While Ss are listening and reading the article, ask them to underline any words they don't know. When the audio program is finished, have Ss write the new vocabulary words on the board.
- Point to each word on the board. Read it aloud. Ask Ss to repeat. Give a brief explanation of each word, or ask Ss who are familiar with the word to explain it. If Ss prefer to look up the new words in their dictionaries, allow them to do so.
- Encourage Ss to guess the meaning of each of the words from the context of the article. For example, if a S writes *budget* on the board, ask another S to read aloud the fourth paragraph of the article. Write the following equation on the board:

  $3,900 *(monthly income / salaries)*
  −500 *(payment each month for credit card debt)*
  $3,400 *(monthly budget for all living expenses)*
- Explain that a monthly budget is the amount of money a person or family has to spend each month.

Learner persistence *(individual work)*

- Self-Study Audio CD track 27 Exercise 2 is recorded on the CD at the back of the Student's Book. Ss can listen to the CD at home for reinforcement and review. They can also listen for self-directed learning when class attendance is not possible.

Comprehension check

- Direct Ss' attention to Exercise **3A**. Read the instructions aloud.
- Ask individual Ss to read the questions. Make sure that all Ss understand the questions.
- Have Ss work in pairs to ask and answer the rest of the questions with a partner.
- Ask several pairs to answer the comprehension questions for the rest of the class.

Presentation

- Focus Ss' attention on Exercise **3B**. Read the instructions for number 1 to the class.
- Have Ss find *credit card* in the first paragraph of the reading. Ask a S to read the sentence in which *credit card* first appears. Make sure that all Ss find *credit card* in sentence 1, underline it, and understand the task.
- Ss complete the exercise individually. Walk around and help as needed.
- Ss in pairs. Ask Ss to show each other where they underlined the words from number 1 of Exercise **3B**. Check that all Ss have underlined all the appropriate words.

Practice

- Direct Ss' attention to number 2 of Exercise **3B**. Read the instructions aloud.
- Focus Ss' attention on the first part of number 2. Model the task. Ask a S to read aloud the two-word combinations in number 1 of Exercise **3B**. Ask Ss if the first word in each combination is a noun or an adjective. (It is a noun.)
- Focus Ss' attention on the second part of number 2 of Exercise **3B**. Model the task. Ask a different S to read again the two-word combinations in number 1 of Exercise **3B**. Ask Ss if the second word in each combination is a noun or an adjective. (It is a noun.)
- Tell Ss that these are noun + noun combinations, or compound nouns. Explain that combining the nouns gives the words a particular meaning.
- Focus Ss' attention on number 3 of Exercise **3B** and read the instructions aloud. Model the task. Ask Ss which definition on the right side corresponds to *credit card*. Elicit: *letter "b."* Ask a S to read the definition aloud. Tell Ss to complete the exercise by writing the appropriate letters in the blanks.
- Ss complete the exercise individually. Help as needed.

Comprehension check

- Write the numbers *1–5* on the board. Ask individual Ss to write the letter of each of the answers for number 3 of Exercise **3B**. Correct as needed.

- Focus Ss' attention on number 4 of Exercise **3B**. Read the instructions aloud.
- Model the task. Ask Ss to brainstorm other noun + noun combinations they see in the community. Write them on the board. For example: *community center*, *fire station*, *senior citizen*, *adult education*.
- Ask Ss to work in small groups to continue brainstorming noun + noun combinations. Help as needed. Allow Ss to use dictionaries to look up words if they wish to do so.

Application

- Focus Ss' attention on Exercise **3C**. Read the instructions aloud.
- Ss complete the exercise in small groups. Help as needed.

Evaluation

- Direct Ss' attention to the lesson focus on the board.
- Books closed. Ask individual Ss to retell the main points of the article "A Credit Card Nightmare." Encourage Ss to talk about the problem and solution in the article.
- Ask Ss to tell you some of the noun + noun combinations that were used in this article. If Ss can't remember some of the combinations, write on the board the first word of the phrases from number 1 of Exercise **3B**. Ask Ss to think of the second noun to complete the two-word combinations.
- Check off each part of the lesson focus as Ss demonstrate an understanding of what they have learned in the lesson.

Learner persistence (individual, pairs)

- You may wish to assign Extended Reading Worksheets from the *Online Teacher's Resource Room* for Ss to complete outside of class. The purpose of these worksheets is to encourage Ss to read for pleasure in English outside of the English class. The worksheets can also be assigned as extended reading in class.

More Ventures, Unit 7, Lesson D	
Workbook, 20–30 min.	
Add Ventures, 30–45 min.	
Collaborative, 30–45 min.	www.cambridge.org/myresourceroom
Extended Reading and worksheet, 45–60 min.	
Student Arcade, time varies	www.cambridge.org/venturesarcade

3 After you read

A Check your understanding.

1. When did Mr. and Mrs. Kim get their first credit card?
2. When did their problems begin?
3. How did they pay for everything?
4. Mrs. Kim says, "It was a nightmare!" What does she mean?
5. Who is Dolores Delgado, and how did she help the Kims?
6. Do you think the Kims will have financial problems in the future? Why or why not?

B Build your vocabulary.

1. Find these words in the reading, and underline them.

credit card	family budget	minimum payments
debt counselor	interest rates	

2. Work with a partner. Circle the correct answers.

   1. Look at the words in Exercise B1. They are compound nouns. In each of the two-word combinations, the first word is:

      (a.) a noun   b. an adjective

   2. Look at the words again. The second word is:

      (a.) a noun   b. an adjective

3. Match each compound noun with its meaning.

   1. credit card _b_
   2. interest rate _d_
   3. minimum payment _c_
   4. debt counselor _e_
   5. family budget _a_

   a. a spending plan that a family makes for itself
   b. a small plastic card that allows you to buy something now and pay for it later
   c. the smallest payment you can make each month on a credit card
   d. the rate – percentage – of interest that you must pay each month on a credit card balance
   e. a person who helps you solve financial problems

4. Work with your classmates. Write other *noun* + *noun* combinations.

   (Answers will vary.) _____ _____

C Talk with your classmates. Ask and answer the questions.

1. How many credit cards do you have? What interest rate do you pay?
2. Do you think credit cards are helpful or harmful? Why?
3. Do you think a family budget is important? Why or why not?

LESSON E Writing

1 Before you write

A **Talk** with a partner. Look at the picture. What is the problem? What do you suggest?

B **Read** the letter from a newspaper advice column.

THE MONEY MAN

Dear Money Man,

   I recently got a new job in a downtown office. I need to look nice every day. I've never worked in an office before, and I don't have the right clothes. Most of the women wear suits to work. How can I get a new wardrobe without spending my entire salary? Can you give me advice?

Not Clothes Crazy

Work with a partner. Answer the questions.

1. What is the woman's problem?
2. What do you suggest?

- Write a letter of advice
- Introduce *first*, *second*, *third*, and *finally* to list ideas in order

Warm-up and review

- Before class. Write today's lesson focus on the board.
  Lesson E:
  Write a letter that gives advice about saving money
  Use first, second, third, and finally to list your ideas in order
- Begin class. Books closed. Focus Ss' attention on the words *saving money* in the lesson focus. Ask Ss to brainstorm some ways to save money. Write their ideas on the board, for example: *cook at home instead of eating at restaurants, get a job that pays more money, shop at discount stores.*

Presentation

- Books open. Focus Ss' attention on the picture in Exercise **1A**. Ask: *What do you see?* Elicit appropriate responses.
- Read the instructions aloud for Exercise **1A**.
- Ss discuss the picture and offer suggestions in pairs. Walk around and help as needed.
- Ask two pairs to answer the questions for the rest of the class.

Practice

- Direct Ss' attention to Exercise **1B**. Read the instructions aloud. Ask Ss if they know what an advice column is. If you did the expansion activity with advice columns in Lesson B, remind Ss that people write letters to advice columnists telling them their problems, and then they look for a response to their letters in the newspaper.
- Focus Ss' attention on the title of the advice column. Have a S read the title aloud. Ask Ss why they think the advice columnist is called *Money Man*.

▼ **Culture tip**
Focus Ss' attention on the picture in the advice column. Ask Ss who they think it is. Tell Ss that there are several well-known advice columnists. *Dear Abby* is one of the most well known. The columnist's picture is often featured in this type of article. Ask Ss where they can find advice columns and what people usually ask advice about. Encourage Ss to clip advice columns from newspapers and magazines and to share them with classmates.

- Ask Ss to read the advice column silently. Guide Ss to underline any words they don't know. Write the words on the board. Encourage Ss to use context clues to guess the meaning of each new word.
- Focus Ss' attention on the name *Not Clothes Crazy* in the signature line. Explain that letter writers often prefer to be anonymous, since they don't want other people to know their problems. Tell Ss that people often think of a name that describes their problem or situation.
- Ask Ss what they think *Not Clothes Crazy* means. Elicit an appropriate response, or tell Ss if they don't know, for example: *She's not crazy about clothes. She doesn't like expensive clothes that much.*

Comprehension check

- Direct Ss' attention to the second part of the instructions for Exercise **1B**, and read it aloud.
- Pairs ask and answer the questions. Remind Ss that they can use the modal *could* when giving suggestions to the letter writer, for example: *She could borrow a suit from a friend.* Help as needed.

Expansion activity (individual, whole group)

- Ask Ss to brainstorm money problems for which they need advice. Write Ss' ideas on the board, for example: *I don't have enough money to pay my rent. I've worked at my job without getting a raise for two years. My landlord is going to raise the rent. I need new clothes for a job interview. I can't pay my doctor's bills.*
- Tell Ss to choose a problem on the board or to think of a different one. Ask them to write a letter to *Money Man* asking for advice about their problem. Encourage Ss to describe the problem and end the letter by asking for advice, using the letter in Exercise **1B** as a guide.
- Ss complete the activity individually. Walk around and help as needed.
- Ask volunteers to read their letters aloud. Invite the class to offer suggestions to the letter writer, and write the suggestions on the board.
- Ask Ss to post their letters around the room. Copy the suggestions from the board onto poster paper and display the suggestions, especially if they reflect real issues and solutions that might affect Ss.

Presentation

- Direct Ss' attention to Exercise **1C** and read the instructions aloud.
- Tell Ss that this is the answer that the advice columnist wrote back to *Not Clothes Crazy*.
- Ask Ss to read the response to the letter silently.

> Read the tip box aloud. Tell Ss that sequence words such as *first*, *second*, *third*, and *finally* are used to organize ideas and put them in time order. Ask Ss to underline these words in the letter. Have Ss brainstorm other times when ordinal numbers are used. Write Ss' responses on the board, for example: *dates (November first)*, *street numbers (Second Street)*, etc.

Practice

- Direct Ss' attention to the second part of Exercise **1C**. Read the instructions aloud. Encourage Ss to find the four suggestions that *Money Man* makes to *Not Clothes Crazy*.
- Ss complete the exercise with a partner. Walk around and help as needed.
- Ask several pairs to answer the question for the rest of the class.

Application

- Direct Ss' attention to Exercise **2**. Read the instructions aloud. Have Ss look at the picture. Tell Ss that they are going to read a letter that the father in the picture wrote to *Money Man*.
- Ask Ss to read the letter silently. When they are finished, ask: *Who wrote the letter?* (Fast-Food Dad.) *Why does he call himself this name?* (Because his family eats at fast-food restaurants three or four times a week.) *What's the problem?* (The family can't afford to eat at restaurants this often.) *Why does the family always eat at fast-food restaurants?* (Because the parents work full-time, and they're too tired to cook after work.)
- Tell Ss to think of a response to write to *Fast-Food Dad*. Encourage them to use the response in Exercise **1C** as a guide.
- Ss complete the exercise individually. Walk around and help as needed.

Learner persistence (individual work)

- If you have Ss who have difficulty writing, sit with them and help them as the other Ss are writing. Encourage the Ss to make notes of their ideas before writing the letter. If more proficient writers finish early, ask them to sit with the Ss who need help with their writing.

Comprehension check

- Direct Ss' attention to Exercise **3A**. Read the instructions aloud. Ask a S to read the three checklist items to the class.
- Model the task. Direct Ss' attention to the example paragraph in Exercise **1C**. Ask Ss to identify all the checklist items in this paragraph (*The problem is that "Not Clothes Crazy" thinks she has to spend all her money on clothes for her job. The "Money Man" gives four suggestions in his letter of advice. He uses words like "first" and "second" in his letter to list his suggestions.*)
- Ss complete the exercise individually. Walk around and help as needed. If any S checked *No* for one or more of the checklist items, ask the S to revise the paragraph to include the missing items. Read the S's paragraph to make sure that all the checklist items have been included.

Evaluation

- Focus Ss' attention on Exercise **3B**. Read the instructions aloud. This exercise asks Ss to work with a partner to peer-correct their writing. Reading aloud enables the writer to review his or her own writing. Reading to a partner allows the writer to understand the need to write clearly for an audience.
- Ss complete the exercise in pairs. Walk around and help as needed.
- Have several volunteers read their letters to the class. Ask other Ss to comment on suggestions and advice given in the letter.
- Direct Ss' attention to the lesson focus on the board.
- Check off each part of the lesson focus as Ss demonstrate an understanding of what they have learned in the lesson.

More Ventures, Unit 7, Lesson E	
Workbook, 20–30 min.	
Add Ventures, 30–45 min.	www.cambridge.org/myresourceroom
Collaborative, 30–45 min.	

C **Read** the answer from the Money Man.

> **Dear Not Clothes Crazy,**
>
> It's important to look nice at your job, but you don't need to spend all your money on clothes. I have a few suggestions. First, why don't you buy a black suit with a skirt, jacket, and pants? Then wear a different blouse and jewelry every day for a different look. Second, you could shop at thrift stores. They often have excellent used clothes at very cheap prices. Third, how about talking to the other women in your office? They can tell you about good places to shop. Finally, you should make a monthly budget and follow it carefully. Following a budget is the best way to manage your money.
>
> **Money Man**

> Use words like *first*, *second*, *third*, and *finally* to list your ideas.

Work with a partner. What does the Money Man suggest?

2 Write

Read the letter. Write an answer. Start with the problem and write two or more suggestions. Use Exercises 1A, 1B, and 1C to help you.

> **Dear Money Man,**
>
> My wife and I have three young children. We both work full-time. When we come home from work, we are very tired and don't want to cook. We eat in fast-food restaurants three or four times a week. It's very expensive. Last night, the bill was $44! How can we save money on dinner?
>
> **Fast-Food Dad**

3 After you write

A **Check** your writing.

	Yes	No
1. I started with the problem.	☐	☐
2. I wrote two or more suggestions.	☐	☐
3. I used words like *first* and *second* to list my suggestions.	☐	☐

B **Share** your writing with a partner.

1. Take turns. Read your letter to a partner.
2. Comment on your partner's letter. Ask your partner a question about the letter. Tell your partner one thing you learned.

LESSON F Another view

1 Life-skills reading

TOWN BANK — CHECKING ACCOUNTS

Choose the plan that's right for you!

	Regular Checking	Premium Checking
Monthly Service Fee	$8	$12
Minimum Daily Balance (to waive the monthly service fee)	$1,000	$5,000
Earn Interest	No	Yes
ATM and Bank Card	Free	Free
Free Checks	No	Yes
Free Internet Banking	Yes	Yes
Free Internet Bill Paying	No	Yes
Free Money Orders and Traveler's Checks	No	Yes

A Read the questions. Look at the bank brochure. Fill in the answer.

1. What does the Regular Checking plan offer?
   - Ⓐ a free bank card
   - Ⓑ free checks
   - Ⓒ free money orders
   - Ⓓ none of the above

2. What does the Premium Checking plan offer?
   - Ⓐ a free ATM card
   - Ⓑ free Internet bill paying
   - Ⓒ free traveler's checks
   - ● all of the above

3. With Premium Checking, how much do you need in your account to avoid a monthly service fee?
   - Ⓐ $0
   - Ⓑ $12
   - Ⓒ $1,000
   - ● $5,000

4. Which kind of checking account offers free Internet banking?
   - Ⓐ Premium Checking
   - Ⓑ Regular Checking
   - ● both *a* and *b*
   - Ⓓ neither *a* nor *b*

B Talk with your classmates. Ask and answer the questions.

1. Do you have a checking account? Do you pay a monthly fee? What services does your bank offer you?

2. Which of the accounts from Town Bank do you think is better? Why?

Warm-up and review

- Before class. Write today's lesson focus on the board.

  Lesson F:
  Compare checking accounts
  Review unit vocabulary and grammar
  Complete the self-assessment

- Begin class. Books closed. If possible, bring some bank brochures to class and show them to Ss. Explain that these are called *brochures*.

- Review vocabulary from the unit. Ask Ss to tell you some of the words they learned about money and finances. Write Ss' ideas on the board, for example: *balance, cash, credit card, debt, financing, interest, checks*.

Learner persistence *(whole group)*

- Making class relevant to the lives of Ss is important in order to keep learners involved. Many Ss will have checking accounts and know how to write checks; however, there may be some Ss who do not. If possible, create a blank check template with blanks for the date, name of the payee, amount, memo and signature. Create a fake name, address, checking account, and bank routing number. Pass out the blank checks to Ss. Pair Ss who are unfamiliar with writing checks with Ss who are familiar with the process. Have Ss work together to write out the checks. Confirm that Ss have written the checks correctly. Remind Ss always to keep a record of their checks and an accurate balance.

Presentation

- Books open. Direct Ss' attention to the chart in Exercise 1. Tell Ss that this is an example of a brochure from a bank. Have a S read aloud the title and subheading of the brochure. Ask Ss to skim the chart and underline any unfamiliar words. Invite Ss to write the new words on the board.

- Point to each word on the board and read it aloud. Have Ss repeat.

- Ask if any Ss can explain the meaning of the words on the board. Allow Ss to use dictionaries.

- Invite eight Ss to read aloud each of the categories in the chart. Have a class discussion about the differences between the two checking accounts. Ask: *Which account has a cheaper monthly service fee?* (Regular checking.) *How much do the ATM and Bank Card cost in both accounts?* (They are free.) *Which account includes free checks?* (Premium checking.)

Practice

- Direct Ss' attention to Exercise **1A** and read the instructions aloud. This task helps prepare Ss for standardized-type tests they may have to take. Make sure that Ss understand the task. Have Ss individually scan for and fill in the answers.

Comprehension check

- Check answers with the class. Make corrections as needed.

Application

- Direct Ss' attention to Exercise **1B**. Read the instructions aloud. Ask two Ss to read the questions to the class. Make sure that Ss understand the meaning of each question.

- Have pairs ask and answer the questions. Walk around and help as needed.

Community building *(whole group)*

- Ask Ss which bank they think is the best one in their community. Encourage them to give reasons for thinking this bank is the best. Ss can help one another learn about good places in the community to do their banking by talking to other Ss in the class.

Expansion activity *(whole group)*

- Encourage numeracy skills and life-skills practice by balancing an imaginary checkbook. Draw a model page on the board from a checking account record book. Ask Ss to practice balancing a checking account. Read figures to the Ss and have them calculate the sums. Stop when Ss realize that there is no money left in the account. For example, write $700.00 in the balance column. Tell Ss to deduct $20.00 for transportation. Then add $200.00 for a paycheck, deduct $100.00 for food, $300.00 for rent, etc. Continue adding and subtracting. Encourage Ss to suggest subtractions and additions until they reach zero or less.

Warm-up and review

- Books closed. Write two sentences on the board. *I get tired. I take a break.* Then write _____ *dressed* and _____ *a bus* and have Ss guess whether you use *get* or *take* in front of each.

  Once Ss have guessed the correct answers, elicit complete answers from Ss utilizing each form on the board, for example: *I get dressed at 8 o'clock each morning.*

Presentation

- Books open. Direct Ss' attention to the grammar chart in **2A**. Read the *get* and *take* collocations aloud. Ask Ss to repeat.

- Explain that a *collocation* consists of two words that have special meaning when they are together. Write *get dressed* on the board. Say the words and have Ss repeat. Explain that *get dressed* means to put on clothes. Write *take notes* on the board. Say the words and have Ss repeat. Explain that *take notes* means to write notes about what happens during a class or meeting.

Practice

- Books open. Direct Ss' attention to the instructions in **2A**. Read the instructions aloud. Ask two Ss to read aloud the first example dialog: *Do you get sick very often? No, I hardly ever get sick.* Ask two Ss to read aloud the second dialog: *Have you taken a vacation recently? Yes, I have. I took a vacation to Florida last year.* Ask Ss what the collocation is in the first dialog (*get sick*). Ask Ss what the collocation is in the second dialog (*take a vacation*).

- Ss complete the activity in pairs. Review the correct answers with the class.

- Direct Ss' attention to the instructions in **2B**. Read the instructions aloud. Ask a S to read the example sentences. Ss complete the activity in pairs. Encourage each S to share a few sentences about a person in their group.

Expansion activity (group discussion)

- Write on the board: *Is it a good idea to take a vacation? Why or why not?* Write down Ss' answers on the board. If you have time, discuss additional questions, such as: *What do you like to take pictures of? How often do you take a nap during the week?*

Evaluation

- Before asking students to turn to the self-assessment on page 139, do a quick review of the unit. Have Ss turn to Lesson A. Ask the class to talk about what they remember about this lesson. Prompt Ss, if necessary, with questions, for example: *What are the conversations about on this page? What vocabulary is in the pictures?* Continue in this manner to review each lesson quickly.

- **Self-assessment** Read the instructions for Exercise **3**. Ask Ss to turn to the self-assessment page and complete the unit self-assessment. The self-assessments are also on the *Online Teacher's Resource Room*. If you prefer to collect the assessments and save them as part of each S's portfolio assessment, print out the unit self-assessment from the *Resource Room*, ask students to complete it, and collect and save it.

- If Ss are ready, administer the unit test on pages T-180–T-181 of this Teacher's Edition (or on the Assessment Audio CD / CD-ROM).

More Ventures, Unit 7, Lesson F	
Workbook, 20–30 min.	
Add Ventures, 30–45 min.	www.cambridge.org/myresourceroom
Collaborative, 30–45 min.	

2 Grammar connections: collocations with *get* and *take*

Use *get* with adjectives and some nouns.	Use *take* with other nouns.
get dressed	take a bus / a train / a taxi / a plane
get engaged / married / divorced	take notes / a test / a class
get lost / confused	take a break / a nap
get sick / better	take a bath / a shower
get upset / nervous / tired	take a vacation / a trip
get a job / laid off / fired	take pictures / photos

A **Talk** with a partner. Point to a circle. Your partner asks a question using *get* or *take*. Answer the question. Take turns.

> **A** Do you get sick very often?
> **B** No, I don't. I hardly ever get sick.

> **A** Have you taken a vacation recently?
> **B** Yes, I have. I took a vacation to Florida last year.

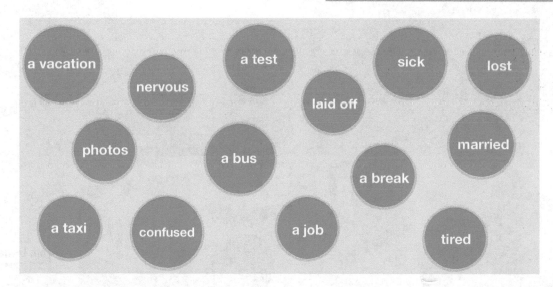

B **Share** information about your partner.

> Manuel doesn't get sick very often.

> Anton took a vacation last year. He went to Florida.

3 Wrap up

Complete the **Self-assessment** on page 139.

LESSON **A**
Listening

1 **Before you listen**

A What do you see?

B What is happening?

C What's the story?

Warm-up and review

- Before class. Write today's lesson focus on the board.

  Lesson A:
  Employment

- Begin class. Books closed. Direct Ss' attention to the lesson focus. Point to *employment.* Say the word aloud. Have Ss repeat. Ask Ss what they think of when they hear the word *employment.* Write their ideas on the board, for example: *jobs, work, occupations, salary.*

- Ask: *What are some ways that people hear about jobs?* Elicit appropriate responses, such as: *from friends, relatives, the newspaper, the Internet, on store windows, on bulletin boards.* Ask Ss what types of jobs they might be interested in.

Community building (whole group)

- Write *job interview* on the board. Say the words aloud and have Ss repeat. Ask Ss to share stories of job interviews they've had. Invite Ss to suggest *dos* and *don'ts* of interviewing for a job, for example: *Do dress nicely. Don't chew gum. Do have a typed résumé. Don't avoid eye contact.*

▼**Teaching tip**
Asking Ss to start thinking about job interviews will prepare them for later discussions in the unit; it will also help some Ss reach their job goals.

Presentation

- Books open. Set the scene. Direct Ss' attention to the first picture on page 96. Ask the question in Exercise **1A**: *What do you see?* Elicit and write on the board as much vocabulary as possible about all four pictures. Explain any unfamiliar words.

▼**Teaching tip**
Before class, review the audio script for Exercise **2A** on page 97 in the Student's Book. There are several words relating to office equipment and interviews that Ss will hear on the audio in this lesson and that are pictured on this page. You may want to elicit and pre-teach this vocabulary, for example: *personnel manager, resume, office machines, computer, fax machine, scanner, copying machine,* etc.

- Direct Ss' attention to the question in Exercise **1B**: *What is happening?* Read it aloud. Divide the class into four groups.

- Assign each group one of the pictures from the story. Ask group members to discuss what is happening in their groups' picture. Walk around the room and elicit full sentences from each group, for example: *Tony is sending a fax. Tony is writing his resume.*

- Tell each group to share their answers with the class.

Practice

- Read aloud the question in Exercise **1C**: *What's the story?* Ask each group to combine what their classmates described happening in each picture to create a story. Encourage them to add their own details. Ask each group to choose one student to write down the group's story.

- Walk around the room and ensure Ss understand the activity. Help each group as needed.

- Ask each group to choose a reader. The reader from each group shares the group's story with the class. Encourage Ss to compare the similarities and differences between the groups' stories.

Presentation

- Books open. Direct Ss' attention to Exercise **2A**. Ask Ss to listen for the main idea. Read the instructions aloud. Explain that after listening to the conversation, Ss will ask and answer questions in the exercise in pairs.
- Ask a S to read the questions in Exercise **2A** aloud. Tell Ss to listen for this information as the audio program is played or read.
- Class Audio CD2 track 15 Play or read the audio program (see audio script, page T-161).
- Ask Ss if they understood everything in the listening. Write any unfamiliar words on the board, and help Ss understand the meaning.
- Elicit answers to the questions.
- Focus Ss' attention on Exercise **2B**. Read the instructions aloud. Have Ss read the chart with information about Tony. Explain any unfamiliar words.
- Ask Ss to create questions with the words in the *Topic* column in the chart. Write the questions on the board, for example: *What job is he applying for? What does he want to do? What is his home country? Where was he born? What is his current job? Where is he working?*, etc.

▼ **Teaching tip**
Correct question formation often continues to pose problems for Ss. Whenever possible, take the opportunity to encourage Ss to practice forming questions.

- Class Audio CD2 track 15 Play or read the audio program (see audio script, page T-161). Guide Ss to listen for details about Tony to complete the chart. Model the task. Pause the program after Mr. Leong says: *I understand you're interested in the job of shipping-and-receiving clerk.* Ask: *What job is Tony applying for?* Elicit the correct response. Point to where *shipping-and-receiving clerk* is written in the chart. Tell Ss to listen and complete the chart.
- Elicit answers from Ss and write them on the board.
- Class Audio CD2 track 15 Play or read the audio program again (see audio script, page T-161). Ss listen and check their answers.

Learner persistence (individual work)

- Self-Study Audio CD track 28 Exercises **2A** and **2B** are recorded on the CD at the back of the Student's Book. Ss can listen to the CD at home for reinforcement and review. They can also listen to the CD for self-directed learning when class attendance is not possible.

Practice

- Focus Ss' attention on Exercise **3A**. Tell Ss that the story in this exercise is a summary of the conversation they heard in the audio program.
- Direct Ss' attention to the words in the word bank. Say each word aloud. Ask Ss to repeat. Explain any unfamiliar words.
- Ss complete the exercise individually. Walk around and help as needed.

Comprehension check

- Class Audio CD2 track 16 Play or read the audio program (see audio script, page T-161). Ss listen and check their answers. Repeat the audio program as needed.
- Write the numbers *1–7* on the board. Ask individual Ss to come to the board to write their answers.

Learner persistence (individual work)

- Self-Study Audio CD track 29 Exercise **3A** is recorded on the CD at the back of the Student's Book. Ss can listen to the CD at home for reinforcement and review. They can also listen for self-directed learning when class attendance is not possible.

Application

- Focus Ss' attention on Exercise **3B**. Read the instructions aloud.
- Ss complete the exercise in pairs. Walk around and help as needed.
- Ask several pairs to ask and answer the questions for the rest of the class.

Evaluation

- Direct Ss' attention to the lesson focus on the board. Ask Ss to look at the pictures on page 96 and to make sentences using words from Exercise **3A**.
- Check off the lesson focus as Ss demonstrate an understanding of what they have learned in the lesson.

More Ventures, Unit 8, Lesson A	
Workbook, 15–30 min.	
Add Ventures, 30–45 min. **Collaborative,** 30–45 min.	www.cambridge.org/myresourceroom
Student Arcade, time varies	www.cambridge.org/venturesarcade

Unit Goals
Identify questions and answers in a job interview
Recognize and produce key elements in a thank-you letter for a job interview
Recognize occupations in which there is job growth

2 Listen

STUDENT TK 28
CLASS CD2 TK 15

A **Listen** and answer the questions.

1. Who are the speakers?   2. What are they talking about?

STUDENT TK 28
CLASS CD2 TK 15

B **Listen again.** Complete the chart with information about Tony.

Topic	Tony's answers
1. job he is applying for	*shipping-and-receiving clerk*
2. native country	*Peru*
3. current job	*teacher's assistant*
4. strengths	*responsible, reliable*
5. shift he prefers	*day shift*

3 After you listen

A **Read.** Complete the story.

background   degree   employed   gets along   personnel   reliable   strengths

> Tony has been working as a teacher's assistant for about a year. He is also going to college part-time to get a _____degree_____ in accounting. Right now, Tony is at a job
> 1
> interview with Mr. Leong, the _____personnel_____ manager.
> 2
> Mr. Leong asks about Tony's _____background_____. Tony says he is from Peru and has
> 3
> been living in the United States for two years. Next, Mr. Leong asks about Tony's
> work experience, and Tony says that now he is _____employed_____ at a school. Finally,
> 4
> Mr. Leong asks about Tony's personal _____strengths_____. Tony says he is responsible and
> 5
> _____realiable_____, and he _____gets along_____ with everybody. Mr. Leong says he will contact
> 6   7
> Tony next week.

STUDENT TK 29
CLASS CD2 TK 16

Listen and check your answers.

B **Talk** with a partner. Ask and answer the questions.

Have you ever had a job interview? What happened?

☑ Listen for and identify an applicant's answers to questions in a job interview   **UNIT 8   97**

LESSON B Present perfect continuous

1 Grammar focus: questions and statements

Questions

| Have you **been living** here **for** a long time? |
| Has Tony **been working** here **for** a long time? |

| How long **have** you **been looking** for a job? |
| How long **has** Tony **been working** as a teacher's assistant? |

Short answers

| Yes, I **have.** | No, I **haven't.** |
| Yes, he **has.** | No, he **hasn't.** |

Since October.
For about a year.

Statements

I've **been waiting for** a long time.

Lida **has been waiting since** 2:00.

We've **been waiting all** morning.

Time words
for (a long time)
since (2:00)
all (morning)

USEFUL LANGUAGE

Use *since* with specific times.
Since 2011.
Use *for* with periods of time.
For two months.

Turn to page 144 for a complete grammar chart and explanation.

2 Practice

A **Write.** Complete the sentences. Use the present perfect continuous.

1. **A** How long ___*has*___ Talia ___*been practicing*___ for her driving test?
   (practice)
   B For about three months.

2. **A** ___*Have*___ you ___*been working*___ here for a long time?
   (work)
   B No, I haven't. I started six days ago.

3. **A** How long ___*has*___ Yin ___*been looking*___ for a job?
   (look)
   B Since last year.

4. **A** ___*Has*___ Mr. Rivera ___*been interviewing*___ people all day?
   (interview)
   B Yes, he has.

5. **A** How long ___*have*___ you ___*been waiting*___ to get an interview?
   (wait)
   B Since March.

6. **A** How long ___*have*___ they ___*been going*___ to night school?
   (go)
   B All year.

Listen and check your answers. Then practice with a partner.

CLASS CD2 TK 17

Lesson objectives
- Introduce the present perfect continuous
- Ask and answer *How long* and *Yes / No* questions with the present perfect continuous

Warm-up and review

Before class: Write today's lesson focus on the board.

Lesson B:
Present perfect continuous
How long? questions
Yes / No questions

- Books open. Begin class. Direct Ss' attention to the pictures on page 96. Ask questions about the pictures, such as: *Where is Tony in the first picture?* (at an elementary school.) *What's his job?* (teaching assistant.) *How long has he been working there?* (a year.) *Do you remember some of Tony's strengths?* (reliable, meets deadlines, gets along with everyone.)

Presentation

Focus on meaning / personalize

- Books closed. Direct Ss' attention to the lesson focus on the board. Read it aloud.

▼**Useful language**

Read the Useful language box aloud. Remind Ss that we use *for* for a period of time and *since* for the starting point. Give an example from your life, for example: *I have been living here for four years. I have been living here since 2009.*

Divide the board into two columns with *Point in time* and *Length of time* as headings.

Write the time phrases in the appropriate columns. Explain that the sentences talk about an action that started in the past and continues to now, and because of this, they use the present perfect continuous.

<u>Point in time</u>   <u>Length of time</u>
since 2009   for four years

- Ask three Ss *How long?* questions, such as: *How long have you been living here? How long have you been studying in this school?* Elicit answers and write the time phrases in the appropriate columns on the board.

Focus on form

- Books open. Direct Ss' attention to the Questions and Short answers charts in Exercise **1**. Read aloud the questions and short answers. Ask Ss to repeat. Direct Ss' attention to the Statements chart. Read aloud each statement. Ask Ss to repeat. Explain that all the sentences are in the present perfect continuous form. Remind Ss that the present perfect continuous is used to talk about actions that started in the past, continue to now, and will probably continue in the future.

Teacher's notes

1. The word *all* can be used before most time words, such as *all day, all year,* and *all morning,* and are usually used with the present perfect continuous, for example: *I have been working all day.*

2. Some verbs, like *know,* are rarely used in the continuous, such as: *I'm knowing her for a year.* or *I've been knowing her for a year. Know* describes a state, which is a condition or situation that exists, not an action. Other common non-continuous verbs are *like, want, believe,* and *have.*

Practice

- Focus Ss' attention on Exercise **2A**. Read the instructions aloud.
- Model the task. Ask two Ss to read aloud the example question and answer. Guide Ss to complete the exercise by filling in the blanks with the present perfect continuous form of the verb that is under each blank.
- Ss complete the exercise individually. Help as needed.

Comprehension check

- Direct Ss' attention to the second part of the instructions in Exercise **2A**. Read it aloud.
- Class Audio CD2 track 17 Play or read the audio program (see audio script, page T-161). Ss listen and check their answers. Repeat the audio program as needed.
- Write the numbers *1–6* on the board. Ask individual Ss to come to the board to write only the answers. Have other Ss read aloud the complete questions and answers. Correct as needed.
- Tell Ss to practice asking and answering the questions in pairs.

LESSON B Present perfect continuous

Presentation
- Direct Ss' attention to the pictures in Exercise **2B**. Ask Ss to look at Picture 1. Ask: *What's happening?* Elicit an appropriate response, such as: *Sandra is talking on the phone. She is in her office. She is working.*
- Ask Ss to look at Picture 2. Ask: *What's happening?* Elicit an appropriate response, such as: *Ron is waiting for a bus. It's morning. He's looking at his watch.*
- Continue describing the action in each of the remaining pictures.

Practice
- Read the instructions aloud. Read the phrases under each picture. Explain any unfamiliar words.
- Model the task. Ask two Ss to read the dialog aloud. Ss complete the exercise with a partner. Walk around and help as needed.
- Read aloud the second part of the instructions for Exercise **2B**.
- Ask a S to read the example sentence aloud. Tell Ss to complete the exercise by writing one sentence for the action listed under each of the pictures.
- Ss complete the exercise individually. Walk around and help as needed.
- Write the numbers *1–6* on the board. Ask individual Ss to come to the board to write their sentences.
- Have other Ss read the sentences aloud. Ask Ss if the sentences are written correctly. Make corrections on the board as needed. Leave the answers on the board for the Expansion activity.

Application
- Direct Ss' attention to Exercise **3A**. Read the instructions aloud.
- Model the task. Ask two Ss to read aloud the example questions and answers.
- Hold up the Student's Book. Show Ss the chart. Lead Ss to see where the answer to the question is written in the example. Point to the name *Josefina*. Tell Ss to write only the Ss' names in the chart who answer *Yes* to the question.
- If space allows, encourage Ss to stand up and walk around so that they can talk to as many classmates as possible.
- Direct Ss' attention to Exercise **3B**. Read the instructions aloud.
- Ask Ss to share one piece of information about their classmates, for example: *(Student's name) has cooked for herself for three years.*

Expansion activity *(small groups)*
- Write on the board: *What are your hobbies?* Say the question and ask Ss to repeat. Ask Ss the meaning of *hobbies*. Elicit answers such as: *An activity you enjoy doing in your free time.*
- Tell Ss to ask another S the question and then ask: *How long have you been (doing the hobby)?*
- Model the activity with a S. Have the S ask you the questions on the board, for example: *What are your hobbies?* (I like writing stories.) *How long have you been writing stories?* (For about 10 years.)
- Ss work in small groups to ask each other the questions. Walk around the room. Make sure Ss are asking and answering the questions correctly and using correct pronunciation. Write on the board any words that Ss aren't pronouncing well. After Ss are finished, point to each of the words in turn. Say each word aloud. Have Ss repeat.
- Encourage Ss to ask all their group members the questions.
- Invite several Ss to share their classmates' hobbies and how long they have been doing them.

Evaluation
- Direct Ss' attention to the lesson focus on the board. Focus Ss' attention on the pictures on page 96.
- Ask Ss questions about Tony using *How long?* and the present perfect continuous form, for example: *How long has Tony been living in the United States?* Elicit answers utilizing the present perfect continuous, such as: *He's been living in the United States for two years.*
- Check off each part of the lesson focus as Ss demonstrate an understanding of what they have learned in the lesson.

More Ventures, Unit 8, Lesson B:	
Workbook, 15–30 min.	
Add Ventures, 30–45 min. **Collaborative,** 30–45 min.	www.cambridge.org/myresourceroom
Student Arcade, time varies	www.cambridge.org/venturesarcade

B **Talk** with a partner. Ask and answer questions.

> A How long has Sandra been talking on the phone?
> B For 20 minutes.

Sandra

1. talk / for 20 minutes

Ron

2. wait / since 8:00

Latifa

3. study / all morning

Jerry

4. practice keyboarding / since 10:30

Felix and Pablo

5. paint the house / for two days

Sharon

6. work in the restaurant / since 2011

Write a sentence about each picture.

Sandra has been talking on the phone for 20 minutes.
(Answers will vary.)

3 Communicate

A **Talk** with your classmates. Find a person who does each activity. Ask how long the person has been doing it. Complete the chart.

> A Do you drive?
> B Yes, I do.

> A How long have you been driving?
> B For about six years. / Since 2007.

Activity	Name	How long?
drive	*Josefina*	*for six years / since 2007*
cook for yourself	*(Answers will vary.)*	
attend this school		
work in this country		
play soccer		
use a computer		

B **Share** information about your classmates.

☑ Use present perfect continuous   **UNIT 8**   **99**

LESSON C Phrasal verbs

1 Grammar focus: separable phrasal verbs

Statements

Alfred **handed out** the papers.
He **handed** the papers **out**.
He **handed** them **out**.

Common separable phrasal verbs

call back	hand out	turn down
clean up	put away	turn off
fill out	throw out / away	turn up

Turn to page 147 for a complete grammar chart and explanation.

USEFUL LANGUAGE

papers → them
application → it

2 Practice

A Write. Complete the sentences.

1. She's **handing out** papers.
   She's ___handing___ the papers ___out___.
   She's ___handing___ them ___out___.

2. He's ___throwing away___ the cups.
   He's **throwing** the cups **away**.
   He's ___throwing___ them ___away___.

3. He's ___turning up___ the volume.
   He's ___turning___ the volume ___up___.
   He's **turning** it **up**.

4. She's **filling out** a job application.
   She's ___filling___ the application ___out___.
   She's ___filling___ it ___out___.

Listen and check your answers.

CLASS CD2 TK 18

Warm-up and review

Before class: Write today's lesson focus on the board.

Lesson C:
Separable phrasal verbs (sometimes called two-word verbs)

- Books open. Begin class. Direct Ss' attention to the pictures on page 96. Ask what Tony is doing and how long he has been doing it, for example: *In picture 1, what is Tony doing?* (He is helping a student read.) *How long has he been helping her?* Tell Ss to guess. (for about 10 minutes.) *In picture 4, what is Mr. Leong doing?* (He's interviewing Tony.) *How long has he been interviewing Tony?* (for 20 minutes.)

Presentation

Focus on meaning / personalize

- Books closed. Direct Ss' attention to the lesson focus on the board. Read it aloud. Write *turn* on the board. Elicit what *turn* means (to go around, to move in a circle). Ask Ss to think of two-word verbs, or phrasal verbs, that begin with *turn*, such as: *turn down, turn over, turn up, turn in, turn on, turn off.* If Ss cannot come up with any, point to the light switch as a cue.
- Explain that the meaning of the whole phrasal verb is different from the meaning of the individual words themselves.

Focus on form

- Books open. Direct Ss' attention to the Statements chart in Exercise **1**. Read aloud the three statements. Ask Ss to repeat. Direct Ss' attention to the separable phrasal verb chart. Read each one aloud. Ask Ss to repeat.
- Direct Ss' attention to the direct object pronoun *them* in the last sentence in Statements.
- Review subject and object pronouns. Write the subject pronouns on the board in one column: *I, you, he, she, it, we, they.* Elicit the object pronouns for each (*me, you, him, her, it, us, them*), and write them in a column beside the subject pronouns. Explain that object pronouns can be used in separable phrasal verbs, and they must come between the two words in the phrasal verb.

- Write on the board: *The teacher handed out the worksheets.* Say: *What is the phrasal verb?* (handed out.) *What's another way to say this sentence?* (The teacher handed the worksheets out.) *How would you say the same sentence with the object pronoun "them"?* (The teacher handed them out.) *Can you say, "The teacher handed it out"?* (No.) *Why?* (because *worksheets* is plural.)

Practice

- Direct Ss' attention to Exercise **2A**. Read the instructions aloud.
- Have Ss focus on Picture 1. Ask: *What do you see?* Elicit answers, for example: *A meeting. A woman is handing out papers.* Continue asking about the remaining pictures.
- Model the task. Ask a S to read aloud the example sentences in number 1. Lead Ss to notice the three different ways that the sentences are written. Tell them that the sentences all have the same meaning.
- Ss complete the exercise individually. Walk around and help as needed.

Comprehension check

- Read aloud the second part of the instructions for Exercise **2A**.
- Class Audio CD2 track 18 Play or read the audio program (see audio script, page T-161). Ss listen and check their answers.
- Write the numbers *1–4* on the board. Ask individual Ss to come to the board to write the sentences. Make corrections on the board as needed.

Presentation

- Books closed. Write *requests* on the board. Say the word aloud. Have Ss repeat. Ask Ss what *requests* are. Elicit appropriate responses, for example: *Requests are ways of asking people to help you.* Tell Ss that they are going to practice making requests.
- Ask Ss to give examples of ways of making requests, such as: *Would you mind _____? Could you please _____? Please _____.*

Practice

- Books open. Focus Ss' attention on Exercise **2B**. Read the instructions aloud. Direct Ss' attention to Picture 1. Ask: *What do you see?* Elicit: *A room with the lights on.* Continue with the remaining pictures.
- Model the task. Ask two Ss to read the example conversation to the class.

▼ Useful language
Read the Useful language box aloud. Explain that this tip shows which pronouns to use when referring to some of the items in the pictures. Ask Ss which pronouns they should use for the other words in the exercise. Elicit: *lunchroom – it; trash – it; books – them.*

- Ss complete the exercise in pairs. Walk around and help as needed.
- Direct Ss' attention to the second part of the instructions for Exercise **2B**. Read it aloud. Then read the example sentence.
- Ss complete the exercise individually. Walk around and help as needed.
- Ask several Ss to read their sentences to the class.

▼ Useful language
Read the Useful language box aloud. Ask Ss what *polite* means. Elicit: *formal, good manners, courteous,* etc. Say each polite request. Ask Ss to repeat. Encourage Ss to practice making polite requests in Exercise **2B** with *Would you please _____?* or *Could you please _____?*

Comprehension check

- Write the numbers *1–6* on the board. Ask individual Ss to come to the board to write their sentences from the second part of Exercise **2B**. Have different Ss read the sentences aloud. Ask: *Are the sentences correct?* Make corrections as needed.

Expansion activity *(whole group)*

- **Materials needed** Before class, prepare index cards with phrasal verbs. Write a verb on one card and its preposition on another card. Make enough cards so that each S in the class has at least one.
- Distribute at least one card to each S. Ask Ss to find a S with a matching card, for example *off* matches *turn*. Get phrasal verbs from the lesson or from the list in the Student's Book on page 147. When Ss find a match, ask them to come to the board to write a sentence in three ways using their phrasal verb. One sentence should keep the phrasal verb together, another should separate it, and the third should use a subject or object pronoun. Correct the sentences with the class.

Application

- Direct Ss' attention to Exercise **3A**. Read the instructions aloud.
- Have Ss look at the questions in the exercise. Ask individual Ss to read the questions to the class.
- Ss ask and answer the questions in a small group. Help as needed.
- Direct Ss' attention to the second part of the instructions for Exercise **3B**. Read it aloud.
- Ask Ss to share information about their classmates with the rest of the class.

Evaluation

- Direct Ss' attention to the lesson focus on the board. Ask Ss to look at the pictures on page 96 and make sentences using phrasal verbs, such as: *Mr. Leong is going to call Tony back about the job. After school, Tony will clean up the classroom.*
- Encourage Ss to make polite requests using the phrasal verbs in the grammar chart in Exercise **1** on page 100, for example: *Would you please call me back? Could you please turn the volume down?*
- Check off each part of the lesson focus as Ss demonstrate an understanding of what they have learned in the lesson.

More Ventures, Unit 8, Lesson C	
Workbook, 15–30 min.	
Add Ventures, 30–45 min.	www.cambridge.org/myresourceroom
Collaborative, 30–45 min.	
Student Arcade, time varies	www.cambridge.org/venturesarcade

B **Talk** with a partner. Make requests. Use the verbs in the box.

A Please turn the lights off.
B OK. I'll turn them off.

call back	throw out
clean up	turn down
put away	turn off

1. lights

2. heat

3. lunchroom

4. Mr. Jones

5. trash

6. books

Write sentences about each picture.

Please turn the lights off.
(Answers will vary.)

3 Communicate

A **Work** in a small group. Ask and answer the questions.

1. Have you ever filled out an application form?
   Where? When?

2. Did you put anything away last night?
   What was it?

3. Is there someone you need to call back? Who?

4. What things do you want to throw away?

5. What things do you turn on, off, or up?

6. Is there anything you need to clean up?
   What is it?

B **Share** information about your classmates.

LESSON D Reading

1 Before you read

Talk with your classmates. Answer the questions.

1. How many dates are in the reading? What are they?
2. What is the reading about?
3. What is a *blog*? Have you ever seen one?

> Scan the text for specific information. Look quickly to find dates. When you find the information you need, stop reading.

2 Read

STUDENT TK 30
CLASS CD2 TK 19

Read the blog. Listen and read again.

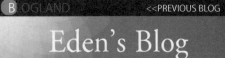

BLOGLAND   <<PREVIOUS BLOG   NEXT BLOG >>   SEARCH

Eden's Blog

→ Monday 9/29

I had my interview today! I gave the interviewer a big smile and a <u>firm</u> handshake. I answered her questions with <u>confidence</u>. I'll let you know if I get the job.

→ Thursday 9/25

Great news! One of the companies from the job fair finally called me back! I've been preparing for the job interview all day. I'm really excited. I'm going to have a practice interview with some classmates today. That will prepare me for the real one.

→ Wednesday 9/24

I've been feeling depressed about the job search lately, but my counselor at school told me I shouldn't give up. He said I need to be <u>patient</u>. Today, I organized my papers. I made lists of the places I have applied to and the people I have talked to. I also did some more research online.

→ Tuesday 9/16

Today, I went to a job <u>fair</u> at my college. I filled out several applications and handed out some résumés. There were about 20 different companies there. Several of them said they were going to call me back. Wish me luck!

→ Monday 9/15

Hello fellow job searchers! I have been looking for a job for several weeks. Everyone tells me that it's <u>critical</u> to <u>network</u>, so I've been telling everyone I know. I've been calling friends, relatives, and teachers to tell them about my job search. If you have any good job-searching tips, please share them with me!

Warm-up and review

- Before class. Write today's lesson focus on the board.

  Lesson D:
  Read and understand "Eden's Blog"
  Practice new vocabulary
  Scan for specific information
  Use context to identify parts of speech and guess meaning

- Begin class. Books closed. Focus Ss' attention on the word *blog* in the lesson focus. Ask Ss if they know what a blog, or Web log, is. Elicit or explain: *A blog is a Web site that one or more people make to share information about their life or interests.*

- Ask Ss if they have read or written blogs before. If any Ss say *Yes*, ask them what the blog was about. If no Ss have experience with blogs, give some examples of blogs, such as travel, work, or political blogs.

Expansion activity *(individual work)*

- If you have access to a computer lab, you might want to ask Ss to do a "blog" search. Tell them to look up topics that interest them so that they can see what a real blog looks like.

- Ask Ss to write down information about a blog they have read. Write on the board: *Name of blog; name of blogger; topic of blog; Is the blog interesting to you? Why or why not?*

- Ask several Ss to share information about their blogs with the rest of the class.

Presentation

- Books open. Direct Ss' attention to Exercise **1**. Read the instructions aloud.

> Read the tip box aloud. Explain to Ss that *scan* means to read quickly to look for particular information. In the case of looking for dates for the first question, eyes should locate one quickly and then look for the next date.

- Ask Ss to find the answer to the first question by scanning the blog. Encourage Ss to tell you the number of dates in the reading and what they are. (9/15, 9/16, 9/24, 9/25, 9/29)

- Ask a S to read the second and third questions aloud. Have Ss work with a partner to answer the questions.

Practice

- Focus Ss' attention on the picture in Exercise **2**. Ask Ss what they see (a picture of a young woman). Tell Ss that the picture is of a woman called Eden, who wrote this blog. The blog is about her job search.

- Read the instructions aloud for Exercise **2**. Have Ss read the blog silently.

- Ask Ss to write any unfamiliar words on the board. Encourage Ss to guess the meaning of these words from context.

- 🎧 Class Audio CD2 track 19 Play or read the audio program and ask Ss to read along silently (see audio script, page T-161). Repeat the audio program as needed.

- Ask Ss if they understood the blog. Ss may not have understood phrases such as *it's critical to network.* Allow Ss to use their dictionaries to look up words that are new to them, or explain that *critical* means very important; lead them to see that the description of *to network* is in the reading: *. . . I've been telling everyone I know. I've been calling friends, relatives, and teachers to tell them about my job search.*

Learner persistence *(individual work)*

- 🎧 Self-Study Audio CD track 30 Exercise **2** is recorded on the CD at the back of the Student's Book. Ss can listen to the CD at home for reinforcement and review. They can also listen for self-directed learning when class attendance is not possible.

LESSON D Reading

Presentation

- Read the instructions for Exercise **3A** aloud.
- Model the task. Ask a S to read aloud the first date in the exercise. Ask: *What happened on Monday, 9/15?* Tell Ss to scan the article for the date and to read the blog entry. Elicit: *She's been telling everyone about her job search.*
- Guide Ss to write the letter *d* in the blank in number 1. Have Ss continue the exercise by matching the dates on the left with the activities on the right.
- Ss complete the exercise individually. Walk around and help as needed.
- Write the numbers *1–5* on the board. Ask individual Ss to come to the board to write their answers to Exercise **3A**. Have different Ss read aloud the dates and Eden's activities on those dates. Ask: *Are the answers correct?* Make corrections on the board as needed.

Comprehension check

- Direct Ss' attention to Exercise **3B**. Read the questions aloud.
- Ss work in pairs to ask and answer the questions. Walk around and help as needed.

> ▼**Culture note**
> Read the note aloud to be sure that Ss understand the meaning of *blog*, a blended word that combines the words *Web* and *log*. Tell Ss that blogs have become very popular and are commonly used by politicians, newspaper columnists, actors, singers, employers, and job seekers, as well as by people like themselves. You might want to challenge your Ss by discussing why people are using blogs or are interested in reading them.

Practice

- Direct Ss' attention to Exercise **3C**. Read the instructions aloud.
- Model the task. Ask a S to read number 1 aloud. Have another S read aloud the dictionary entry for *critical*. Have Ss answer the question in number 1 of Exercise **3C**. (three definitions)
- Direct Ss' attention to number 2 of Exercise **3C**. Read the instructions aloud.
- Ask Ss to name parts of speech. Write them on the board with their dictionary abbreviations, for example: *noun (n), verb (v), adjective (adj), adverb (adv), preposition (prep).*
- Model the task. Read the first blog entry, in which the word *critical* is written. Tell Ss to underline the word. Ask: *What part of speech is "critical" in this sentence?* (adjective) Ask Ss why they think it is an adjective, for example: *In this sentence "critical" means very important,*

or essential. It describes "networking," which is a noun. Adjectives describe nouns. The dictionary entry says "adj," which is short for "adjective."

- Tell Ss to find each of the words in the reading, to underline each word, and to locate it in a dictionary. Have Ss write the part of speech and the definition in the chart.
- Ss complete the exercise individually. Walk around and help as needed.
- Have Ss work with a partner to compare their answers in number 2 of Exercise **3C**. Ask Ss if their answers are the same or different. If answers are different, talk about which answer is correct.
- Ask individual Ss to read their answers to the class. Make corrections as needed.

Application

- Focus Ss' attention on Exercise **3D**. Read the instructions aloud.
- Ss work in pairs to ask and answer the questions. Help as needed.
- Ask several pairs to share what they learned about their partner with the rest of the class.

Evaluation

- Books closed. Direct Ss' attention to the lesson focus on the board. Write on the board the vocabulary words in number 2 from Exercise **3C**. Ask Ss to use these words to talk about "Eden's Blog."
- Check off each part of the lesson focus as Ss demonstrate an understanding of what they have learned in the lesson.

Learner persistence (individual, pairs)

- You may wish to assign Extended Reading Worksheets from the *Online Teacher's Resource Room* for Ss to complete outside of class. The purpose of these worksheets is to encourage Ss to read for pleasure in English outside of the English class. The worksheets can also be assigned as extended reading in class.

More Ventures, Unit 8, Lesson D	
Workbook, 15–30 min.	
Add Ventures, 30–45 min. **Collaborative,** 30–45 min. **Extended Reading and worksheet,** 45–60 min.	www.cambridge.org/myresourceroom
Student Arcade, time varies	www.cambridge.org/venturesarcade

3 After you read

A Scan the blog for Eden's activities. Match them with the dates.

1. Monday 9/15 _d_
2. Tuesday 9/16 _e_
3. Wednesday 9/24 _c_
4. Thursday 9/25 _a_
5. Monday 9/29 _b_

a. She had a practice interview with her classmates.
b. She had a job interview.
c. She organized her papers.
d. She's been telling everyone about her job search.
e. She went to a job fair.

B Check your understanding.

1. Who wrote the blog?
2. How long has she been looking for a job?
3. Who did she network with?
4. How did she get a job interview?
5. How did she practice for the interview?

CULTURE NOTE

Blog comes from the words *Web log*. Readers, or visitors, can visit the Web site and write comments or just read.

C Build your vocabulary.

1. Read the dictionary entry for *critical*. How many definitions are there?

> **critical** /adj/ **1** saying that someone or something is bad or wrong **2** giving opinions on books, plays, films, etc. **3** very important; essential – **critically** /adv/

2. Find the vocabulary in the reading. Underline the words. Find each word in a dictionary. Copy the part of speech and the definition that best fits the reading.

Vocabulary	Part of speech	Definition
1. critical	*adjective*	*very important; essential*
2. network	*verb*	*to talk to people about jobs*
3. fair	*noun*	*a place to learn about jobs and companies*
4. patient	*adjective*	*calmly waiting for something to happen*
5. firm	*adjective*	*strong*
6. confidence	*noun*	*the feeling that you are good at something*

D Talk with a partner. Ask and answer the questions.

1. What is your most critical goal right now?
2. If you are trying to find a job, who can you network with?
3. How can you show confidence in a job interview?

LESSON E Writing

1 Before you write

A **Talk** with a partner. Who do you send thank-you letters to? Make a list. Share your list with the class.

B **Read** the thank-you letter.

> 4 South Avenue, Apt. 303
> Kansas City, MO 64115
> September 30, 2013
>
> Janice Hill
> Personnel Manager
> Smart Shop
> 1255 Front Street
> Kansas City, MO 64114
>
> Dear Ms. Hill:
>
> I would like to thank you for the job interview I had with you on Monday, September 29th. I appreciate the time you spent with me. Thank you for showing me around the store and introducing me to some of the employees. I felt very comfortable with them.
>
> Thank you again for your time. I hope to hear from you soon.
>
> Sincerely,
>
> *Eden Babayan*
> Eden Babayan

Work with a partner. Answer the questions.

1. Who wrote the letter?
2. Who did she write it to?
3. What is the writer's address?
4. What is Ms. Hill's address?
5. What information is in the first sentence?
6. How many times did the writer say thank you?
7. How does the writer end the letter?

Lesson objectives
- Write a thank-you letter
- Understand what to include in a thank-you letter

Warm-up and review

- Before class. Write today's lesson focus on the board.

  Lesson E:

  Read and write a thank-you letter following a job interview

- Begin class. Books closed. Focus Ss' attention on the words *thank-you letter* in the lesson focus on the board. Say it aloud and have Ss repeat.

- Books open. Focus Ss' attention on Exercise **1A**. Read the instructions. Ss work with a partner and share their work with the class.

▼ **Culture tip**

Explain that in American culture, some people like to send and receive thank-you notes after receiving a birthday, wedding, or graduation gift, for example, or after spending the weekend at someone's home. Discuss if this is common in Ss' cultures and what they say in these letters.

Presentation

- Tell Ss that today's lesson is about writing a thank-you letter after a job interview. Explain that it is a good idea to send a thank-you letter or an e-mail message to the person or people who interviewed you. Tell the class that sending a thank-you letter or a thank-you note shows that you are interested in getting the job; it also shows the interviewer that you appreciated the time that he or she took to interview you.

- Direct Ss' attention to Exercise **1B**. Read the instructions aloud. Tell Ss that they are going to read a thank-you letter that was written after a job interview. Ask: *What's the date on the letter?* (September 30, 2013.) *Who lives at 4 South Avenue, Apt. 303?* (Eden Babayan.) *Who is the personnel manager at Smart Shop?* (Janice Hill.)

- Ask Ss to read the letter silently. Make sure that Ss understand all the words in the letter.

Practice

- Focus Ss' attention on the second part of Exercise **1B**. Read the instructions aloud.

- Ss work in pairs to ask and answer the questions. Walk around and help as needed.

Comprehension check

- Write the numbers *1–7* on the board. Ask individual Ss to write the answers in short form on the board. Tell Ss that they don't need to write complete sentences for their answers.

- Ask different Ss to read the questions and answers aloud. Ask: *Are the answers correct?* Make corrections on the board as needed.

Expansion activity (student pairs)

- Review the format for writing a formal letter. Draw a template on the board. Block out the following parts:

  the return address

  the date

  the address of the person to whom the letter is addressed

  the person to whom the letter is being written

  the greeting (or salutation)

  the body with paragraph indents

  the closing

  the signature

- Ask Ss to tell you what to put in each block. Ss can use this template later for reference when planning and writing their own business or thank-you letters.

LESSON E Writing

Presentation

- Books closed. Tell Ss to imagine that they have just had a job interview and are now going to write a thank-you letter to the personnel manager who interviewed them.
- Elicit a list and write on the board reasons why you might want to thank the interviewer, for example: *for taking the time to interview you, for explaining the job to you, for taking you to lunch, for introducing you to people, for taking you on a tour of the factory, office, or store.*

Expansion activity (student pairs)

- If time allows, ask Ss to role-play an interview between a job applicant and a personnel manager so that Ss can write about the interview after practicing it in class.
- Ask Ss to brainstorm questions that might be asked in a job interview. Write Ss' questions on the board, such as: *Have you ever done this type of work before? How many years of experience do you have doing this type of work?*
- Tell Ss to practice the job interview with a partner, with one person playing the applicant and the other, the personnel manager.
- When Ss are finished, ask them to switch roles. Ask pairs to perform their role plays for the class.

Practice

- Books open. Direct Ss' attention to Exercise 1C. Read the instructions aloud.
- Model the task. Tell Ss to think of the name and address of the person to whom they are writing the thank-you letter. Allow Ss to use a local phone book to look up the addresses of real businesses in your city or town, or tell Ss to make up an address to use for a business.
- Ss complete the exercise individually. Tell Ss that they can plan to write a thank-you letter for the job interview they have just role-played or for a different job interview.

▼**Teaching tip**

Ss may not be familiar with the word *specific* in the third question in Exercise 1C. Tell Ss that here, *specific* refers to a particular thing that you appreciated about the interview. Ask Ss to find an example of a specific thing that Eden said she appreciated in the example letter in Exercise 1B on page 104. (*Thank you for showing me around the store and introducing me to some of the employees.*) Tell Ss that it is important to mention something specific in the letter to show that you are writing about that particular interview and not writing the same letter to all the people who interview you.

Application

- Focus Ss' attention on Exercise 2. Read the instructions aloud.

Read the tip box aloud. Ask Ss to find each of the items in the tip in the example letter in Exercise 1B.

- Ss individually complete the exercise of writing the thank-you letter. Help as needed.
- Remind Ss to include all information pertaining to a letter, for example: address, date, opening, and closing.

Comprehension check

- Focus Ss' attention on Exercise 3A. This exercise asks Ss to develop skills to review and edit their own writing.
- Ss check their own paragraphs. Help as needed. If any Ss check *No* for one or more of the checklist items, ask them to revise their letters to include the missing information.

Evaluation

- Focus Ss' attention on Exercise 3B. Read the instructions aloud.
- This exercise asks partners to peer-correct their writing. Reading aloud enables the writer to review his or her own writing. Reading to a partner allows the writer to understand the need to write clearly for an audience.
- Listen to Ss as they comment on their partner's letter. Check that partners are giving constructive criticism and are being supportive in their peer review.
- Walk around and listen to Ss as they ask their partner questions about the letter and tell their partner one thing they learned from it.
- Books closed. Direct Ss' attention to the lesson focus on the board. Ask several Ss to read aloud the thank-you letters they wrote in Exercise 2.
- Ask volunteers if these Ss included all the items in the checklist.
- Check off each part of the lesson focus as Ss demonstrate an understanding of what they have learned in the lesson.

More Ventures, Unit 8, Lesson E	
Workbook, 15–30 min.	
Add Ventures, 30–45 min.	www.cambridge.org/myresourceroom
Collaborative, 30–45 min.	

C **Plan** a formal thank-you letter. Complete the information.

Name and address of the person or business you are thanking:
(Answers will vary.)

Reason for saying thank you:

Something specific you appreciate:

2 Write

Write a formal thank-you letter to a person or a business. Say why you are thanking the person and mention something specific that you appreciated. Thank the person again at the end of the letter. Use the letter in Exercise 1B and the information in Exercise 1C to help you.

In a thank-you letter, include:
• why you are thanking the person
• what you appreciate
• another thank you at the end

3 After you write

A **Check** your writing.

	Yes	No
1. My first sentence says why I am thanking the person.	☐	☐
2. I mentioned something specific that I appreciated.	☐	☐
3. I thanked the person again at the end of the letter.	☐	☐

B **Share** your writing with a partner.

1. Take turns. Read your letter to a partner.
2. Comment on your partner's letter. Ask your partner a question about the letter. Tell your partner one thing you learned.

LESSON F Another view

1 Life-skills reading

Job Growth for Occupations Requiring an Associate Degree or Vocational Training, 2006 to 2016			
Occupation	Number * of new jobs	Percent increase in growth	Source of postsecondary education
Dental hygienists	50	30.1	Associate Degree
Environmental science and protection technicians, including health	10	28.0	Associate Degree
Makeup artists, theatrical and performance	1	39.8	Postsecondary vocational award
Manicurists and pedicurists	22	27.6	Postsecondary vocational award
Physical therapist assistants	20	32.4	Associate Degree
Skin care specialists	13	34.3	Postsecondary vocational award
Veterinary technologists and technicians	29	41.0	Associate Degree

* Numbers in thousands

Source: http://www.bls.gov/news.release/ooh.t01.htm

A **Read** the questions. Look at the chart. Fill in the answer.

1. What is not true about the jobs in the chart?

   (A) They require an associate degree.

   (B) They require a bachelor degree.

   (C) They require vocational training.

   (D) There will be more jobs in 2016 than in 2006.

2. Which occupation will have the largest percent increase in growth from 2006–2016?

   (A) dental hygienist

   (B) manicurist

   (C) physical therapist assistant

   (D) veterinary technician

3. What is the growth in number of jobs from 2006–2016 for dental hygienists?

   (A) 50

   (B) 500

   (C) 5,000

   (D) 50,000

4. This chart does not give information about _____.

   (A) environmental protection technicians

   (B) hairdressers

   (C) pedicurists

   (D) theatrical artists

B **Talk** with a partner. Ask and answer the questions.

1. What jobs are growing in your community? Are they the same as the jobs in the chart?

2. Is a job you want on this list?

3. Did anything in this chart surprise you? What was it?

Warm-up and review

- Before class. Write today's lesson focus on the board.
  Lesson F:
  Read and understand a chart comparing job growth in different occupations.
  Review topic vocabulary
  Complete the self-assessment
- Begin class. Books closed. Direct Ss' attention to the words *job growth* in the lesson focus. Say the words aloud. Have Ss repeat. Ask Ss what they think this phrase means. Elicit an appropriate response, such as: *Job growth is how jobs increase in number over a period of time.*
- Ask Ss to say what jobs they would be interested in. Make a list on the board.

Presentation

- Books open. Direct Ss' attention to the chart in Exercise 1. Ask a S to read the title of the chart. Discuss the meaning of *Associate's Degree* and *Postsecondary Vocational Award*. Ask: *What kind of degree or training do the jobs in this chart require?* Elicit: *an associate's degree or Postsecondary Vocational Award.* If Ss don't know what these terms mean, give a brief explanation, for example: *An associate's degree is a two-year degree from a college; a Postsecondary Vocational Award is given in a specific industry or trade.*
- Guide Ss to scan the chart to see if the jobs that were listed on the board in the warm-up are included in the occupations in the chart. If so, ask Ss to look at the chart and say whether the particular job has been growing a lot.
- Ask Ss to skim the information in the chart and underline any occupations that are unfamiliar to them. Allow Ss to use dictionaries to look up any occupations they don't understand.

Expansion activity *(whole group)*

- Practice reading numbers. Ask Ss to read the numbers in the chart aloud. These numbers may be difficult for some Ss and are worth practicing. Remind Ss that the number of new jobs are in the thousands.
- Practice doing simple calculations. Have Ss close their books. On the board, write the numbers from the two columns *2006* and *2016*. Ask Ss to add up the total number of new jobs in three categories, for example *veterinary technologists and technicians*, *dental hygienists*, and *physical therapist assistants* (29,000 + 50,000 + 20,000 = 99,000). Or ask Ss to calculate the difference, for example, the percent increase in growth between *manicurists and pedicurists* and *skin care specialists*: 22% – 13% = 9%. Have Ss check their answers in the book.

Practice

- Direct Ss' attention to Exercise 1A and read the instructions aloud. This task helps prepare Ss for standardized-type tests they may have to take. Make sure that Ss understand the task. Have Ss individually scan for and fill in the answers.

Comprehension check

- Check answers with the class. Make sure that Ss followed the instructions and filled in their answers.

Application

- Direct Ss' attention to Exercise 1B and read the instructions aloud. Ask a S to read the questions to the class.
- Ss complete the exercise in pairs. Help as needed.
- Ask several pairs to share what they learned from their partner with the rest of the class.

Expansion activity *(whole group)*

- Make a copy of the following chart for each S in your class:

Names:	1.	2.	3.	4.	5.
What are your career goals?					
What can you do to reach your career goals?					

- Have each S talk to five Ss in the class.
- Model the activity. Hold up the chart. Ask two Ss to read the questions to the class.
- Guide Ss to write in the first row of the chart the names of the Ss they interview and to take notes on these Ss' answers.
- Ask several Ss to share what they learned with the rest of the class.

Warm-up and review

- Books closed. Ask Ss questions with *How long?* and the present perfect continuous: *How long have you been studying English? How long have you been working at your current job?* Ensure Ss reply using *for* in their answer, for example: *I've been working at my current job for three years.*

Presentation

- Books open. Direct Ss' attention to the grammar chart in **2A**. Ask a S to read aloud the first sentence: *My classmate is writing in her book right now.* Tell Ss that in this case, we can tell that the action is happening at this exact minute because the speaker is using present continuous only.

- Ask another S to read aloud the second sentence: *I've been writing e-mails for two hours.* Tell Ss that in this case, we can tell the action started in the past and is continuing until the present.

Practice

- Direct Ss' attention to the instructions in **2A**. Read the instructions aloud. Ensure Ss understand the activity. Ask a pair of Ss to read the dialog aloud.

- Split the class into small groups. Pass out pennies to each group. Ss play the game. Walk around and help as needed.

- Direct Ss' attention to the instructions in **2B**. Read the instructions aloud. Ask two Ss to read the example sentences. Ss complete the exercise in pairs. Encourage each S to share a sentence about a person in their group.

Expansion activity *(group discussion)*

- Ask Ss: *What are your hobbies?* Elicit or tell Ss that a *hobby* is an activity people do in their free time. Write Ss' answers on the board, for example: *play the violin, read mystery novels, play soccer.* Ask each Ss how long they have been doing their hobby. Elicit answers using the present continuous, for example: *I've been playing the violin for two years.*

Evaluation

- Before asking students to turn to the self-assessment on page 139, do a quick review of the unit. Have Ss turn to Lesson A. Ask the class to talk about what they remember about this lesson. Prompt Ss, if necessary, with questions, for example: *What are the conversations about on this page? What vocabulary is in the pictures?* Continue in this manner to review each lesson quickly.

- **Self-assessment** Read the instructions for Exercise **3**. Ask Ss to turn to the self-assessment page and complete the unit self-assessment. The self-assessments are also on the *Online Teacher's Resource Room.* If you prefer to collect the assessments and save them as part of each S's portfolio assessment, print out the unit self-assessment from the *Resource Room*, ask students to complete it, and collect and save it.

- If Ss are ready, administer the unit test on pages T-182–T-183 of this Teacher's Edition (or on the Assessment Audio CD / CD-ROM).

More Ventures, Unit 8, Lesson F	
Workbook, 15–30 min.	
Add Ventures, 30–45 min.	www.cambridge.org/myresourceroom
Collaborative, 30–45 min.	

2 Grammar connections: present continuous and present perfect continuous

Use the *present continuous* to talk about an activity that is happening at the moment of speaking.	Use the *present perfect continuous* to talk about an activity that started in the past and continues to the present.
My classmate **is writing** in her book right now.	I**'ve been writing** e-mails for two hours.

A **Work** in a small group. Play the game. Write your name on a small piece of paper. Flip a coin to move your paper. Then tell your group your answer to the question in the square. Use the present continuous or the present perfect continuous in your answer. Take turns.

= 1 space

= 2 spaces

"Choose someone in the classroom. What is he/she wearing?" OK. I'll describe Tonya. She's wearing . . .

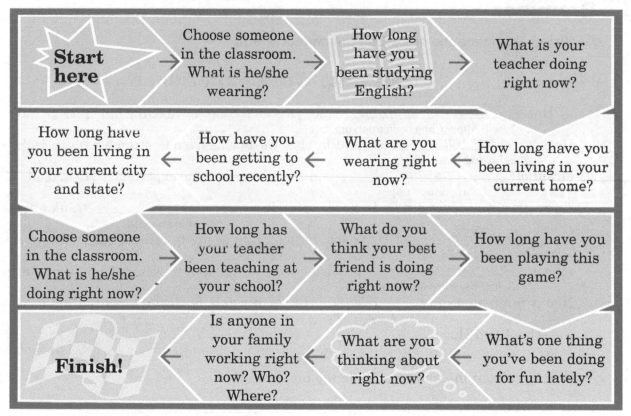

Start here

Choose someone in the classroom. What is he/she wearing?

How long have you been studying English?

What is your teacher doing right now?

How long have you been living in your current city and state?

How have you been getting to school recently?

What are you wearing right now?

How long have you been living in your current home?

Choose someone in the classroom. What is he/she doing right now?

How long has your teacher been teaching at your school?

What do you think your best friend is doing right now?

How long have you been playing this game?

Finish!

Is anyone in your family working right now? Who? Where?

What are you thinking about right now?

What's one thing you've been doing for fun lately?

B **Share** information about your classmates.

Tonya is wearing a red and blue sweater.

3 Wrap up

Complete the **Self-assessment** on page 139.

☑ Scan a chart for information; contrast present continuous and present perfect continuous **UNIT 8 107**

Review

CLASS CD2 TK 20

Listen. Put a check (✓) under the correct name.

	Clara	John
1. wants an SUV		✓
2. thinks a small car is better	✓	
3. says an SUV is more comfortable		✓
4. wants to take friends for a ride		✓
5. wants to keep taking the bus	✓	
6. wants to save money to buy a house	✓	

Talk with a partner. Check your answers.

2 Grammar

A Write. Complete the story. Use the correct words.

Getting Work Experience

Hao ___*has been applying*___ for jobs as a computer technician since October.
1. will apply / has been applying
He ___*has had*___ several interviews, but he hasn't gotten a job yet. He's
2. is having / has had
afraid of ___*applying*___ again until he gets some experience. His friend
3. applying / apply
Terry gave him some good advice. He said Hao ___*should*___ think about
4. could / should
___*volunteering*___ at Hao's son's school. Hao wants to call the school because the
5. volunteer / volunteering
school ___*has been having*___ problems with the computer system for a few months.
6. has been having / has
Hao is interested in ___*helping*___. It would be a win-win situation for both
7. help / helping
the school and Hao.

B Write. Look at the answers. Write the questions.

1. **A** Who *has been applying for a job* ?

   B Hao has been applying for a job.

2. **A** What *job has he been looking for* ?

   B He has been looking for a job as a computer technician.

3. **A** Where *does Hao want to volunteer* ?

   B Hao wants to volunteer at his son's school.

Talk with a partner. Ask and answer the questions.

Lesson objectives
- Review vocabulary and grammar from Units 7 and 8
- Introduce linking sounds

UNITS 7&8

Warm-up and review

- Before class. Write today's lesson focus on the board.
  Review unit:
  Review vocabulary and grammar from Units 7 and 8
  Practice linking sounds
- Begin class. Books closed. Review vocabulary and grammar from Units 7 and 8. Ask Ss: *My friend spends too much money on clothes. What should she do? My friend wants to find a nice restaurant for Valentine's Day. What could he do? What are you thinking about doing after class? What are you interested in doing in the future? How long have you been living in the United States? How long have you been studying English? Do you throw away or recycle plastic bottles?*

Presentation

- Books open. Direct Ss' attention to Exercise **1**. Read the instructions aloud. Tell Ss that they will hear a conversation between two friends, John and Clara.

- Class Audio CD2 track 20 Model the task. Play or read only the first part of the conversation on the audio program (see audio script, page T-161). Pause the program after John says: *I'm interested in buying a used SUV.*
- Ask Ss what an SUV is. Elicit: *An SUV is a type of car. It stands for Sport Utility Vehicle.*
- Direct Ss' attention to number 1 in the chart (*wants an SUV*) and ask. *Who wants an SUV?* (John) Tell Ss to check John's name for number 1.
- Ask individual Ss to read the remaining phrases in the chart. Say: *Listen and check the correct boxes.*

- Class Audio CD2 track 20 Play or read the complete audio program (see audio script, page T-161). Ss listen and check the boxes. Repeat the audio program as needed.

Comprehension check

- Read aloud the second part of the instructions for Exercise **1**. Model the task. Ask a S: *Who thinks a small car is better, John or Clara?* Elicit: *Clara.*
- Guide Ss to ask their partner questions to find what their partner checked. Help as needed.
- Ask several Ss to make sentences about John and Clara using the information in the chart.

Expansion activity *(whole group)*

- Write on the board: *Public transportation* and *Private car.* Ask Ss to name types of public transportation (train, subway, bus, etc.)

- Have Ss stand in two lines facing each other. Ss in one line will argue the advantages of public transportation. Ss in the other line will argue the advantages of driving in a personal car. Have Ss debate the pros and cons with the person facing them. Then have Ss move to the right and begin the debate with a new partner. Continue until Ss have had a chance to debate with several partners.

Practice

- Review *could*, *should*, and the present perfect continuous. Have Ss say or write sentences with each.

▼**Teaching tip**
In multilevel classes, create small heterogeneous groups. Encourage the Ss in the group who are comfortable with this review of grammar to help those who are less comfortable.

- Read the instructions for Exercise **2A** aloud. Point out that in this exercise, Ss choose the correct word or words to complete each sentence. This exercise does not ask Ss to change the word forms. Ask a S to read aloud the example sentence in the story and explain why *has been applying* completes the sentence correctly. Tell Ss to continue reading the story and filling in the blanks.
- Ss complete the exercise individually. Help as needed.
- Write the numbers *1–7* on the board. Have Ss come to the board to write the answers only.
- Read the complete story aloud using Ss' answers. Correct as needed.

Comprehension check

- Direct Ss' attention to Exercise **2B**. Read the instructions aloud. This exercise reviews question formation by asking questions related to the reading *"Getting Work Experience."*
- Read the instructions aloud. Model the task. Focus Ss' attention on the answer in number 1. Ask: *What question can you ask to get this answer?*
- Ss work individually to write the questions. Help as needed.
- Check answers with the class. Ask for volunteers to read their questions to the class. Correct as needed.
- Read aloud the second part of the instructions for Exercise **2B**.
- Pairs ask and answer the questions. Help as needed.

Review

Presentation

- Books closed. Write on the board: *linking sounds*. Explain that linking sounds describe the sound of joining an end consonant in a word with the beginning vowel of the word that follows it, for example: *clean up*. This makes the phrase sound like *cle-nup*; *think about* sounds like *thin-kabout*.
- Ask Ss to name the vowels in English. (a, e, i, o, u) Explain that all other letters are consonants.
- Write several phrases on the board from Exercise **3A**. Ask Ss to circle the end consonant in the first word of the phrase. Have other Ss underline the beginning vowel of the word that follows it. Ask Ss to repeat the words. Stress the linking sounds in these phrasal verbs.

> ▼ **Teaching tip**
> These pronunciation exercises are presented to make Ss aware of certain sound features in English. They are not presented as an exhaustive study of pronunciation. Their purpose is to raise Ss' awareness.

- Books open. Direct Ss' attention to Exercise **3A**. Read the instructions aloud.
- 🔘 Class Audio CD2 track 21 Play or read the complete audio program (see audio script, page T-161).
- Repeat the audio program. Pause after each phrase to allow Ss time to repeat. Play the audio program as many times as needed. Focus Ss' attention on the pronunciation of the linking letters on page 109.

Practice

- Direct Ss' attention to Exercise **3B**. Read the instructions aloud.
- 🔘 Class Audio CD2 track 22 Model the task. Play or read the audio program (see audio script, page T-162). Ss listen and repeat the conversations. Repeat the program as needed. Ask Ss to look at the linking sounds in the phrasal verbs and repeat them after you: *clea-nup*; *thro-wout*; *tur-nup*; *pu-ton*.

Comprehension check

- Direct Ss' attention to Exercise **3C**. Read the instructions aloud.
- Ss work in pairs to complete the exercise. Walk around and listen to their pronunciation. Write any words or phrases on the board that Ss had trouble pronouncing. Point to the words. Say each word aloud. Ask Ss to repeat.

- Invite four pairs to say the conversations for the rest of the class. Ask the class: *Did you hear the linking sounds?* Have Ss repeat if they are not linking the words correctly.
- Ask Ss to repeat some of the phrasal verbs after you and draw a linking line between the consonant and vowel, for example: *intereste-din*; *fil-lout*; *loo-karound*; *thin-kabout*.

> ▼ **Teaching tip**
> Encouraging Ss to pronounce linking sounds correctly will make Ss' pronunciation sound less accented and more natural. It will also make the rhythm of the language more typical of standard English. In addition, it will help Ss better understand English speakers.

Application

- Focus Ss' attention on Exercise **3D**. Read the instructions aloud.
- Ask a S to read the example question to the class.
- Model the task. Ask a S to make up a question with the phrasal verb *turn up*, such as: *Can you turn up the volume, please?* Write the question and answer on the board, and draw the linking line between the end consonant and the beginning vowel of the phrasal verb. Ask Ss to repeat. Correct as needed.
- Ss complete the exercise individually. Walk around and help as needed.
- Ss in pairs. Tell Ss to ask their partner the questions that they wrote. Walk around and listen to Ss' pronunciation as they ask and answer the questions.

Evaluation

- Direct Ss' attention to the lesson focus on the board.
- Focus Ss' attention on the phrasal verbs in Exercise **3A**. Ask Ss to read the phrasal verbs aloud, being careful to pronounce the linking sounds correctly.
- Check off each part of the lesson focus as Ss demonstrate an understanding of what they have learned in the lesson.

3 Pronunciation: linking sounds

A Listen to the phrasal verbs. Pay attention to the linking sounds.

CLASS CD2 TK 21

1. clean up
2. think about
3. turn up

4. fill out
5. interested in
6. throw out

7. put on
8. tired of

Listen again and repeat.

B Listen and repeat. Pay attention to the linking sounds in the phrasal verbs.

CLASS CD2 TK 22

1. A What do you need to do?
   B I have to clean up the kitchen.
   A Can I help?
   B Sure. Could you throw out the trash?
   A I'd be happy to.

2. A Don't you think it's cold in here?
   B It's a little cold.
   A Why don't you turn up the heat?
   B That costs too much money. You can put on my jacket.

C Talk with a partner. Practice the conversations. Pay attention to the linking sounds in the phrasal verbs.

1. A Do you need some help?
   B I'm interested in applying for a job here.
   A OK. Just fill out this application, and return it to me.
   B Thanks.
   A Don't forget to put your name on it.

2. A May I help you?
   B I may be interested in buying a big-screen TV.
   A We have some great deals. Let me show you.
   B Thanks, but I'd like to just look around some more.

3. A Do you want to go to a movie tonight?
   B What do you think about just staying home?
   A That's fine. There's a good game on TV.
   B OK. First help me clean up the kitchen. Then we can watch the game.

4. A I want to register for English classes.
   B Fill out this form, please.
   A Can you help me?
   B Sure. I just need to put away these papers.
   A Thank you.

D Write four questions. Use the words in Exercise 3A. Ask your partner. Remember to connect the sounds.

Did you clean up the kitchen last night?

1. *(Answers will vary.)* _____
2. _____
3. _____
4. _____

LESSON A
Listening

1 Before you listen

A What do you see?

B What is happening?

C What's the story?

UNIT 9

Objectives
- ... to the topic
- ...dents know about the topic
- ... by talking about the pictures
- ...ocabulary
- ...ning skills

- Find out what stu...
- Preview the unit...
- Practice key vo...
- Practice liste...

Warm-up and review

- Before class. Write today's lesson focus on the board.
  Lesson A:
  Crime and community action
- Begin class. Books closed. Direct Ss' attention to the words *community action* on the board. Say the words aloud and have Ss repeat. Ask Ss what the words mean. Remind Ss that they learned the word *community* in Unit 3 in the context of talking about neighbors. Elicit appropriate responses, for example: *"Community action" means that the neighborhood works together to do something or to get something done, such as neighbors helping neighbors in an emergency.*
- Focus Ss' attention on the word *crime* and ask Ss to define it, for example: *"Crime" is breaking the law.* Elicit examples of small or petty crimes (exceeding the speed limit by 5 miles.) and big crimes (theft or robbery.).
- Tell Ss that the next lesson is about a robbery. Write *robbery* on the board. Say it aloud. Have Ss repeat. Ask Ss what the verb form of the word *robbery* is. Elicit: *rob.* Ask what a person who robs someone is called. Elicit: *A robber.* Write *robber* on the board. Ask Ss to identify the parts of speech of each word again. Write on the board next to each word: *robbery (noun)*; *rob (verb)*; *robber (noun).* Say each word aloud and have Ss repeat.

Presentation

- Books open. Set the scene. Direct Ss' attention to the two pictures on page 110. Ask the question in Exercise **1A**: *What do you see?* Elicit and write on the board as much vocabulary as possible about the two pictures. Explain any unfamiliar words.
- Direct Ss' attention to the question in Exercise **1B**: *What is happening?* Read it aloud. Divide the class into pairs. Assign each pair a number from 1 to 2 to correspond to one of the two pictures in the story. Guide partners to talk about what is happening in the picture that corresponds to their number.

Practice

- Read aloud the question in Exercise **1C**: *What's the story?* Help Ss create the story by asking the class a few questions, for example: *Who is the man in Picture 1? What does he have in his hand? What do you see in the room? What has happened? What time is it? Who are the people in Picture 2? What time is it? How do they look? What is missing from the room? Who do you think the woman is talking to?*
- Ask several pairs to create a story based on the pictures and to share the story with the class.

Presentation

- Books open. Direct Ss' attention to Exercise **2A**. Have Ss listen for the main idea. Read the instructions aloud. Explain that after listening to the conversation, Ss in pairs will ask and answer questions in the exercise.
- Ask a S to read the questions in Exercise **2A** aloud. Tell Ss to listen for this information as the audio program is played or read.

- Class Audio CD2 track 23 Play or read the audio program (see audio script, page T-162).
- Ask Ss if they understood everything in the listening exercise. Write any unfamiliar words on the board, and help Ss understand the meaning of each word.
- Elicit answers to the questions.
- Focus Ss' attention on Exercise **2B**. Read the instructions aloud. Have Ss read the chart that contains information about Monica. Explain any unfamiliar words.
- Tell Ss to listen for details in the conversation and to take notes to complete the chart. Explain that taking notes means to write information in short form, without using complete sentences.

- Class Audio CD2 track 23 Play or read the audio program again (see audio script, page T-162). Pause the program after Monica says: *Someone broke into our house tonight.* Point to where *someone broke into* is written in the chart. Tell Ss to listen and complete the chart. Play or read the rest of the audio program.
- Elicit answers from Ss and write them on the board.

- Class Audio CD2 track 23 Play or read the audio program again (see audio script, page T-162). Ss listen and check their answers.
- Write the numbers *1–5* on the board. Ask several Ss to come to the board and write their answers in note form. Make corrections as needed.

Learner persistence (individual work)

- Self-Study Audio CD track 31 Exercises **2A** and **2B** are recorded on the CD at the back of the Student's Book. Ss can listen to the CD at home for reinforcement and review. They can also listen to the CD for self-directed learning when class attendance is not possible.

Practice

- Focus Ss' attention on Exercise **3A**. Tell Ss that the story in this exercise is a summary of the conversation they heard in the audio program.
- Direct Ss' attention to the words in the word bank. Say each word aloud. Ask Ss to repeat. Explain any unfamiliar words.
- Ss complete the exercise individually. Walk around and help as needed.

▼ Teaching tip

It might be helpful to explain the difference betwe[...] *steal*. Write both verbs on the board. Explain that yo[...] rob someone and steal something. Illustrate the examp[...] by asking about the story: *What did the robber steal?* (a TV, a DVD player, etc) *Who was robbed?* (Monica was robbed.)

Comprehension check

- Class Audio CD2 track 24 Play or read the audio program (see audio script, page T-162). Ss listen and check their answers. Repeat the audio program as needed.
- Write the numbers *1–8* on the board. Ask individual Ss to come to the board to write their answers.

Learner persistence (individual work)

- Self-Study Audio CD track 32 Exercise **3A** is recorded on the CD at the back of the Student's Book. Ss can listen to the CD at home for reinforcement and review. They can also listen for self-directed learning when class attendance is not possible.

Application

- Focus Ss' attention on Exercise **3B**. Read the instructions aloud.
- Ss complete the exercise in pairs. Walk around and help as needed.
- Ask several pairs to retell their discussion to the rest of the class.

Evaluation

- Direct Ss' attention to the lesson focus on the board. Ask Ss to look at the pictures on page 110 to make up a conversation between Monica and Samantha (or between Monica and her husband), using the words in Exercise **3A**.
- Check off each part of the lesson focus as Ss demonstrate an understanding of what they have learned in the lesson.

More Ventures, Unit 9, Lesson A	
Workbook, 20–30 min.	
Add Ventures, 30–45 min.	www.cambridge.org/myresourceroom
Collaborative, 30–45 min.	
Student Arcade, time varies	www.cambridge.org/venturesarcade

Describe a crime and suggest solutions
Write about an emergency
Interpret a chart about the safest states in the U.S.

2 Listen

STUDENT TK 31
CLASS CD2 TK 23

A **Listen** and answer the questions.

1. Who are the speakers?   2. What are they talking about?

STUDENT TK 31
CLASS CD2 TK 23

B **Listen again.** Take notes. Answer the questions.

1. What happened at Monica and Todd's house?	*someone broke into it*
2. Where were Monica and Todd when the robbery happened?	*at their neighbors' house*
3. What did the robber steal?	*TV, DVD player, jewelry, cash*
4. How has the neighborhood changed?	*more crime now*
5. What does Samantha think they should do?	*start a Neighborhood Watch program*

3 After you listen

A **Read.** Complete the story.

broke into   come over   crime   got in   mess   robbed   robber   stole

> Monica calls Samantha with bad news. While Monica and Todd were out, someone
> ___*broke into*___ their home and ___*stole*___ their TV, DVD player, jewelry, and some
>   1   2
> cash. Monica is upset because the ___*robber*___ took her mother's ring. She says the
>   3
> person ___*got in*___ through a window in the back bedroom.
>   4
> Samantha is worried. She says they never used to have so much ___*crime*___
>   5
> in their neighborhood. She tells Monica that last week someone ___*robbed*___ their
>   6
> neighbor Mr. Purdy, too. Samantha thinks they should start a Neighborhood Watch
> program. Monica agrees, but first, she needs to clean up the ___*mess*___ in her
>   7
> house. Samantha offers to ___*come over*___ and help.
>   8

STUDENT TK 32
CLASS CD2 TK 24

Listen and check your answers.

B **Talk** with a partner.

Tell about a crime that happened to you or someone you know.

LESSON B Past continuous

1 Grammar focus: questions and answers

Questions	Answers	
What **was** Beth **doing** yesterday morning?	She **was cleaning** her house.	
What **were** the neighbors **doing** at 10:00?	They **were watching** TV.	

Questions	Answers	
Was Maria **visiting** a neighbor last night?	Yes, she **was**.	No, she **wasn't**.
Were they **watching** a movie at 8:30?	Yes, they **were**.	No, they **weren't**.

wasn't = was not
weren't = were not

Turn to page 145 for a complete grammar chart and explanation.

2 Practice

A Write. Complete the sentences. Use the past continuous.

What were you doing at 8:30 last night?

1. **Roberto and Maya**: We _____were watching_____
   (watch)
   a movie at the Rialto Theater.

2. **Mi Young**: I _____was studying_____ English
   (study)
   at home last night.

3. **Ciro**: I _____was driving_____ to work.
   (drive)

4. **Magda and Luis**: We _____were eating_____ dinner at
   (eat)
   Kate's Kitchen Restaurant.

5. **Ilian and Francine**: We _____were attending_____ a Neighborhood
   (attend)
   Watch meeting.

6. **Susana**: I _____was babysitting_____ my grandchildren at my daughter's house.
   (babysit)

7. **Claudia**: I _____was baking_____ a cake for my daughter's birthday party.
   (bake)

8. **Leila and Mark**: We _____were painting_____ the kitchen.
   (paint)

Listen and check your answers.

CLASS CD2 TK 25

Lesson objectives
- Introduce the past continuous
- Ask and answer *What* and *Yes / No* questions with the past continuous

Warm-up and review

Before class: Write today's lesson focus on the board. *Lesson B:*
Past continuous questions and answers

- Books open. Begin class. Direct Ss' attention to the pictures on page 110. Ask the questions on page 111, Exercise **2B**. Elicit the answers.

Presentation

Focus on meaning / personalize

- Books closed. Direct Ss' attention to the lesson focus on the board. Read it aloud. Say: *I was watching TV at 7:00 p.m. last night. What about you? What were you doing at 7:00 p.m. last night?* Elicit answers, for example: *watching TV, studying English.* Ss do not need to answer in full sentences.
- Write on the board: *I was watching TV at 7:00 p.m. last night. Is a specific time talked about?* (Yes, 7:00 p.m.) *Did the action start before 7:00 p.m.?* (Yes.) *Did the action continue after 7:00 p.m.?* (Yes.)
- Underline *was watching*. Explain that this tense is called the *past continuous*, and that it is used to talk about actions that were happening at a specific time in the past. The actions were not completed at that time.

Focus on form

- Books open. Direct Ss' attention to the Questions and Short answers charts in Exercise **1**. Read each question and answer, and have Ss underline the past continuous verb in each in their books.

What <u>was</u> Beth <u>doing</u> yesterday morning?
She <u>was cleaning</u> her house.
What <u>were</u> the neighbors <u>doing</u> at 10:00?
They <u>were watching</u> TV.
Was Maria <u>visiting</u> a neighbor last night?
Yes, she <u>was</u>. / No, she <u>wasn't</u>.
Were they <u>watching</u> a movie at 8:30?
Yes, they <u>were</u>. / No, they <u>weren't</u>.

- Elicit or explain how to form the past continuous: *was / were* + base verb + *-ing* (present participle).
- Review when to use *was* or *were*. Write *I, you, he, she, it, we, you,* and *they* in a list on the board. Read each pronoun, elicit *was* or *were*, and write it on the board beside the correct pronoun. Point out that questions that begin with *was* or *were* only need short answers.
- Tell Ss that the spelling rules for the past continuous are the same for all verb + *-ing* forms. Refer Ss to the section on page 146 that has the spelling rules for gerunds.

Practice

- Focus Ss' attention on Exercise **2A**. Read the instructions aloud.
- Set the scene. Ask Ss to look quickly at the exercise and then ask: *Who is questioning the people in the exercise?* Ask: *What do you think? Why is he asking this question?*
- Ask two Ss to read the first example. Tell Ss to complete the exercise by filling in the blanks with the past continuous form of the verbs that are written below the blanks.
- Ss complete the exercise individually. Help as needed.

Comprehension check

- Direct Ss' attention to the second part of the instructions for Exercise **2A**. Read it aloud.
- Class Audio CD2 track 25 Play or read the audio program (see audio script, page T-162). Ss listen and check their answers. Repeat the audio program as needed.
- Write the numbers *1–8* on the board. Ask several Ss to write their answers on the board. Ask other Ss to read the complete question and answers to the class. Make corrections as needed.

LESSON **B** Past continuous

Presentation

- Direct Ss' attention to the picture in Exercise **2B**. Ask: *What do you see?* Elicit an appropriate response, such as: *A family is in the living room. Bill is reading the newspaper. Jon and Sandra are playing cards. Judy is talking on the phone. etc.* Ask: *What time is it?* (7:00 p.m.)

> ▼ **Teaching tip**
> Review family relationships and assign each of the people in the picture a family label, for example: *mother, father, grandmother, grandfather, brother, older sister, younger sister.* You could also assign labels such as *aunt, uncle, friend, cousin.* Have the class agree on how the people in the picture are related and use these relationships in the exercise.

- Read the instructions aloud.
- Focus Ss' attention on the word bank. Say each verb aloud. Ask Ss to repeat. If Ss are unfamiliar with any of the verbs, ask them to identify each verb with a family member in the picture to illustrate the meaning.
- Model the task. Have two Ss read aloud the example conversation. Pairs complete the exercise.
- Ask several pairs to say the questions and answers for the class.

Practice

- Read aloud the second part of the instructions for Exercise **2B**.
- Ask a S to read the example sentence to the class.
- Ss complete the exercise individually. Walk around and help as needed.

Comprehension check

- Write the numbers *1–7* on the board. Ask individual Ss to come to the board to write their sentences.
- Have other Ss read the sentences aloud. Ask Ss if the sentences are written correctly.

Application

- Direct Ss' attention to Exercise **3A**. Read the instructions aloud.
- Model the task. Ask two Ss to read the example conversation to the class.

- Hold up the Student's Book. Point to where the name *Sergio* is written. Tell Ss to write the names of the Ss they speak to in this column of the chart, the time they ask about in the second column, and the action in the third column.
- Ss complete the exercise in small groups. Help as needed.
- Direct Ss' attention to Exercise **3B**. Read the instructions aloud.
- Ask as many Ss as possible to share with the class the information they learned about their classmates.

Expansion activity *(small groups)*

- **Materials needed** Enough copies of a current newspaper to give to small groups in your class.
- Tell Ss to look at the pictures in the paper. Write on the board: *What was he or she doing in the picture? What were they doing in the picture? What was he or she wearing in the picture?*
- Model the activity. Show the class a picture from the newspaper. Ask questions about the picture using the past continuous. Listen as Ss describe the action. Write the correct past continuous sentences on the board.
- Ss continue the activity in pairs. Help as needed.
- Ask several pairs to stand up and show a picture to the class. Have them ask and answer questions about the picture by using the past continuous form.

Evaluation

- Direct Ss' attention to the lesson focus on the board.
- Books open. Tell Ss to ask and answer questions about the actions in the big picture on page 110, using the past continuous form, for example: *What was the robber doing at 10:30 last night? The robber was taking things in the bedroom. What was he doing at 11:00? He was running away.*
- Check off each part of the lesson focus as Ss demonstrate an understanding of what they have learned in the lesson.

More Ventures, Unit 9, Lesson B	
Workbook, 15–30 min.	
Add Ventures, 30–45 min. **Collaborative,** 30–45 min.	www.cambridge.org/myresourceroom
Student Arcade, time varies	www.cambridge.org/venturesarcade

B Talk with a partner. Look at the picture. Ask and answer questions. Use the past continuous and the verbs in the box.

A What was Bill doing at 7:00 p.m.?
B He was reading.

knit   play a game   read   sew   sleep   talk   watch TV

Write a sentence about each person.

Bill was reading.
(Answers will vary.)

3 Communicate

A Work in a small group. Ask and answer questions. Take notes in the chart.

A Sergio, were you at home at 9:00 a.m. yesterday?
B Yes, I was.
A What were you doing?
B I was sleeping.

Name	Time	Action
Sergio	*9:00 a.m.*	*was sleeping*
(Answers will vary.)		

B Share information about your classmates.

LESSON C Past continuous and simple past

1 Grammar focus: adverb clauses with *when* and *while*

When the fire **started**, Maxine and Joel **were sleeping**.

While Maxine and Joel **were sleeping**, a fire **started** in the kitchen.

Maxine and Joel **were sleeping** when the fire **started**.

A fire **started** in the kitchen while Maxine and Joel **were sleeping**.

Turn to page 148 for a complete grammar chart and explanation.

2 Practice

A Write. Complete the sentences. Use the past continuous or simple past.

1. While Dad ____*was working*____ in the
   garden, a thief ____*stole*____ his car.
   (work)
   (steal)

2. I ____*was eating*____ lunch when the fire
   (eat)
   alarm suddenly ____*went off*____.
   (go off)

3. Ali ____*fell*____ off a ladder while
   (fall)
   he ____*was painting*____ the ceiling.
   (paint)

4. When the earthquake ____*started*____, the students ____*were taking*____ a
   (start)
   (take)
   test.

5. I ____*was making*____ a right turn when another car ____*hit*____ the
   (make)
   (hit)
   back of my car.

6. While we ____*were camping*____, it suddenly ____*began*____ to rain.
   (camp)
   (begin)

7. Mr. and Mrs. Gomez ____*were jogging*____ in the park when a dog
   (jog)
   ____*began*____ to chase them.
   (begin)

8. While Diana ____*was working*____ outside, a stranger ____*drove*____ up to
   (work)
   (drive)
   her house.

Listen and check your answers.

CLASS CD2 TK 26

114 UNIT 9

Lesson objective

- Introduce past continuous and simple past using *when* and *while*

Warm-up and review

Before class: Write today's lesson focus on the board.
Lesson C:
Past continuous and simple past verb tense
<u>*when*</u> *clauses*
<u>*while*</u> *clauses*

- Books open. Begin class. Direct Ss' attention to the picture on page 113. Say: *This picture is of a family at 7:00 p.m. last night.* Ask past continuous questions about the family, and write Ss' answers on the board, for example: *What was Bill doing at 7:00?* (He was reading a newspaper.) *What was Elisa doing?* (She was knitting.) *What were Jon and Sandra doing?* (They were playing checkers.)

- Have S volunteers come to the board and underline the past continuous verbs in each sentence.

Presentation

Focus on meaning/personalize

- Books closed. Direct Ss' attention to the lesson focus on the board. Read it aloud. Ask two or three Ss what they were doing last night at 7:00 p.m. Write their names and answers on the board. Ss do not have to answer in full sentences, for example: *Roberto / studying English, Maria / watching TV, Omar / sleeping.*

- Say: *Last night at 7:00 p.m., I called (Roberto).* Write on the board: *Roberto was studying when I called.* Ask: *What was Roberto doing?* (studying.) *What interrupted him?* (my call.)

- Write on the board: *I called Roberto while he was studying.* Ask: *Do these two sentences mean the same – I called Roberto while he was studying.* and *When I called Roberto, he was studying?* (Yes.)

Focus on form

- Books open. Direct Ss' attention to the charts in Exercise 1. Read the first two statements aloud. Ask Ss to repeat. Write them on the board. Ask: *What is the difference between the beginning of the first and second statements?* (The first begins with *while*; the second begins with *when*.)

- Ask: *What is the verb tense in the "while" clause?* (past continuous.) *What is the verb tense in the "when" clause?* (simple past.)

- Summarize by saying: *The past continuous is used to express a longer action that was interrupted by another action. We use the simple past tense to express a short action that interrupts the longer action.*

- Direct Ss' attention to the second two statements in Exercise 1. Read the statements aloud. Ask Ss to repeat.

- Have Ss look for commas in all four statements. Remind Ss of the comma placement in clauses: If the *when* or *while* clause is at the beginning of a sentence, a comma is used after the clause; if the clause is at the end of the sentence, the comma is not used.

Practice

- Direct Ss' attention to Exercise 2A. Read the instructions aloud. Have Ss focus on the picture in the exercise. Ask: *What was happening?* Elicit an appropriate response, such as: *A man was working in the garden when someone broke into his car.*

- Model the task. Ask a S to read the example sentence to the class. Tell Ss to complete the exercise by filling in the blanks with the correct form of the verb.

- Ss complete the exercise individually. Walk around and help as needed.

Comprehension check

- Read aloud the second part of the instructions in Exercise 2A.

- Class Audio CD2 track 26 Play or read the audio program (see audio script, page T-162). Ss listen and check their answers.

- Write the numbers *1–8* on the board. Ask individual Ss to come to the board to write their answers. Make corrections as needed.

▼**Culture tip**
It might be helpful to tell Ss that in an emergency, they can call 911, the telephone number for the police and fire departments. Discuss the information that Ss will need to give to the person on the phone (their name, the kind of emergency, their address, the cross streets, their telephone number, etc.). Remind Ss to speak slowly, clearly, and calmly.

Presentation

- Books open. Direct Ss' attention to the pairs of pictures in the exercise. Ask Ss what the woman was doing in the first picture. Elicit an appropriate response, such as: *The woman was working on her computer.* Focus Ss' attention on the next picture. Ask: *What happened?* Elicit: *A tree fell on her house.* Continue describing the remaining pictures.

Practice

- Read the instructions aloud. Model the task. Ask two Ss to read aloud the example question and answer. Tell Ss that they can include the *when* or *while* clause at the beginning or at the end of their sentences. Have Ss suggest other ways of describing the first set of pictures and write their sentences on the board to model possible forms:

  While the woman was working, a tree fell on her house.
  A tree fell on her house while she was working.
  She was working when a tree fell on her house.
  When a tree fell on her house, she was working.

- Ss work in pairs to complete the exercise. Walk around and help as needed.

▼ **Teaching tip**
It might be helpful to encourage Ss to ask themselves: *What was happening? Then what happened?* Being able to identify each clause will help them determine whether to use *while* (with the past continuous) or *when* (with the simple past).

- Direct Ss' attention to the second part of the instructions for Exercise **2B**. Read it aloud. Then read the example sentence.
- Ss complete the exercise individually. Walk around and help as needed.
- Ask several Ss to read their sentences to the class.

Comprehension check

- Write the numbers *1–4* on the board. Ask volunteers to come to the board to write their sentences from the second part of Exercise **2B**. Have different Ss read the sentences aloud. Ask: *Are the sentences correct?* Invite other Ss to come to the board to make corrections.

Application

- Direct Ss' attention to Exercise **3A**. Read the instructions aloud.
- Model the task. Tell Ss about a situation that happened to you or a friend, or make up a situation.
- Ss work with a partner to ask and answer the questions. Help as needed.
- Direct Ss' attention to Exercise **3B**. Read the instructions aloud.
- Model the task. Ask a S what he or she learned about his or her partner in Exercise **3A**. Ask the S to describe the event that happened to the partner.
- Continue the exercise by asking different Ss to share information they learned about their partner with the rest of the class.

▼ **Teaching tip**
Before Ss begin to do Exercise **3A**, be sure to tell them that the situation they discuss with their partner will be shared with the class. Do this to make sure that Ss will not talk about events they do not wish the entire class to hear.

Evaluation

- Direct Ss' attention to the lesson focus on the board.
- Write on the board:
  1. *I was walking to school when _____.*
  2. *I was talking on the phone when _____.*
  3. *While I was driving to class, _____.*
  4. *While I was doing my homework, _____.*
  5. *When you called me, _____.*
- Have Ss read the first part of the first sentence on the board and make up an ending, such as: *I was walking to school when I saw my friend on the street.* Tell Ss to complete each of the sentences using the correct verb form.
- Check off each part of the lesson focus as Ss demonstrate an understanding of what they have learned in the lesson.

More Ventures, Unit 9, Lesson C	
Workbook, 15–30 min.	
Add Ventures, 30–45 min.	www.cambridge.org/myresourceroom
Collaborative, 30–45 min.	
Student Arcade, time varies	www.cambridge.org/venturesarcade

B **Talk** with a partner. Look at the pictures. Ask and answer questions. Use *when* or *while*.

> **A** What happened?
> **B** While the woman was working, a tree fell on her house.

work   fall   drive   run out of gas

eat   get a parking ticket   cook dinner   the lights go out

Write sentences about what happened.

The woman was working when a tree fell on her house.
(Answers will vary.)

3 Communicate

A **Work** with a partner. Describe a situation that happened to you. Answer the questions.

1. What happened?
2. When and where did it happen?
3. What were you doing when it happened?

B **Share** information about your partner.

LESSON D Reading

1 Before you read

Look at the picture. Answer the questions.

1. Who are the people in the picture?
2. What do you think is happening?
3. How do they probably feel?

2 Read

STUDENT TK 33
CLASS CD2 TK 27

Read the newspaper article. Listen and read again.

Home Is More Than a Building
Claypool, AZ

A few months ago, Pedro Ramirez, 45, lost his job in a grocery store. To pay the bills, he got a part-time job at night. Several days later, Pedro's wife, Luisa, gave him a big surprise. She was pregnant with their sixth child. Pedro was happy but worried. "How am I going to <u>support</u> another child without a full-time job?" he wondered.

That evening, Pedro and Luisa got some more news. A fire was coming near their home. By the next morning, the fire was very close. The police ordered every family in the neighborhood to <u>evacuate</u>. The Ramirez family moved quickly. While Pedro was <u>gathering</u> their legal documents, Luisa <u>grabbed</u> the family photographs, and the children put their pets – a cat and a bird – in the family's van. Then, the family drove to the home of Luisa's sister, one hour away.

About 24 hours later, Pedro and Luisa got very bad news. The fire <u>destroyed</u> their home. They lost almost everything. With no home, only part-time work, and a baby coming, Pedro was even more worried about the future.

For the next three months, the Ramirez family stayed with Luisa's sister while workers were rebuilding their home. Many <u>generous</u> people helped them during that difficult time. Friends took them shopping for clothes. <u>Strangers</u> left gifts at their door. A group of children collected $500 to buy bicycles for the Ramirez children.

Because of all the help from friends and neighbors, the Ramirez family was able to rebuild their lives. Two months after the fire, Luisa mailed out holiday cards with this <u>message</u>: "Home is more than a building. Home is wherever there is love."

In a story, time phrases show changes in time.
A few months ago, . . .
Several days later, . . .
That evening, . . .

Lesson objectives

- Introduce and read "Home Is More Than a Building"
- Practice using new topic-related vocabulary
- Recognize time phrases that show changes in time
- Use context clues

Warm-up and review

- Before class. Write today's lesson focus on the board.
  Lesson D:
  Read and understand "Home Is More Than a Building"
  Practice new vocabulary
  Recognize time phrases that show changes in time
  Use context clues to guess the meaning of words
- Begin class. Books closed. Ask Ss if they read newspapers. Ask Ss who say *Yes* to tell about the kinds of articles they like to read. In addition, ask Ss if they read newspapers or magazines in English.

▼ **Teaching tip**
Encourage Ss to read newspapers and magazines in English outside of class. Tell Ss that they will improve their vocabulary if they read at least one article from an English-language newspaper or magazine each week. Tell Ss that they don't need to look up every word they don't understand in the article. They can use context clues to guess the meaning of an unfamiliar word and can look up only those words that prevent them from understanding the main ideas of the article.

- Focus Ss' attention on the title on the board: *"Home Is More Than a Building."* Tell Ss that they are going to read a newspaper article with this title. Ask Ss what they think the title means. Elicit appropriate responses, such as: *A home is what you make it to be – it is a place for your family, a place to grow up in, a place of love and memories – not just a building made of materials. Home can be a country or a community,* etc.

▼ **Culture tip**
Ask Ss if they agree with the idea that a home is more than a building. Many Ss may have left their "home" and do not feel "at home" where they live now. If you have Ss who feel this way, it may help to have a discussion about these feelings and about how to make a home wherever you are.

Presentation

- Books open. Direct Ss' attention to Exercise **1**. Read the instructions aloud.
- Focus Ss' attention on the picture. Ask Ss the questions and write their ideas on the board.

Practice

- Read the instructions aloud for Exercise **2**. Ask Ss to read the article silently before listening to the audio program.

Read the tip box aloud. Ask Ss to look for examples of the time phrases listed in the tip box as they read the newspaper article. Guide Ss to underline the phrases. Explain that the phrases indicate how long ago something happened in the story.

- ◉ Class Audio CD2 track 27 Play or read the audio program and ask Ss to read along (see audio script, page T-162). Repeat the audio program as needed.
- While Ss are listening and reading the article, ask them to underline any words they don't know. When the audio program is finished, ask Ss to write the new vocabulary words on the board.
- Point to each word on the board. Say it and ask Ss to repeat. Give a brief explanation of each word, or ask Ss who are familiar with the word to explain it. Encourage Ss to guess the meaning of each word from context clues in the article. Allow Ss to look up the new words in their dictionaries.

Learner persistence (individual work)

◉ Self-Study Audio CD track 33 Exercise **2** is recorded on the CD at the back of the Student's Book. Ss can listen to the CD at home for reinforcement and review. They can also listen for self-directed learning when class attendance is not possible.

Expansion activity (whole group)

- Write the word *rebuilding* on the board. Say the word and ask Ss to repeat. Underline the prefix *re-*. Tell Ss that this prefix means "to do something again."
- Suggest that Ss brainstorm other words with this prefix. Write the words on the board, for example: *reuse, recycle, repaint, redo.*
- Ask Ss to make sentences with the words to practice using them in context. Model the activity. Say: *When we reuse something, we use it again.*
- Listen to Ss' examples. Correct as needed.

Comprehension check

- Direct Ss' attention to Exercise 3A. Read the instructions aloud.
- Ask individual Ss to read the sentences, one at a time. Make sure all Ss understand the sentences.
- Remind Ss that *scan* means "to read quickly to look for specific information." Encourage Ss to scan the article for time phrases to help them place the events in order.
- Model the task. Ask a S to read the first sentence in the article. Ask: *What is the time phrase in this sentence?* Elicit: *A few months ago.* Say: *Write the number 1 next to "Pedro lost his job" because this event happened first.*
- Ss complete the exercise individually. Walk around and help as needed.
- Select seven Ss (in a large class include several groups of seven). Assign one sentence from Exercise 3A to each S. Ask these Ss to come to the front of the class and line themselves up in the order of the events in the story. In order, each S reads his or her sentence. Ask the class if this order is correct.
- Have a S write his or her sequence of numbers on the board. Correct answers as needed.

Practice

- Focus Ss' attention on Exercise 3B. Read the instructions aloud.
- Model the task. Ask Ss to scan for the word *support* in the article (in last sentence of the first paragraph). Ask a S to say where the word is and to read the sentence. Have Ss underline the word.
- Focus Ss' attention on the multiple-choice options in number 1. Ask Ss which letter they think describes the word *support* best. Elicit: *letter "a."* Ask Ss why they chose this option. Elicit an appropriate response, such as: *Because Pedro is worried about paying for necessary things for another baby.*
- Ss complete the task individually. Walk around and help as needed.
- Ss in pairs. Ask Ss to show each other where they underlined the vocabulary words in the article. Make sure that Ss have underlined all eight vocabulary words.
- Write the numbers 1–8 on the board. Ask individual Ss to come to the board to write the letter of each of the answers.
- Ask other Ss to read the words and the definitions that correspond to the letters on the board. Ask the class if the definitions are correct. Make corrections on the board as needed.

Application

- Direct Ss' attention to Exercise 3C. Read the instructions aloud.
- Ask a S to read the questions to the class. Make sure that all Ss understand the questions.
- Model the task. Read the first question to the class again. Ask for a volunteer to answer it.
- Ss complete the exercise in pairs. Help as needed.

▼ **Teaching tip**
It is important to be sensitive to your Ss' experiences. In some cases, responding to these questions may bring back painful memories that some Ss would prefer not to share with the class.

Community building *(whole group)*

- If your school has a counselor, consider asking that person to visit your class to talk about the resources available in the community to help in the event of a fire or another emergency. Ask the counselor to discuss the different agencies and how they can help people handle unexpected emergencies.

Evaluation

- Direct Ss' attention to the lesson focus on the board.
- Books closed. Ask individual Ss to retell the main points of the article "Home Is More Than a Building." Encourage Ss to use appropriate time phrases to talk about the article.
- Write on the board the vocabulary words from Exercise 3B. Ask Ss to use each word in a sentence to demonstrate that they understand the meaning.
- Check off each part of the lesson focus as Ss demonstrate an understanding of what they have learned in the lesson.

Learner persistence *(individual, pairs)*

- You may wish to assign Extended Reading Worksheets from the *Online Teacher's Resource Room* for Ss to complete outside of class. The purpose of these worksheets is to encourage Ss to read for pleasure in English outside of the English class. The worksheets can also be assigned as extended reading in class.

More Ventures, Unit 9, Lesson D	
Workbook, 15–30 min.	
Add Ventures, 30–45 min.	www.cambridge.org/myresourceroom
Collaborative, 30–45 min.	
Extended Reading and worksheet, 45–60 min.	
Student Arcade, time varies	www.cambridge.org/venturesarcade

3 After you read

A **Check** your understanding. Scan the reading. Look for the time phrases. Write numbers to show the order of events.

_1_ Pedro lost his job.

_7_ Luisa mailed out holiday cards.

_5_ The fire destroyed Pedro and Luisa's home.

_3_ Pedro and Luisa heard about a fire near their home.

_4_ The police ordered people in the neighborhood to evacuate.

_2_ Luisa told Pedro she was pregnant.

_6_ The Ramirez family stayed with Luisa's sister for three months.

B **Build** your vocabulary.

Find the words in the story and underline them. Circle the definitions that best match the reading.

1. support
   a. pay for necessary things
   b. find
   c. say that you agree with someone

2. evacuate
   a. clean
   b. go inside a house
   c. leave a dangerous place

3. gathering
   a. separating
   b. a group of things
   c. collecting

4. grabbed
   a. took quickly
   b. held someone with force
   c. stole

5. destroyed
   a. broke completely
   b. killed
   c. hurt

6. generous
   a. critical
   b. giving
   c. sad

7. strangers
   a. family
   b. friends
   c. people you don't know

8. message
   a. medical treatment
   b. communication
   c. a person who brings things

C **Talk** with a partner. Ask and answer the questions.

1. Tell your partner about an emergency situation that happened to you or your family. What happened?

2. Has someone been generous to you or your family? How?

3. How do you feel about accepting help from strangers?

LESSON E Writing

1 Before you write

A **Talk** with a partner. Think about an emergency. Answer the questions.

1. **Who** did it happen to?
2. **What** happened?
3. **When** did it happen?
4. **Where** did it happen?
5. **Why** or **how** did it happen?

B **Read** the story.

Fire in Our Backyard

One evening last summer, my husband and I were preparing dinner together. My husband was cooking outside, and I was setting the table inside. Suddenly, my husband ran into the kitchen and shouted, "There's a fire in the backyard!" I ran outside and saw fire in the bushes next to our fence. I was really scared because my 70-year-old parents live next door. Luckily, my husband acted quickly. He called the fire department and then started putting water on the fire. The firefighters arrived quickly, and they easily put out the fire. They said a coal from the barbecue started it.

My parents were very surprised when they saw the firefighters. They were watching the news in the living room, and they never knew there was a problem. My father said, "Let's go back and watch the news. Maybe we're on TV!"

Lesson objectives

- Write a story about an emergency
- Organize a story using *who, what, when, where, why*, and *how* questions
- Practice using the past continuous

Warm-up and review

- Before class. Write today's lesson focus on the board.

  Lesson E:
  Read and write about an emergency
  Use questions to organize a story

- Begin class. Books closed. Focus Ss' attention on the word *emergency* in the lesson focus. Ask Ss to brainstorm different types of emergencies. Write Ss' ideas on the board, such as: *health emergencies (heart attack, stroke, etc.), fire, flood, tornado, earthquake.*

- Ask Ss to brainstorm question words and write them on the board. Write *Who* on the board as an example. Elicit: *What, When, Where, Why,* and *How.*

- Guide Ss to look carefully at the pictures on page 110 and to ask questions using the question words. Write the correctly formed questions on the board. Elicit appropriate answers such as: *Who was robbed? When did the robbery happen?*

- Be sure Ss understand the meaning of the question words and the correct way to respond.

▼ **Teaching tip**

Ss may have missed or do not remember Lesson A on page 110 of this unit. Therefore, any appropriate questions and answers about Lesson A should be encouraged. These questions and answers do not have to mimic the conversation or summary in the lesson. The task is to review questions, not necessarily to review the story in Lesson A.

Presentation

- Books open. Focus Ss' attention on Exercise **1A**. Read the instructions aloud. Ss work with a partner and then share their discussion with the class.

Practice

- Direct Ss' attention to the picture in Exercise **1B**. Have Ss use their visual literacy skills to answer the question: *What do you see?* Elicit a description of the picture, such as: *There is a fire between two backyards. The bushes caught fire. Two firefighters are putting out the fire with water. The two families who live near the fire are surprised and worried.*

- Read the instructions aloud. Then read the title to the class. Tell Ss that they are going to read about the fire that is shown in the picture.

- Have Ss read the story silently. Tell Ss to underline any words they don't know.

- Ask Ss to write any new words on the board. Have other Ss explain the words if they know them, or encourage Ss to try to guess the meaning of the words from context.

Expansion activity *(student pairs)*

- Ask Ss to look at the opening pictures of previous units (pages 2, 6, 18, 32, 44, 58, 70, 84, or 110).

- Tell Ss to pick one of the opening pictures and use the questions in Exercise **1A** to tell a story about the pictures.

  Option Assign opening pictures to pairs of students.

- Ask Ss to share the stories they create with the class.

Learner persistence *(whole group)*

- Reviewing material as a class helps reinforce information for Ss who have been in class and keeps Ss who have missed lessons from falling behind. Encourage Ss to look through the first eight units of the Student's Book and to ask questions about anything they do not remember or still do not understand. Take time to review whenever possible.

Comprehension check

- Direct Ss' attention to the second part of the instructions for Exercise 1B. Read it aloud.
- Ask individual Ss to read the questions to the class.
- Model the task. Ask a S the first question. Elicit: *The story is about a woman, her husband, and her parents.*
- Ss work with a partner to ask and answer the questions. Walk around and help as needed.
- Ask several pairs to ask and answer the questions for the rest of the class.

Practice

- Direct Ss' attention to Exercise 1C. Read the instructions aloud. Remind Ss that they already thought of an emergency in Exercise 1A of this lesson. Tell Ss that they can write about the same emergency if it happened to them or to someone they know, or they can think of a different emergency. Explain that Ss can also write a plan for an imagined emergency.
- Model the task. Hold up the Student's Book. Point to the chart and the blank space after the first question. Say: *Write your answers in note form here.*
- Ss complete the exercise individually. Walk around and help as needed.

Application

- Focus Ss' attention on Exercise 2. Read the instructions aloud.

> Read the tip box aloud. Remind Ss that their stories should answer the questions in the tip box. Tell Ss to refer to their answers in Exercise 1C to check to see that they included the answers to all these questions in their stories.

- Ss complete the exercise individually. Walk around and help as needed.

Learner persistence *(individual work)*

- If you have Ss in your class who have difficulty writing on their own, you could also suggest that they copy the story "Fire in Our Backyard" but change the story to refer to the people in the picture. In that case, the story would begin: *One evening last summer, Mr. and Mrs. Lee were preparing dinner together. Mrs. Lee's husband was cooking outside. . . .*

Comprehension check

- Direct Ss' attention to Exercise 3A. Read the instructions aloud. Ask a S to read the three checklist items to the class. This exercise asks Ss to develop skills to review and edit their own writing.
- Ss check their own stories. Walk around and help as needed. If any Ss check *No* for one or more of the checklist items, ask them to revise their story to include the missing information or to edit their story to correct grammar and punctuation.

Evaluation

- Focus Ss' attention on Exercise 3B. Read the instructions aloud. This exercise asks Ss to work together to peer-correct their writing. Reading aloud enables the writer to review his or her own writing. Reading to a partner allows the writer to understand the need to write clearly for an audience.
- Have partners take turns reading their stories. Walk around and help as needed.
- Listen to Ss as they ask their partner a question about the story and comment on one thing they learned from it.
- Encourage Ss to read their stories to the class. Have individual Ss comment on what they learned from their classmates' stories.
- Direct Ss' attention to the lesson focus on the board. Encourage Ss to give examples of question words and to ask questions about the story using the question words.
- Check off each part of the lesson focus as Ss demonstrate an understanding of what they have learned in the lesson.

More Ventures, Unit 9, Lesson E	
Workbook, 15–30 min.	
Add Ventures, 30–45 min.	www.cambridge.org/myresourceroom
Collaborative, 30–45 min.	

Work with a partner. Answer the questions.

1. Who is the story about?
2. When did it happen?
3. Where did it happen?
4. What were the people doing when the story started?
5. What was the emergency?
6. Why was the writer scared?
7. How did the story end?

C **Write** a plan for a story about an emergency that happened to you or someone you know. Answer the questions.

1. Who is the story about?	*(Answers will vary.)*
2. Where did it happen?	
3. When did it happen?	
4. What were the people doing when the story started?	
5. What was the emergency?	
6. How did the story end?	

2 Write

Write a story about an emergency that happened to you or someone you know. Give the story a title and write a concluding sentence. Use the information from Exercises 1B and 1C to help you.

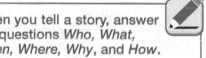

When you tell a story, answer the questions *Who, What, When, Where, Why,* and *How.*

3 After you write

A **Check** your writing.

	Yes	No
1. I gave my story a title.	☐	☐
2. My story answers the questions *Who, What, When, Where, Why,* and *How.*	☐	☐
3. I wrote a concluding sentence.	☐	☐

B **Share** your writing with a partner.

1. Take turns. Read your story to a partner.
2. Comment on your partner's story. Ask your partner a question about the story. Tell your partner one thing you learned.

☑ Write a story about an emergency that answers the questions *Who, What, When, Where, Why,* and *How.* **UNIT 9** **119**

LESSON F Another view

Life-skills reading

Safest States in the United States	
2007	**2010**
1 North Dakota	1 New Hampshire
2 Vermont	2 Vermont
3 Maine	3 North Dakota
4 New Hampshire	4 Maine
5 Wyoming	5 Idaho
18 New Jersey	15 New York
20 New York	19 New Jersey
30 Illinois	30 Ohio
39 Texas	36 California
42 California	42 Arizona
43 Florida	43 Maryland

Source: Crime State Rankings 2007 and 2010

A **Read** the questions. Look at the chart. Fill in the answer.

1. Which state had the same rank in 2007 and 2010?
   - Ⓐ Florida
   - ● Vermont
   - Ⓒ California
   - Ⓓ New York

2. Which state became less safe in 2010?
   - Ⓐ New York
   - Ⓑ California
   - ● North Dakota
   - Ⓓ New Hampshire

3. Which state became safer in 2010?
   - Ⓐ Maine
   - Ⓑ Vermont
   - Ⓒ New Jersey
   - ● New Hampshire

4. Which state had a different rank in 2007 and 2010?
   - Ⓐ North Dakota
   - Ⓑ New Jersey
   - ● both *a* and *b*
   - Ⓓ neither *a* nor *b*

B **Talk** with your classmates. Ask and answer the questions.

1. Do you feel safe where you live? Why?
2. Where do you think is the safest place to live?
3. Where do you think is the most dangerous place to live?

Lesson objectives

- Practice reading and understanding a chart comparing safety in various states in the U.S.
- Use the present continuous for three different purposes
- Complete the self-assessment

Warm-up and review

- Before class. Write today's lesson focus on the board.

  Lesson F:
  Read and understand a chart comparing safety in different states in the U.S.
  Review topic vocabulary
  Complete the self-assessment

- Begin class. Books closed. Focus Ss' attention on the words *U.S. states* in the lesson focus. Say the words and ask Ss to repeat. Have Ss create a list of names of as many states as they can brainstorm. Write the states on the board.

- If possible, bring a map of the United States to class, or point to a map if there is one in the classroom. Ask individual Ss to volunteer to point out the states written on the board.

- Focus Ss' attention on the word *safety* in the lesson focus. Guide Ss to see that this is the noun form of the word *safe*. Ask Ss to guess which state is the safest state in the U.S. Point to the states on the map that Ss guess to be the safest. Ask Ss to guess which state is the least safe. Point to the states on the map that Ss guess to be the least safe.

Presentation

- Books open. Direct Ss' attention to the chart in Exercise **1**. Lead Ss to see that this is a chart comparing safety in different states.

- Write the word *rank* on the board. Say the word aloud. Ask Ss what they think it means. Elicit, or tell Ss if they don't know: *A rank is a position in a comparison.* Tell Ss that the chart shows the rank, or position, of the safest states in the U.S. in 2007 and 2010, with number 1 being the safest state and number 43 being the least safe state.

- Ask: Which state in the chart was the safest in 2007? (North Dakota.) Ask: *Which state in the chart was the safest in 2010?* (New Hampshire.) Ask: *Which state in the chart was the least safe in 2007?* (Florida.) *What about in 2010?* (Maryland.)

▼**Teaching tip**
It might be helpful to explain that this chart shows only the top five safest states and the rank of a few other states. That is why other numbers and states are not included in the chart.

Practice

- Direct Ss' attention to Exercise **1A** and read the instructions aloud. This task helps prepare Ss for standardized-type tests they may have to take. Make sure that Ss understand the task. Have Ss individually scan for and fill in the answers.

Comprehension check

- Check answers with the class. Ask Ss to read the questions and their answers aloud. Make corrections as needed.

Application

- Direct Ss' attention to Exercise **1B**. Read the instructions aloud. Ask three Ss to read the questions to the class. Make sure that Ss understand the meaning of each question.

- Discuss these questions as a class.

Community building (small groups)

- Brainstorm ways that Ss can prevent crime and feel safer.

- Put poster board or large pieces of paper around the room. Ask Ss to form groups in front of each of the posters or pieces of paper. Before class, write a different suggestion for safety on each poster or piece of paper, for example: *Always walk with another person when it is dark or in less safe neighborhoods. Don't leave valuable items in cars. Walk on lighted streets, even if it means going out of your way. Set up a neighborhood watch. Lock all doors. Report crimes if you see them.*

- Give the groups markers and ask them to write additional safety tips on the poster board or pieces of paper.

- Discuss the ideas from the different groups.

- Make a *Crime Buster* poster of Ss' ideas. Ask Ss to draw illustrations of the safety advice and attach them to the poster. Keep the poster in class and continue to talk about safety when time allows.

Warm-up and review

- Books closed. Ask Ss questions with the past continuous. *What were you doing last night at 8 p.m.?* Ensure Ss reply using the past continuous.
- Write on the board: *When the fire started, both families were inside their houses.* Ask Ss how we can change the order of this sentence so that there is no comma. Elicit the correct answer and write it on the board (*Both families were inside their houses when the fire started.*)

Presentation

- Books open. Direct Ss' attention to the grammar chart in **2A**. Ask three Ss to read the sentences. Tell Ss to compare the sentences. Ask: *What do these sentences have in common?* Elicit the answer: *They all use the present continuous.*
- Ask Ss to define the present continuous. Elicit answers, such as: *The present continuous tells us what's happening right now.* Tell Ss that, in addition to describing current actions, present continuous can also describe ongoing events and events in the near future.

Practice

- Direct Ss' attention to the instructions in **2A**. Read the instructions aloud. Ensure Ss understand the activity. Ask a pair of Ss to read the dialog aloud.
- Split the class into small groups. Have Ss ask one another questions. Walk around and help as needed.
- Direct Ss' attention to the instructions in **2B**. Read the instructions aloud. Ask two Ss to read the example sentences. Ss complete the exercise in pairs. Encourage each S to share a sentence about a person in their group.

Evaluation

- Before asking students to turn to the self-assessment on page 140, do a quick review of the unit. Have Ss turn to Lesson A. Ask the class to talk about what they remember about this lesson. Prompt Ss, if necessary, with questions, for example: *What are the conversations about on this page? What vocabulary is in the pictures?* Continue in this manner to review each lesson quickly.
- **Self-assessment** Read the instructions for Exercise **3**. Ask Ss to turn to the self-assessment page and complete the unit self-assessment. The self-assessments are also on the *Online Teacher's Resource Room.* If you prefer to collect the assessments and save them as part of each S's portfolio assessment, print out the unit self-assessment from the *Resource Room,* ask students to complete it, and collect and save it.
- If Ss are ready, administer the unit test on pages T-184–T-185 of this Teacher's Edition (or on the Assessment Audio CD / CD-ROM).

More Ventures, Unit 9, Lesson F	
Workbook, 15–30 min.	
Add Ventures, 30–45 min.	www.cambridge.org/myresourceroom
Collaborative, 30–45 min.	

2 Grammar connections: three uses of the present continuous

Events happening now	Farah **is wearing** new jeans right now.
Ongoing events	I**'m studying** in the library this week.
Events in the near future	Hiro **isn't working** next Saturday.

A **Work** in a small group. Complete the chart.

> **A** What are you doing tonight, Farah?
> **B** I'm studying English.

	Name: _____	Name: _____	Name: _____
1. What are you doing tonight?	*(Answers will vary.)*		
2. What are you looking at right now?			
3. What are you watching on TV this week?			
4. What are you doing next Saturday?			
5. What are you thinking about right now?			
6. What classes are you taking this term?			

B **Work** with a partner. Look at the questions in Exercise 2A. Answer the questions.

1. Which questions are about events happening now? _____
2. Which questions are about ongoing events? _____
3. Which questions are about events in the near future? _____

3 Wrap up

Complete the **Self-assessment** on page 140.

☑ Interpret a chart about the safest states in the U.S.;
use the present continuous for three different purposes **UNIT 9** 121

LESSON A
Listening

1 **Before you listen**

Talk about the pictures.

A What do you see?

B What is happening?

C What's the story?

Lesson objectives

- Introduce students to the topic
- Find out what students know about the topic
- Preview the unit by talking about the pictures
- Practice key vocabulary
- Practice listening skills

Warm-up and review

- Before class. Write today's lesson focus on the board.

  Lesson A:
  Vacation plans

- Begin class. Books closed. Direct Ss' attention to the words *vacation plans* on the board. Say the words aloud and have Ss repeat. Ask Ss to brainstorm ideas that come to mind when they think of vacations. Write Ss' responses on the board, for example: *no work, no school, bus, plane, car, go home to see my family*.

- Discuss ways in which people get information about vacations and about things to do in their free time, for example: *through friends and family, the Internet, airlines, bus companies, newspapers*.

- If any Ss have recently had vacation time, ask how they spent their time and if they planned the vacation.

▼**Teaching tip**
Because of their personal situations, some Ss may not have much or any vacation time. It is important to be sensitive to these Ss. Do not spend too much time talking about personal vacation time, but rather keep the discussion more focused on free time.

Presentation

- Books open. Set the scene. Direct Ss' attention to the first picture on page 122. Ask the question in Exercise **1A**: *What do you see?* Elicit and write on the board as much vocabulary as possible about the picture. Explain any unfamiliar words. Continue eliciting words to describe the three remaining pictures.

- Direct Ss' attention to the question in Exercise **1B**: *What is happening?* Read it aloud. Draw three vertical lines on the board, creating four columns. Write the headings *Picture 1, Picture 2, Picture 3*, and *Picture 4* above the columns. Ask Ss to say a few sentences to describe what is happening in each picture. Write Ss' ideas in the correct column on the board.

- Guide Ss to see that the exercises on the opening page enable them to use and develop their visual literacy skills as well as their language skills.

Practice

- Direct Ss' attention to the question in Exercise **1C**: *What's the story?* Tell Ss that they are going to work with a partner to create a story from the pictures. One S writes the story as pairs work together.

▼**Teaching tip**
Encourage Ss to be creative. At this point, there is no single correct story.

▼**Teaching tip**
If you have a multilevel class, this would be a good time to pair a S who feels more confident with speaking skills with a S who feels more comfortable with writing skills. Encourage pairs to be supportive as they work together to create the story.

- Ask a S to begin the story. Write several suggestions or sentence-starters on the board. Then have partners work together to continue the story.

- Ask Ss from several pairs to tell their story to the class.

Presentation

- Book open. Direct Ss' attention to Exercise **2A**. Have Ss listen for the main idea. Read the instructions aloud. Explain that after listening to the conversation, Ss in pairs will ask and answer questions in the exercise.

- Ask a S to read the questions in Exercise **2A** aloud. Tell Ss to listen for this information as the audio program is played or read.

- 🎧 Class Audio CD2 track 28 Play or read the audio program (see audio script, pages T-162–T-163).

- Ask Ss if they understood everything in the listening exercise. Write any unfamiliar words on the board and help Ss understand the meaning.

- Elicit answers to the questions.

- Focus Ss' attention on Exercise **2B**. Read the instructions aloud. Have Ss read the chart for information about transportation and lodging. Explain any unfamiliar words.

▼ **Teaching tip**

It might be helpful to explain that *one-way* means there is no return trip. You will travel in only one direction – from here to your destination. *Round-trip* means there is a return trip. You will travel to a destination and back to your starting place. *Airfare* is the cost of an airplane ticket. *Campsite* is a place where people can sleep outside, usually in tents, when they *go camping.*

▼ **Culture note**

Read the note at the bottom of the page. Explain that in most hotels there is usually an additional charge of a room tax that increases the advertised cost of the room. There can also be additional charges for using the telephone, watching a movie on TV, or taking food from the in-room snack bar. Coffee and tea in the room are usually free.

- 🎧 Class Audio CD2 track 28 Guide Ss to listen for details about Ricardo and Felicia's travel plans. Model the task. Play or read the audio program again (see audio script, pages T-162–T-163). Pause the program after Ricardo says: *we can get a round-trip ticket for $200.* Ask: *How much is the cost of the round-trip airfare per person?* Elicit: *$200.* Show Ss where in the chart to write $200. Tell Ss to listen and complete the chart. Play or read the rest of the audio program.

- Elicit answers from Ss and write them on the board.

- 🎧 Class Audio CD2 track 28 Play or read the audio program again (see audio script, pages T-162–T-163). Ss listen and check their answers.

- Have several Ss come to the board to write their answers. Ask Ss to repeat the numbers after you to practice reading and saying numbers with dollars and percentages.

Learner persistence (individual work)

- 🎧 Self-Study Audio CD track 34 Exercises **2A** and **2B** are recorded on the CD at the back of the Student's Book. Ss can listen to the CD at home for reinforcement and review. They can also listen to the CD for self-directed learning when class attendance is not possible.

Practice

- Focus Ss' attention on Exercise **3A**. Read the instructions aloud. Tell Ss that the story in this exercise is a summary of what happened in the pictures on the previous page and of the conversation they heard.

- Direct Ss' attention to the words in the word bank. Say each word aloud. Ask Ss to repeat. Explain any unfamiliar words.

- Ss complete the exercise individually. Walk around and help as needed

Comprehension check

- 🎧 Class Audio CD2 track 29 Play or read the audio program (see audio script, page T-163). Ss listen and check their answers. Repeat the audio program as needed.

- Write the numbers *1–8* on the board. Ask individual Ss to come to the board to write their answers.

Learner persistence (individual work)

- 🎧 Self-Study Audio CD track 35 Exercise **3A** is recorded on the CD at the back of the Student's Book. Ss can listen to the CD at home for reinforcement and review. They can also listen for self-directed learning when class attendance is not possible.

Application

- Focus Ss' attention on Exercise **3B**. Read the instructions aloud.

- Ss complete the exercise with a partner. Help as needed.

Evaluation

- Direct Ss' attention to the lesson focus on the board. Ask Ss to look at the pictures on page 122 and make sentences using the words from the word bank in Exercise **3A**.

- Check off each part of the lesson focus as Ss demonstrate an understanding of what they have learned in the lesson.

More Ventures, Unit 10, Lesson A	
Workbook, 15–30 min.	
Add Ventures, 30–45 min.	www.cambridge.org/myresourceroom
Collaborative, 30–45 min.	
Student Arcade, time varies	www.cambridge.org/venturesarcade

Unit Goals	**Discuss** vacation plans
	Read about a tourist attraction
	Get information from a hotel advertisement

2 Listen

STUDENT TK 34
CLASS CD2 TK 28

A Listen and answer the questions.

1. Who are the speakers?   2. What are they talking about?

STUDENT TK 34
CLASS CD2 TK 28

B Listen again. Complete the chart.

	San Francisco	**Camping**
Transportation	Round-trip airfare per person: $ _200_	Gas for the car: $ _100_
Lodging	Hotel per night: $ _250_ Tax: _14_ %	Campsite per night: $ _35_

3 After you listen

A Read. Complete the story.

> **CULTURE NOTE**
>
> Advertisements for hotels do not include the room tax. The tax adds 7% to 16% per night to the cost of the room.

book a flight	days off	reserve	tax
camping	discounts	round-trip	tourist

Felicia is exhausted. She needs a vacation. Her husband, Ricardo, says he can ask his boss for a few ___days off___ . Felicia would like to go to San Francisco.
                                  1
They look for special travel ___discounts___ on the Internet. If they _book a flight_ at
                              2   3
least seven days ahead, they can get a ___round-trip___ ticket for less than $200. On
                                        4
the other hand, hotel room rates will be high because summer is the most popular

___tourist___ season. Also, there is a room ___tax___ on hotel rooms in San
       5   6
Francisco. They figure out that a three-day trip to San Francisco will cost

almost $1,200.

Felicia and her husband decide to change their plans. If they go ___camping___,
                                                                        7
they will save a lot of money and their daughter will have more fun. Felicia's

husband will ___reserve___ the campsite after he talks to his boss.
                  8

STUDENT TK 35
CLASS CD2 TK 29

Listen and check your answers.

B Talk with a partner. Answer the question.

Which would you prefer: a trip to San Francisco or camping in the mountains?

LESSON **B** Conditionals

1 Grammar focus: future real

> If the fare **is** cheap enough, we **will fly**.
>
> If the weather **is** bad, she **won't go swimming**.

> We **will fly if** the fare **is** cheap enough.
>
> She **won't go swimming if** the weather **is** bad.

Turn to page 148 for a grammar explanation.

USEFUL LANGUAGE

won't = will not

2 Practice

A **Write.** Complete the sentences. Use the simple present or future form of the verbs. Circle the future conditional clause.

1. Annette and William _____will take_____ their children to Sea Adventure next month
   (take)
   if William _____gets_____ a few days off.
   (get)

2. If they _____get_____ a discount, they _____will reserve_____ a room at a hotel.
   (get)   (reserve)

3. If prices _____are_____ too high, they _____will not take_____ an expensive vacation.
   (be)   (not / take)

4. We _____will have_____ a picnic on Saturday if it _____does not rain_____.
   (have)   (not / rain)

5. If you _____give_____ me the money, I _____will buy_____ the concert tickets.
   (give)   (buy)

6. If you _____come_____ to Chicago, we _____will meet_____ you at the airport.
   (come)   (meet)

7. They _____will fly_____ to Miami next month if they _____don't find_____ a cheap flight.
   (fly)   (find)

8. We _____will not go_____ camping if the weather _____is_____ too hot.
   (not / go)   (be)

CLASS CD2 TK 30

Listen and check your answers.

Lesson objectives

- Introduce future conditional clauses with *if*
- Ask and answer questions about future possibility

Warm-up and review

Before class: Write today's lesson focus on the board.
Lesson B:
Clauses with if

- Books open. Begin class. Direct Ss' attention to the pictures on page 122. Ask questions such as the following: *Where will Ricardo and Felicia go on vacation?* (They'll go to Big Bear Lake.) *What will they do there?* (They will go camping.) *Why won't they stay in a hotel?* (because it is too expensive.)

Presentation

Focus on meaning / personalize

- Books closed. Direct Ss' attention to the lesson focus on the board. Read it aloud. Divide the board into two columns with *Name* and *Activity* as headings. Say: *The weather might be good this weekend. If the weather is good, I will take a walk. What about you? What will you do if the weather is good?* Write Ss' answers on the board. For example:

Name	Activity
José	play soccer
Ana	barbecue outside

- Ask questions with *will* about the information on the board, such as: *What will José do if the weather is good?* (play soccer.) *Will Ana barbecue outside if the weather is good?* (Yes.)

- Write on the board: *If the weather is good this weekend, José will play soccer. If the weather is good, Ana will barbecue outside.* Ask: *Are the sentences about now, the past, or the future?* (the future.) *How do you know?* (will.) *Will they do those things for sure or maybe?* (maybe.) *What part of the sentence tells you "maybe"?* (if.)

- Explain that these sentences express future possibility. This means that it is possible that something will happen but only if a certain condition is in place, for example: *José will only play soccer if the weather is good.*

Focus on form

- Books open. Direct Ss' attention to the charts in Exercise **1**. Read the first two statements. Ask Ss to repeat. Direct Ss attention to the first statement. Ask: *Will they definitely fly?* (No.) *What will make them decide to fly?* (whether the fare is cheap.)
  Have Ss circle: *If the fare is cheap enough.* Ask: *What tense is the verb "is"?* (present.) Say: *This is the dependent clause.* Ask: *What is the main clause?* (we will fly.) *Why is it the main clause?* (It can stand alone as a sentence.) *What tense is used in the main clause?* (future.)

- Direct Ss' attention to the bottom chart in Exercise **1**. Read each statement aloud and ask Ss to repeat. Ask Ss: *Do these two sentences mean the same as the first two sentences?* (Yes.) Explain that the *if* clause can be at the beginning or end of the sentence.

▼ **Useful language**

Read the *Useful language* box aloud then direct Ss attention to the examples of *won't* in the language chart.

Practice

- Focus Ss' attention on Exercise **2A**. Read the instructions aloud.

- Model the task. Ask two S to read aloud the example sentence. Tell Ss to complete the exercise by filling in the blanks with the correct form of the verb below. Tell Ss that they will use either *will* plus the verb or the simple present tense (as part of the *if* clause).

- Ss complete the exercise individually. Help as needed.

Comprehension check

- Focus Ss' attention on the second part of the instructions for Exercise **2A**. Read it aloud.

- 🔊 Class Audio CD2 track 30 Play or read the complete audio program (see audio script, page T-163). Ss listen and check their answers. Repeat the audio program as needed.

- Write the numbers *1–8* on the board. Ask several Ss to come to the board to write their answers. Ask other Ss to read aloud the complete sentences. Correct as needed.

LESSON B Conditionals

Presentation

- Direct Ss' attention to the pictures for Exercise **2B**. Ask Ss to look at the first picture in number 1. Ask: *What's John doing?* Elicit an appropriate response such as: *He's playing soccer.* Ask: *How's the weather?* (It's sunny. It's fine. It's good.)

- Ask Ss to look at the second picture in number 1. Ask: *What's he doing now?* Elicit an appropriate response, such as: *He's watching a movie at home.* Ask: *How's the weather now?* (It's rainy. It's raining. It's bad. It's awful.) Continue describing the action in the remaining sets of pictures.

Practice

- Read the instructions aloud. Then read the two phrases under each set of pictures. Explain any unfamiliar words.

- Model the task. Ask two Ss to read the example questions and answers to the class. Be sure that Ss understand that the first picture in each set shows what John will do in good weather. The second picture in each set shows what John will do if the weather isn't good.

- Ss complete the exercise with a partner. Walk around and help as needed.

- Read the second part of the instructions for Exercise **2B**.

- Ask two Ss to read the example sentences aloud. Tell Ss that they will write two sentences, such as the ones in the example, for each set of pictures.

- Ss complete the exercise individually. Walk around and help as needed.

▼ **Useful language**

Read the *Useful language* box aloud and then direct Ss' attention to the example of *He'll* in the language chart.

Comprehension check

- Write the numbers *1–4* on the board. Ask individual Ss to come to the board to write their sentences.

- Have other Ss read the sentences aloud. Ask Ss if the sentences are written correctly. Have different Ss correct them on the board as needed.

Expansion activity *(student pairs)*

- Ask Ss to think about what they will do this weekend if the weather is good or if the weather is bad.

- Write on the board: *What will you do this weekend if the weather is good? What will you do if the weather is bad?*

- Model the activity. Invite a S to ask you the two questions written on the board. Respond with your real plans, or make up some plans.

- Ss work with a partner to ask and answer the questions. Make sure that all Ss both ask and answer the questions. Walk around and help as needed.

- Ask several pairs to ask and answer the questions for the rest of the class.

Application

- Direct Ss' attention to Exercise **3A**. Read the instructions aloud. Explain any unfamiliar vocabulary.

- Model the task. Ask two Ss to read aloud the example question and answer.

- Hold up the Student's Book. Show Ss where the answer to the question is written in the chart.

- Ss complete the exercise with a partner. Walk around and help as needed.

- Direct Ss' attention to Exercise **3B**. Read the instructions aloud.

- Ask as many Ss as possible to share their partner's plans with the rest of the class.

Evaluation

- Direct Ss' attention to the lesson focus on the board.

- Tell Ss to use future conditional clauses with *if* to make sentences about the pictures on page 125.

- Check off each part of the lesson focus as Ss demonstrate an understanding of what they have learned in the lesson.

More Ventures, Unit 10, Lesson B	
Workbook, 15–30 min.	
Add Ventures, 30–45 min.	www.cambridge.org/myresourceroom
Collaborative, 30–45 min.	
Student Arcade, time varies	www.cambridge.org/venturesarcade

B **Talk** with a partner. Ask and answer questions about the pictures.

A What will John do if the weather is good?
B He'll play soccer.

A What will he do if the weather isn't good?
B He'll watch a movie.

USEFUL LANGUAGE

He'll = He will

1. John

play soccer   watch a movie

2. Melinda and Pedro

go hiking   go shopping

3. Ken

go swimming   clean the house

4. Andrea

work in the garden   read a book

Write a sentence about each picture.

If the weather is good, John will play soccer.
He'll watch a movie if the weather isn't good.
(Answers will vary.)

3 Communicate

A **Work** with a partner. Ask and answer questions. Take notes in the chart.

A What will you do if you have time off in the summer?
B I'll visit my family in Mexico.

1. have time off in the summer	*visit family in Mexico*
2. have a three-day weekend	*(Answers will vary.)*
3. get some extra money	
4. the weather is beautiful next weekend	

B **Share** information about your partner.

LESSON C Future time clauses

1 Grammar focus: clauses with *before* and *after*

Before Kim **takes** a vacation, he **will finish** school.
After Kim **finishes** school, he **will take** a vacation.

Kim **will finish** school **before** he **takes** a vacation.
Kim **will take** a vacation **after** he **finishes** school.

Turn to page 148 for a grammar explanation.

2 Practice

A Write. Complete the sentences. Use the correct form of the verb.

1. Kara _____*will talk*_____ to a travel agent before she _____*books*_____ a flight.
   (talk)   (book)

2. Before Cynthia _____*leaves*_____ for Puerto Rico, she _____*will buy*_____ some
   (leave)   (buy)
   new clothes.

3. Donald _____*will take*_____ a taxi to the hotel after he _____*picks up*_____ his baggage.
   (take)   (pick up)

4. The campers _____*will make*_____ a fire before they _____*cook*_____ their dinner.
   (make)   (cook)

5. After they _____*finish*_____ eating, they _____*will clean up*_____ the campsite.
   (finish)   (clean up)

6. I _____*will call*_____ you after I _____*return*_____ from my trip.
   (call)   (return)

7. After I _____*get*_____ my passport, I _____*will make*_____ the reservations.
   (get)   (make)

8. Before we _____*go*_____ to Mexico, we _____*will learn*_____ some words in Spanish.
   (go)   (learn)

9. Jack _____*will lock*_____ the doors before he _____*leaves*_____ for the airport.
   (lock)   (leave)

Listen and check your answers.

CLASS CD2 TK 31

Warm-up and review

Before class: Write today's lesson focus on the board.

Lesson C:
<u>before</u> *clauses with future meaning*
<u>after</u> *clauses with future meaning*

- Books open. Begin class. Direct Ss' attention to the pictures on page 125. Point to the pictures and say: *Tell me what John will do if the weather is good.* (If the weather is good, John will play soccer.)

- Write on the board: *John will play soccer if the weather is good.* Ask: *What is the dependent clause?* (if the weather is good) *What verb tense is used in the "if" clause?* (present) *What is the main clause?* (John will play soccer) *What tense is used in the main clause?* (future tense) Ask similar questions about Melinda and Pedro, Ken, and Andrea. Elicit answers in the conditional.

Presentation

Focus on meaning / personalize

- Books closed. Direct Ss' attention to the lesson focus on the board. Say: *After I go home today, I will eat lunch. What about you? What will you do after you go home today?* (clean the house) Elicit responses from three or four Ss, and write the answers on the board, for example: *José will eat lunch after he goes home.* And under that, write: *After José goes home, he will eat lunch.*

- Then write on the board a full sentence with *before*, for example: *José will go home before he eats lunch.*

Focus on form

- Books open. Direct Ss' attention to the charts in Exercise **1**. Read the first two statements aloud. Ask Ss to repeat. Ask: *What will Kim do first?* (finish school.) *What will Kim do second?* (take a vacation.)

- Ask the following questions about the first statement: *What is the main clause?* (he will finish school) *What is the dependent clause?* (before Kim takes a vacation) *What verb tense is used in the main clause?* (future) *What verb tense is used in the dependent clause?* (present) Remind Ss that these sentences follow the same pattern as the *if* sentences in Lesson B.

- Direct Ss' attention to the next two statements in the chart. Read them aloud. Ask Ss to repeat.

- Ask what the difference is between the two sets of sentences. Elicit or explain: *The before and after clauses are at the beginning in the first set of statements.* Ask: *What punctuation is used when the before and after clauses come first in the statements?* (a comma)

Practice

- Direct Ss' attention to Exercise **2A**. Read the instructions aloud.

- Model the task. Have a S read the example sentence aloud. Tell Ss to complete the exercise by filling in the blanks with the correct verb forms: simple present or future.

- Ss complete the exercise individually. Help as needed.

Comprehension check

- Read aloud the second part of the instructions for Exercise **2A**.

- Class Audio CD2 track 31 Play or read the audio program (see audio script, page T-163). Ss listen and check their answers.

- Write the numbers *1–9* on the board. Have Ss come to the board to write their answers.

Presentation

- Books closed. Ask Ss if they have flown on an airplane before. If any Ss say *Yes*, ask them to brainstorm the procedure of getting onto the airplane on the day of the flight. Write the sequence Ss tell you in list form on the board, for example: *1. Check in at your airline's ticket counter. 2. Go through security. 3. Walk or ride to the gate that your airplane leaves from. 4. Wait in the gate area until your flight is announced. 5. Show your boarding pass and picture ID to the person at the gate. 6. Get on the airplane.*

▼ **Teaching tip**
Ss may not know the vocabulary for getting onto an airplane. Write these words or phrases on the board: *check in*, *ticket counter*, *security*, *boarding pass*, *picture ID*, and *gate*. Explain each one.

Practice

- Books open. Direct Ss' attention to Picture 1 in Exercise **2B**. Ask Ss what they see. Elicit an appropriate response, such as: *A woman is going on a trip. She is checking in for her flight.* Ask Ss what they see in Picture 2. Elicit: *The woman is going through security. Continue with the remaining pictures.*
- Read the instructions aloud. Model the task. Ask two Ss to read the example sentences aloud. Point out that the pictures and the words cue sentences with *before* and *after.*
- Ss work in pairs to complete the exercise. Help as needed.
- Direct Ss' attention to the second part of the instructions for Exercise **2B**. Read it aloud. Then read the example sentence.
- Ss complete the exercise individually. Help as needed.

Comprehension check

- Write the numbers *1–6* on the board. Ask individual Ss to come to the board to write their sentences from the second part of Exercise **2B**.
- Ask other Ss to read the sentences aloud. Correct as needed.

Application

- Direct Ss' attention to Exercise **3A**. Read the instructions aloud.
- Ss work individually to think of a vacation location and three things they need to do before the trip. Help as needed.
- Direct Ss' attention to Exercise **3B**. Read the instructions aloud.
- Model the task. Ask two Ss to read aloud the example questions and answers.

- Ss conduct the interview in pairs and write notes in the chart. Help as needed.
- Direct Ss' attention to Exercise **3C**. Read the instructions aloud.
- Ask Ss to use their notes to share information they learned about their partner's plans.

Expansion activity *(individual work, whole group)*

- Remind Ss that they can use *before* and *after* to describe the order of events. They can also use sequencing words, such as *first, second, third, then, after that,* and *finally.*
- Encourage Ss to use these sequencing words and *before* and *after* to tell the story of Anita in Exercise **2B**. Choose several Ss to be the recorders to write the sentences with these words as they hear them in the story.
- Begin the story, for example: *Anita has always wanted to visit her family in Japan. Today is the big day. She has been looking forward to this trip for a long time. She needs to get to the airport early because there will be a lot of things to do when she arrives.*
- Ask a S to continue the story with *First*. The S must continue speaking and explaining what Anita will do until you say *Stop*. (*She'll check in. She'll give her ticket to the ticket agent. She'll show her passport. She'll tell the agent how excited she is*, etc.) Ask another S to pick up the story with *Second*. (*Second, she'll go through security. She'll show her boarding pass*, etc.) That S continues until you say *Stop*. Ask another S to pick up the story. Continue until you reach Picture 6 and *Finally*. (*Finally, she will turn off her cell phone and be on her way.*)

Evaluation

- Direct Ss' attention to the lesson focus on the board.
- Focus Ss' attention on the pictures on page 122. Ask Ss to make sentences about Felicia and Ricardo using *before* and *after* clauses with future meaning, for example: *They will compare costs before they reserve a campsite.*
- Check off each part of the lesson focus as Ss demonstrate an understanding of what they have learned in the lesson.

More Ventures, Unit 10, Lesson C	
Workbook, 15–30 min.	
Add Ventures, 30–45 min.	www.cambridge.org/myresourceroom
Collaborative, 30–45 min.	
Student Arcade, time varies	www.cambridge.org/venturesarcade

B **Talk** with a partner. Anita is going to the airport. Talk about her plans. Use *before* or *after*.

> **A** After Anita checks in, she'll go through security.
> **B** Before Anita goes through security, she'll check in.

1. check in

2. go through security

3. buy a cup of coffee

4. read a newspaper

5. get on the plane

6. turn off her cell phone

Write sentences about Anita. Use *before* and *after*.

Anita will go through security after she checks in.
(Answers will vary.)

3 Communicate

A **Imagine** you are going to take a weekend trip. Choose the location. Write three things you need to do before the trip.

B **Interview** a partner. Take notes in the chart.

> **A** Where will you go on your trip?
> **B** To the mountains.
> **A** What will you do first?
> **B** I'll reserve a campsite.
> **A** What will you do after you reserve a campsite?
> **B** I'll pack warm clothes.
> **A** What will you do after that?
> **B** I'll pack my camping supplies.

You
Location:
1. _____
2. _____
3. _____
Your partner
Location:
1. _____
2. _____
3. _____

C **Share** information about your partner.

LESSON D Reading

1 Before you read

Look at the picture. Answer the questions.

1. What do you see on the postcard?
2. Would you like to visit this place? Why or why not?

2 Read

STUDENT TK 36
CLASS CD2 TK 32

Read the article from a tourist guidebook. Listen and read again.

The ROCK — SAN FRANCISCO'S BIGGEST TOURIST ATTRACTION

Alcatraz, a small, rocky island in the middle of San Francisco Bay, was once the most famous <u>prison</u> in the United States. For a period of 29 years, from 1934 to 1963, over 1,500 dangerous criminals lived in the prison's 378 <u>cells</u>. People believed that it was impossible to <u>escape</u> from Alcatraz Island. However, in 1962, two brothers, John and Clarence Anglin, and another man named Frank Morris, escaped on a raft made of raincoats. A famous movie, *Escape from Alcatraz*, tells this amazing story. Other famous prisoners who lived on the island included Al Capone, the gangster, and Robert Stroud, the "Birdman of Alcatraz."

Alcatraz prison closed in 1963. The island became a national park, and since then it has been a major <u>attraction</u> for tourists from all over the world. These days, many people call Alcatraz by its popular name, "The Rock."

In the summer, it is wise to buy tickets to the island <u>in advance</u> because the <u>ferries</u> <u>sell out</u>. Evening tours are less crowded. The <u>admission</u> prices listed include the ferry, tickets, and an audio tour.

General admission	
Adult (18–61)	$36.00
Junior (12–17)	$34.50
Child (5–11)	$26.00
Senior (62+)	$34.50

> Words between commas sometimes explain the words before them.
>
> *For a period of 29 years, **from 1934 to 1963**, . . .*

Lesson objectives

- Introduce and read "The Rock"
- Practice using new topic-related vocabulary
- Use context clues

Warm-up and review

- Before class. Write today's lesson focus on the board.

  Lesson D:
  Read and understand "The Rock"
  Use context clues to guess the meanings of words

- Begin class. Books closed. Ask Ss what tourist guide books are used for. Write Ss' ideas on the board, for example: *To tell you what to see and do in a place, to give you a map of a tourist attraction, to give you a short history about a place you are visiting.*

▼ **Teaching tip**

If possible, bring to class some tourist brochures from tourist attractions in your area. Tell Ss that these are examples of tourist guides. Pass them around to introduce Ss to the kind of article (genre) they will be reading in Exercise **2**.

Presentation

- Books open. Focus Ss' attention on the postcard photo in Exercise **1**. Ask: *What is the city in the postcard?* Elicit, or tell Ss that San Francisco is a city in California.
- Read the instructions aloud. Direct Ss' attention to the questions.
- Answer the questions with the class and discuss why or why not Ss would like to visit the place pictured in the postcard.

Practice

- Focus Ss' attention on the article in Exercise **2**. Ask a S to read the title of the article and the first sentence to the class.
- Write *Alcatraz* on the board. Ask Ss if they have heard of it. If any Ss say *Yes*, ask them what they know about Alcatraz. If Ss say *No*, tell them that they are going to read an article from a tourist guide about a place in San Francisco called Alcatraz.
- Write *tourist attraction* on the board. Point to the words. Say them and ask Ss to repeat. Tell Ss that a tourist attraction is a place that people like to visit and learn about. It attracts tourists. Ask Ss to brainstorm other tourist attractions in the United States: Elicit examples, such as: *the Grand Canyon, the Empire State Building, Mount Rushmore, the Everglades.*
- Read the instructions aloud for Exercise **2**. Ask Ss to read the article silently before listening to the audio program.

- ⊙ Class Audio CD2 track 32 Play or read the audio program and ask Ss to read along (see audio script, page T-163). Repeat the audio program as needed.
- While Ss are listening and reading the article, ask them to underline any words they don't know. When the audio program is finished, have Ss write the new words on the board.
- Point to each word on the board. Read it aloud and have Ss repeat. Give a brief explanation of the words, or ask Ss who are familiar with the words to explain them. If some Ss prefer, they can look up the new words in their dictionaries.

Read the tip box aloud. Ask: *When was the period of 29 years in the article?* Elicit: *From 1934 to 1963.* Tell Ss that the purpose of putting words between commas is to define or explain what the words outside the commas mean.

Learner persistence *(individual work)*

⊙ Self-Study Audio CD track 36 Exercise **2** is recorded on the CD at the back of the Student's Book. Ss can listen to the CD at home for reinforcement and review. They can also listen for self-directed learning when class attendance is not possible.

▼ **Culture tip**

The article refers to several characters in the history of Alcatraz; however, Ss may not be familiar with some of the names. You might explain that John and Clarence Anglin were in prison for bank robbery when they made their famous escape from Alcatraz. Frank Morris was also in prison for robbery and other crimes. All three men escaped and were never seen again. Some people believe they must have drowned in the icy waters around Alcatraz, but recent studies have shown that they could have survived. Clint Eastwood starred in *Escape from Alcatraz*, a movie about their escape. Explain that Al Capone was a famous gangster in Chicago during the Prohibition Era of the 1920's and that Robert Stroud was serving a prison term for murder. While in prison, Stroud became an authority on birds and bird diseases, keeping nearly 300 canaries in his cell. *The Birdman of Alcatraz*, starring Burt Lancaster, is a famous movie based on Stroud's life.

Comprehension check

- Direct Ss' attention to Exercise **3A**. Read the questions aloud.
- Ss work with a partner to ask and answer the questions. Help as needed.

Practice

- Direct Ss' attention to Exercise **3B**. Read the instructions aloud for number 1.
- Have Ss focus on the words in the word bank. Say each word and have Ss repeat.
- Model the task. Call Ss' attention to the word *attraction* in the title of the article. Have Ss underline the word. Tell them to continue to look in the article for the words in the word bank and to underline the words as they find them.
- Ss complete the task individually. Walk around and help as needed.
- Ss in pairs. Ask Ss to show each other where they underlined the words in the article. Make sure that all Ss have underlined all the words from the word bank.
- Direct Ss' attention to number 2 in Exercise **3B**. Read the instructions aloud.
- Model the task. Focus Ss' attention on the example "think-aloud" in the exercise. Ask a S to read it aloud.
- Ss complete the exercise with a partner. Walk around and listen to Ss' ideas. Make sure that partners have access to dictionaries for this exercise.
- Ask individual Ss to share their guesses about the meaning of each word in the word bank. Encourage them to explain how they used context clues to figure out the meaning of each of the words. Ask Ss if the dictionary meaning was similar to the meaning they guessed.

Comprehension check

- Focus Ss' attention on number 3 in Exercise **3B**. Model the task. Ask a S to read the first sentence aloud, filling in the blank with *attraction*.
- Ss complete the exercise individually. Walk around and help as needed.

- Write the letters *a–h* on the board in list form. Ask individual Ss to come to the board to write the answer (word only) next to the letter.
- Ask Ss to read the completed sentences aloud using the answers on the board. Ask: *Is the answer correct?* Make corrections on the board as needed.

Application

- Focus Ss' attention on Exercise **3C**. Read the instructions aloud.
- Ask three Ss to read the questions in Exercise **3C** to the class. Make sure that all Ss understand the questions.
- Ss complete the exercise with a partner. Walk around and help as needed.
- Ask several pairs to ask and answer the questions for the rest of the class.

Evaluation

- Books closed. Direct Ss' attention to the lesson focus on the board.
- Ask individual Ss to retell the main points of the article, *The Rock: San Francisco's Biggest Tourist Attraction*.
- Check off each part of the lesson focus as Ss demonstrate an understanding of what they have learned in the lesson.

Learner persistence (individual, pairs)

- You may wish to assign Extended Reading Worksheets from the *Online Teacher's Resource Room* for Ss to complete outside of class. The purpose of these worksheets is to encourage Ss to read for pleasure in English outside of the English class. The worksheets can also be assigned as extended reading in class.

More Ventures, Unit 10, Lesson D	
Workbook, 15–30 min.	
Add Ventures, 30–45 min.	www.cambridge.org/myresourceroom
Collaborative, 30–45 min.	
Extended Reading and worksheet, 45–60 min.	
Student Arcade, time varies	www.cambridge.org/venturesarcade

3 After you read

A Check your understanding.

1. What is Alcatraz?
2. Why did dangerous criminals go to Alcatraz?
3. What happened in 1962?
4. How long has Alcatraz been a tourist attraction?
5. How much is admission for a ten-year-old child?
6. How much is admission for a three-year-old child?

B Build your vocabulary.

1. Find the following words in the reading. Underline them.

admission	cells	ferries	prison
attraction	escape	in advance	sell out

2. Work with a partner. Guess the meaning of the words. Note the clues that helped you. Then use a dictionary to check your guesses.

> I guess that *attraction* means a place tourists want to visit. My clue was the phrase "biggest tourist attraction" in the title. The dictionary definition of *attraction [noun]* is "a thing or place that tourists like to see or visit."

3. Complete the sentences. Use the words from Exercise B1.

a. The Empire State Building in New York is a famous tourist ___attraction___.

b. General ___admission___ to the museum is $36.00 for adults.

c. Tickets to popular music concerts often ___sell out___ very quickly.

d. We bought our tickets six months ___in advance___.

e. To get to the Ellis Island Immigration Museum in New York, you have to take one of the ___ferries___ from Manhattan.

f. Alcatraz used to be a ___prison___. Then it became a national park.

g. Each prisoner in Alcatraz lived in one of the 378 ___cells___.

h. Thirty-six men tried to ___escape___ from Alcatraz.

C Talk with a partner. Ask and answer the questions.

1. Tell about a popular tourist attraction in a city you have visited. What was the cost of admission?
2. What kinds of tickets do you usually buy in advance?
3. Have you ever taken a ferry ride? Where did you go?

☑ Read an article about a tourist attraction; guess the meaning of words from context clues **UNIT 10 129**

LESSON E Writing

1 Before you write

A Work with a partner. Write the name of a tourist attraction in your community. Make a list of things to do or see there.

Attraction: *(Answers will vary.)*

1. _____

2. _____

3. _____

B Read the paragraph.

COUNTY FAIRS

One of the biggest tourist attractions in many cities in the United States is the county fair. A fair has something for everyone. It has a beautiful flower show and a photography exhibit. <u>If you have children, they will love the Ferris wheel and the fast rides.</u> <u>If you like animals, you can watch many different animal competitions.</u> The winner in each competition gets a blue ribbon. A fair also has displays of new products, such as cleaning products and cooking tools. <u>When you get hungry, you can buy food from one of the many booths.</u> <u>After you have eaten dinner, you can listen to a concert of live music until late in the evening.</u> Many fairs end with spectacular fireworks. There really is something for everyone at a fair.

Lesson objectives
- Write about a tourist attraction
- Introduce complex sentences

Warm-up and review

- Before class. Write today's lesson focus on the board.

  Lesson E:
  Read and write about a tourist attraction
  Use complex sentences
- Begin class. Books closed. Focus Ss' attention on the words *tourist attraction* in the lesson focus on the board. Read the words aloud and have Ss repeat.
- Ask Ss about tourist attractions in other countries. Write Ss' responses on the board, along with the city and country where these attractions are found.
- Point to some of the tourist attractions on the board. Ask the Ss who mentioned them: *Why is this a popular place for tourists? What is special about it?*

▼ **Teaching tip**
Be sensitive to your Ss' background, prior experience, and the political history of their countries or cultures. Many important national monuments and other tourist attractions may have been destroyed during your Ss' lifetime. Refrain from discussing tourist attractions in Ss' countries if this is the case.

Presentation

- Books open. Direct Ss' attention to Exercise 1A. Read the instructions aloud.
- Model the task. Ask Ss to brainstorm attractions in your community. Write Ss' responses on the board.
- Choose one of the attractions on the board. Ask: *What can you do or see here?* Write Ss' responses in a list on the board.

▼ **Teaching tip**
Do not erase this list of attractions from the board. You will need to use it as an example for the writing exercise that follows on page 131 of the Student's Book.

- Ss in pairs. Tell Ss to choose one of the tourist attractions on the board or to think of another one in your community.
- Ss complete the exercise in pairs. Help as needed.

Practice

- Direct Ss' attention to Exercise 1B. Read the instructions aloud. Tell Ss that they are going to read about a tourist attraction in San Diego, California.
- Focus Ss' attention on the pictures above the paragraph. Ask: *What do you see?* Point to each picture in turn, and write Ss' responses on the board. You may need to tell Ss the name of the item in each picture: *a Ferris wheel, an animal competition,* and *food booths.*
- Have Ss read the paragraph silently. Ask them to underline any words they do not know. Tell Ss to write the new words on the board. Encourage Ss to use context clues in the article to guess the meaning of any unfamiliar words.

Expansion activity (student pairs)

- Write on the board: *What, Where, Who, When, Why, How many.*
- Ask Ss to brainstorm questions they can ask about the paragraph by using the question words on the board. Elicit appropriate questions and write them on the board, such as: *What is the tourist attraction? Where is it? Who likes to go to this attraction? When do people visit this tourist attraction? Why is it a tourist attraction? How many different types of food booths are there?*
- Ss in pairs. Tell Ss to ask each other questions about the paragraph. Walk around and listen as Ss ask and answer questions with a partner.
- Ask several pairs to ask and answer questions for the rest of the class.

Community building (whole group)

- If your community has a county fair, ask Ss if they go to it or have ever gone. If so, ask Ss to describe what they saw at the fair, how much it cost, etc. Based on Ss' descriptions, ask other Ss if they would like to go to the county fair.

LESSON E Writing

Presentation

- Direct Ss' attention to Exercise 1C. Read the instructions aloud.
- Ask Ss if they know what the word *outline* means. Explain that an outline is a plan for organizing ideas for writing and includes only the main ideas of a paragraph.

Practice

- Model the task. Ask a S to read aloud the example main idea of the paragraph. Ask Ss to add an example or a supporting detail of the main idea, such as: *If you like flowers, the fair has a beautiful flower show.* Tell Ss to write this example in number 1 of the outline.
- Ss complete the exercise individually. Walk around and help as needed.
- Ask five Ss to read their examples aloud. Ask the class if they agree that these are good examples or details that support the main idea.
- Ask a S to read the conclusion to the class. Explain that a conclusion brings the paragraph to an end. In this case, the conclusion restates the main idea.

Read the tip box aloud. Ask two Ss to read aloud the example complex sentences. Explain that complex sentences often include *if* and *when* clauses. Explain that Ss can also use *before* and *after* clauses to make complex sentences.

- Focus Ss' attention on Exercise 1D. Read the instructions aloud.
- Model the task. Refer Ss to the writing tip box. Tell them that these are two complex sentences from the paragraph. Have Ss underline these two complex sentences in the paragraph before they find and underline two additional complex sentences.
- Ss complete the exercise with a partner. Walk around and help as needed.
- Ask four Ss to read aloud the complex sentences from the paragraph.

Application

- Focus Ss' attention on Exercise 2. Read the instructions aloud.
- Ss complete the task individually. Walk around and help as needed.

Comprehension check

- Direct Ss' attention to Exercise 3A.
- This exercise asks Ss to develop skills to review and edit their own writing. Ss check their own paragraphs against the checklist or rubric. Help as needed. If any Ss check *No* for any of the checklist items, ask them to revise and edit their paragraphs to include the missing information.

Evaluation

- Focus Ss' attention on Exercise 3B. Read the instructions aloud.
- This exercise enables Ss to work together to peer-correct their writing. Reading aloud enables the writer to review his or her own writing. Reading to a partner allows the writer to understand the need to write clearly for an audience.
- Ss complete the exercise in pairs. Walk around and help as needed.
- Listen to Ss as they ask their partner a question about the paragraph and tell their partner one thing they learned from it.
- Direct Ss' attention to the lesson focus on the board. Ask several Ss to read aloud the paragraphs they wrote for Exercise 2. Have other Ss tell if these paragraphs contain complex sentences and include all the items in the checklist.
- Check off each part of the lesson focus as Ss demonstrate an understanding of what they have learned in the lesson.

More Ventures, Unit 10, Lesson E	
Workbook, 15–30 min.	
Add Ventures, 30–45 min.	www.cambridge.org/myresourceroom
Collaborative, 30–45 min.	

C Complete the outline. Write five examples of things to do at the county fair.

Topic sentence: *A fair has something for everyone.*

Examples:

1. (Answers will vary.)
   _____

2. _____
   _____

3. _____
   _____

4. _____
   _____

5. _____
   _____

> Use complex sentences to make your writing more interesting. Complex sentences are sentences with a dependent clause.
>
> *If you have children, they will love the Ferris wheel and the fast rides.*
>
> *When you get hungry, you can buy food from at least 25 different booths.*

Conclusion: *There really is something for everyone at a fair.*

D Work with a partner. Look at the paragraph in Exercise 1B. Find four complex sentences. Underline them.

2 Write

Write a paragraph about a tourist attraction in your city. Include the topic sentence, at least three examples, and a conclusion. Use at least two complex sentences in your paragraph. Before you write, make an outline. Use Exercises 1B and 1C to help you.

3 After you write

A Check your writing.

	Yes	No
1. My paragraph has a topic sentence and a conclusion.	☐	☐
2. My paragraph has at least three examples.	☐	☐
3. My paragraph has complex sentences with *before*, *after*, *when*, or *if*.	☐	☐

B Share your writing with a partner.

1. Take turns. Read your paragraph to a partner.
2. Comment on your partner's paragraph. Ask your partner a question about the paragraph. Tell your partner one thing you learned.

LESSON F Another view

Life-skills reading

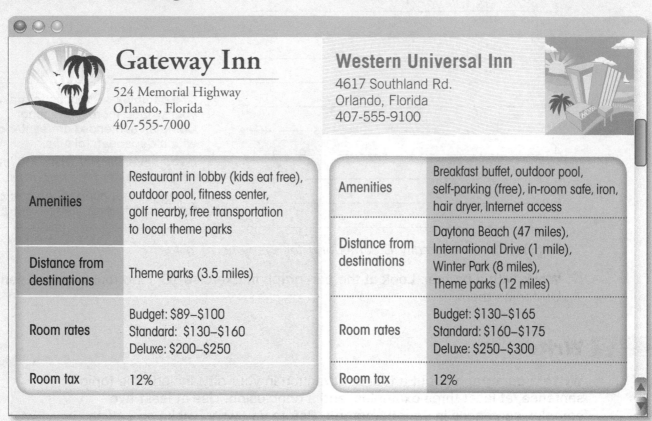

Gateway Inn

524 Memorial Highway
Orlando, Florida
407-555-7000

Amenities	Restaurant in lobby (kids eat free), outdoor pool, fitness center, golf nearby, free transportation to local theme parks
Distance from destinations	Theme parks (3.5 miles)
Room rates	Budget: $89–$100 Standard: $130–$160 Deluxe: $200–$250
Room tax	12%

Western Universal Inn

4617 Southland Rd.
Orlando, Florida
407-555-9100

Amenities	Breakfast buffet, outdoor pool, self-parking (free), in-room safe, iron, hair dryer, Internet access
Distance from destinations	Daytona Beach (47 miles), International Drive (1 mile), Winter Park (8 miles), Theme parks (12 miles)
Room rates	Budget: $130–$165 Standard: $160–$175 Deluxe: $250–$300
Room tax	12%

A **Read** the questions. Look at the hotel information. Fill in the answer.

1. What is the rate for a standard room at the Gateway Inn?
   - (A) $89–$100
   - ● $130–$160
   - (C) $160–$175
   - (D) $200–$250

2. Where can children eat for free?
   - (A) Daytona Beach
   - ● Gateway Inn
   - (C) Western Universal Inn
   - (D) none of the above

3. How far is the Western Universal Inn from the theme parks?
   - (A) 3.5 miles
   - (B) 8 miles
   - (C) 10 miles
   - ● 12 miles

4. Where is self-parking free?
   - (A) Gateway Inn
   - ● Western Universal Inn
   - (C) neither *a* nor *b*
   - (D) both *a* and *b*

B **Talk** with a partner. Ask and answer the questions.

Which hotel do you prefer? Why?

Lesson objectives

- Practice reading and understanding a hotel Web site
- Use the present perfect for three different purposes
- Complete the self-assessment

Warm-up and review

- Before class. Write today's lesson focus on the board.

  Lesson F:
  Read and understand a hotel Web site
  Review topic-related vocabulary
  Complete the self-assessment

- Begin class. Books closed. Direct Ss to the words *hotel Web site* in the lesson focus. Ask Ss: *What information is included in a hotel Web site?* Elicit and write on the board: *room rates, address, phone number, nearby tourist attractions,* etc.

- Tell Ss that they will read a Web site comparing two hotels in Orlando, Florida.

- Ask Ss if they have been to Orlando. Ask: *What are some famous tourist attractions in Orlando?* Elicit the names of some theme parks in Orlando (Disney World, Sea World, etc.).

Presentation

- Books open. Direct Ss' attention to the Web site in Exercise 1. Ask: *Which hotels are on this Web page?* Elicit: *Gateway Inn and Western Universal Inn.*

- Write *amenities* on the board. Say it and have Ss repeat. Ask Ss if they know what this word means. Explain that amenities are features customers look for in a hotel such as a pool, a restaurant, or a fitness center. Amenities make a hotel stay nicer.

- Ask: *What are the amenities at the Gateway Inn? What are the amenities at the Western Universal Inn?* (Ss can read the amenities from the chart.)

- Ask: *Which hotel is less expensive?* (the Gateway Inn.)

Practice

- Direct Ss' attention to Exercise 1A. Read the instructions aloud. This task helps prepare Ss for standardized-type tests they may have to take. Make sure that Ss understand the task. Have Ss individually scan for and fill in the answers.

Comprehension check

- Go over the answers to Exercise 1A with the class. Make sure that Ss followed the instructions and filled in the answers.

- Make correctons as needed.

Application

- Direct Ss' attention to Exercise 1B. Read the instructions aloud. Ask a S to read the questions to the class.

- Ss complete the exercise with a partner. Help as needed.

- Ask Ss to share what they learned from their partner with the rest of the class.

Expansion activity *(whole group)*

- Give a copy of the following chart to each S, or ask them to copy it from the board:

Names:	1.	2.	3.	4.	5.
Where do you stay when you go on trips?					
What do you like to do when you are on a trip?					

- Tell Ss that they are going to talk to five Ss in the class. Guide Ss to talk about trips they have gone on or about trips they would like to take.

- Tell Ss to write each S's name in the first row of the column and the S's answers in the next two rows, going down. Guide Ss to write the answers in note form.

- Model the activity. Ask a S the two questions. Write answers in note form on the board.

- Ask several Ss to share what they learned about their classmates with the rest of the class.

Warm-up and review

- Books closed. Ask each Ss to make a list of two to three cities or countries they have visited. Tell Ss to share their list with a partner. Walk around the room, and ensure Ss are using the present perfect and complete sentences, for example: *I have been to San Francisco.*

- Ask individual Ss to tell the rest of the class about places they have visited. Ask Ss questions about their statements, for example: *How many times have you been to San Francisco?*

- Tell Ss to change their classmates' sentences so that *the I* pronoun is replaced by the student's name. For example: *Anita has been to San Francisco two times.* Write the sentences on the board.

Presentation

- Books open. Direct Ss' attention to the grammar chart in **2A**. Ask three Ss to read the sentences. Tell Ss to compare the sentences. Ask *What do these sentences have in common?* Elicit the answer: *They all use the present perfect.*

- Ask Ss to define the present perfect. Elicit answers such as *The present perfect tells us about an action that started in the past and continues into the present.* Tell Ss that, in addition to describing things that began in the past and continue into the present, present perfect can also describe events that happened or were repeated before now.

Practice

- Direct Ss' attention to the instructions in **2A**. Read the instructions aloud. Ensure Ss understand the activity. Ask a pair of Ss to read the dialog aloud. Tell Ss that when they're asking about items such as: *hasn't missed a class since the beginning of the term*, the question should still be affirmative. *(Have you missed a class since the beginning of the term?)*

- Split the class into small groups. Have Ss ask one another questions. Walk around and help as needed.

- Direct Ss' attention to the instructions in **2B**. Read the instructions aloud. Ask two Ss to read the example sentences. Ss complete the exercise in pairs. Encourage each S to share a sentence about a person in their group.

Evaluation

- Before asking students to turn to the self-assessment on page 140, do a quick review of the unit. Have Ss turn to Lesson A. Ask the class to talk about what they remember about this lesson. Prompt Ss, if necessary, with questions, for example: *What are the conversations about on this page? What vocabulary is in the pictures?* Continue in this manner to review each lesson quickly.

- **Self-assessment** Read the instructions for Exercise **3**. Ask Ss to turn to the self-assessment page and complete the unit self-assessment. The self-assessments are also on the *Online Teacher's Resource Room*. If you prefer to collect the assessments and save them as part of each S's portfolio assessment, print out the unit self-assessment from the *Resource Room*, ask students to complete it, and collect and save it.

- If Ss are ready, administer the unit test on pages T-186–T-187 of this Teacher's Edition (or on the Assessment Audio CD / CD-ROM).

- If Ss are ready, administer the final test on pages T-188–T-190 of this Teacher's Edition (or on the Assessment Audio CD / CD-ROM).

More Ventures, Unit 10, Lesson F	
Workbook, 15–30 min.	
Add Ventures, 30–45 min.	www.cambridge.org/myresourceroom
Collaborative, 30–45 min.	

2 Grammar connections: three uses of the present perfect

Events that began in the past and continue to now	Keiko **has taken** English classes for six years.
Events that have happened before now (time unclear)	Jason **has been** to Canada.
Events that were repeated before now	I **have flown** on a plane six times.

A Talk with your classmates. Complete the chart.

A Have you been to another country on vacation, Elena?
B No, I haven't.
A Have you been to another country on vacation, Jason?
C Yes, I have. I've been to Canada.

Find someone who . . .	Name
has been to another country on vacation.	
has taken English classes for more than five years.	
hasn't missed a class since the beginning of the term.	
hasn't changed his/her hairstyle in the last five years.	
has flown on a plane more than once.	
has seen snow.	
has shopped online a lot recently.	
hasn't sent a text message in the last 24 hours.	
has lived in the same place for more than ten years.	
has lived in this country for less than a year.	
hasn't traveled by bus before.	

B Share information about your classmates.

Jason has been to Canada on vacation.

Keiko has taken English classes for six years.

3 Wrap up

Complete the **Self-assessment** on page 140.

Review

1 Listening

CLASS CD2 TK 33

Listen. Put a check (✓) under *Yes* or *No*.

	Yes	No
1. Brad Spencer was missing for two nights.		✓
2. He disappeared Sunday.	✓	
3. He was camping with his friends.		✓
4. He was wearing only a T-shirt and shorts.	✓	
5. When the park police found him, he was playing his guitar.		✓
6. If Brad returns to the park, he's going to stay on the trails.	✓	

Talk with a partner. Check your answers.

2 Grammar

A Write. Complete the story. Use the correct words.

A Problem in Chicago

Tina Foster is visiting Chicago for the first time. While she ___was taking___

1. took / was taking

a walk in Lincoln Park early this morning, she ___lost___ her wallet

2. lost / was losing

with all her cash, identification, and credit cards. When she got back to her hotel, she

realized that her wallet ___was missing___. She is going to ___search___

3. missed / was missing   4. search / searching

the park. If she ___doesn't find___ her wallet, she ___will call___

5. doesn't find / didn't find   6. calls / will call

the credit card companies. After she ___cancels___ her credit cards, she

7. cancels / canceled

___will go___ to the nearest police station and file a police report.

8. will go / goes

B Write. Look at the answers. Write the questions.

1. **A** Who *is visiting Chicago for the first time* ?

   B Tina Foster is visiting Chicago for the first time.

2. **A** What *was Tina doing when she lost her wallet* ?

   B Tina was taking a walk when she lost her wallet.

3. **A** Where *will she file a police report* ?

   B She will file a police report at the nearest police station.

Talk with a partner. Ask and answer the questions.

Lesson objectives
- Review vocabulary and grammar from Units 9 and 10
- Practice the unstressed vowel (schwa)

UNITS 9&10

Warm-up and review

- Before class. Write today's lesson focus on the board.
  Review unit:
  Review vocabulary and grammar from Units 9 and 10
  Practice unstressed vowel sound
- Begin class. Books closed. Ask Ss if they listen to the radio to hear news reports in English. If Ss say *Yes*, ask them if it is easy or difficult to understand the news reports. Have Ss tell why.

▼ **Teaching tip**
Encourage Ss to listen to the radio and watch TV programs in English to improve language skills.

- Tell Ss that they are going to listen to a news report about a missing person. Explain that a missing person is a person who has disappeared unexpectedly. People often call the police to help them find a missing person. They also file a Missing Person's report with the police.

Presentation

- Books open. Direct Ss' attention to Exercise 1. Read the instructions aloud.
- 🔊 Class Audio CD2 track 33 Model the task. Play or read only the first part of the news report on the audio program (see audio script, page T-163). Pause the program after the reporter says: *Park police have found a Denver man who was missing overnight in Rocky River National Park.*
- Direct Ss' attention to number 1 in the chart (*Brad Spencer was missing for two nights.*) and ask: *Was Brad missing for two nights?* Elicit: *No, he was only missing overnight, or for one night.*
- Tell Ss to check *No* for number 1.
- Ask five Ss to read aloud the remaining sentences in the chart. Explain any unfamiliar words. Say: *Now listen and check the correct boxes.*
- 🔊 Class Audio CD2 track 33 Play or read the complete audio program (see audio script, page T-163). Ss listen and check the boxes in the chart. Repeat the program as needed.

Comprehension check

- Read aloud the second part of the instructions for Exercise 1.
- Ss work with a partner to complete the exercise. Help as needed.
- Ask Ss to make sentences about the news report using the information in the chart.

Expansion activity (small groups)

- Put Ss in groups of four. Have each group choose who will be the director, the newscaster, the missing person, and the wife or husband of the missing person. Tell Ss to prepare and practice giving a news report based on the information in the chart and the audio script for Exercise 1.
- Encourage Ss to ask questions and make statements with the past continuous and *if* and *while*, for example: *While I was bird watching, I got lost.* Or *If I go hiking again, I'll bring food with me.*
- Ask groups to present their newscast to the class. If possible, tape-record it to play back later.

Practice

- Review *if, while, when, before,* and *after.* Write the words on the board. Ask Ss to say or write sentences with each to confirm their understanding of the key grammar points.
- Direct Ss' attention to Exercise 2A. Ask: *What is the title of this story?* ("A Problem in Chicago") Ask: *Where is Chicago? Is it a big city or a small town? What types of problems can you have when visiting a big city?* Elicit appropriate responses.
- Read the instructions for Exercise 2A aloud. Point out that in this exercise, Ss choose the correct word (or words) to complete each sentence. This exercise does not ask Ss to change the word forms.
- Have a S read the example and explain the answer. Tell Ss to continue reading the story and filling in the blanks.
- Write the numbers 1–8 on the board. Ask Ss to come to the board to write only the answers. Correct answers.

Comprehension check

- Direct Ss' attention to Exercise 2B. This exercise reviews question formation by asking questions related to the reading "A Problem in Chicago."
- Read the instructions aloud. Model the task. Ask a S to read the answer to number 1. Ask: *What is the question for this answer?* Elicit: *Who is visiting Chicago for the first time?*
- Ss complete the questions individually.
- Check answers with the class. Ask for volunteers to read their questions. Correct as needed.
- Read aloud the second part of the instructions for Exercise 2B. Pairs ask and answer the questions.

Review

Presentation

- Books closed. Write *unstressed vowel sound* on the board. Ask Ss to tell you the vowels in English, or write them on the board: *a, e, i, o, u.*
- Explain that when these vowels are not stressed, they are all pronounced the same way. They sound like "uh." This is the schwa sound. Tell Ss that words have both stressed and unstressed sounds.
- Write several words on the board from Exercise **3A** and point out the stressed and unstressed sounds. Say each word and have Ss repeat.

▼ **Teaching tip**
These pronunciation exercises are presented to make Ss aware of certain sound features in English. They are not presented as an exhaustive study of pronunciation. Their purpose is to raise Ss' awareness.

- Books open. Direct Ss' attention to Exercise **3A**. Read the instructions aloud. Explain that the colored letters are unstressed; the letters with a mark over them are stressed; the dashes separate the syllables in the words.
- Class Audio CD2 track 34 Play or read the complete audio program (see audio script, page T-163).
- Repeat the audio program. Pause after each word to allow Ss time to repeat. Play the audio program as many times as needed. Focus Ss' attention on the pronunciation of the colored letters on page 135.

Practice

- Direct Ss' attention to Exercise **3B**. Read the instructions aloud.
- Class Audio CD2 track 35 Model the task. Play or read the first sentence on the audio program. (See audio script page T-163) Write the sentence on the board. Ask Ss to underline the unstressed vowel in the words. Correct as needed.
- Class Audio CD2 track 35 Play or read the remaining audio program (see audio script, page T-163). Ss listen and underline the unstressed vowel in the words. Most of the words are repeated from Exercise **3A**. Repeat the audio program as needed.
- Focus Ss' attention on the second part of the instructions for Exercise **3B**. Read the instructions aloud. Tell Ss to show their partners the unstressed vowels they underlined in the words. Ask: *Are your answers the same or different?* Monitor the answers. Correct any mistakes that Ss make.

Comprehension check

- Direct Ss' attention to Exercise **3C**. Read the instructions aloud.
- Ss complete the exercise with a partner. Walk around and listen to Ss' pronunciation. Write on the board any words that Ss had trouble pronouncing. Point to the words. Say them aloud. Ask Ss to repeat.
- Ask several pairs to say the conversations for the class. Ask the class: *Did they pronounce the unstressed vowel sounds correctly?* Have Ss repeat if they are not pronouncing these sounds correctly.

▼ **Teaching tip**
Encouraging Ss to pronounce unstressed vowel sounds correctly will make Ss' pronunciation sound less accented and more natural. It will also make the rhythm of the language more typical of standard English. In addition, it will help Ss better understand the reduced sounds of English speakers.

Application

- Focus Ss' attention on Exercise **3D**. Read the instructions aloud.
- Ask a S to read aloud the example question. Make sure that the S correctly pronounces the unstressed vowel sound in *upset.* Model the task. Ask a S to make up a question with the word *about*, the second word in Exercise **3A**, for example: *What do you think about the weather today?* Ask another S to answer the question. Write the question on the board and underline the unstressed vowel (*a*) in the word *about.* Say the word and have Ss repeat. Correct pronunciation as needed.
- Ss complete the exercise individually. Help as needed.
- Ss in pairs. Tell Ss to ask their partner the questions they wrote. Walk around and listen to Ss' pronunciation as they ask and answer the questions.

Evaluation

- Direct Ss' attention to the lesson focus on the board.
- Ask individual Ss questions about Exercise **1**. For example: *What happened to Brad Spencer? What was he wearing when he disappeared? What was he doing when he disappeared? If you go hiking, what will you take with you?* Make sure that Ss answer the questions in complete sentences.
- Focus Ss' attention on the words in Exercise **3A**. Ask Ss to read the words aloud, being careful to pronounce the unstressed vowel sounds correctly.
- Check off each part of the lesson focus as Ss demonstrate an understanding of what they have learned in the lesson.

3 Pronunciation: unstressed vowel

CLASS CD2 TK 34

A **Listen** to the unstressed vowel sounds in these words. Unstressed vowels sound like "uh."

1. **u**p-sét
2. **a**-bóut
3. fá-m**i**-ly
4. éx-tr**a**
5. trá-v**e**l

6. p**o**-líce
7. v**a**-cá-ti**o**n
8. dán-g**e**-r**ou**s
9. S**a**-mán-th**a**
10. phó-t**o**-graphs

> The unstressed vowels are in **green**.

Listen again and repeat.

CLASS CD2 TK 35

B **Listen and repeat.** Then underline the unstressed vowels in these words.

1. Samantha is upset.
2. Where's the travel agent?
3. The prison is dangerous.
4. It's about seven o'clock.

5. Did you take photographs?
6. Call the police!
7. She'll think about visiting her family.
8. I need a vacation.

Talk with a partner. Compare your answers.

C **Talk** with a partner. Practice the conversations. Pay attention to the unstressed vowel sounds in **green**.

1. A There was a lot of excitement at the Community Adult School yesterday!

   B What are you talking about?

   A There was a fire in the kitchen!

   B Did the fire department come?

   A Yes. A student heard the smoke alarm and called 911 right away.

2. A Betty is going to Washington next week!

   B Are you serious? Won't that cost a lot?

   A Well, she probably got a cheap ticket.

   B Is she traveling with her family?

   A No. Her husband's going to take care of the children.

D **Write** five questions. Use the words in Exercise 3A. Ask a partner your questions. Remember to pay attention to the unstressed vowel sound.

What makes you get upset?

1. *(Answers will vary.)*
2. _____
3. _____
4. _____
5. _____

Self-assessments

Overview

Each unit of *Ventures 3* Student's Book ends with a self-assessment. Self-assessments allow students to reflect on what they have learned and to decide whether they need more review of the material.

How self-assessments help students

■ It is not possible for English language teachers to teach students all the English they need to know. Therefore, it is important that teachers help students develop strategies for learning and for measuring their learning. One important strategy is self-assessment. With self-assessment, students become aware of their own learning and focus on their own performance. Being able to self-assess is important for developing learner autonomy. This autonomy will equip students for lifelong learning.

■ Self-assessment allows students to participate in the assessment process. Responsibility for learning shifts from the teacher to the students as self-assessment makes the students more aware of their role in learning and monitoring their own performance.

■ Self-assessment can also contribute to learner persistence. Learners will continue to attend classes when they have verification that learning has taken place. They can measure this learning when they complete the self-assessment checklists.

How self-assessments help teachers

■ Teachers can use the results of the self-assessments to identify areas that need further instruction or review. They can use the results to meet with students and discuss items that have been mastered as well as those that need further study.

■ The information on the self-assessment forms can also be used at the beginning of the unit to identify and discuss the learning objectives of the unit. In this way, students will have a clear understanding of the learning goals. If they know what the learning objectives are, they can better monitor their own progress. This results in greater learner gains, which is gratifying to both students and teachers.

Self-assessment in *Ventures*

■ Each self-assessment asks students to write eight new words they have learned and to rate the skills and functions they feel they have mastered or have not mastered. Students then decide if they are ready to take the unit test to confirm this acquisition of unit language. The self-assessments are in an easy-to-use form, making it easier for students to check how they feel they are progressing.

■ If students feel they need additional study for a particular unit, the *Ventures* series provides additional practice in the Workbook and Add Ventures.

■ The Online Teacher's Resource Room contains the same self-assessments that are found in the Student's Book. However, online, each unit's self-assessment is on its own page and can be printed, distributed to, and completed by the student after each unit and placed in his or her learner portfolio. It can also be given to students to keep as a personal record of their progress.

UNIT 1 Personal information

A **Vocabulary** Write eight new words you have learned.

_____   _____   _____   _____

_____   _____   _____   _____

B **Skills and functions** Read the sentences. Rate yourself. Circle 3 (*I agree.*) OR 2 (*I'm not sure.*) OR 1 (*I can't do this.*).

I can ask and answer questions using verbs + gerunds: **Do** you **enjoy dancing**? I **love dancing**.	3 2 1
I can use **more than**, **less than**, and **as much as** to compare likes and interests: I like reading **more than** watching TV.	3 2 1
I can use **must** for logical conclusions: Ella isn't answering her phone. She **must be** busy.	3 2 1
I can predict what I am going to read by looking at the title and pictures.	3 2 1
I can write a paragraph with a topic sentence and supporting details.	3 2 1

C **What's next?** Choose one.

☐ I am ready for the unit test.   ☐ I need more practice with _____.

UNIT 2 At school

A **Vocabulary** Write eight new words you have learned.

_____   _____   _____   _____

_____   _____   _____   _____

B **Skills and functions** Read the sentences. Rate yourself. Circle 3 (*I agree.*) OR 2 (*I'm not sure.*) OR 1 (*I can't do this.*).

I can ask and answer present perfect questions with **How long**, **for**, and **since**: **How long has** he **been** here? He **has been** here **for two years** / **since January**.	3 2 1
I can ask and answer present perfect *Yes / No* questions with **ever**: **Have** you **ever studied** French? No, I **haven't**.	3 2 1
I can distinguish between simple past and present perfect: She **moved** to Chicago in 2008. She **has lived** in Chicago for six years.	3 2 1
I can find examples in a reading.	3 2 1
I can write a paragraph that uses examples to support my ideas.	3 2 1

C **What's next?** Choose one.

☐ I am ready for the unit test.   ☐ I need more practice with _____.

UNIT 3 Friends and family

A **Vocabulary** Write eight new words you have learned.

_____ _____ _____ _____

_____ _____ _____ _____

B **Skills and functions** Read the sentences. Rate yourself. Circle 3 (*I agree.*) OR
2 (*I'm not sure.*) OR 1 (*I can't do this.*).

I can give reasons using **because of** and **because**: *I can't reach the smoke alarm **because of** the high ceiling.* ***Because** the ceiling is high, I can't reach the smoke alarm.*	3 2 1
I can use **too** and **enough**: *The ceiling is **too high**. He **isn't tall enough** to reach the ceiling.*	3 2 1
I can use **be able to** to talk about ability: *Jose **is able to play** the guitar.*	3 2 1
I can identify the main idea, facts, and examples in a reading.	3 2 1
I can write a letter of complaint.	3 2 1

C **What's next?** Choose one.

☐ I am ready for the unit test.   ☐ I need more practice with _____.

UNIT 4 Health

A **Vocabulary** Write eight new words you have learned.

_____ _____ _____ _____

_____ _____ _____ _____

B **Skills and functions** Read the sentences. Rate yourself. Circle 3 (*I agree.*) OR
2 (*I'm not sure.*) OR 1 (*I can't do this.*).

I can ask and answer questions using the present perfect with **lately** and **recently**: ***Have** you **gained** weight **recently**? No, I **have lost** weight **lately**.*	3 2 1
I can ask and answer questions with **used to**: ***Did** you **use to** exercise? I **used to** exercise a lot, but now I don't.*	3 2 1
I can report commands using **tell**: *She **told us to walk** quickly.*	3 2 1
I can identify the topic of a text by reading the introduction and conclusion.	3 2 1
I can write a paragraph with a topic sentence.	3 2 1

C **What's next?** Choose one.

☐ I am ready for the unit test.   ☐ I need more practice with _____.

UNIT 5 Around town

A **Vocabulary** Write eight new words you have learned.

_____   _____   _____   _____

_____   _____   _____   _____

B **Skills and functions** Read the sentences. Rate yourself. Circle 3 (*I agree.*) OR 2 (*I'm not sure.*) OR 1 (*I can't do this.*).

I can use verbs + infinitives in questions and answers: *Where do you **plan to go**? I **plan to go** to the park.*	3 2 1
I can ask and answer questions using the present perfect with **already** and **yet**: ***Have** you **already bought** the tickets? No, I **haven't bought** them **yet**.*	3 2 1
I can use verbs + infinitives and verbs + gerunds: *I **want to go** to the mall. I **enjoy going** to the mall.*	3 2 1
I can guess if a word has a positive or negative meaning.	3 2 1
I can use an informal writing style in an e-mail.	3 2 1

C **What's next?** Choose one.

☐ I am ready for the unit test.   ☐ I need more practice with _____.

UNIT 6 Time

A **Vocabulary** Write eight new words you have learned.

_____   _____   _____   _____

B **Skills and functions** Read the sentences. Rate yourself. Circle 3 (*I agree.*) OR 2 (*I'm not sure.*) OR 1 (*I can't do this.*).

I can use adverb clauses with **when**: ***When** she **feels** tired, she **takes** a break.*	3 2 1
I can use adverb clauses with **before** and **after**: ***Before** she **eats**, she **reads**. She **eats after** she **reads**.*	3 2 1
I can use **one**, **some**, **any**, **it**, and **them** to refer to nouns: *Do you have <u>a pencil</u>? Sure. Here's **one**.* *Did you read <u>the e-mails</u>? Yes, I read **them**.*	3 2 1
I can identify a definition, an explanation, or an example in a reading.	3 2 1
I can use words and phrases to signal the conclusion of my paragraph.	3 2 1

C **What's next?** Choose one.

☐ I am ready for the unit test.   ☐ I need more practice with _____.

UNIT 7 Shopping

A **Vocabulary** Write eight new words you have learned.

_____   _____   _____   _____

_____   _____   _____   _____

B **Skills and functions** Read the sentences. Rate yourself. Circle 3 (*I agree.*) OR 2 (*I'm not sure.*) OR 1 (*I can't do this.*).

I can make suggestions using **could** and give advice using **should**: *You could get a smaller car. You should open a savings account.*	3 2 1
I can use gerunds after prepositions in questions and statements: *What are you interested in doing? I'm interested in cooking.*	3 2 1
I can use collocations with **get** and **take**: *Janet got laid off. Then she took a vacation.*	3 2 1
I can identify problems and solutions in a reading.	3 2 1
I can use words like **first**, **second**, and **finally** to list my ideas.	3 2 1

C **What's next?** Choose one.

☐ I am ready for the unit test.   ☐ I need more practice with _____.

UNIT 8 Work

A **Vocabulary** Write eight new words you have learned.

_____   _____   _____   _____

_____   _____   _____   _____

B **Skills and functions** Read the sentences. Rate yourself. Circle 3 (*I agree.*) OR 2 (*I'm not sure.*) OR 1 (*I can't do this.*).

I can ask and answer questions using the present perfect continuous: *How long have you been living here? I have been living here for a long time.*	3 2 1
I can use separable phrasal verbs: *He handed out the papers. He handed them out.*	3 2 1
I can distinguish between the present continuous and the present perfect continuous: *Mark is reading a book right now. I've been reading this magazine for an hour.*	3 2 1
I can scan a reading for specific information.	3 2 1
I can write a thank-you letter.	3 2 1

C **What's next?** Choose one.

☐ I am ready for the unit test.   ☐ I need more practice with _____.

UNIT 9 Daily living

A **Vocabulary** Write eight new words you have learned.

_____   _____   _____   _____

_____   _____   _____   _____

B **Skills and functions** Read the sentences. Rate yourself. Circle 3 (*I agree.*) OR
2 (*I'm not sure.*) OR 1 (*I can't do this.*).

I can use the past continuous in questions and answers: *What **were** you **doing** yesterday morning? I **was watching** TV.*	3 2 1
I can use *while* with the past continuous and *when* with the simple past: ***While** I **was sleeping**, the fire **started**. **When** the fire **started**, I **was sleeping**.*	3 2 1
I can use the present continuous in three ways: *Tom **is sleeping** right now.* *Chu **is living** with his parents. Omar **isn't coming** to the party tomorrow.*	3 2 1
I can use time phrases in a reading to sequence events.	3 2 1
I can write a paragraph with details answering *Wh-* questions.	3 2 1

C **What's next?** Choose one.

☐ I am ready for the unit test.   ☐ I need more practice with _____.

UNIT 10 Free time

A **Vocabulary** Write eight new words you have learned.

_____   _____   _____   _____

_____   _____   _____   _____

B **Skills and functions** Read the sentences. Rate yourself. Circle 3 (*I agree.*) OR
2 (*I'm not sure.*) OR 1 (*I can't do this.*).

I can use future real conditionals with *if*: *I **will fly** if the fare **is** cheap.*	3 2 1
I can use future time clauses with ***before** and **after***: *He'**ll finish** school **before** he **finds** a job. **After** he **finishes** school, he'**ll find** a job.*	3 2 1
I can use present perfect in three ways: *Mohamed **has lived** in Miami for a year.* *Luz **has been** to Miami. I **have visited** Miami three times.*	3 2 1
I can find the explanation of words in a reading.	3 2 1
I can use complex sentences in writing.	3 2 1

C **What's next?** Choose one.

☐ I am ready for the unit test.   ☐ I need more practice with _____.

Reference

Verbs + gerunds

A gerund is the base form of a verb + -ing. Gerunds often follow verbs that talk about preferences. Use a gerund like a noun: *I love dancing.*

Spelling rules for gerunds

- For verbs ending in a vowel-consonant pair, repeat the consonant before adding -ing:
  stop → stopping   *get → getting*

- For verbs ending in silent -e, drop the e before -ing:
  dance → dancing   *exercise → exercising*

  but:

  be → being   *see → seeing*

Questions

Do	I	enjoy dancing?
	you	
	we	
	they	
Does	he	
	she	
	it	

Affirmative statements

I	enjoy	dancing.
You		
We		
They		
He	enjoys	
She		
It		

Negative statements

I	don't enjoy	dancing.
You		
We		
They		
He	doesn't enjoy	
She		
It		

Verbs gerunds often follow

avoid	feel like	love	quit
can't help	finish	mind	recommend
dislike	hate	miss	regret
enjoy	like	practice	suggest

Gerunds after prepositions

Prepositions are words like *in, of, about,* and *for.* Prepositions are often used in phrases with adjectives (*excited about, interested in*) and verbs (*think about*). Gerunds often follow these phrases.

Wh- questions: *What*

What	am	I	tired of doing?
	are	you	
		we	
		they	
	is	he	
		she	
		it	

Affirmative statements

I	am	tired of working.
You		
We	are	
They		
He		
She	is	
It		

Phrases gerunds often follow

afraid of	famous for	nervous about	thank (someone) for
amazed by	good at	plan on	think about
angry at	happy about	pleased about	tired of
bad at	interested in	sad about	worried about
excited about	look forward to	talk about	

Verbs + infinitives

An infinitive is *to* + the base form of a verb. Infinitives often follow verbs that talk about future ideas. See below for a list of verbs that infinitives often follow.

Wh- questions: *Where*

		I	
		you	
	do	we	
Where		they	want to go?
		he	
	does	she	
		it	

Affirmative statements

I		
You	want to go	
We		to the park.
They		
He		
She	wants to go	
It		

Yes / No questions

	I	
	you	
Do	we	
	they	want to go?
	he	
Does	she	
	it	

Short answers

	I			I		
	you	do.		you	don't.	
	we			we		
Yes,	they		No,	they		
	he			he		
	she	does.		she	doesn't.	
	it			it		

don't = do not
doesn't = does not

Verbs infinitives often follow

agree	hope	need	promise
can / can't afford	intend	offer	refuse
decide	learn	plan	volunteer
expect	manage	prepare	want
help	mean	pretend	would like

Present perfect

The present perfect is *have* or *has* + past participle. Use the present perfect to talk about actions that started in the past and continue to now. See page 146 for a list of past participles with irregular verbs.

Use *how long* + present perfect to ask about length of time.
Use *for* with a period of time to answer questions with *how long*.
Use *since* with a point in time to answer questions with *how long*.

Wh- questions: *How long*

How long	have	I / you / we / they	been	here?
	has	he / she / it	been	

Affirmative statements: *for* and *since*

I / You / We / They	have been	here	for two hours.
He / She / It	has been		since 6:00 p.m.

Use *ever* with the present perfect to ask *Yes / No* questions about things that happened at any time before now.

haven't	=	have not
hasn't	=	has not

Yes / No questions: *ever*

Have	I / you / we / they	ever	been late?
Has	he / she / it	ever	been late?

Short answers

Yes,	I / you / we / they	have.
Yes,	he / she / it	has.

No,	I / you / we / they	haven't.
No,	he / she / it	hasn't.

Use *recently* and *lately* with the present perfect to talk about things that happened in the very recent past, not very long ago.

Yes / No questions: *recently* and *lately*

Have	I / you / we / they	been	early recently?
Has	he / she / it		early lately?

Use *already* and *yet* with the present perfect to talk about actions based on expectations.

Affirmative statements: *already*

I / You / We / They	have	already	eaten.
He / She / It	has		

Negative statements: *yet*

I / You / We / They	haven't	eaten	yet.
He / She / It	hasn't		

Present perfect continuous

The present perfect continuous is *have* or *has* + *been* + present participle. Use the present perfect continuous to talk about actions that started in the past, continue to now, and will probably continue in the future.

Yes / No questions

Have	I	
	you	been sitting here for a long time?
	we	
	they	
Has	he	
	she	
	it	

Short answers

Yes,	I	have.
	you	
	we	
	they	
	he	has.
	she	
	it	

No,	I	haven't.
	you	
	we	
	they	
	he	hasn't.
	she	
	it	

Wh- questions: *How long*

How long	have	I	been sitting here?
		you	
		we	
		they	
	has	he	
		she	
		it	

Affirmative statements: *for* and *since*

I	have been sitting here	for an hour. since 10 a.m.
You		
We		
They		
He	has been sitting here	
She		
It		

used to

Used to talks about things that happened in the past. Use *used to* to talk about a past situation or past habit that is not true now.

Yes / No questions

Did	I	use to arrive late?
	you	
	we	
	they	
	he	
	she	
	it	

Short answers

Yes,	I	did.
	you	
	we	
	they	
	he	
	she	
	it	

No,	I	didn't.
	you	
	we	
	they	
	he	
	she	
	it	

didn't = did not

Affirmative statements

I	used to arrive late.
You	
We	
They	
He	
She	
It	

Past continuous

Use the past continuous to talk about actions that were happening at a specific time in the past. The actions were not completed at that time.

Wh- questions: *What*

What	was	I	doing last night?
	were	you	
		we	
		they	
	was	he	
		she	
		it	

Affirmative statements

I	was	working.
You	were	
We		
They		
He	was	
She		
It		

Yes / No questions

Was	I	working?
Were	you	
	we	
	they	
Was	he	
	she	
	it	

Short answers

Yes,	I	was.
	you	were.
	we	
	they	
	he	was.
	she	
	it	

No,	I	wasn't.
	you	weren't.
	we	
	they	
	he	wasn't.
	she	
	it	

wasn't = was not
weren't = were not

could and *should*

Use *could* to give suggestions. Use *should* to give advice. *Should* gives stronger advice than *could*.

Wh- questions: *What*

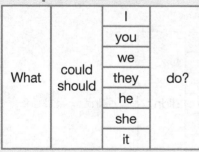

What	could should	I	do?
		you	
		we	
		they	
		he	
		she	
		it	

Affirmative statements

I	could should	go home.
You		
We		
They		
He		
She		
It		

Negative statements

I	couldn't shouldn't	go home.
You		
We		
They		
He		
She		
It		

couldn't = could not
shouldn't = should not

Irregular verbs

Base form	Simple past	Past participle	Base form	Simple past	Past participle
be	was / were	been	leave	left	left
become	became	become	lose	lost	lost
begin	began	begun	make	made	made
break	broke	broken	meet	met	met
bring	brought	brought	pay	paid	paid
build	built	built	put	put	put
buy	bought	bought	read	read	read
catch	caught	caught	ride	rode	ridden
choose	chose	chosen	run	ran	run
come	came	come	say	said	said
cost	cost	cost	see	saw	seen
cut	cut	cut	sell	sold	sold
do	did	done	send	sent	sent
drink	drank	drunk	set	set	set
drive	drove	driven	show	showed	shown
eat	ate	eaten	sing	sang	sung
fall	fell	fallen	sit	sat	sat
feel	felt	felt	sleep	slept	slept
fight	fought	fought	speak	spoke	spoken
find	found	found	spend	spent	spent
fly	flew	flown	stand	stood	stood
forget	forgot	forgotten	steal	stole	stolen
get	got	gotten / got	swim	swam	swum
give	gave	given	take	took	taken
go	went	gone	teach	taught	taught
have	had	had	tell	told	told
hear	heard	heard	think	thought	thought
hide	hid	hidden	throw	threw	thrown
hit	hit	hit	understand	understood	understood
hold	held	held	wake	woke	woken
hurt	hurt	hurt	wear	wore	worn
keep	kept	kept	win	won	won
know	knew	known	write	wrote	written

Spelling rules for regular past participles

- To form the past participle of regular verbs, add -ed to the base form:
  listen → *listened*

- For regular verbs ending in a consonant + -y, change y to i and add -ed:
  study → *studied*

- For regular verbs ending in a vowel + -y, add -ed:
  play → *played*

- For regular verbs ending in -e, add -d:
  live → *lived*

Grammar explanations

Separable phrasal verbs

A phrasal verb is a verb + preposition. The meaning of the phrasal verb is different from the meaning of the verb alone.

He *handed out* the papers to the class. = He *gave* the papers to the class.

A separable phrasal verb can have a noun between the verb and the preposition.

He *handed **the papers** out*.

A separable phrasal verb can have a pronoun between the verb and the preposition.

He *handed **them** out*.

Common separable phrasal verbs

call back	cut off	find out	look up	throw away / out
call up	do over	give back	pick out	turn down
clean up	fill in	hand in	put away / back	turn off
cross out	fill out	hand out	shut off	turn up
cut down	fill up	leave on	tear up	

Comparisons

Use *more than*, *less than*, and *as much as* to compare nouns and gerunds. A gerund is the base form of a verb + *-ing*. It is often used as a noun. You can compare activities by using gerunds and *more than*, *less than*, and *as much as*.

I enjoy *walking more than driving*.

She likes *cooking less than eating*.

They enjoy *singing as much as dancing*.

Giving reasons and explanations with *because of* phrases and *because* clauses

Use a *because of* phrase or a *because* clause to give an explanation. A *because of* phrase is the part of the sentence that begins with *because of* and has a noun phrase. A *because* clause is the part of the sentence that begins with *because* and has a subject and verb. Use a comma (,) when the *because of* phrase or *because* clause begins the sentence.

I came to Ohio *because of my children*.
Because of my children, I came to Ohio.

I came to Ohio *because my children are here*.
Because my children are here, I came to Ohio.

Adjectives with *too* and *enough*

Use *too* + adjective to talk about more than the right amount.

The ladder is *too tall*.

Use adjective + *enough* to talk about the right amount of something.

The ladder is *tall enough* to reach the ceiling.

Use *not* + adjective + *enough* to talk about less than the right amount.

The ladder is *not tall enough*.

Capitalization rules

Capitalize the first, last, and other important words in titles.	**M**y **S**trategies for **L**earning **E**nglish **S**alsa **S**tarz at **C**entury **P**ark **E**scape from **A**lcatraz
Capitalize letters in abbreviations.	**TV** (television) **DVD** (digital video disc or digital versatile disc) **ATM** (automated teller machine or automatic teller machine)
Capitalize titles when they follow a name.	Latisha Holmes, **P**resident, Rolling Hills Neighborhood Watch Janice Hill, **P**ersonnel **M**anager, Smart Shop

Adverb clauses

A clause is a part of a sentence that has a subject and a verb. A dependent clause often begins with time words such as *when*, *before*, and *after*. The dependent clause can come at the beginning or end of a sentence. Use a comma (,) after a dependent clause that comes at the beginning of a sentence. Do not use a comma when a dependent clause comes at the end of a sentence.

when: Use *when* + present time verbs to talk about habits.

> *When I have a lot to do*, I make a to-do list.
> I make a to-do list *when I have a lot to do*.

before: Use *before* to order events in a sentence. *Before* introduces the second event.

Use *before* with the simple present to talk about habits.

> First, she reads the newspaper. Second, she eats breakfast. =
> She reads the newspaper *before she eats breakfast*.
> *Before she eats breakfast*, she reads the newspaper.

Use *before* with the simple present and future to talk about future plans.

> First, he'll finish school. Second, he'll take a vacation. =
> He'll finish school *before he takes a vacation*.
> *Before he takes a vacation*, he'll finish school.

after: Use *after* to order events in a sentence. *After* introduces the first event.

Use *after* with the simple present to talk about habits.

> First, I eat dinner. Second, I watch the news. =
> I watch the news *after I eat dinner*.
> *After I eat dinner*, I watch the news.

Use *after* with the simple present and future to talk about future plans.

> First, he'll finish school. Second, he'll take a vacation. =
> He'll take a vacation *after he finishes school*.
> *After he finishes school*, he'll take a vacation.

when and **while**: Use *when* or *while* with the past continuous and simple past to show that one past action interrupted another past action.

Use *when* with the simple past for the action that interrupted.

> They were sleeping *when the fire started*.
> *When the fire started*, they were sleeping.

Use *while* with the past continuous to show the action that was happening before the interruption.

> The fire started *while they were sleeping*.
> *While they were sleeping*, the fire started.

if: Use *if* clauses to talk about future possibility. Use the simple present in the clause with *if*. Use the future in the other clause to talk about what could happen.

> She won't go *if the weather is bad*.
> *If the weather is bad*, she won't go.

Projects

Overview

The *Ventures* projects are optional material to be used at the completion of a unit. There is one project per unit, and most of the projects can be completed in one class period.

The Online Teacher's Resource Room contains the same projects that are found on pages T-150–T-154. Each unit's project can be printed and distributed to students after each unit. Projects are valuable activities because they extend students' learning into a real-world context. They work within the unit topic, but they also go beyond the Student's Book.

These projects are designed to be fun and practical, with the goal of helping students become more independent while learning to live in a new culture and speak a new language.

Project set-up and materials

Projects may be done in class as a group activity or outside of class, individually.

Some projects will need the teacher to gather simple materials to be used in class. For example, some require large poster paper, index cards, or authentic materials such as store ads and copies of the local newspaper. In order to complete other projects, students will need access to a computer that is linked to the Internet.

Skills learned through the projects

Students learn different skills through these projects. For example, half the projects involve use of the Internet. Students search for information using key words. This is an essential skill that most students will need to use in English. In addition, the projects encourage students to practice other essential life skills, such as working collaboratively to make a poster or a booklet, looking up information on community resources, and learning to manage their study time better by making a wall chart.

Community building and learner persistence

Ventures projects help build community inside and outside the classroom as students work together, using materials such as local newspapers and flyers to find information. Building community, in turn, helps to promote learner persistence. As students apply essential life skills, they will become more confident in their English skills and will be more motivated to come to class to learn additional skills that will help them in daily life.

UNIT 1 Personality types

A **Use the Internet.**

Find a free personality survey.

Take the survey.

Copy or print out the results.

Keywords (personality surveys)

B **Make a chart.**

Write three things about your personality from the survey.

Do you agree or disagree with the survey? Check (✓) your answer.

	Agree	Disagree
I like to be with people.	✓	
I like to think about the future.		✓
I like to talk about my feelings.	✓	

C **Share your information.**

Show your chart to your classmates.

Talk about the survey.

UNIT 2 Strategies for learning English

A **Make a list.**

What are some strategies you have used to learn English?

Share your strategies with a partner.

B **Make a chart.**

Write some strategies you want to try.

Set goals. When will you start using these strategies?

Strategy	Goal
Write new words in my notebook	after class
Listen to English on the radio.	tonight
Talk to my neighbors.	this weekend

C **Share your information.**

Talk to your classmates about your strategies.

Make a class booklet of learning strategies.

UNIT 3 Volunteer opportunities

A Use the Internet.

Find information about a place to volunteer in your city.
Write the names of three places.

Keywords (your city), volunteer opportunities

B Take notes. Answer these questions.

1. Where can you volunteer?
2. What can you do there?
3. What is the telephone number?

Name	Volunteer work	Telephone number
Senior Center	deliver meals	555-3068
Heart Hospital	greet visitors	555-4752
Brown Elementary School	help students do their homework	555-4231

C Share your information.

Tell your class about the places and the volunteer work.

How many classmates want to volunteer? Where do they want to volunteer?

UNIT 4 Health tips

A Make a list.

Write three ways to stay healthy.

Ways to stay healthy:

Exercise.

Eat well.

Get plenty of sleep.

B Make a chart.

Write three ways to stay healthy.
Write examples of these three ways.

C Share your information.

Talk about your ideas.
Make a class poster.
What are the best ideas?
Take a class vote.

Ways to stay healthy	Examples
Exercise.	walk, run, swim, ride a bike
Eat well.	eat fresh fruit and vegetables, drink lots of water
Get plenty of sleep.	go to bed early

UNIT 5 Weekend activities

A **Use the Internet.**

Find the entertainment section of your local newspaper online.

Find information about weekend activities in your city.

Keywords (name of your local newspaper), entertainment

B **Take notes. Answer these questions.**

1. What is the activity?
2. When is the activity?
3. Where is the activity?

Activity	When	Where
Jazz concert	Thursday: 8:00 p.m.	Town Park
Garden show	Saturday and Sunday: 9:00 a.m.–9:00 p.m.	Civic Center
Art show	Friday: 10:00 a.m.–5:00 p.m.	15 Main Street

C **Share your information.**

Tell your classmates about the activities.

Make a class wall chart of weekend activities.

Discuss with your classmates. Who would like to go to each activity?

UNIT 6 Tips for managing time

A **Make a list.**

What are ways to manage your study time?

Write three ideas.

1. Find a quiet and comfortable place to study.
2. Decide what time of day is best for you to study.
3. Make a list of what you have to study.

B **Interview your classmates.**

Find two more ways to manage study time. Write them in your chart.

C **Share your information.**

Make a class wall chart.

Talk about ways to manage your study time.

UNIT 7 Shopping

A   **Think about shopping.**

What do you want to buy?

Choose one: a car, a computer, a big-screen TV, furniture, or appliances.

B   **Find an ad.**

Find an ad from two different stores for the item you want to buy.

Look in this week's paper. Look in the mail for a flyer. Look on TV.

C   **Make a chart.**

Write information about your ads.

Write the name of the item.

Write the name of the stores.

Write the price of the item in each store.

Item	Sam's TV Discount Store	A & B Electronics
TV	$2,900.00	$3,100.00

D   **Share your information.**

Find a picture of the item you want to buy.

Paste it on a piece of paper.

Write the price and any other information you find.

Show it to the class, and compare stores.

UNIT 8 Job interview

A   **Use the Internet.**

Find common interview questions.

Keywords   interview questions

> What experience do you have?
> What are your goals?
> Do you have any questions?

B   **Make a chart.**

Write some interview questions.

C   **Answer the questions.**

Write your answers.

Questions	Answers
What experience do you have?	I've been a salesperson for ten years.
What are your goals?	I'd like to be a manager. I enjoy working with people.
Do you have any questions?	Yes. When can I start?

D   **Share your information.**

Show your questions and answers to a partner.

Tell the class about your partner.

UNIT 9 Home safety

A Think about your house or apartment.
Check (✓) the things you have.
Answer the questions.

	How many?	Where?
☐ fire extinguisher		
☐ smoke alarm		
☐ fire alarm		
☐ first-aid kit		
☐ other:		

B Make a list.
Write things you need for your
house or apartment.

> fire alarm
> other: evacuation plan

C Share your information.
Talk with your classmates.
Make a list of important safety items for the home.

UNIT 10 Hotel search

A Use the Internet.
Find information about a hotel in your city or a city you would like to visit.
If possible, print pictures of the hotel.

Keywords (city name), hotels

B Make a chart.
Write the name of the hotel.
Write the address.
Write other information.

Name	Address	Telephone	Rates	Other
Hilltop Hotel	87 Hilltop Road San Antonio, TX	210-555-8376	$79.00– $109.00	free breakfast pool parking: $5.00 a day

C Share your information.
Make a poster about your hotel.
Show your poster to your class.
Talk about the different hotels.
Where would the class like to stay? Take a class vote.

Class audio script

Welcome

Page 3, Exercise 2A – CD1, Track 2

A Hi, Silvia. What do you want to do in the future?

B I want to open my own beauty salon someday.

A What steps do you need to take?

B First, I need to go to beauty school for two years.

A What's the next step after that?

B Second, I need to take an exam to get my license.

A And after that?

B Third, I need to work in a salon to get experience.

A That sounds great. Do you have any other goals?

B I hope to become a business owner in five years. I don't want to work for anyone else.

Page 4, Exercise 3A – CD1, Track 3

1. Javier Molina works at a grocery store.
2. He puts groceries in bags for customers.
3. Javier is working at the store right now.
4. He is helping a woman with her bags of groceries.
5. He is talking to the woman.
6. He works every day from 9 a.m. to 5 p.m.
7. He likes his job, but he wants to do something different in the future.
8. Javier is going to cooking school at night.
9. He wants to be a chef at a restaurant.
10. He is planning to graduate from cooking school in six months.

Page 4, Exercise 3B – CD1, Track 4

Oksana Petrova is from Russia. She is living in Philadelphia right now. She works at an elementary school. She has a job as a teacher's assistant. She is working at the school right now. She is helping the students with math at the moment.

Oksana wants to become a teacher in the U.S. She studies English every evening. She plans to take elementary education classes at the community college next year. She is saving her money right now, because college classes are very expensive. She also is looking for another part-time job. She needs to pay her bills every month.

Page 5, Exercises 4A and 4B – CD1, Track 5

1. Diego Mata moved to the United States in 2005.
2. He got a job at a gas station.
3. He also took classes in English and auto mechanics.
4. Diego will finish his classes in auto mechanics next month.
5. He will look for a job when he is finished.
6. Diego liked his job at the gas station.
7. He will also like working as a mechanic.
8. He lived in an apartment last year.
9. He will move to a house next year.
10. He will also get married next summer.

Page 5, Exercise 4C – CD1, Track 6

1. A When did you move to this city?
   B I moved here in 2011.
2. A How long will you stay here?
   B Maybe I will stay here for one more year.
3. A Where did you live before you moved here?
   B I lived in Taiwan.
4. A How long will you study English in the future?
   B I will study English for two more years.

Unit 1: Personal information

Page 7, Exercises 2A and 2B – CD1, Track 7

A Hey, Danny, I am so tired this morning. I need a break. Let's get a cup of coffee.

B You're always tired on Mondays, Fernando. So, how was your weekend? Wild, as usual?

A Yeah, I guess. You know I like dancing, right? Well, last night, my girlfriend and I went to that new Cuban dance club – Club Havana.

B Oh, the one on, uh, Fourteenth Street?

A Yeah. Fourteenth Street. The place was full of people, and the music was incredible. We danced until, oh, it was about 1:30 in the morning. . . . Hey, you know what? You should come with us next time.

B Me? No. Oh, no. I don't like dancing.

A You're kidding. You don't like dancing? You really don't like dancing?

B Yeah, well, you know, Fernando, you're really outgoing and friendly, but I'm not outgoing. I'm not a party animal like you. I'm kind of shy. When I was a kid, I disliked going to parties, and I never learned how to dance.

A Really? That's too bad. But then, what do you enjoy doing?

B OK. This weekend, for example, I had a really nice, quiet weekend. I worked on my car, I watched some TV, I studied for my business class, and . . .

A Wow, Danny! You mean you were home the whole time? You didn't go anywhere?

B Nope. I was home alone the whole weekend. Well, I went to the auto-parts store. See, I like staying home more than going out. But I'd like to find a girlfriend who likes staying home, too.

A A girlfriend? How are you going to find a girlfriend if you stay home all the time?

B Good question. Come on. Let's get back to work.

Page 7, Exercise 3A – CD1, Track 8

Fernando and Danny are talking about their weekend. Fernando is a very friendly and outgoing person. He enjoys dancing. Last night, he went to a dance club and stayed until late. Danny thinks Fernando is a party animal.

Danny is different from Fernando. He is shy and quiet. He dislikes dancing. Danny was home alone the whole weekend. He likes staying at home more than going out. He wants a girlfriend who likes staying home, too.

Page 8, Exercise 2A – CD1, Track 9

1. Does Katrina like shopping for clothes online?
2. My brother enjoys playing soccer.
3. Mrs. Tanaka doesn't mind getting up early.
4. I love listening to the birds in the morning.
5. Do you mind going to the movies by yourself?
6. Do you enjoy being alone?
7. Most people don't enjoy paying bills every month.
8. Winston dislikes doing English homework.

Page 10, Exercise 2A – CD1, Track 10

1. Sally enjoys cooking more than washing dishes.
2. Sally likes washing dishes less than cooking.
3. Alfredo loves listening to music as much as playing an instrument.
4. Alfredo enjoys playing an instrument as much as listening to music.
5. Pam likes working less than going to school.
6. Pam enjoys going to school more than working.
7. Marta enjoys painting more than jogging.
8. Marta likes jogging less than painting.

Page 12, Exercise 2 – CD1, Track 11

Your Personality and Your Job

What is the perfect job for you? It depends a lot on your personality. People think, act, and feel in different ways, and there are interesting jobs for every kind of person. Three common personality types are outgoing, intellectual, and creative.

Outgoing people enjoy meeting others and helping them. They are good talkers. They are friendly, and they get along well with other people. They often become nurses, counselors, teachers, or social workers.

Intellectual people like thinking about problems and finding answers to hard questions. They often enjoy reading and playing games like chess. Many intellectual people like working alone more than working in a group. They may become scientists, computer programmers, or writers.

Creative people enjoy making things. They like to imagine things that are new and different. Many of them become artists such as painters, dancers, or musicians. Architects, designers, and photographers are other examples of creative jobs.

Before you choose a career, think about your personality type. If you want to be happy in your work, choose the right job for your personality.

Unit 2: At school

Page 19, Exercises 2A and 2B – CD1, Track 12

A Hi, Alex.
B Hi, Bella.
A How long have you been in the library?
B For about two hours.
A How's it going?
B Um, not great.
A Why? What's the matter?
B I'm so discouraged. Look at this mess! I have to finish reading this book. Then I have to write a paper and study for a test. Where do I start!
A Well, Alex, have you ever tried making a to-do list?
B A to-do list?
A Yeah. You make a list of all the things you have to do. Then you do the most important things first.
B A to-do list. No, I've never tried that. I usually try to do six things at the same time. Let's see. Right now, the most important thing is to finish reading this book. But it's so boring. I can't concentrate.
A You need to be more active, Alex. Don't just read the book. You know, underline important ideas, write notes, repeat the main ideas to yourself. Those things will help you concentrate.

B Hmm. I think I can do that. But there's another problem.
A What's that?
B Too many new words! I can't remember all of them.
A Hmm. Well, here's an idea. Write important words on index cards. Take the cards with you, and study them everywhere – on the bus, during your break at work, and before you go to bed . . .
B OK, OK! I get it: study smarter – not harder. Thanks, Bella.

Page 19, Exercise 3A – CD1, Track 13

Alex has been at the library for a long time, and he is discouraged. He has many things to do. He needs to study for a test and write a paper. He needs to finish reading a book, but he can't concentrate. He says the book is boring.

Alex's friend Bella gives him some study advice. First, she tells Alex to make a list of all the things he needs to do. Next, she says he has to be a more active reader. Finally, she tells him to write vocabulary words on index cards and study them when he has free time. With Bella's help, Alex plans to study smarter, not harder.

Page 20, Exercise 2A – CD1, Track 14

1. A How long has Manya been in the computer lab?
   B Since six o'clock.
2. A How long has Avi known Bella?
   B For four months.
3. A How long has Kayla worked at the library?
   B Since September.
4. A How long has Mrs. Bateson taught at the adult school?
   B For 20 years.
5. A How long have you lived in Canada?
   B For one year.
6. A How long has Omar had two jobs?
   B Since last year.

Page 22, Exercise 2A – CD1, Track 15

1. A Has Laura ever talked to her school counselor?
   B No, she hasn't.
2. A Have you ever forgotten your teacher's name?
   B Yes, I have.
3. A Has Joseph ever read a book in English?
   B No, he hasn't. But he wants to.
4. A Have Mary and Paula ever been late to school?
   B No, they haven't.
5. A Have you ever tried to speak English with your neighbors?
   B Yes, I have.
6. A Has Tomas ever taken the wrong bus to school?
   B No, he hasn't.

Page 24, Exercise 2 – CD1, Track 16

Strategies for Learning English

Have you ever felt discouraged because it's hard to speak and understand English? Don't give up!

Here are three strategies to help you learn faster and remember more.

Strategy # 1 – Set goals.

Have you ever set goals for learning English? When you set goals, you decide what you want to learn. After you determine your purpose for learning, you can make a plan to help you reach your goals. Maybe your goal is to learn more vocabulary. There are many ways to do this. For example, you can read in English for 15 minutes every day. You can also learn one new word every day.

Strategy # 2 – Look for opportunities to practice English.

Talk to everyone. Speak with people in the store, at work, and in the park. Don't worry about making mistakes. And don't forget to ask questions. For example, if your teacher uses a word you don't understand, ask a question like "What does that word mean?"

Strategy # 3 – Guess.

Don't try to translate every word. When you read, concentrate on clues such as pictures or other words in the sentence to help you understand. You can also make guesses when you are talking to people. For example, look at their faces and hand gestures – the way they move their hands – to help you guess the meaning.

Set goals, look for opportunities to practice, and guess. Do these things every day, and you will learn more English!

Review: Units 1 and 2

Page 30, Exercise 1 – CD1, Track 17

A How long have you been here, Marisol?
B Umm . . . about two months.
A Really? You're a good student, Marisol. How did you learn English so quickly?
B Well, Vladimir, I ask a lot of questions in class. When I don't understand the teacher, I raise my hand and ask him to explain. I enjoy learning that way.
A I'm too shy to raise my hand in class.
B Well, why don't you ask the teacher your questions after class?
A Yeah. That's a good idea. Sometimes I just ask the person next to me.
B Oh, so then you're not so shy.
A Actually, I'm not really very outgoing, you know. . . . Hey, Marisol, do you write vocabulary on index cards so you can study on the bus? That's what I do.
B Well, I don't have much time to study like that. But I talk to my co-workers a lot. I listen to their conversations and learn new words that way. I like talking to them.
A And you know, I like talking to you. You give me great ideas, Marisol. Thanks a lot. See you next time.

Page 31, Exercise 3A – CD1, Track 18

1. She loves playing cards with friends.
2. He hates working in the garden.
3. Do you like being alone?
4. She enjoys cooking less than eating.
5. I like living in the city.
6. How long has Shen studied English?
7. He's been here for six months.
8. Have you ever studied Korean?

Page 31, Exercise 3B – CD1, Track 19

1. What is the perfect job for you?
2. The perfect job depends on your personality.
3. Have you ever felt discouraged?
4. Have you ever set goals for learning English?
5. What does that word mean?
6. Intellectual people often enjoy working alone.

Unit 3: Friends and family

Page 33, Exercises 2A and 2B – CD1, Track 20

A Hello?
B Maria? Hi, It's Ana.
A Hey. Hi, Ana. How are you?
B Good, thanks. But I've been super busy. . . . Listen, Maria, do you have a minute to talk? Are you eating dinner?
A No, we've eaten. What's up?
B Well, I need a favor.
A Sure, Ana, what is it?
B The smoke alarm in my kitchen is beeping. *Beep, beep, beep.* I need to change the battery, but the ceiling's too high. Can I borrow your ladder?
A Sure, but I have a better idea. Um, Daniel can come over and change the battery for you.
B Really? Are you sure he has enough time?
A Oh, Ana, you know Daniel. He is never too busy to help a neighbor. He'll come over in five minutes.
B Thanks. I really appreciate it. I owe you one. See you . . .
A Wait, Ana, I want to ask you something. Did you hear our noisy neighbors last Saturday night? They had a party until three in the morning. Because of the noise, we couldn't sleep at all.
B Gosh, that's too bad, Maria. I didn't hear anything. But you should complain to the manager.
A Yeah, I know. I'll do it tomorrow.

Page 33, Exercise 3A – CD1, Track 21

Ana and Maria are neighbors. Ana calls Maria because she needs a favor. The smoke alarm in Ana's kitchen is beeping. She needs to change the battery, but the ceiling in her kitchen is too high. Ana asks to borrow Maria's ladder.

Maria says her husband, Daniel, will come over with a ladder and help Ana. Ana says, "I owe you one." This means she appreciates Maria and Daniel's help, and she will do a favor for them in the future.

Next, Maria tells Ana about their noisy neighbors. The neighbors had a party on Saturday night. Because of the noise, Maria and Daniel couldn't sleep. Ana tells Maria that she should complain to the apartment manager.

Page 34, Exercise 2A – CD1, Track 22

A Nice Surprise

Lei wanted to bake a cake because it was her neighbor Margy's birthday. Lei needed to go to the store because she didn't have any flour. However, her car had a flat tire. Because of this problem, she couldn't drive to the store. She couldn't walk to the store because of the distance. It was more than a mile away. Lei had a clever idea. She went to Margy and asked to borrow a cup of flour. Margy was happy to help because she had a lot of flour and she was a good neighbor. Two hours later, Lei returned to Margy's house with a beautiful cake. When Margy opened the door, Lei shouted, "Happy birthday!" Margy was very surprised and happy. Because of the nice surprise, Margy had a wonderful birthday!

Page 36, Exercise 2A – CD1, Track 23

Too Far to Visit

My neighbors – the Mansours – have four children. Their house isn't big enough. Mr. and Mrs. Mansour think it's too expensive to live in the city. Their rent is too high. Last weekend, the Mansours bought a house outside the city. It has four bedrooms. It's big enough for the whole family. However, the new house is too far from Mr. Mansour's job, so he's going to look for a new job. Mr. Mansour is an experienced engineer. He's experienced enough to find a new job. I will miss the Mansours. I probably can't visit them. Their new house isn't close enough for me to visit.

Page 38, Exercise 2 – CD1, Track 24

Neighborhood Watch Success Story
by Latisha Holmes, President, Rolling Hills Neighborhood Watch

People often ask me about the role of Neighborhood Watch. My answer is *Because of Neighborhood Watch, our neighborhood is safer and nicer.* Members of Neighborhood Watch help each other and look after the neighborhood. For example, we look after our neighbors' houses when they aren't home. We help elderly neighbors with yard work. Once a month, we get together to paint over graffiti.

Last Wednesday, the Neighborhood Watch team had another success story. Around 8:30 p.m., members of our Neighborhood Watch were out on a walk. Near the Corner Café, they noticed two men next to George Garcia's car. George lives on Rolling Hills Drive. The men were trying to break into the car.

Suddenly, the car alarm went off. The men ran away and got into a car down the street. But they weren't quick enough. Our Neighborhood Watch members wrote down the car's license plate number and called the police. Later that night, the police arrested the two men.

I would like to congratulate our Neighborhood Watch team on their good work. Because so many people participate in Neighborhood Watch, Rolling Hills is a safer neighborhood today.

For information about Neighborhood Watch, please call 773-555-1234.

Unit 4: Health

Page 45, Exercises 2A and 2B – CD1, Track 25

A Hello, Stanley. I haven't seen you for some time. How've you been?
B Busy. I've been working really hard.
A I see. So what brings you here today?
B Well, you know, I've always been healthy, but, uh, I've been really tired lately.
A Uh-huh. Well, let's take a look at your chart. . . . Ah, I see you've gained 20 pounds since last year.
B Yeah. I used to exercise a lot, but now I just work. Work, eat, and sleep.
A Well, you know, gaining weight can make you feel tired, Stanley. You need to start exercising again. Can you try walking for 30 minutes each day?
B I don't have time. I'm working a lot these days – sometimes 10, even 12, hours a day.
A Hmm. Well, then, can you walk or ride a bicycle to work? And at work, don't use the elevator. Take the stairs.
B Well, I guess, I can try.
A Good. Now, let's see. You also have high blood pressure. Tell me about your diet. What have you eaten since yesterday?
B Well, last night I had a hamburger with fries and a soft drink.
A Fat, salt, and sugar! They're all bad for your blood pressure, Stanley. What about today?
B I haven't eaten anything today.
A No breakfast? Well, of course you feel tired! You need to change your diet, Stanley. Eat more fish and more vegetables. Give up fast food. No hamburgers! No fries! They're really bad for your health.
B That's really hard. I'm so busy right now. I don't have time to –
A Listen, Stanley. You're 40 years old. Do you want to have a heart attack? This is my advice. You need to make real changes, or you'll need to start taking pills and all kinds of medication.
B OK. I'll try.

Page 45, Exercise 3A – CD1, Track 26

Stanley is at the doctor's office. His health has always been good, but he has been really tired lately. The doctor looks at Stanley's chart. He sees a couple of problems. One problem is Stanley's weight. He has gained 20 pounds. Another problem is his blood pressure. The doctor tells him he needs regular exercise – for example, walking or riding a bike. He also tells Stanley to change his diet – to eat more fish and vegetables. If Stanley doesn't do these things, he will need to take pills and other medication. Stanley wants to be healthy, so he is going to try to follow the doctor's advice.

Page 46, Exercise 2A – CD1, Track 27

Lola has been unhappy recently. She hasn't gone to the gym lately. And she hasn't watched her weight. She hasn't eaten healthy food, either. She has gained a lot of weight, and her blood pressure has gone up, too.

William has started to get in shape lately. He has lost weight recently. His blood pressure has gone down, too. He has given up hamburgers, french fries, and soft drinks. But he hasn't given up ice cream!

Page 48, Exercise 2A – CD1, Track 28

1. **A** Did he use to stay up all night?
   B Yes, he did, but he goes to bed early now.
2. **A** How often do you eat meat?
   B I used to eat meat every night, but now I usually have fish.
3. **A** Did you use to drive to work?
   B Yes, I did, but now I ride my bike.
4. **A** What do you usually do after work?
   B We used to go straight home, but now we take dance classes twice a week.
5. **A** Do you exercise every day?
   B I used to exercise every day, but now I exercise only on weekends.

Page 50, Exercise 2 – CD1, Track 29

Two Beneficial Plants

Since the beginning of history, people in every culture have used plants to stay healthy and to prevent sickness. Garlic and chamomile are two beneficial plants.

Garlic is a plant in the onion family. The green stem and the leaves of the garlic plant grow above the ground. The root – the part under the ground – is a bulb with sections called cloves. They look like the pieces of an orange. The bulb is the part that people have traditionally used for medicine. They have used it for insect bites, cuts, earaches, and coughs. Today, some people also use it to treat high blood pressure and high cholesterol.

Chamomile is a small, pretty plant with flowers that bloom from late summer to early fall. The flowers have white petals and a yellow center. Many people use dried chamomile flowers to make tea. Some people give the tea to babies with upset stomachs. They also drink chamomile tea to feel better when they have a cold or the flu, poor digestion, or trouble falling asleep.

For thousands of years, people everywhere have grown garlic, chamomile, and other herbal medicines in their gardens. Today, you can buy them in health-food stores. You can get them in dried, powdered, or pill form.

Review: Units 3 and 4

Page 56, Exercise 1 – CD1, Track 30

A Hello?
B Hi, Sara. This is Jenny. Remember me?
A Hey, Jenny! How have you been lately? We haven't talked in ages!
B Sorry about that, Sara. I used to have time to call friends after work. I just don't have enough time now.
A That's too bad. I have lots of time now that I work part-time! I used to work 50 hours a week; now I only work 20. But I've gotten lazy! I used to exercise a lot more.
B You're lucky you have free time, Sara. Because of my schedule, I eat fast food and don't exercise regularly. I used to cook healthy food for myself. Not anymore!
A It sounds like we both need to start taking care of ourselves, the way we used to do.
B I have an idea, Sara. Let's meet a few evenings a week and take a walk. I sit all day. I used to take the stairs at work, but I don't even do that anymore!
A I really like your idea. We can motivate each other. And we can catch up on each other's lives, too!

Page 57, Exercise 3A – CD1, Track 31

1. this morning
2. sore throat
3. That's too bad!
4. health problems
5. the neighbors
6. on South Street
7. they are
8. this month
9. asked them
10. three times
11. How are things?
12. thanks

Page 57, Exercise 3B – CD1, Track 32

1. **A** Where's Tommy this morning?
   B He's sick. He has a sore throat.
   A That's too bad!
   B He often has health problems.
   A I'm sorry to hear that.
2. **A** The neighbors on South Street are really noisy.
   B Yes, they are.
   A This month, I've asked them three times to be quiet.
   B Let's write them a letter.
   A That's a good idea.

Unit 5: Around town

Page 59, Exercises 2A and 2B – CD1, Track 33

A Mei, I'm so glad tomorrow is Friday. It's been a long week.
B That's for sure. Hmm. What would you like to do this weekend, Wen?
A Well, there are a few movies we haven't seen yet, or we could go to a concert downtown.
B Oh, we can't afford to go to concerts, Wen. They're too expensive. And I'm sort of tired of going to the movies.
A OK, so let's do something different on Sunday, something we haven't done yet this summer.
B Like what? Got any ideas?
A Let's check the newspaper for community events. Maybe we'll find something free right here in the neighborhood. Let's take a look. . . . Hmm. We have a lot of options. Here's something interesting. There's a concert in the park on Sunday at noon, admission is free.
B And here, look, there's a free walking tour of the gardens on Sunday at eleven o'clock.
A Here's another option, Mei. The Museum of Art is free the first Sunday of every month. There's an exhibit of modern art showing now. The museum opens at 10:00 a.m.
B Oh. And here's something at the library: free storytelling for children on Sunday at 10:30. Everything is happening on the same day at the same time! What do you want to do, Wen?
A Why don't we go to the library first?
B OK.
A Then, let's plan to go to the concert if the weather is nice. And then maybe later, we can go to the art museum.
B Yeah. That sounds good. I'll check the weather forecast for the weekend. Then we can decide.

Page 59, Exercise 3A – CD1, Track 34

It is Thursday. Wen and Mei are talking about their plans for the weekend. They can't afford to spend a lot of money on entertainment. They decide to check the newspaper for free community events on Sunday. They have many options. There's an outdoor concert in the park, a walking tour of the gardens, a modern art exhibit at the art museum, and storytelling for children at the library. All these events have free admission.

The problem is that all these things are happening on Sunday at the same time. Mei and Wen decide to take their son to the storytelling first. Then, if the weather is nice, they will go to the concert. Later, they might go to the art museum.

Page 60, Exercise 2A – CD1, Track 35

1. **A** How much do you expect to pay for the concert?
   B No more than $25.00.

2. **A** What have you decided to do for your birthday?
   B I'm going to an exhibit at the art museum.
3. **A** Can you afford to buy a ticket for the show?
   B Not really. I need to start saving money.
4. **A** What did you agree to do next weekend?
   B We agreed to go to the park.
5. **A** How does Tom intend to get to the park?
   B He's going to ride his bike.
6. **A** Have you ever refused to go on a trip with your family?
   B No, I haven't.
7. **A** Did they promise to visit their relatives this weekend?
   B Yes, they did.

Page 62, Exercise 2A – CD1, Track 36

1. It's 11:00 p.m. The salsa concert has already ended.
2. It's 8:00 a.m. The science museum opens at nine. It hasn't opened yet.
3. It's July 5th. The Independence Day parade has already finished.
4. It's the beginning of August. School begins in September. School activities haven't begun yet.
5. It's 2:00 a.m. The dance club stays open until 3:00. It hasn't closed yet.
6. It's Friday evening. The weekend has already started.
7. It's 7:45 p.m. The movie starts at 8:00. We haven't missed the movie yet.
8. It's Monday. I've already bought tickets for next Sunday's soccer game.

Page 64, Exercise 2 – CD1, Track 37

Salsa Starz at Century Park

If you missed the outdoor concert at Century Park last Saturday evening, you missed a great night of salsa music and dancing – and the admission was free!

The performers were the popular band Salsa Starz. Bandleader Ernesto Sanchez led the five-piece group and two dancers. Sanchez is a versatile musician. He sang and played maracas and guitar. The other musicians were also superb. The group's excellent playing and great energy galvanized the crowd. No one sat down during the entire show!

However, the evening had some problems. At first, the sound level of the music was excessive. I had to wear earplugs. Then, the level was too low. The change in sound was irritating. In addition, the stage was plain and unremarkable. I expected to see lights and lots of color at the performance. The weather was another problem. The night started out clear. By 10:00 p.m., some ominous black clouds moved in, and soon it started to rain. The band intended to play until eleven, but the

show ended early because of the rain.

Century Park has free concerts every Saturday evening in July and August. If you haven't attended one of these concerts yet, plan to go next weekend. But take an umbrella!

Unit 6: Time

Page 71, Exercises 2A and 2B – CD2, Track 2

A Winston, what are you doing?
B I'm thinking.
A No, you're not. You're procrastinating. You always procrastinate. I'm getting very impatient with you! I asked you to take out the trash two hours ago, and you haven't done it yet.
B Aw, Mom.
A Do you have homework?
B Yeah, but . . . I can't decide what to do first.
A Hmm. Would you like some help?
B Well, uh, yeah, I guess.
A OK. So, why don't you make a to-do list. You know, write down all the tasks you have to do.
B OK. I've got . . . math, an English essay, and a history project.
A Uh-huh. What else?
B I have to practice guitar. I have a lesson tomorrow.
A And don't forget the trash. Write that down, too.
B OK. Now what?
A Prioritize. What are you going to do first, second, third, and so on?
B Well, guitar is first. It's the most fun.
A Nuh-uh. I don't think so. Homework and chores are first. Guitar is last.
B OK. Should I start with math, English, or history?
A Hmm. When are they due?
B Math and English are due tomorrow.
A And the history project?
B The deadline is next week. On Tuesday.
A OK. So do math and English tonight. You can do the history project over the weekend.
B OK, math and English tonight. Which one should I do first?
A Well, I always do the hardest thing first.
B English is a lot harder than math.
A OK. So English, then math, then guitar. But before you do anything . . .
B Yeah, I know. Take out the trash.
A Right.

Page 71, Exercise 3A – CD2, Track 3

Winston is listening to music in his room. His mother comes in and tells him to stop procrastinating. She is very impatient because he isn't taking out the trash and he isn't doing his homework.

Winston has too many things to do. His mother suggests making a to-do list. First, she tells him to list all the tasks he needs to do. Next, she tells him to prioritize – to put his tasks in

order of importance. His mother says he needs to do his homework and chores first. He decides to do his English and math homework first because they are due the next day. He also has a history project, but the deadline is next Tuesday. After he finishes his homework, he will practice guitar. But before he does anything else, he has to take out the trash.

Page 72, Exercise 2A – CD2, Track 4

1. When you have many things to do, make a to-do list.
2. When you have a deadline, write it on your calendar.
3. Don't let people interrupt you when you need to concentrate.
4. When you want to focus on a task, turn off the television.
5. When you feel tired, take a break.
6. Give yourself a reward when you finish something difficult.
7. Don't procrastinate when you have a deadline.
8. When you are tired, don't do difficult tasks.

Page 74, Exercise 2A – CD2, Track 5

1. After Bonnie takes a shower, she gets dressed.
2. Bonnie takes a shower before she gets dressed.
3. Before Bonnie makes coffee, she gets dressed.
4. Bonnie makes coffee after she gets dressed.
5. Bonnie brings in the newspaper before she eats breakfast.
6. Bonnie eats breakfast after she brings in the newspaper.
7. After Bonnie eats breakfast, she leaves for work.
8. Before Bonnie leaves for work, she eats breakfast.

Page 76, Exercise 2 – CD2, Track 6

Rules About Time

Every culture has rules about time. These rules are usually unspoken, but everybody knows them.

In some countries such as the United States, England, and Canada, punctuality is an unspoken rule. It is important to be on time, especially in business. People usually arrive a little early for business appointments. Business meetings and personal appointments often have strict beginning and ending times. When you are late, other people might think you are rude, disorganized, or irresponsible.

These countries also have cultural rules about time in social situations. For example, when an invitation for dinner says 6:00 p.m., it is impolite to arrive more than five or ten minutes late. On the other hand, when the invitation is for a party from 6:00 to 8:00 or a reception from 3:30 to 5:30, you can arrive anytime between those hours. For public events with specific starting times – movies, concerts, sports events –

you should arrive a few minutes before the event begins. In fact, some theaters do not allow people to enter if they arrive after the event has started.

Other cultures have different rules about time. In Brazil, it is not unusual for guests to arrive an hour or two after a social event begins. In the Philippines, it is not uncommon for people to miss scheduled events – a class or an appointment – to meet a friend at the airport. Many Filipinos believe that relationships with people are more important than keeping a schedule.

Review: Units 5 and 6

Page 82, Exercise 1 – CD2, Track 7

A Hey, Minh. So where do you plan to go on vacation?

B I've decided to visit my family in Vietnam.

A Fantastic. Have you bought your tickets yet?

B Not yet, Trina. I plan to buy them this week. What about you? What do you plan to do during your vacation?

A Well, I want to go to Las Vegas.

B Las Vegas?

A Yeah. I've already made my reservations. My husband and I won three free nights at a big hotel.

B You're kidding! How did you win that?

A We just filled out a form at a shopping mall.

B Wow! Is it really free?

A I think so. But when we get there, we have to listen to a lecture about vacation time-shares.

B Do you intend to buy a place in a hotel for vacations?

A No, but we intend to have fun in a free one.

Page 83, Exercise 3A – CD2, Track 8

1. Study English.
2. Start the computer.
3. Tell the story.
4. What state do you live in?
5. Go to the store.
6. Students need to study.
7. Let's see the Salsa Starz.
8. Stop procrastinating.

Page 83, Exercise 3B – CD2, Track 9

1. A Hi, Stuart. I'm going to the store. What do you need?
   B Can you get me some stamps? It's the first of the month, and I have to pay bills.
   A Sure.
   B Thanks. I'll start writing the checks now and stop procrastinating.
2. A Hello, Stephanie.
   B Hi, Steve. Are you still a student here?
   A Yes. I'm studying appliance repair.
   B Really? Maybe you can fix my stove when you're finished.
   A I hope so.

Unit 7: Shopping

Page 85, Exercises 2A and 2B – CD2, Track 10

A Julie, look at this car! "Automatic transmission, air-conditioning, leather seats, sun roof, power windows . . ." It's got everything, and it's only $27,500.

B Ken, are you crazy? With tax and fees, that's about $30,000! We can't afford $30,000 for a car! Where . . . where are we going to get the money? The balance in our savings account is less than $8,000!

A No problem. Look here. It says, "Special financing available. Only 4 percent interest with 60 months to pay off the loan!"

B Sixty months to pay! That's five years! We're going to pay for that car every month for five years. Ken, you know I'm afraid of getting into debt. We have bills to pay every month, and we need to save money for college for the kids.

A Well, Julie, tell me: Do we need a car, or don't we need a car? Our old one always needs repair, and it's . . .

B OK, OK. We do need a car. But we don't need a new car. We could look for a used car. Let's go across the street and look. I'm sure we can find a good used car for $10,000 or even less than that.

A Yeah, but, Julie, look at this car. It's a beauty! We should get it. We can buy the car on credit. Everybody does it!

B No, not everybody! My father always paid cash for everything. He didn't even have a credit card!

A Well, your father never had any fun. And, I'm not your father!

Page 85, Exercise 3A – CD2, Track 11

Ken and his wife, Julie, are looking at cars. Ken wants to buy a new car that costs over $27,000. Julie thinks that they can't afford to spend that much money. The balance in their savings account is less than $8,000. She's afraid of getting into debt. But Ken says they can get financing to help pay for the new car. The interest rate is low, and they can take five years to pay off the loan. Ken isn't worried about buying things on credit.

Julie disagrees. She suggests that they could buy a used car. She says her father never had a credit card. He always paid cash for everything.

Page 86, Exercise 2A – CD2, Track 12

1. A My rent is going up again. What should I do?
   B Here's my advice. You're a good tenant. I think you should talk to your landlord.
2. A I have to fix my credit. What should I do?
   B You should talk to a debt counselor. He can help you.

3. A Can you suggest a nice restaurant? It's my wife's birthday.
   B You could try Chao's. Or how about Anita's?
4. A It's my niece's sixteenth birthday next week. What could I get her?
   B Why don't you get tickets to a concert? Or you could buy her a CD.
5. A That vocational school is very expensive. I can't afford it. Can you give me any advice?
   B Well, you're a good student. I think you should apply for a scholarship.
6. A I need a new car. Where do you suggest I look for one?
   B How about looking in the newspaper? Or you could look online.

Page 88, Exercise 2A – CD2, Track 13

1. I'm worried about paying interest on my credit card balance.
2. Rob is afraid of getting into debt. He pays for everything with cash.
3. Have you thought about opening a checking account?
4. Elizabeth is happy about finding an apartment she can afford.
5. Elena is excited about starting classes at the community college.
6. I'm tired of making payments on my car.
7. Franco isn't interested in applying for a loan.
8. Thank you for lending me money for school.
9. We're thinking about buying a house.
10. They were worried about getting a loan.

Page 90, Exercise 2 – CD2, Track 14

A Credit Card Nightmare

Sun Hi and Joseph Kim got their first credit card a week after they got married. At first, they paid off the balance every month.

The couple's problems began after they bought a new house. They bought new furniture, a big-screen television, and two new computers. To pay for everything, they applied for more and more credit. Soon they had six different credit cards, and they were more than $18,000 in debt.

"It was a nightmare!" says Mrs. Kim. "The interest rates were 19 percent to 24 percent. Our minimum payments were over $750 a month. We both got second jobs, but it wasn't enough. I was so worried about paying off the debt, I cried all the time."

Luckily, the Kims found a solution. They met Dolores Delgado, a debt counselor. With her help, they looked at all of their living expenses and made a family budget. They combined their six credit card payments into one monthly payment with a lower interest rate.

Now, their monthly budget for all living expenses is $3,400. Together they earn $3,900 a month. That leaves $500 for paying off their debt.

"We've cut up our credit cards," says Mr. Kim. "No more expensive furniture! In five years, we can pay off our debt. Now we know. Credit cards are dangerous!

Unit 8: Work

Page 97, Exercises 2A and 2B – CD2, Track 15

A Good morning, Tony. Thanks for coming in. I'm Ken Leong, personnel manager for the company.

B Nice to meet you, Mr. Leong.

A So, I have your résumé right here, and I understand you're interested in the job of shipping-and-receiving clerk.

B Yes, that's right. I'm applying for the shipping-and-receiving clerk position.

A OK. I'd like to ask you a few questions.

B Sure, go ahead.

A Uh. First of all, could you tell me a little about your background? Where are you from? What kind of work have you done?

B Well, I was born in Peru and lived there for 18 years. I finished high school there, and then I came here with my family. I've been living here for two years.

A OK. And are you currently employed?

B Uh. Sorry?

A Are you working now?

B Yes, I've been working part-time as a teacher's assistant at an elementary school for about a year. And I'm also going to community college at night. I want to get a degree in accounting.

A Oh. That's good. What office machines can you use?

B Uh. I can use a computer, a fax machine, a scanner, and a copying machine.

A Excellent. Those skills will be useful in this job. You'll need to take inventory and order supplies. Now, Tony, can you tell me about some of your strengths?

B Um. Excuse me?

A Your strengths – you know, your personal qualities. What makes you a good person for this job?

B Well, I'm very responsible and reliable. If I have a deadline, I come in early or stay late to finish the job. Also, I get along with everyone. I never have problems working with people. I like everyone, and they like me.

A That's great. Can you work any shift?

B Well, I prefer the day shift because I have classes at night.

A OK, Tony. There's going to be an opening in the day shift soon. I'll get back to you next week sometime.

B Thank you, Mr. Leong. I appreciate that. It was nice to meet you.

A You, too. I'll give you a call.

Page 97, Exercise 3A – CD2, Track 16

Tony has been working as a teacher's assistant for about a year. He is also going to college part-time to get a degree in accounting. Right now, Tony is at a job interview with Mr. Leong, the personnel manager.

Mr. Leong asks about Tony's background. Tony says he is from Peru and has been living in the United States for two years. Next, Mr. Leong asks about Tony's work experience, and Tony says that now he is employed at a school. Finally, Mr. Leong asks about Tony's personal strengths. Tony says he is responsible and reliable, and he gets along with everybody. Mr. Leong says he will contact Tony next week.

Page 98, Exercise 2A – CD2, Track 17

1. **A** How long has Talia been practicing for her driving test?
   B For about three months.
2. **A** Have you been working here for a long time?
   B No, I haven't. I started six days ago.
3. **A** How long has Yin been looking for a job?
   B Since last year.
4. **A** Has Mr. Rivera been interviewing people all day?
   B Yes, he has.
5. **A** How long have you been waiting to get an interview?
   B Since March.
6. **A** How long have they been going to night school?
   B All year.

Page 100, Exercise 2A – CD2, Track 18

1. She's handing out papers.
   She's handing the papers out.
   She's handing them out.
2. He's throwing away the cups.
   He's throwing the cups away.
   He's throwing them away.
3. He's turning up the volume.
   He's turning the volume up.
   He's turning it up.
4. She's filling out a job application.
   She's filling the application out.
   She's filling it out.

Page 102, Exercise 2 – CD2, Track 19

Eden's Blog

Monday 9/29

I had my interview today! I gave the interviewer a big smile and a firm handshake. I answered her questions with confidence. I'll let you know if I get the job

Thursday 9/25

Great news! One of the companies from the job fair finally called me back! I've been preparing for the job interview all day. I'm really excited. I'm going to have a practice interview with some classmates today. That will prepare me for the real one.

Wednesday 9/24

I've been feeling depressed about the job search lately, but my counselor at school told me I shouldn't give up. He said I need to be patient. Today, I organized my papers. I made lists of the places I have applied to and the people I have talked to. I also did some more research online.

Tuesday 9/16

Today, I went to a job fair at my college. I filled out several applications and handed out some résumés. There were about 20 different companies there. Several of them said they were going to call me back. Wish me luck!

Monday 9/15

Hello fellow job searchers! I have been looking for a job for several weeks. Everyone tells me that it's critical to network, so I've been telling everyone I know. I've been calling friends, relatives, and teachers to tell them about my job search. If you have any good job-searching tips, please share them with me!

Review: Units 7 and 8

Page 108, Exercise 1 – CD2, Track 20

A Hey, hi, John!

B Oh, hi, Clara.

A What a long week. I'm glad it's Friday.

B Me, too, Clara. And look! The bus is on time today!

A And you don't have to drive in all that rush-hour traffic.

B I know. But I've been taking this bus a long time, and I'm thinking about buying a car. I'm interested in finding a used SUV.

A An SUV? You should think about buying a smaller car. You can save a lot more money. And you can save on gas, too.

B Hey, I'm a big guy. I can't fit in a small car. I'm worried about getting a car that's too small for me. . . . But, hey, you could get a smaller car. I'll come to work with you and save my gas money. Then I can buy my SUV and take my friends for a ride after work.

A Sorry, John. I'm not interested in buying a car. I like the bus just fine. I'm saving my money to buy a house someday. Oh, here's my stop! See you Monday!

Page 109, Exercise 3A – CD2, Track 21

1. clean up
2. think about
3. turn up
4. fill out
5. interested in
6. throw out
7. put on
8. tired of

Page 109, Exercise 3B – CD2, Track 22

1. **A** What do you need to do?
   B I have to clean up the kitchen.
   A Can I help?
   B Sure. Could you throw out the trash?
   A I'd be happy to.
2. **A** Don't you think it's cold in here?
   B It's a little cold.
   A Why don't you turn up the heat?
   B That costs too much money. You can put on my jacket.

Unit 9: Daily living

Page 111, Exercises 2A and 2B – CD2, Track 23

A Hello?
B Samantha, this is Monica.
A Monica! I've been waiting for you to call. But, um, you sound really strange. Are you OK?
B Well, actually, no! I'm not. . . . Not at all. Somebody broke into our house tonight.
A Broke into your house? That's terrible! When? How?
B Well, around 7:30, we went over to the Morenos' next door to watch a movie. And while we were there, someone broke into our house and robbed us. They stole our TV, DVD player, jewelry, and some cash. I still can't believe it.
A Ugh. That's awful. How did the robber get in?
B He broke a window in the back bedroom. You should see the mess – there's glass all over the floor, and there are books and CDs and clothes all over the place. And, Samantha, they took my mother's ring. I'm so upset.
A Oh, did you call the police?
B Of course. They've already been here.
A What's happening to our neighborhood? We never used to have so much crime. When the kids were little, we didn't even lock the front door!
B Well, I'm just glad we weren't home when it happened.
A Oh, Monica, I feel so bad for you. And I'm worried. Did you hear someone robbed Mr. Purdy last week, too, while he was out taking a walk? I think we should start a Neighborhood Watch program, don't you?
B Yeah, we've been talking about that for months. I agree, it's time we finally did it. But right now, I have to clean up this mess.
A Do you want me to come over, Monica? I could help you clean up.
B You're the best, Samantha. Yeah, come as quickly as you can. Thanks.

Page 111, Exercise 3A – CD2, Track 24

Monica calls Samantha with bad news. While Monica and Todd were out, someone broke into their home and stole their TV, DVD player, jewelry, and some cash. Monica is upset because the robber took her mother's ring. She says the person got in through a window in the back bedroom.

Samantha is worried. She says they never used to have so much crime in their neighborhood. She tells Monica that last week someone robbed their neighbor Mr. Purdy, too. Samantha thinks they should start a Neighborhood Watch program. Monica agrees, but first she needs to clean up the mess in her house. Samantha offers to come over and help.

Page 112, Exercise 2A – CD2, Track 25

What were you doing at 8:30 last night?

1. We were watching a movie at the Rialto Theater.
2. I was studying English at home last night.
3. I was driving to work.
4. We were eating dinner at Kate's Kitchen Restaurant.
5. We were attending a Neighborhood Watch meeting.
6. I was babysitting my grandchildren at my daughter's house.
7. I was baking a cake for my daughter's birthday party.
8. We were painting the kitchen.

Page 114, Exercise 2A – CD2, Track 26

1. While Dad was working in the garden, a thief stole his car.
2. I was eating lunch when the fire alarm suddenly went off.
3. Ali fell off a ladder while he was painting the ceiling.
4. When the earthquake started, the students were taking a test.
5. I was making a right turn when another car hit the back of my car.
6. While we were camping, it suddenly began to rain.
7. Mr. and Mrs. Gomez were jogging in the park when a dog began to chase them.
8. While Diana was working outside, a stranger drove up to her house.

Page 116, Exercise 2 – CD2, Track 27

Home Is More Than a Building

A few months ago, Pedro Ramirez, 45, lost his job in a grocery store. To pay the bills, he got a part-time job at night. Several days later, Pedro's wife, Luisa, gave him a big surprise. She was pregnant with their sixth child. Pedro was happy but worried. "How am I going to support another child without a full-time job?" he wondered.

That evening, Pedro and Luisa got some more news. A fire was coming near their home. By the next morning, the fire was very close. The police ordered every family in the neighborhood to evacuate. The Ramirez family moved quickly. While Pedro was gathering their legal documents, Luisa grabbed the family photographs, and the children put their pets – a cat and a bird – in the family's van. Then, the family drove to the home of Luisa's sister, one hour away.

About 24 hours later, Pedro and Luisa got very bad news. The fire destroyed their home. They lost almost everything. With no home, only part-time work, and a baby coming, Pedro was even more worried about the future.

For the next three months, the Ramirez family stayed with Luisa's sister while workers were rebuilding their home. Many generous people helped them during that difficult time. Friends took them shopping for clothes. Strangers left gifts at their door. A group of children collected $500 to buy bicycles for the Ramirez children.

Because of all the help from friends and neighbors, the Ramirez family was able to rebuild their lives. Two months after the fire, Luisa mailed out holiday cards with this message: "Home is more than a building. Home is wherever there is love."

Unit 10: Free time

Page 123, Exercises 2A and 2B – CD2, Track 28

A I'm so exhausted! I really need a vacation.
B You know, my work is pretty slow right now. I can talk to my boss. Maybe he'll give me a few days off.
A Oh, Ricardo, what a great idea. We haven't had a family vacation in two years.
B Where would you like to go, Felicia?
A We could go to San Francisco. Michelle's six – she's old enough to enjoy it, don't you think?
B Well, let's see if there are any deals on any of the Internet travel sites. . . . Look, if we book a flight seven days ahead, we can get a round-trip ticket for $200.
A That's not too expensive. Are there any discounts for children?
B Hmm. Let's see . . . I don't think so.
A Oh, that's too bad. What about hotel rates?
B Not cheap. Summer is the height of the tourist season. If we stay in a nice hotel, it's going to cost at least $250 a night.
A Plus the room tax, don't forget. You have to add on an extra 14 percent or something like that.
B Right. I forgot about that. So if the three of us take this trip, and if we stay in San Francisco just three days, it's going to cost almost $1,200.
A That's a lot to spend for just a three-day vacation, Ricardo. Maybe we should just go camping instead.
B Yeah, you're probably right. We could go to Big Bear Lake. If we do that, how much will it cost?

A Well, gas will probably cost about $100, the campsite will cost about $35 a night, and then there's food – but that won't be too much if we grill hamburgers.

B Michelle will probably have more fun camping, too.

A I agree. So what do you think? Should we make a reservation?

B I'll reserve the campsite after I talk to my boss tomorrow.

A I hope he says yes. We really need a vacation.

Page 123, Exercise 3A – CD2, Track 29

Felicia is exhausted. She needs a vacation. Her husband, Ricardo, says he can ask his boss for a few days off. Felicia would like to go to San Francisco. They look for special travel discounts on the Internet. If they book a flight at least seven days ahead, they can get a round-trip ticket for less than $200. On the other hand, hotel room rates will be high because summer is the most popular tourist season. Also, there is a room tax on hotel rooms in San Francisco. They figure out that a three-day trip to San Francisco will cost almost $1,200.

Felicia and her husband decide to change their plans. If they go camping, they will save a lot of money and their daughter will have more fun. Felicia's husband will reserve the campsite after he talks to his boss.

Page 124, Exercise 2A – CD2, Track 30

1. Annette and William will take their children to Sea Adventure next month if William gets a few days off.
2. If they get a discount, they'll reserve a room at a hotel.
3. If prices are too high, they won't take an expensive vacation.
4. We'll have a picnic on Saturday if it doesn't rain.
5. If you give me the money, I'll buy the concert tickets.
6. If you come to Chicago, we'll meet you at the airport.
7. They'll fly to Miami next month if they find a cheap flight.
8. We won't go camping if the weather is too hot.

Page 126, Exercise 2A – CD2, Track 31

1. Kara will talk to a travel agent before she books a flight.

2. Before Cynthia leaves for Puerto Rico, she'll buy some new clothes.
3. Donald will take a taxi to the hotel after he picks up his baggage.
4. The campers will make a fire before they cook their dinner.
5. After they finish eating, they'll clean up the campsite.
6. I'll call you after I return from my trip.
7. After I get my passport, I'll make the reservations.
8. Before we go to Mexico, we'll learn some words in Spanish.
9. Jack will lock the doors before he leaves for the airport.

Page 128, Exercise 2 – CD2, Track 32

The Rock: San Francisco's Biggest Tourist Attraction

Alcatraz, a small, rocky island in the middle of San Francisco Bay, was once the most famous prison in the United States. For a period of 29 years, from 1934 to 1963, over 1,500 dangerous criminals lived in the prison's 378 cells. People believed that it was impossible to escape from Alcatraz Island. However, in 1962, two brothers, John and Clarence Anglin, and another man named Frank Morris escaped on a raft made of raincoats. A famous movie, *Escape from Alcatraz*, tells this amazing story. Other famous prisoners who lived on the island included Al Capone, the gangster, and Robert Stroud, the "Birdman of Alcatraz."

Alcatraz prison closed in 1963. The island became a national park, and since then, it has been a major attraction for tourists from all over the world. These days, many people call Alcatraz by its popular name, "The Rock."

In the summer, it is wise to buy tickets to the island in advance because the ferries sell out. Evening tours are less crowded. The admission prices listed include the ferry, tickets, and an audio tour.

General admission:
Adult (18–61), $36.00
Junior (12–17), $34.50
Child (5–11), $26.00
Senior (62 or older), $34.50

Review: Units 9 and 10

Page 134, Exercise 1 – CD2, Track 33

A This is a KPST Radio special report.

B Park police have found a Denver man who was missing overnight in Rocky River National Park. Brad Spencer disappeared sometime on Sunday after camping Saturday night at Timber Creek. His wife, Paula Spencer, became worried when he didn't return to their campsite Sunday evening. Mrs. Spencer told KPST News . . .

C When I talked to Brad early Sunday, he was planning a short hike. It was a beautiful day, and he was wearing only a T-shirt and shorts. I got really worried when he wasn't back by eight o'clock in the evening. It was getting cold and dark. That's when I decided to call the park police.

B Paula's husband, Brad, got lost while he was bird-watching. Fortunately, he was carrying matches, and he was able to start a fire to keep warm. When park rangers found him around six o'clock Monday morning, he was sleeping next to the fire, over a mile from the closest trail. A happy and hungry Mr. Spencer told KPST . . .

D I learned a good lesson. If I ever go hiking here again, I'm going to carry food and stay on the trails!

A This is Roberta Chang with KPST Radio.

Page 135, Exercise 3A – CD2, Track 34

1. upset
2. about
3. family
4. extra
5. travel
6. police
7. vacation
8. dangerous
9. Samantha
10. photographs

Page 135, Exercise 3B – CD2, Track 35

1. Samantha is upset.
2. Where's the travel agent?
3. The prison is dangerous.
4. It's about seven o'clock.
5. Did you take photographs?
6. Call the police!
7. She'll think about visiting her family.
8. I need a vacation.

tests, midterm test, and final test help
rs assess students' mastery of the material
the *Ventures 3* Student's Book.

- Each of the ten unit tests covers one unit.
- The midterm test covers Units 1–5.
- The final test covers Units 6–10.
- Each test assesses listening, grammar, reading, and writing.

Students' performance on the tests helps to determine what has been successfully learned and what may need more attention. Successful completion of a test can also give students a sense of accomplishment.

Getting ready for a test

- Plan to give a unit test shortly after students have completed a unit and have had time for a review. The midterm should follow completion of Unit 5 and the review lesson for Units 5 and 6. The final test should follow completion of Unit 10 and the review lesson for Units 9 and 10. Tell students when the test will be given. Encourage students to study together and to ask you for help if needed.
- Explain the purpose of the test and how students' scores will be used.
- Prepare one test for each student. The tests may be photocopied from the Teacher's Edition, starting on page T-165, or printed from the Assessment Audio CD / CD-ROM.
- Schedule approximately 30 minutes for each unit test and 1 hour for the midterm and final tests. Allow more time if needed.
- Locate the audio program for each test's listening section on the Assessment Audio CD / CD-ROM. The CD is a hybrid. It will work in both a stereo and a computer CD-ROM drive.

Giving a test

- During the test, have students use a pencil and an eraser. Tell students to put away their Student's Books and dictionaries before the test.
- Hand out one copy of the test to each student.
- Encourage students to take a few minutes to look through the test without answering any of the items. Go through the instructions to make sure students understand them.

- Tell students that approximately 5 minutes of the unit test (10 minutes of the midterm and final tests) will be used for the listening section.
- When playing the listening section of the test, you may choose to pause or repeat the audio program if you feel that students require more time to answer. The audio script appears in the Teacher's Edition on page T-191. The script can also be printed from the Assessment Audio CD / CD-ROM and read aloud in class.

Scoring

- You can collect the tests and grade them on your own. Alternatively, you can have students correct their own tests by going over the answers in class or by having students exchange tests with a partner and correcting each other's answers. The answer key is located in the Teacher's Edition on page T-194. It can also be printed from the Assessment Audio CD / CD-ROM.
- Each test has a total score of 100 points. Each unit test has five sections worth 20 points each. The midterm and final tests have five sections worth 12.5 or 25 points each.

Track list for test audio program

Track 1: Introduction
Track 2: Unit 1 Test
Track 3: Unit 2 Test
Track 4: Unit 3 Test
Track 5: Unit 4 Test
Track 6: Unit 5 Test
Track 7: Midterm Test
Track 8: Unit 6 Test
Track 9: Unit 7 Test
Track 10: Unit 8 Test
Track 11: Unit 9 Test
Track 12: Unit 10 Test
Track 13: Final Test

Name: _____

Date: _____

Score: _____

TEST
UNIT 1 Personal information

A Listening

TRACK 2

1 Listen. Circle the correct answer.

1. What are Greg and Neil talking about?
   a. their job   b. their weekend   c. their girlfriends

2. Where are Greg and Neil?
   a. at work   b. at the beach   c. at home

3. Greg and Neil are
   a. co-workers   b. friends   c. relatives

TRACK 2

2 Listen again. Put a check (✓) under the correct name.

	Neil	Greg
1. likes playing cards with friends	☐	☐
2. dislikes socializing	☐	☐
3. went to the beach	☐	☐
4. enjoys jogging	☐	☐
5. dislikes working out	☐	☐
6. is kind of shy	☐	☐
7. has a new girlfriend	☐	☐

B Grammar

Complete the sentences. Use gerunds.

be	learn	stand	take	talk

1. We love _____ languages.

2. My friend doesn't mind _____ alone.

3. Do you dislike _____ on the phone?

4. I hate _____ in line!

5. She doesn't enjoy _____ out the trash.

© Cambridge University Press 2014 Photocopi

C Grammar

Complete the sentences. Use *more than*, *less than*, and *as much as*.

1. Marta enjoys _____. (socializing / reading)
2. Marta likes _____. (working out / watching TV)
3. Marta likes _____. (playing sports / dancing)
4. She likes _____. (reading / working out)
5. She enjoys _____. (watching TV / dancing)

D Reading

Read the story. Then read the sentences. Are they correct? Circle *Yes* or *No*.

The Wrong Job

My brother, Danny, has the wrong job for his personality. He's a writer and works in his apartment alone. He stays at home during the week and doesn't meet people at his job. The problem is that he likes working with others more than working alone.

Danny is a very outgoing person. He enjoys meeting new people as much as he enjoys socializing. He likes talking to everyone. When he's not working, he goes out dancing and visits friends. Danny gets bored being alone. He calls people to chat all the time. He likes writing, but maybe he has the wrong job.

I think being a writer is not a good job for Danny. He needs a job to fit his personality. Next week, I will talk to Danny about his job. He knows he is bored, and he knows being a writer doesn't suit him, but he needs my help. He should take my advice if he wants to be happy at work. Don't you agree?

1. Danny's brother thinks Danny has the right job.   Yes   No
2. Danny likes working alone more than working with others.   Yes   No
3. Danny likes visiting friends.   Yes   No
4. Danny doesn't meet new people at his job.   Yes   No
5. A writer is a good job for Danny's personality.   Yes   No

E Writing

Write a paragraph about the right job for Danny. Write sentences with *like* or *enjoy*. Use adjectives to describe Danny's personality. Use a separate piece of paper.

Name: _____

Date: _____

Score: _____

TEST
UNIT 2 At school

A Listening

1 Listen. Circle the correct answer.

TRACK 3

1. What are Tanya and Omar talking about?

   a. their school   b. learning English   c. their families

2. Where are they?

   a. at the library   b. at work   c. at school

3. Tanya and Omar are

   a. classmates   b. friends   c. co-workers

2 Listen again. Put a check (✓) under the correct name.

TRACK 3

	Tanya	Omar
1. has been at the school for one day	☐	☐
2. has been at the school for one month	☐	☐
3. practices English with co-workers	☐	☐
4. reads the newspaper in English	☐	☐
5. dislikes using a dictionary	☐	☐
6. knows more English vocabulary	☐	☐
7. is going to start a new strategy for learning English	☐	☐

B Grammar

Complete the sentences. Write the correct word.

1. How long _____ Ana known
   (have / has)

   Manya?

2. He has _____ here since
   (be / been)

   February.

3. I have taught him _____ one
   (for / since)

   year.

4. Alex has _____ that job for
   (have / had)

   five months.

5. She has worked there _____
   (for / since)

   last week.

C Grammar

Complete the sentences. Use *ever* and the present perfect.

1. _____ to your neighbors?
   (you / talk)

2. _____ her books?
   (Jameela / forget)

3. _____ French?
   (he / study)

4. _____ lost?
   (you / be)

5. _____ the wrong homework?
   (Laura and Joseph / do)

D Reading

Read the story. Then read the sentences. Are they correct? Circle *Yes* or *No*.

Problems at School

Kayla is a new high school student. She has been in the United States for two months and has learned to speak English quickly. She has practiced speaking a lot with her neighbors, but high school is different. Kayla has to speak, read, and write in English. Kayla isn't a very active reader, so this is more difficult. Also, she has to study for a lot of classes. And of course, there are so many new words to know!

Kayla is discouraged. Since she started high school in September, Kayla has gotten bad grades. She has done the homework every day. She has practiced with her neighbors. She has studied for tests, but her teacher says that Kayla doesn't always understand. She says that Kayla doesn't ask enough questions in class. Her counselor says that Kayla needs to concentrate when she reads and develop strategies for learning new words in English. Kayla hasn't ever had so much trouble in school. Now, she doesn't enjoy school as much as she did before. Often she can't wait until school is over. Have you ever felt this way about school?

1. Kayla has been a high school student for two years.	Yes	No
2. Kayla has lived in the United States for two months.	Yes	No
3. High school has been difficult for Kayla.	Yes	No
4. Kayla has had problems learning vocabulary.	Yes	No
5. Kayla has always had bad grades.	Yes	No

E Writing

Write a paragraph about three strategies to help Kayla learn more words in English. Use a separate piece of paper.

Name: _____

Date: _____

Score: _____

TEST
UNIT 3 Friends and family

A Listening

1 Listen. Circle the correct answer.

1. What is the relationship between Daniel and Alfredo?

  a. co-workers   b. classmates   c. neighbors

2. Where are they?

  a. at home   b. at work   c. at school

3. Who are they talking about?

  a. Alfredo's wife   b. Alfredo's daughter   c. Alfredo's son

2 Listen again. Put a check (✓) under the correct name.

	Daniel	Alfredo
1. is the first speaker	☐	☐
2. comes over to his neighbor's apartment	☐	☐
3. borrows a dictionary	☐	☐
4. can't use the computer	☐	☐
5. doesn't complain about the noise	☐	☐
6. does a favor	☐	☐
7. appreciates a favor	☐	☐

B Grammar

Complete the sentences. Use _because_ or _because of_.

1. She complained _____ the noise.
2. Pam borrowed the ladder _____ she needed to paint the ceiling.
3. They couldn't come to the party _____ their son was sick.
4. I couldn't drive _____ a flat tire.
5. The alarm doesn't work _____ it needs a new battery.

C Grammar

Complete the sentences. Use _too_ or _enough_.

1. The apartment has two bedrooms. It is _____ for my wife and me and our son.
  (big)

2. She has worked for only one month. She is not _____ for the new job.
  (experienced)

3. The houses in that neighborhood look expensive. The prices are _____ for us.
  (high)

4. Their house is _____ from my house. I can only
   (far)

   visit once a year!

5. Our apartment is not _____ to our jobs. We're going to have to move.
   (close)

D Reading

Read the story. Then read the sentences. Are they correct? Circle *Yes* or *No*.

The New Neighbors

Yesterday, Sally, my neighbor, came over and had coffee. We discussed our new neighbors, Mr. and Mrs. Holmes, and their two children. I told her that when I met Mr. and Mrs. Holmes, their two children were running up and down the hallway. They were knocking on all the doors and ringing all the doorbells. I asked them to watch their children. So did the other neighbors. Next, Sally told me that she met Mr. and Mrs. Holmes a few days later. This time, the children had matches and were trying to light a newspaper outside her door! She was so surprised because Mr. and Mrs. Holmes didn't say anything to the children.

Then, I told Sally that I tried to visit the Holmes' apartment last week. There was very loud music at 3:30 in the afternoon, and I was concerned. I rang the bell, but there was no answer. The parents weren't there. Afterward, Sally told me she also heard loud music from their apartment last Friday. It was 1:00 in the morning! On Saturday, she went to the apartment. Again, no one answered the door. Sally and I have decided that we need to do something about our new neighbors. We're going to write a letter to our landlord!

1. Sue and Sally complained to each other about the new neighbors.   Yes   No
2. Sally met the Holmes family the same day as Sue.   Yes   No
3. Sue rang the bell because she wanted to welcome them.   Yes   No
4. Because of the Holmes children, the building is not safe.   Yes   No
5. Sally wants to write a letter to Mr. and Mrs. Holmes.   Yes   No

E Writing

Write a letter of complaint to the landlord of Sue and Sally's apartment building. Use *enough* or *too*. Include the date, the name of the person they are writing, the reason, examples of problems, and what they want. Use a separate piece of paper.

Name: _____

Date: _____

Score: _____

TEST
UNIT 4 Health

A Listening

TRACK 5

1 Listen. Circle the correct answer.

1. What is their relationship?

   a. sisters   b. friends   c. boss and worker

2. When did they last see each other?

   a. yesterday   b. last week   c. a long time

3. Where are they?

   a. at home   b. in a public place   c. at the doctor's office

TRACK 5

2 Listen again. Put a check (✓) under the correct name.

	Sheila	Joy
1. is the first speaker	☐	☐
2. has been busy	☐	☐
3. has started a new diet	☐	☐
4. used to eat unhealthy food	☐	☐
5. hasn't exercised recently	☐	☐
6. needs to change her diet	☐	☐
7. hasn't eaten yet	☐	☐

B Grammar

Complete the sentences. Use the present perfect.

1. The doctor _____ my blood pressure recently.
   (check)

2. Elisa _____ to the gym lately.
   (not / gone)

3. I _____ salt, fat, and sugar recently.
   (give up)

4. Ahmet _____ really tired lately.
   (be)

5. I _____ recently.
   (not / sleep)

C Grammar

Complete the sentences. Use *use to* or *used to*.

1. Did you _____ skip breakfast?
2. She _____ stay up late, but now she goes to bed early.
3. I _____ drive to work, but now I walk.
4. Did he _____ eat fatty foods?
5. He _____ go straight home, but now he goes to the gym.

D Reading

Read the story. Then read the sentences. Are they correct? Circle *Yes* or *No*.

Joseph's Healthy Change

Recently, I have decided to follow my doctor's advice about eating and exercising. Before, I used to just work, eat, and sleep. I didn't exercise enough, and I was always tired. Lately, I have made healthy changes. I used to drive to work, but now I walk to work or ride my bike. At work, I used to take the elevator. Lately, I have started taking the stairs. I've joined a gym, too. Now, I have so much more energy than I used to have.

Because of my high blood pressure, I have also had to change my diet. I used to eat too much fat, salt, and sugar. My doctor explained that my diet made me unhealthy. So, now I eat more fish, vegetables, and fruits. Also, I used to skip breakfast. But I have started eating three meals a day. I never knew that eating three meals is healthier than eating just one meal. In two months, I have lost weight – about ten pounds.

At first, all these changes were really difficult; but I changed because my health is important. Next time I go to my doctor, he will be very happy. Since I have taken his advice, my blood pressure is lower. Now, I don't need pills or medication!

1. Joseph used to walk or ride his bike to work.   Yes   No
2. He didn't use to take the elevator, but now he does.   Yes   No
3. Joseph eats breakfast, lunch, and dinner.   Yes   No
4. He's lost ten pounds in the last ten months.   Yes   No
5. He used to need medication.   Yes   No

E Writing

Write a paragraph about habits that you have changed. Write about your habits before and now. Use *used to . . . , but now* and *lately* in your paragraph. Use a separate piece of paper.

Name: _____

Date: _____

Score: _____

TEST
UNIT 5 Around town

A Listening

TRACK 6

1 Listen. Circle the correct answer.

1. What are they talking about?

   a. weekend plans   b. places in the city   c. relationships

2. Who is Joe?

   a. Sharon's husband   b. Renee's friend   c. their brother

3. What does Sharon want to do?

   a. get out more   b. stay at home   c. go shopping

4. What does Joe like to do?

   a. go to museums   b. watch sports   c. take tours

TRACK 6

2 Listen again. Put a check (✓) next to the events Renee and Sharon talk about.

☐ salsa concert   ☐ walking tour

☐ staying home   ☐ trip to the beach

☐ new art exhibit   ☐ soccer game

☐ community fair   ☐ fun party

☐ science museum   ☐ school activities

B Grammar

Complete the sentences. Use verbs + infinitives.

1. Did they _____ their bills?
        (promise / pay)

2. When does Andrea _____ her new job?
        (hope / start)

3. What time do you _____ Ernesto?
        (plan / meet)

4. Have you ever _____ in a helicopter?
        (wanted / ride)

5. What have you _____ this weekend?
        (decided / do)

C Grammar

Complete the sentences. Use *already* or *yet*.

1. It's Friday morning. The weekend hasn't started _____ !

2. It's 7:05. The movie has _____ begun.

3. The museum opens at 10:00. It's 9:30. The museum
   hasn't opened _____.

4. We haven't paid our rent _____!

5. It's Thursday. We've _____ made plans for next weekend.

D Reading

Read the story. Then read the sentences. Are they correct? Circle *Yes* or *No*.

Weekend Plans

Linda and Benito are talking about their plans for the weekend. Lately, the weather has been perfect, so they hope to spend time outside. Although the weekend is only two days, they intend to do a lot. They have already bought tickets to an outdoor concert Friday night. It's going to be a salsa concert with lots of musicians and singers. Linda and Benito love salsa music. They expect to dance a lot.

On Saturday, they plan to spend a day at the beach. Linda and Benito have already bought beach chairs and swimsuits – they really expect to have fun. They both love to swim and surf. They want to get a tan, too. Later that evening, Benito would like to take Linda to an outdoor restaurant for dinner. Because Linda loves to see the sunset, she is really excited.

On Sunday, they plan to go to a baseball game. Benito loves baseball – he hopes to catch a home run ball. Even if he doesn't, he expects to have a good time. Benito and Linda are very excited about their plans. They can't wait until the weekend arrives. They just hope the weather forecast promises to keep the rain away!

1. Linda and Benito intend to go to the beach.   Yes   No
2. They are planning outdoor activities for the weekend.   Yes   No
3. They can't afford the tickets to the outdoor concert.   Yes   No
4. They have decided on options if it rains.   Yes   No
5. It has been raining lately.   Yes   No

E Writing

Write a paragraph about your plans for next weekend. Use verbs such as *decide, intend, would like,* and *plan*. Also use *already* and *yet*. Use a separate piece of paper.

MIDTERM TEST
UNITS 1–5

A Listening

1 Listen. Circle the correct answer.

TRACK 7

1. Who are mother and daughter?

   a. Amelia and Elsa   b. Elsa and Ana   c. Amelia and Ana

2. How does Elsa feel?

   a. lonely   b. worried   c. excited

2 Listen again. Put a check (✓) under the correct name.

TRACK 7

	Amelia	Elsa	Ana
1. worried about her daughter	☐	☐	☐
2. hasn't made friends	☐	☐	☐
3. is discouraged	☐	☐	☐
4. gives advice to join a team	☐	☐	☐
5. likes exercising	☐	☐	☐
6. isn't outgoing	☐	☐	☐
7. tells about storytelling	☐	☐	☐
8. appreciates the advice	☐	☐	☐

B Grammar

Complete the sentences. Choose the correct word.

1. I don't mind _____ up desserts.
   (to give / giving)

2. How long has Jenny _____ at the school?
   (taught / teach)

3. Mr. Lee hopes _____ rich one day.
   (being / to be)

4. _____ the weather, they decided to stay home.
   (Because of / Because)

5. She _____ to be shy, but now she's a party animal.
   (used / was)

C Grammar

Complete the sentences.

| enough | ever | for | much | yet |

1. She enjoys reading as _____ as watching TV.

2. Have you _____ complained to your landlord?

3. We have known him _____ one year.

4. He isn't old _____ to walk to school alone.

5. They haven't done their homework _____.

D Reading

Read the story. Then read the sentences. Are they correct? Circle *Yes* or *No*.

Marie's Problem

Recently, Marie moved to the United States. Since last summer, she has tried to get used to her new life, but things are different here. In her country, Haiti, Marie hated to stay home. She didn't use to be shy, but she is now. She and her husband used to go to cafés or dance clubs every weekend. She used to go out with friends to the movies, too. Now, she dislikes going out. Marie's problem is English. Because she is uncomfortable speaking it, she stays at home.

Marie hates speaking English because sometimes people don't understand her. She has had to ask questions many times before people understand her. She practices English in her classes, but she isn't outgoing enough to practice with her neighbors. Her children have learned to speak English quickly because they enjoy socializing with other children and they speak English with their new friends. Her husband has already made friends because of his job. And he knew a lot of English before they moved.

Her husband has told her to watch TV programs in English, but Marie likes watching programs in her first language more than watching them in English. It's too difficult to understand when there are so many new words! Marie is unhappy. She has been unhappy since she arrived from her country. This summer, she would like to go out with friends to restaurants and the movies. Marie needs to find some good strategies to help her learn English.

1. In her country, Marie disliked staying home.   Yes   No
2. Marie is worried about people understanding her.   Yes   No
3. Marie has already learned to speak English well.   Yes   No
4. She is too shy to speak English with her neighbors.   Yes   No
5. Her children refuse to make friends.   Yes   No

6. Her husband speaks English at his job.   Yes   No

7. Her husband has suggested practicing with her neighbors.   Yes   No

8. Marie prefers watching TV in English.   Yes   No

9. Marie has enjoyed being in the United States.   Yes   No

10. Marie has already started using new strategies to learn English.   Yes   No

E Writing

1. Write a plan for a paragraph about strategies to help Marie improve her English. Write four strategies and one or two examples for each one. Use the chart below.

Strategy	Examples

2. Write a paragraph about strategies to help Marie improve her English. Write at least three strategies and one or two examples for each one. Use the chart above and the reading in Exercise D to help you. Use a separate piece of paper.

Name: _____

Date: _____

Score: _____

TEST
UNIT 6 Time

A Listening

TRACK 8

1 Listen. Circle the correct answer.

1. What are they talking about?

   a. a birthday party   b. English class   c. weekend plans

2. What does Sally ask Lola?

   a. to go shopping   b. to come to dinner   c. to work on a project

3. Why can't Lola accept Sally's invitation?

   a. She's sick.   b. She's out of town.   c. She's busy.

4. When are they going to get together?

   a. next week   b. Friday   c. Sunday

TRACK 8

2 Listen again. Complete Lola's to-do list.

Things to Do

1. _____
2. _____
3. _____
4. _____
5. _____
6. _____

B Grammar

Combine the sentences. Use *when*.

1. You have many chores. You need to prioritize.

   When _____, _____.

2. Your projects are due on Monday. Don't procrastinate over the weekend.

   _____ when _____.

3. You're talking to your children. Don't be impatient.

   When _____, _____.

4. You have a deadline. Plan your tasks.

   When _____, _____.

5. Don't turn on the television. You need to focus.

   _____ when _____.

C Grammar

Read Lola's schedule. Write sentences with *before* and *after*.

Lola's Evening Schedule	
3:30 go to the supermarket	5:15 eat dinner
4:10 meet the children at the bus stop	6:00 clean the kitchen
4:30 start preparing dinner	6:30 leave for evening class

1. go to the supermarket / meet the children

   After Lola _____, _____.

2. meet the children / start preparing dinner

   Before _____, _____.

3. start preparing dinner / meet the children

   After _____, _____.

4. eat dinner / clean the kitchen

   _____ after _____.

5. clean the kitchen / leave for class

   _____ before _____.

D Reading

Read the journal entry. Then read the sentences. Are they correct? Circle *Yes* or *No*.

> My son, Stanley, is only 12 years old, but he has already learned to manage his time well. Every Sunday, he makes a to-do list. He writes deadlines in his calendar. During the week, he does all his chores before he starts his homework. He puts the dishes away, takes out the trash, and helps Megan, his little sister, with her homework. After he helps Megan, he works on his homework. He doesn't procrastinate. When a project is due on Friday, he tries to finish it on Wednesday or Thursday. He gets all his work done before he watches any TV.
>
> I am very different from Stanley. I don't prioritize well. I really need to learn some time-management skills from my son! Parents can learn a lot from their children, too.

1. Before the week begins, Stanley writes deadlines in his calendar.   Yes   No
2. He does his chores after he starts his homework.   Yes   No
3. Before he does his homework, he helps Megan.   Yes   No
4. He usually starts a project when it is due.   Yes   No
5. When he has done all his work, he watches TV.   Yes   No

E Writing

Write a paragraph about your daily activities. Use *when, before,* and *after*.
Use a separate piece of paper.

TEST
UNIT 7 Shopping

A Listening

TRACK 9

1 Listen. Circle the correct answer.

1. What is their relationship?

   a. parent and child   b. husband and wife   c. brother and sister

2. Why do they want a computer?

   a. to pay their bills   b. to do research   c. to help kids with homework

3. What is important to them as they decide?

   a. the cost   b. the brand   c. the amount of memory

4. Which way will they pay?

   a. with a credit card   b. with cash   c. with a check

TRACK 9

2 Listen again. Complete the chart.

	How much?
1. cost of used computer	
2. cost of used printer	
3. cost of new computer and printer	
4. amount of financing	
5. amount of debt	
6. cost of online service (every month)	

B Grammar

Complete the sentences. Use *could* or *should*.

1. **A** It's difficult to get to work on time. The bus is not reliable! What should I do?

   B Maybe you _____ think about buying a used car.

2. **A** We're afraid of going into debt. What do you suggest we do?

   B You and your husband _____ set up a monthly budget.

3. **A** I need a credit card. Can you give me any advice?

   B You _____ look for a credit card with low interest rates.

4. **A** Can you suggest a good online company?

   B You _____ try talking to the computer teacher. She knows a lot about getting online.

5. **A** My son wants to go to college, but we can't afford it. Do you have any advice?

   B You and your son _____ apply for a loan.

C Grammar

Complete the sentences. Use gerunds.

1. I'm worried about _____ him the money.
   (lend)

2. Dolores is afraid of _____ into debt.
   (get)

3. Gregory is excited about _____ his new job.
   (start)

4. We're not happy about _____ interest on our credit card balance.
   (pay)

5. I'm interested in _____ a used car.
   (buy)

D Reading

Read the letter to Money Man. Then read the sentences. Are they correct?
Circle *Yes* or *No*.

Dear Money Man,

My husband and I have two children in high school. My husband works full-time as an auto mechanic, and I work as a babysitter. Our daughter, Ana, is 14. She won't wear the clothes we bought her last year. Our son, Juan, is 16. He complains about his clothes, too. They want a new wardrobe every month! They also ask for new cell phones and expensive video games.

We understand their requests. They want to be like the other students at the high school. But they should be more concerned with their schoolwork! And we're worried about getting into credit card debt because of our children. We want to buy nice things for them, but we want to pay more than the minimum payment on our credit card bill every month, too. Can you give us advice?

No Debt for Us

1. The parents don't understand their children's requests.   Yes   No
2. Ana wants a new cell phone and a computer.   Yes   No
3. Juan doesn't like his clothes.   Yes   No
4. Ana and Juan have part-time jobs.   Yes   No
5. The parents want to pay more than the minimum payment.   Yes   No

E Writing

Write an answer to No Debt for Us. Use *could* and *should*. Use words like *first*, *second*, *third*, and *finally* to list your suggestions. Use a separate piece of paper.

TEST
UNIT **8** Work

A Listening

TRACK 10

1 Listen. Circle the correct answer.

1. What is their relationship?
   a. interviewer and applicant   b. supervisor and employee   c. counselor and student

2. What does Janice talk about?
   a. her work experience   b. her education   c. her hobbies

3. Where are they?
   a. at home   b. at the store   c. in an office

4. What is the outcome?
   a. Janice gets a job.   b. No job is available.   c. Ms. Rivera will contact her.

TRACK 10

2 Listen again. Complete the chart.

Topic	Information
1. job she is applying for	
2. degree	
3. years in this country	
4. current occupation	
5. three strengths Janice mentions	
6. one strength Ms. Rivera mentions	

B Grammar

Complete the sentences. Use the present perfect continuous.

1. How long _____ they _____ for a degree?
   (study)

2. _____ you _____ in this country for a long time?
   (live)

3. How long _____ Josefina _____ at her job?
   (work)

4. _____ Ken _____ his English?
   (practice)

5. How long _____ you _____?
   (wait)

C Grammar

Complete the sentences.

1. He's filling out an application.

   He's _____ the application _____.

2. She's putting them away.

   She's _____ the pots.

3. He's turning up the volume.

   He's _____ it _____.

4. She's cleaning the kitchen up.

   She's _____ the kitchen.

5. He's calling his wife back.

   He's _____ his wife.

D Reading

Read the story. Then read the sentences. Are they correct? Circle *Yes* or *No*.

> Sandra Jones has been working as a clerk at a supermarket for two years. She doesn't like working the night shift, and she wants to work with more people. She has been looking for a new job for three weeks. She has called everyone she knows to tell them about her job search, and she has done a lot of research online. She also went to a job fair at a community college and filled out several applications.
>
> Yesterday, she had a job interview with Mr. Leong, the personnel manager at The Best Haircuts. There is an opening for a full-time position as a receptionist. Mr. Leong asked her questions about her past work experience, her current job, and her strengths. She answered his questions with confidence because she knows she is a reliable and responsible worker.
>
> After the interview, Mr. Leong showed her around the hair salon. He also introduced her to some of the employees. Finally, he promised to call her back next week. Before she left, Sandra gave him a big smile and a firm handshake. Sandra really wants the job. She is also a good person for the job because she gets along with everybody.

1. Sandra has been working as a receptionist.   Yes   No
2. She has been looking for a new position for two weeks.   Yes   No
3. Sandra doesn't like to work at night.   Yes   No
4. Mr. Leong asked Sandra about her strengths.   Yes   No
5. Mr. Leong called Sandra back two hours after the interview.   Yes   No

E Writing

Write a formal thank-you letter to Mr. Ken Leong from Sandra Jones. Use the information in Exercise D to help you. The address of The Best Haircuts is 35 South Third Street, Milwaukee, WI 53215. Include reasons for saying thank you, something specific you appreciate, and an ending for the letter. Use a separate piece of paper.

TEST
UNIT 9 Daily living

A Listening

TRACK 11

1 Listen. Circle the correct answer.

1. 1. Where are they?

   a. at home   b. at a meeting   c. at a barbecue

2. What is their relationship?

   a. family   b. classmates   c. neighbors

3. What is the purpose of their conversation?

   a. to prevent crime   b. to help the Wongs   c. to get to know each other

4. How do they feel?

   a. happy   b. bored   c. concerned

TRACK 11

2 Listen Complete the chart.

Questions	Answers
1. What happened at the Wongs' house?	
2. What did the robber steal?	
3. How did he get in?	
4. What did everyone use to do?	
5. What do they have to remember?	
6. When will they meet again?	

B Grammar

What were they doing at 9:00 last night?

Complete the sentences. Use the past continuous.

1. My daughter _____ her homework.
                               (do)

2. I _____ my favorite TV show.
               (watch)

3. We _____ up the kitchen.
               (clean)

4. He _____ a meeting at our children's school.
               (attend)

5. The neighbors _____ cards with friends.
                   (playing)

C Grammar

Complete the sentences. Use the past continuous or simple past.

1. When the phone _____, she _____ dinner.
   (ring)   (cook)

2. He _____ when the alarm _____.
   (sleep)   (go off)

3. While we _____ to school, it _____ to snow.
   (drive)   (start)

4. While they _____ to us, their young child _____ many times.
   (talk)   (interrupt)

5. I _____ when the dog _____ to bark.
   (study)   (begin)

D Reading

Read the journal entry. Then read the sentences. Are they correct? Circle
Yes or *No*.

> About three years ago, before I moved to the United States, I was
> living in my country, El Salvador. One night, while my sister Maria and I
> slept, our grandmother was reading a book in the living room. Suddenly,
> my grandmother started to shout. I heard a very loud sound. Then, my
> grandmother grabbed us out of bed, and we ran out of the house. I was really
> scared. Someone told me it was an earthquake.
>
> Luckily, there was no damage to our house or the other houses on our street.
> But unfortunately, houses in other parts of the country were destroyed.
>
> The day after the earthquake, my friend Lena, who lived next door to
> me, was surprised to learn about the earthquake. She and her family were
> sleeping while everybody else in our neighborhood ran around and shouted.
> Nothing – not even an earthquake – prevents them from sleeping!

1. The writer used to live in El Salvador.   Yes   No
2. The writer was reading a book when the story started.   Yes   No
3. The emergency was an earthquake.   Yes   No
4. There was damage to the writer's house.   Yes   No
5. The writer's friend was scared during the earthquake.   Yes   No

E Writing

Write a story about an emergency that happened to you or someone you
know. Use a separate piece of paper.

Use these questions to help you: *Who is the story about? When did it
happen? Where did it happen? What were people doing when the story
started? What was the emergency? How did the story end?*

TEST
UNIT 10 Free time

A Listening

🎧 TRACK 12

1 Listen. Circle the correct answer.

1. What are they talking about?

   a. someone's visit   b. a weekend trip   c. a business trip

2. What is their relationship?

   a. brother and sister   b. travel agent and customer   c. husband and wife

3. Why do they need a hotel?

   a. His sister isn't home.   b. His brother's house is full.   c. His mother is sick.

4. How do they feel?

   a. excited   b. stressed   c. angry

🎧 TRACK 12

2 Listen again. Complete the chart.

	Cost
1. Airfare to Chicago	
2. Hotel room per night	
3. Room tax per night	
4. Food for the weekend	
5. Babysitting	
6. Total cost	

B Grammar

Complete the sentences. Use the simple present or future form of the verbs.

1. If my husband _____ a few days off, we _____ on vacation.
   (get)   (go)

2. They _____ if there _____ a room tax.
   (ask)   (be)

3. If we _____ discounts, we _____ a lot of money.
   (find)   (save)

4. She _____ her English if she _____.
   (not / improve)   (not / practice)

5. If he _____ for discounts, it _____ too much.
   (look)   (not / cost)

Name: _____

Date: _____

C Grammar

Complete the sentences. Use the simple present or future form of the verbs.

1. Before the children _____, she _____ dinner.
   (arrive)   (cook)

2. After the alarm _____, she _____.
   (go off)   (get up)

3. We _____ to school before it _____ to snow.
   (drive)   (start)

4. Our parents _____ with us after they _____ our trip to
   (speak)   (book)

   New York.

5. Before Sam _____ the dog, he _____ doing the dishes.
   (walk)   (finish)

D Reading

Read the article. Then read the sentences. Are they correct? Circle *Yes* or *No*.

King's World

King's World is a large amusement park with rides, shows, restaurants, and gift stores. It is one of the biggest tourist attractions in our state. It is open from May 1 to September 6, and over 500,000 people visit it every year.

King's World has activities for children, teenagers, and adults. If you are a child, you will like the animal shows and the children's rides. If you are a teenager, you will like the fast rides and the dance competitions. If you are an adult, you will enjoy the concerts and the many different restaurants. After you spend a long day at King's World, you will be tired but happy. Every evening ends at 9:00 p.m. with spectacular fireworks.

General admission is $35.00 for adults and $25.00 for children under 10 years old. It is expensive to take your family there, but you and your family will have a great time. If you want to save some money, you can bring a picnic lunch.

---

1. King's World is open on July 31.   Yes   No
2. General admission for a child under 10 is $35.00.   Yes   No
3. There are animals at King's World.   Yes   No
4. If you are at King's World at 9:00 p.m., you will see fireworks.   Yes   No
5. If you don't bring a picnic lunch, you will not be able to eat.   Yes   No

E Writing

Write a paragraph about your favorite tourist attraction. Include a main idea, three examples of things to do, and a conclusion. Use complex sentences. Use a separate piece of paper.

FINAL TEST
UNITS 6–10

A Listening

🎧
TRACK 13

1 Listen. Circle the correct answer.

1. Where are they?
   a. at the store   b. at school   c. at the police department

2. What is their relationship?
   a. victim and thief   b. police officer and citizen   c. travel agent and customer

3. What are they talking about?
   a. a crime   b. an assignment   c. a ticket

🎧
TRACK 13

2 Listen again. Check _Yes_ or _No_.

	Yes	No
1. A thief has been using Mr. Purdy's credit card.	☐	☐
2. A thief stole Mr. Purdy's plane ticket to Asia.	☐	☐
3. The thief wanted to fly to Asia.	☐	☐
4. The thief wanted $9,000 in cash.	☐	☐
5. Mr. Purdy called his credit card company to report the crime.	☐	☐
6. He has already applied for another credit card.	☐	☐
7. He had to take the day off.	☐	☐

B Grammar

Complete the sentences. Use the correct form of the verbs.

1. Tom _____ to his wife before he makes a decision.
   (talk)

2. While she _____ dinner, the phone rang.
   (cook)

3. When he is worried about something, he _____ trouble sleeping.
   (have)

4. They are excited about _____ on vacation next month.
   (go)

5. How long have you been _____ at this school?
   (study)

C Grammar

Complete the sentences.

away	down	if	in	of

1. She won't go because she is afraid _____ flying.

2. Could you please throw _____ those old newspapers?

3. He is interested _____ becoming a teacher.

4. If you turn _____ the volume, you will be able to hear me.

5. She will call us _____ she needs help.

D Reading

Read the blog. Then read the sentences. Are they correct? Circle *Yes* or *No*.

Syed's Blog

Monday 2/25 My interview went well. While I was on my way home, the employer called to ask me to come back for a second interview! I really hope I get the job.

Friday 2/22 Today, I went to the career center at my college to get advice for the interview. I was worried that I wouldn't make a good impression. The counselor said that if I prepare, I will do fine. He said that I should let the employer know my strengths. I feel better. I'm going to do a practice interview with my wife. The interview is on Monday.

Thursday 2/21 I got a call yesterday from an employer I met at the job fair. He liked my résumé and would like me to come in for an interview. After he called, I told my wife. We are both excited about my interview. I'm a little worried about going on it, too.

Friday 2/15 On Wednesday and Thursday, I went to two different job fairs at my college. Before I went, I made a folder with my résumés and work history. I met several employers and filled out some applications. Many of the employers said that they would call me back. I really hope so!

Tuesday 2/12 Everyone has told me that I should send out a lot of résumés. So, this afternoon I went to the career center at school. After the career counselor helped me, I had more confidence. My résumé has really improved.

Monday 2/11 Hi, fellow job searchers! I really want a job in computer technology. This past month, I've told a lot of my friends that I'm looking for a new position. I've called employers about open positions, too. I haven't seen a job I really like yet, but I will soon.

1. Syed wants a job in computer technology.   Yes   No
2. He filled out applications at the job fairs.   Yes   No
3. Many employers said that they would call Syed back.   Yes   No
4. Syed went to the career center after he went on his interview.   Yes   No

5. Before he met with the career counselor, he was worried. Yes No

6. He was worried that he wouldn't know enough English. Yes No

7. The counselor said that he should prepare for his interview. Yes No

8. On Friday, 2/15, Syed did a practice interview with his wife. Yes No

9. The employer called while Syed was having dinner. Yes No

10. Syed has already gone on his second interview. Yes No

E Writing

Plan a letter to a future employer about your experience, skills, and personal strengths for a new job. Then write a letter to your new employer. Use a separate piece of paper.

How long have you been working?	
What kind of work have you done?	
What skills have you learned?	
What are your personal strengths?	
What type of job do you want? Why?	

Tests audio script

This audio script contains the listening portions of the *Ventures 3* unit tests, midterm test, and final test. A customizable copy is available on the Assessment Audio CD / CD-ROM. You can play the audio program using the Assessment Audio CD / CD-ROM in a computer or a stereo, or you can read the script aloud.

Unit 1: Personal information

Track 2

A Listening

A Hey, Greg. I need a cup of coffee. Want some?

B Sure. Tired, as usual, Neil? Did you have another wild weekend?

A Yeah, well, last night some friends came over and . . . You know I like playing cards, right? Well, we played cards until about two in the morning. Hey, you know what? You should come next time. Do you like playing cards?

B Me? Not really. I don't like socializing much, remember? I'm not a party animal like you.

A Oh, yeah. Right. So, how was your weekend? What did you do?

B Well, I had a really nice, quiet weekend. I went to the beach on Sunday . . . you know I enjoy jogging on the beach . . . and . . .

A Wow, Greg! So you mean you weren't home the whole time?

B Nope. Not this weekend.

A That's good! But you went to the beach to work out? I hate working out! I hate exercising.

B Yeah, well . . . Rita likes jogging, so . . .

A Rita? Who's Rita? Greg, do you have a new girlfriend?

B Yeah, well. You know I'm not outgoing and I'm kind of shy. Well, I met Rita. And now I have a girlfriend who likes staying home, too.

A So, tell me about Rita.

B No way! Come on. Let's get back to work.

Unit 2: At school

Track 3

A Listening

A Hello. I'm Tanya.

B Hi. I'm Omar.

A You're new here, aren't you?

B Uh, yeah. I'm new. I just started yesterday. How long have you been here?

A Oh, for about a month now.

B Wow. Your English is good! How have you learned so quickly?

A Well, I've had a lot of opportunities to improve my English since I came to the United States. I work and so, you know, I speak English with my co-workers in the morning, at my job. Then, I come here to school in the evenings. And I listen to the news

in English and read a newspaper every day. Hey, Omar, have you tried reading newspapers in English?

B No, I can't concentrate, and there are too many new words. I can't remember them all. And I hate using a dictionary all the time.

A Well, here's an idea. Read the newspaper in the morning, and then you can ask me about new words!

B Yeah, that's a good idea! I think I'm going to enjoy learning that way!

Unit 3: Friends and family

Track 4

A Listening

A Oh, hi, Alfredo. How are you?

B Hi, Daniel. I'm fine. Listen. Are you busy? Are you eating?

A No, no. Come on in.

B Thanks, but I can't stay long. Actually, can I ask a favor?

A Sure, Alfredo. What is it?

B Can I borrow a dictionary . . . again?

A Of course.

B I wanted to look up some words online, but I can't use the computer because my son is using it for his homework.

A No problem.

B I'll tell you something. I don't know how he can concentrate. He plays his music too loud and does his homework at the same time. Do you hear the noise?

A No, Alfredo. I don't hear anything. You know, you really can't complain. At least he's doing his homework!

B Well, I guess you're right.

A Now, let me get that dictionary for you.

B Thanks, Daniel. I appreciate it. I owe you one.

Unit 4: Health

Track 5

A Listening

A Sheila, is that you?

B Joy! Hi!

A Wow. I haven't seen you for such a long time!

B Yes, it has been a long time! How have you been?

A I've been busy, as usual. But, you! You look great!

B Well, thanks. I've started a new diet recently.

A Oh, really?

B Yeah. You know, I used to eat unhealthy food all the time. But now I eat more fish and vegetables – no more hamburgers and fries!

A Well, Sheila, you look great.

B And I exercise a lot more, too. Lately, I've been working out about three days a week.

A Really? I haven't exercised for a long time. I should follow my doctor's advice – to get more exercise and change my diet.

B Joy, I have an idea. Have you eaten lunch yet? Can you have lunch with me right now? We can talk about healthy diets and good exercise.

A Thanks, but I've already eaten. How about tomorrow?

B OK. Let's meet tomorrow for lunch!

A Great!

Unit 5: Around town

Track 6

A Listening

A I'm so glad it's Friday! Do you plan to do anything special this weekend, Sharon?

B Not really. I'd like to go to the salsa concert tonight, but Joe and I have agreed to try and save money. We can't afford to go out every weekend. But I want to do something! I'm sort of tired of staying home.

A Well, have you seen the new exhibit at the art museum? Admission is free on Sundays, you know.

B I'd like to go, but Joe isn't interested in art.

A How about the new science museum?

B Really, Joe refuses to go to museums.

A Then let's check the newspaper. This looks interesting . . . a walking tour of homes and gardens, and it's free!

B I'd like to take that tour, but Joe really doesn't like to spend time on things like that.

A Well, here's something your husband would like! There's a soccer game tomorrow afternoon. It's a fund-raiser for the city.

B Let me see. The tickets are cheap. I think Joe would like to help raise money for the city. Good idea, Renee! I'll check with him tonight.

A And, Sharon. I plan to go on that walking tour. Would you like to come with me?

B Oh, Renee. That's a great idea! And maybe we could stop in at the new art exhibit, too.

Midterm Test Units 1–5

Track 7

A Listening

A Hi, Elsa! How are you?
B Hi, Amelia. I'm OK . . . a little tired, I guess. I haven't slept well lately.
A Really? Why?
B I'm worried about my daughter, Ana.
A Why? What's the matter, Elsa?
B Well, I don't know, Amelia. We've lived here for a few months now, but Ana isn't happy. She hasn't made any friends. I hate seeing her alone all the time.
A Have you talked to her about it?
B Oh, yes, I've spoken with her a few times. I've tried to give her some advice, but she's so discouraged.
A Maybe she's shy.
B Well, she had some close friends before we moved here. She used to love to socialize with them.
A Does she like playing sports? Maybe Ana could join a team.
B Well, she likes exercising, but she's not outgoing enough to be on a team.
A How about dancing, Elsa? Does Ana like dancing?
B Oh, yes, she loves dancing! She's already taken years of dance classes.
A So, have you checked out the dance classes at the community center?
B No, I haven't, but that's a great idea!
A And does she enjoy reading? There's storytelling every Saturday at the library. After the storytelling, they talk about books they've read.
B Both of those options sound good. Amelia, I appreciate your advice. Thanks. Maybe I'll sleep better tonight!

Unit 6: Time

Track 8

A Listening

A Hello?
B Lola? Hi. It's Sally.
A Hi, Sally. How are you?
B I'm fine. It's been a long time since we've talked. Listen, I'm calling to see if you can come to my house for dinner on Friday.
A Oh, Sally. Thanks so much, but I don't think I can. I have to go shopping on Friday evening.
B Well, can't you go shopping on Friday afternoon?
A Well, before I go shopping, I have to clean the apartment. See, my relatives are coming to visit.
B Well, how about Saturday?
A Well, see, my relatives arrive on Saturday morning. I have to meet them at the bus station at 11:00. After they arrive, I'm going to drive them to my sister's house.
B Wow, Lola. You're going to be busy this weekend!

A And, Sally, I'm not finished! All my relatives are coming to my apartment for dinner on Saturday. I need to prepare dinner for 15 people!
B Well, after you do all that work for your family, you need to rest and relax on Sunday!
A I can't! I have an English project due on Monday!
B Boy, Lola, you certainly have a big to-do list. Well, maybe you can come for dinner next week, then.
A I'd love to. Thanks, Sally.

Unit 7: Shopping

Track 9

A Listening

A Hey, Rob. You know, I'm thinking about buying a computer. It could help the kids with their homework. They've been asking for one, and I could use it, too.
B How much do computers cost? Can we afford it?
A Well, used computers cost about $300.
B $300. And a printer? How much is a used printer?
A About $100.
B What about a new computer?
A I think a new computer and a new printer cost about $800. You know, we can afford to pay cash for a used computer and printer, but I'm worried about spending $800 for new ones. We'd have to buy them on credit.
B I know, but I prefer a new computer and printer. I know we have enough money in our savings account, so if we use a credit card and pay it off immediately, there'll be no problem.
A Right. So, zero financing, zero interest, zero debt – I like that! And I'm really excited about getting online with my family. I wonder how much that costs?
B I think it's about $30 a month. Hey, let's worry about that later. One thing at a time.
A Great! Let's go tell the kids.

Unit 8: Work

Track 10

A Listening

A Good afternoon, Janice. Thank you for coming. I'm Ms. Rivera.
B Nice to meet you, Ms. Rivera.
A So, I see you're interested in the teacher's assistant job.
B Yes, I'm applying to be a teacher's assistant.
A OK, Janice, I'd like to ask you a few questions. First of all, could you tell me a little about your background?
B Well, you can see from my application that I have a degree in

education from my country. I've been living in this country for two years.
A And are you currently employed?
B No, I'm not. I'm a student. I'm taking English classes at the community college. I've been studying English since I arrived in this country.
A That's excellent, Janice. Now, can you tell me some of your strengths?
B Well, I'm reliable. I'm always on time. And I get along with people, especially children!
A That's important in this job! And I think you have another strength, too.
B Really?
A Yeah. You speak two languages – Spanish and English. That's a very important strength in our schools.
B Oh, thank you! I appreciate that!
A Well, it's been nice to meet you, Janice. I'll get back to you in a few days.
B Thank you, Ms. Rivera. It was very nice to meet you, too.

Unit 9: Daily living

Track 11

A Listening

A Welcome, everybody, to the first meeting of the Neighborhood Watch Program. As you know, crime has become a big problem in the neighborhood recently. Somebody broke into the Wongs' house last Saturday.
B Oh, no! Really?
A Yeah. Somebody broke into their house while they were having a barbecue in their backyard.
C Yeah. Raymond and Eve are really upset. The robber stole a computer, a new TV, and some cash.
D So the robber just walked in the front door while they were cooking in the backyard? That's terrible!
A Yeah, that's right. The front door wasn't locked.
C You know, things have changed. We didn't use to lock our doors when we were home. Now we all have to remember to lock our doors all the time – even when we're home!
D Of course! We don't want that sort of thing to happen again.
A Well, this is why the Neighborhood Watch Program is such a good idea. We have to fight crime in our neighborhood! So tell all your neighbors to come to our next meeting in two weeks.

Unit 10: Free time

Track 12

A Listening

A Look, Kara! Take a look at these cheap flights on the Internet! There's a special discount to Chicago . . . $65!
B Wow. Is that $65 round-trip?

A Yup. $65 round-trip per person. That's amazing! We could visit my brother. I haven't seen him in a very long time.

B That's a great idea. But I refuse to stay with him. There are too many people in that house! Are there any discounts on hotel rates?

A Let me see. Here's the Hotel Chicago for $99 a night.

B That's not too expensive. But don't forget the room tax. That would be about $14 more per night.

A Right. But that's not too much.

B And there's food! We have to eat! But we don't have to go to expensive restaurants. If we're careful, I guess we'll spend only about $150 on food.

A That's about $500 for the weekend. What do you think?

B Well, can your sister babysit Cynthia? If she can babysit Cynthia, you and I will fly to Chicago this weekend!

A I'll make the reservations after I talk to my sister!

Final Test Units 6–10

Track 13

A Listening

A Hello, I'm Officer Gomez. How can I help you?

B Well, I'm very upset. I'd like to file a police report. Someone stole my credit card! And . . .

A Slow down. Start from the beginning. What's your name?

B Purdy. John Purdy. And someone has been using my credit card since last night! My credit card company called me at home last night. Someone – the thief! – was trying to book a round-trip flight to Asia. The airfare was $9,000. Then, the same person wanted $5,000 in cash! . . . With my credit card! The total credit was too much – it was over my credit line – so the credit card company called me. They were concerned.

A Mr. Purdy, it's nice to know your credit card company is reliable.

B Yes, but I can't use that credit card now! What a nightmare! After I file this report, I'll have to apply for another credit card! And I had to take the day off to file this report and file three other credit reports.

A Mr. Purdy, you should calm down a little. Let's see. Do you know how the thief stole your credit card? Is your wallet missing?

B No, I have my wallet. I have no idea how this person got my credit card. What a nightmare!

Tests answer key

Each unit test section is worth 20 points, for a total of 100 points per unit test. Therefore, each listening item is 2 points. All other items are worth 4 points.

Unit 1: Personal information

A Listening

1

1. b   2. a   3. a

2

1. Neil   5. Neil
2. Greg   6. Greg
3. Greg   7. Greg
4. Greg

B Grammar

1. learning   4. standing
2. being   5. taking
3. talking

C Grammar

1. Marta enjoys socializing more than reading.
2. Marta likes working out less than watching TV.
3. Marta likes playing sports as much as dancing.
4. She likes reading less than working out.
5. She enjoys watching TV more than dancing.

D Reading

1. No   4. Yes
2. No   5. No
3. Yes

E Writing

Answers will vary.
Sample answer:

Danny needs a job to fit his personality. He likes writing, and he enjoys talking to people and socializing. He has an outgoing personality and is very friendly. I think an English teacher is a good job for Danny.

Unit 2: At school

A Listening

1

1. b   2. c   3. a

2

1. Omar   5. Omar
2. Tanya   6. Tanya
3. Tanya   7. Omar
4. Tanya

B Grammar

1. has   4. had
2. been   5. since
3. for

C Grammar

1. Have you ever talked to your neighbors?

2. Has Jameela ever forgotten her books?
3. Has he ever studied French?
4. Have you ever been lost?
5. Have Laura and Joseph ever done the wrong homework?

D Reading

1. No   4. Yes
2. Yes   5. No
3. Yes

E Writing

Answers will vary.
Sample answers:

1. Kayla needs to learn more words in English.
2. Kayla can underline new words and important information. She can write the new words in a notebook and look them up.
3. Kayla can practice saying the new words with her classmate.
4. Kayla can also use clues to make guesses about the meanings of words.
5. Kayla learns new words when she writes them down. She goes back and practices them with her classmates. When she guesses meanings, her classmates tell her if she's correct.

Unit 3: Friends and family

A Listening

1

1. c   2. a   3. c

2

1. Daniel   5. Daniel
2. Alfredo   6. Daniel
3. Alfredo   7. Alfredo
4. Alfredo

B Grammar

1. because of   4. because of
2. because   5. because
3. because

C Grammar

1. big enough
2. experienced enough
3. too high
4. too far
5. close enough

D Reading

1. Yes   4. Yes
2. No   5. No
3. No

E Writing

Answers will vary.
Sample answers:

1. October 10, 2011
2. To Whom It May Concern
3. Sue and Sally are writing because they heard loud music. They are also concerned about the children because no one answers the door.
4. Sue heard loud music at 3:30 in the afternoon. When she knocked, no one answered. Sally saw the children trying to start a fire outside her door. Sally also heard loud music at 1:00 in the morning last Friday. Other neighbors were complaining about the children, too.
5. Sue and Sally want the landlord to tell Mr. and Mrs. Holmes to watch their children better. They also want the landlord to tell them to keep the noise down.

Unit 4: Health

A Listening

1

1. b   2. c   3. b

2

1. Joy   5. Joy
2. Joy   6. Joy
3. Sheila   7. Sheila
4. Sheila

B Grammar

1. has checked   4. has been
2. hasn't gone   5. haven't slept
3. have given up

C Grammar

1. use to   4. use to
2. used to   5. used to
3. used to

D Reading

1. No   4. No
2. No   5. Yes
3. Yes

E Writing

Answers will vary.
Sample answer:

My life has changed since I moved to the United States. Before, I used to walk for half an hour to work, but now I take a bus for half an hour. Before, I used to go home and eat lunch with my family, but now I bring my lunch to work. Before, I used to sew my children's clothes for school, but now I buy them every September.

Unit 5: Around town

A Listening

1

1. a   2. a   3. a   4. b

2

Check: salsa concert, staying home, new art exhibit, science museum, walking tour, soccer game

B Grammar

1. promise to pay
2. hope to start
3. plan to meet
4. wanted to ride
5. decided to do

C Grammar

1. yet   4. yet
2. already   5. already
3. yet

D Reading

1. Yes   4. No
2. Yes   5. No
3. No

E Writing

Answers will vary.
Sample answer:

> Next weekend, I plan to go to the park with my family. I intend to have a big picnic with food and drinks. I would like to play basketball and soccer with my children. I intend to sit and chat with my wife, too. I have already taken the day off. But I haven't told my family yet. I want it to be a surprise.

Midterm Test Units 1–5

A Listening

(2.5 points per item)

1

1. c   2. b

2

1. Elsa   5. Ana
2. Ana   6. Ana
3. Ana   7. Amelia
4. Amelia   8. Elsa

B Grammar

(2 points per item)

1. giving   4. Because of
2. taught   5. used
3. to be

C Grammar

(3 points per item)

1. much   4. enough
2. ever   5. yet
3. for

D Reading

(2.5 points per item)

1. Yes   6. Yes
2. Yes   7. No
3. No   8. No
4. Yes   9. No
5. No   10. No

E Writing

Answers will vary. This section is worth 25 points. Score for accuracy, grammar, punctuation, and spelling.
Sample paragraph:

> There are many ways for Marie to improve her English. She can practice with her teacher and her classmates. She can listen to the radio. Many people like to learn the words of songs. She can practice pronunciation and sing the songs. Another idea is to practice with her children and her husband. They can help her, too. When Marie feels comfortable speaking English, she will enjoy living in this country.

Unit 6: Time

A Listening

1

1. c   2. b   3. c   4. a

2

1. Clean the apartment
2. Go shopping
3. Meet relatives at bus station
4. Drive them to sister's house
5. Prepare dinner
6. Do English project

B Grammar

1. When you have many chores, you need to prioritize.
2. Don't procrastinate over the weekend when your projects are due on Monday.
3. When you're talking to your children, don't be impatient.
4. When you have a deadline, plan your tasks.
5. Don't turn on the television when you need to focus.

C Grammar

1. After Lola goes to the supermarket, she meets the children.
2. Before she starts preparing dinner, she meets the children.
3. After she meets the children, she starts preparing dinner.
4. She cleans the kitchen after she eats dinner.
5. She cleans the kitchen before she leaves for class.

D Reading

1. Yes   4. No
2. No   5. Yes
3. Yes

E Writing

Answers will vary.
Sample answer:

> When I get up in the morning, I brush my teeth. After I brush my teeth, I take a bath and get dressed. Before I leave for work, I prepare breakfast for my family. Then I drive to work. After I come home from work, I cook dinner. I usually have to ask my children to do their homework.

Unit 7: Shopping

A Listening

1

1. b   2. c   3. a   4. a

2

1. $300   4. zero
2. $100   5. zero
3. $800   6. $30

B Grammar

1. should   4. could
2. could   5. should
3. should

C Grammar

1. lending   4. paying
2. getting   5. buying
3. starting

D Reading

1. No   4. No
2. No   5. Yes
3. Yes

E Writing

Answers will vary.
Sample answer:

Dear No Debt for Us,

> I agree. You should not get into debt. First, maybe your children could help with the finances of the house. Your daughter could help with the babysitting. Your son could get a part-time job. Second, you and your husband could talk to your children about your monthly budget. You should show them how much money you spend on living expenses like rent and food. Finally, you should help your children understand debt. Someday they will thank you for teaching them!

Money Man

Unit 8: Work

A Listening

1

1. a   2. b   3. c   4. c

2

1. teacher's assistant
2. education
3. two
4. student
5. reliable, on time, gets along with people
6. speak two languages

B Grammar

1. How long have they been studying for a degree?
2. Have you been living in this country for a long time?
3. How long has Josefina been working at her job?
4. Has Ken been practicing his English?
5. How long have you been waiting?

C Grammar

1. He's filling the application out.
2. She's putting away the pots.
3. He's turning it up.
4. She's cleaning up the kitchen.
5. He's calling back his wife.

D Reading

1. No   4. Yes
2. No   5. No
3. Yes

E Writing

Answers will vary.
Sample answer:

Mr. Ken Leong
Personnel Manager
The Best Haircuts
35 South Third Street
Milwaukee, WI 53215

Dear Mr. Leong,

I would like to thank you for the job interview I had with you yesterday. I appreciate the time you spent with me. Thank you for showing me around the shop and for introducing me to some of the employees. I look forward to your call next week.

Sincerely,
Sandra Jones

Unit 9: Daily living

A Listening

1
1. b   2. c   3. a   4. c
2
1. Someone broke in
2. a computer, a TV and cash
3. through the front door
4. not lock doors
5. lock doors
6. in two weeks

B Grammar

1. was doing
2. was watching
3. were cleaning
4. was attending
5. were playing

C Grammar

1. When the phone rang, she was cooking dinner.
2. He was sleeping when the alarm went off.
3. While we were driving to school, it started to snow.
4. While they were talking to us, their young child interrupted many times.
5. I was studying when the dog began to bark.

D Reading

1. Yes   4. No
2. No   5. No
3. Yes

E Writing

Answers will vary.
Sample answer:

Two years ago, I was traveling on a train in Ecuador when I heard the conductor say the train had to stop. There was another train in front of us with problems. Many people were worried because they did not know what happened. I couldn't call anyone. I was worried, too. We had to wait for three hours! Everyone was tired and hungry. Finally, the train started to move again. We never found out what happened.

Unit 10: Free time

A Listening

1
1. b   2. c   3. b   4. a
2
1. $65   4. $150
2. $99   5. free
3. $14   6. $500

B Grammar

1. If my husband gets a few days off, we will go on vacation.
2. They will ask if there is a room tax.
3. If we find discounts, we will save a lot of money.
4. She will not (won't) improve her English if she doesn't practice.
5. If he looks for discounts, it will not (won't) cost too much.

C Grammar

1. Before the children arrive, she will cook dinner.
2. After the alarm goes off, she will get up.
3. We will drive to school before it starts to snow.
4. Our parents will speak with us after they book our trip to New York.
5. Before Sam walks the dog, he will finish doing the dishes.

D Reading

1. Yes   4. Yes
2. No   5. No
3. Yes

E Writing

Answers will vary.
Sample answer:

The State Zoo is the best free tourist attraction. When you go to the State Zoo, you can see all the animals for free. Every month, there is a new baby animal. If you have children, they will love to see the baby animals. After you see all the animals, you can have dinner in the outdoor food court. The State Zoo is always fun.

Final Test Units 6–10

A Listening

(2.5 points per item)
1
1. c   2. b   3. a
2
1. Yes   5. No
2. No   6. No
3. Yes   7. Yes
4. No

B Grammar

(2 points per item)
1. will talk   4. going
2. was cooking   5. studying
3. has

C Grammar

(3 points per item)
1. of   4. down
2. away   5. if
3. in

D Reading

(2.5 points per item)
1. Yes   6. No
2. Yes   7. Yes
3. Yes   8. No
4. No   9. No
5. Yes   10. No

E Writing

Answers will vary. This section is worth 25 points. Score for accuracy, grammar, punctuation, and spelling.
Sample letter:

To Whom It May Concern:

I have been working for ten years. Before I came to the United States, I was a secretary at an insurance company. Now, I work at a department store as a salesperson. I have learned to speak, read, and write in English. I have learned to file, type, and use the computer well. I have also learned to sell clothing and housewares.

Some of my personal strengths are that I am very friendly and outgoing. I get along with most people, especially children. I am also very creative. I would like to be a teacher's assistant because I really love children. I also would really like to work in a classroom where I can be creative.

Sincerely,
Michelle Franklin

Overview

The Online Teacher's Resource Room (www.cambridge.org/myresourceroom) is an additional resource for teachers using the *Ventures 3* Student's Book. The Online Teacher's Resource Room provides reproducible, supplementary materials for use during in-class assessment, whole-class activities, and group work. It provides more than 180 pages of additional material.

What's included in the Online Teacher's Resource Room:

- The **self-assessments** from the *Ventures 3* Student's Book. Each unit self-assessment can be printed out, completed by students, and saved as a portfolio assessment tool.
- The **projects** from the *Ventures 3* Teacher's Edition. Unit projects extend students' learning into real-world context. They work within the unit topic, but they also go beyond the Student's Book.
- **Collaborative Activity Worksheets**. For each lesson in the *Ventures 3* Student's Book, there is a reproducible activity worksheet to encourage collaborative pair and group work in class. In addition, there are **Teaching tips** which provide instructions for using the worksheets in class.
- **Extended Reading Worksheets**. For each unit in *Ventures 3* Student's Book, there is a reproducible reading worksheet. These worksheets encourage students to become independent learners by offering those students who have the time and interest an opportunity to read for pleasure at home. The readings are slightly longer, and slightly more difficult, high-interest material related to the topics and themes of the Student's Book. The exercises that accompany each reading support the understanding of the text, reinforce skills introduced in the Student's Book, expand vocabulary-building strategies, and encourage critical thinking. The worksheets can also be used in class to practice and extend the reading skills and strategies in the Student's Book. The answer key can be printed and distributed to students for self-correction or peer correction.

- A **vocabulary list**. All key vocabulary in *Ventures 3* Student's Book is listed alphabetically, with first occurrence page numbers included for easy reference.
- A **certificate of completion**. To recognize students for satisfactory completion of *Ventures 3*, a printable certificate is included.

Additional resources include:

- A **placement test** that helps place students into the appropriate level of *Ventures*.
- A **Career and Educational Pathways solution** that helps students identify their educational and career goals.
- *Add Ventures* multilevel worksheets designed for use in multilevel classrooms and in classes with differing student-proficiency levels.
- The *Canadian Teacher's Guide*, a valuable tool for teachers using the *Ventures* series in Canada. With an easy-to-use format and clear and simple explanations, it shows teachers how to adapt *Ventures* Student's Books for a Canadian setting.
- The *Multilevel Lesson Planner*. This invaluable part of the *Ventures* series helps instructors who manage a single classroom in which students use different levels of *Ventures* Student's Books.
- Reproducible *Civics Worksheets* for use alongside the *Ventures* series.
- **Audio scripts** for both the class audio program and the Workbook audio program. These audio scripts can be used by teachers who don't have classroom access to a CD player or computer.
- A variety of national and state **correlations** meant to be used as a guide to developing or aligning your program's curriculum with *Ventures*.

Games

Overview

Games provide practice and reinforcement of skills, but in a fun and engaging manner. Students love to play games. Games raise motivation and enjoyment for learning. They can be used as a warm-up, practice, or review activity. The games described below can be adjusted and adapted to the skill level of the class.

1. Conversation Toss

Skills: speaking, listening
Objective: to practice pronunciation, vocabulary, and grammar
Preparation: Prepare a dialog. Bring a soft ball to class

- Write a dialog on the board, for example, a pronunciation dialog from a review unit.
- Read the dialog and ask Ss to repeat, paying special attention to the key pronunciation point.
- Toss a ball to one S to start the dialog again. The S begins the dialog and then tosses the ball to a classmate. The classmate reads the next line of the dialog and then tosses the ball to a third student to continue.
- Continue until all lines of the dialog have been read.

Adaptation: To make the task more difficult, erase a key pronunciation word or two from each sentence so that Ss must fill in the missing word. If a S reads a sentence, but it is not easily understood, encourage classmates to say: *Could you please repeat that?* Offer suggestions for improving pronunciation at those times.

2. Which Part Is It?

Skills: listening, writing
Objective: to increase vocabulary by identifying parts of speech
Preparation: Prepare a list of vocabulary previously learned

- Write the parts of speech you want to practice on the board. For example:

    Noun   Verb   Adjective

- Divide the class into teams of six Ss and assign a number from 1–6 to each team member.

- Call all number 1 Ss to the board and give each one a piece of chalk. Read the first word on the vocabulary list.
- The first S to write the word and label it with the correct part of speech (for example, *digestion – noun*) wins a point for his or her team.
- Call all number 2 Ss to the board and repeat with another word.
- Continue until all Ss have had a chance to come to the board and a winning team is identified.

Adaptation: To make the task more difficult, the point is awarded only if a team member can use the word correctly in a sentence.

3. Take One Away

Skills: listening, speaking
Objective: to practice vocabulary and grammar
Preparation: Prepare a list of complex sentences students can understand from lessons taught

- Divide the class into teams of six Ss. Write a complex sentence that Ss will understand on the board. For example, *I couldn't sleep last night because my neighbors were too noisy.*
- Working in teams, Ss take turns changing one word of the sentence. The sentences can be silly, but they must still make some sense and be grammatically correct. For example:

    S1: *I couldn't sleep last night because my children were too noisy.*

    S2: *I couldn't sleep yesterday because my children were too noisy.*

    S3: *I couldn't sleep yesterday because of my children.*

- Team members must judge whether the sentence is correct. If it is not correct, they must offer a better suggestion.
- Teams continue making sentences until everyone has had a couple of turns or until Ss can make no more changes.
- Ask the member in each team who has made the last change to say his or her sentence to see the difference in the sentences the teams have made.

Adaptation: Assign a note-taker to record the changes. The note-takers from each team read all their team's changes to the class at the end of the game.

4. Variation on *Take One Away*

Skills: listening, speaking
Objective: to practice vocabulary and grammar
Preparation: Prepare a list of complex sentences Ss can understand from lessons taught

- Divide the class into two teams.
- Play as in *Take One Away,* but with two teams competing. Each team takes a turn changing a word in the complex sentence. Each correct change earns one point.
- Teams continue taking turns making changes to the same sentence until one team makes a mistake or cannot change any more words.
- The team with the most points wins.

5. Round Table

Skills: speaking, listening, writing
Objective: to review vocabulary from a unit
Preparation: none

- Ss form groups of four or five. Each group has a blank sheet of paper.
- Announce the topic, usually the unit topic just completed.
- The first S says a word related to the topic, writes the word on the paper, and passes the paper to the next S.
- That S says a new word related to the topic, enters the word on the paper, and passes the paper to the third S, who continues the process.
- Ss can ask for help from their teammates when they cannot think of a new word to add to the list.
- The paper continues to pass around the table until no one can think of another related word.
- A unique way of scoring is to have one group read its first word. If no other group has that word, the first group receives three points. If any other group has that word, the first group receives one point. The first group continues through its list, one word at a time.
- The other groups mark off the words on their lists as they are heard and record one point for each of those words as they know another group has the same word.
- When the first group finishes reading its list, the second group reads only those words that have not already been mentioned. Again, if other groups have the word, they each score one point; if no other group has the word, the first group scores three points.
- Continue until all groups have accounted for all their words.

6. Bingo

Skills: listening, writing
Objective: to review vocabulary
Preparation: Bingo grids (3x3, 3x4, 4x4 . . .)

- Select enough words to fill a Bingo grid. Read and spell each new word and use it in a sentence.
- Ss write each word randomly on their bingo grids.
- When the grids are filled, play Bingo.
- The S who shouts "Bingo" first calls the next game.

Adaptation: Depending on the Ss' familiarity with the words, call the words by saying the word, spelling the word, providing a definition or an example, or giving a synonym or an antonym.

7. Picture It

Skill: speaking
Objective: to review vocabulary
Preparation: sets of vocabulary cards (one per group)

- Ss form groups of three or four. Give each group one set of vocabulary cards.
- One S chooses a card but does not tell the group members the word.
- On a piece of paper, this S draws a picture or pictures representing the word. Point out that the S drawing the picture cannot talk or make gestures.
- The other Ss try to guess the word, using the drawings as clues.
- Ss take turns choosing and drawing words until all words are chosen.

Adaptation: Instead of drawing the words, Ss can act out the words for group members to guess.

8. Prediction Bingo

Skills: reading or listening
Objective: to develop the prereading or prelistening strategy of predicting
Preparation: Bingo grids (3x3, 3x4, 4x4 . . .)

- Provide Ss with the title or topic of a selection to be read or heard from an audio recording.
- In each square of the Bingo grid, Ss enter a word related to that topic that they think will appear in the reading or audio.
- Ss listen to the audio or read the text. When they hear or see a word that is on their Bingo grid, they circle it.
- Ss discuss in small groups their choices, both correct and incorrect, and how they relate to the topic.

9. Disappearing Dialog

Skills: speaking, listening, reading, writing
Objective: to practice learning dialogs
Preparation: none

- Write a dialog on the board.
- Go over the dialog with the whole class, then have selected groups say the dialog.
- Next, have Ss practice the dialog in pairs.
- Erase one word from each line of the dialog each time pairs practice, until all words are gone.
- Have volunteers recite the dialog without support from words on the board.
- Then have Ss add words back to the board until all words are again in place.

10. Moving Dialog

Skills: speaking, listening
Objective: to practice using dialogs
Preparation: none

- Ss stand in two lines (A and B), facing each other as partners.
- Ss in line A have one side of a conversation. Ss in line B have the other side. At a signal, Ss in line A begin the dialog, with Ss in line B responding. The dialog may be two or several lines long, depending on the level of the Ss.
- When Ss have completed the dialog, Ss in line A move one (or more) people to the left and practice the dialog again with a new partner.
- Ss at the end of the line will move to the beginning of the line to find their new partners.

11. Hear Ye, Hear Ye

Skills: listening or reading
Objective: to refine listening skills
Preparation: a reading text or an audio clip; an index card with a word or phrase from the clip on it (one word or phrase for each S or, if not enough words, use the same word multiple times)

- Select an audio clip or a reading segment.
- Provide each S with an index card containing a word or phrase that occurs one or more times in the clip or reading segment.
- Play or read the segment.
- Ss listen, paying particular attention for their word or phrase. They raise, then lower, their index card each time they hear the word.

Adaptation: The audio may be a song, a lecture, or a dialog. Ss can listen for things other than specific words, such as past tense verbs, numbers, or three-syllable words.

Alternatively, Ss can stand up or sit down when they hear their word, rather than raise their cards.

12. Treasure Hunt

Skills: reading, writing
Objective: to develop the reading skill of scanning
Preparation: Enlarge a reading selection from the Student's Book and cut it into paragraphs. Number each one. Create a handout with questions/items to be found in the reading.

- Post the pieces of the reading around the room.
- Ss, individually or in pairs, go around the room and locate specific information to enter into their handout. For example: *Write the words that begin with st.*
- Ss check their answers by reading or reviewing the completed text in their books and sharing their answers as a class.

Adaptation: A short reading selection can be cut into sentences for lower-level Ss.

All classrooms are multilevel in some sense. No two students will ever be exactly the same. Learners vary in demographic factors such as culture and ethnicity, personal factors such as a willingness to take risks and differing learning styles, and experiential factors such as background knowledge and previous education. With all these differences, it will always be a challenge to provide useful learning activities for all members of the class. Yet there are some techniques that make working with a multilevel class more manageable.

1. Group work is one of the best ways of working with a multilevel class. Some tasks, such as watching a video, going on a field trip, or describing a picture, can be performed as a whole group. What will change in a multilevel class is the level of expectation of responses following the shared experience. Other tasks can be performed as a whole group, but the tasks are adapted for the students' levels. This could include interviews with varying difficulty of questions or a project such as a class newspaper, where students of differing levels contribute through activities appropriate to their abilities.

   Smaller, homogeneous groups allow students of the same level the opportunity to work together on activities such as a problem-solving task or a group writing activity. Smaller, heterogeneous groups are good for board games or jigsaw activities where the difficulty of the material can be controlled.

2. Varying the materials or activities is another method of addressing the issue of multiple levels in the classroom. Add Ventures, the multilevel component of *Ventures*, provides activities for learners at differing levels. These materials can be used in the classroom with heterogeneous or homogeneous groups because the answers are the same for all three levels of worksheets.

3. Self-access centers are another kind of classroom management technique. These centers would be located in corners of the classroom and would provide opportunities for learners to work at varying levels. By providing a variety of materials, which can be color-coded for levels of difficulty, students have the opportunity to make choices as to the level they feel comfortable working on. Students can self-correct with answer keys. In this way, students are working towards more learner autonomy, which is a valuable assistant in a multilevel classroom and a good start toward promoting lifelong learning skills.

4. Computer-assisted learning, using computers located within the classroom, can provide self-directed learning through software programs geared to a student's individual ability. Most programs provide immediate feedback to students to correct errors and build in a level of difficulty as a student progresses. Groups of students of like ability can rotate their time on the computer, working in pairs, or students can work individually at their own level.

A multilevel classroom, while challenging to the teacher, should offer each learner appropriate levels of instruction according to the learner's abilities, interests, needs, and experiences, and it should be designed to maximize each learner's educational gains. Good management techniques call for the teacher to provide a mixture of whole class, small group, and individual activities, create a learner-centered class by establishing self-access materials, use computers, and incorporate variety in the difficulty of the tasks and materials given to each student.

Authors' acknowledgments

The authors would like to acknowledge and thank focus group participants and reviewers for their insightful comments, as well as Cambridge University Press editorial, marketing, and production staffs, whose thorough research and attention to detail have resulted in a quality product.

The publishers would also like to extend their particular thanks to the following reviewers and consultants for their valuable insights and suggestions:

Kit Bell, LAUSD division of Adult and Career Education, Los Angeles, CA; **Bethany Bogage**, San Diego Community College District, San Diego, CA; **Leslie Keaton Boyd**, Dallas ISD, Dallas, TX; **Barbara Brodsky**, Teaching Work Readiness English for Refugees – Lutheran Family Services, Omaha, NE; **Jessica Buchsbaum**, City College of San Francisco, San Francisco, CA; **Helen Butner**, University of the Fraser Valley, British Columbia, Canada; **Sharon Churchill Roe**, Acadia University, Wolfville, NS, Canada; **Lisa Dolehide**, San Mateo Adult School, San Mateo, CA; **Yadira M. Dominguez**, Dallas ISD, Dallas, TX; **Donna M. Douglas**, College of DuPage, Glen Ellyn, IL; **Latarsha Dykes**, Broward Collge, Pembroke Pines, FL; **Megan L. Ernst**, Glendale Community College, Glendale, CA; **Megan Esler**, Portland Community College, Portland, OR; **Jennifer Fadden**, Fairfax County Public Schools, Fairfax, VA; **Fotine Fahouris**, College of Marin, Kentfield, CA; **Lynn Francis, M.A, M.S.**, San Diego Community College, San Diego, CA; **Danielle Gines**, Tarrant County College, Arlington, TX; **Katherine Hayne**, College of Marin, Kentfield, CA; **Armenuhi Hovhannes**, City College of San Francisco, San Francisco, CA; **Fayne B. Johnson**; **Martha L. Koranda**, College of DuPage, Glen Ellyn, IL; **Daphne Lagios**, San Mateo Adult School, San Mateo, CA; **Judy Langelier**, School District of Palm Beach County, Wellington, FL; **Janet Les**, Chilliwack Community Services, Chilliwack, British Columbia, Canada; **Keila Louzada**, Northern Virginia Community College, Sterling, VA; **Karen Mauer**, Fort Worth ISD, Fort Worth, TX; **Silvana Mehner**, Northern Virginia Community College, Sterling, VA; **Astrid T. Mendez-Gines,** Tarrant County College, Arlington, TX; **Beverly A. Miller**, Houston Community College, Houston, TX; **José Montes, MS. Ed.**, The English Center, Miami-Dade County Public Schools, Miami, FL; **Suzi Monti**, Community College of Baltimore County, Baltimore, MD; **Irina Morgunova**, Roxbury Community College, Roxbury Crossing, MA; **Julia Morgunova**, Roxbury Community College, Roxbury Crossing, MA; **Susan Otero**, Fairfax County Public Schools, Fairfax, VA; **Sergei Paromchik**, Hillsborough County Public Schools, Tampa, FL; **Pearl W. Pigott**, Houston Community College, Houston, TX; **Marlene Ramirez**, The English Center, Miami-Dade County Public Schools, Miami, FL; **Cory Rayala**, Harbor Service Center, LAUSD, Los Angeles, CA; **Catherine M. Rifkin**, Florida State College at Jacksonville, Jacksonville, FL; **Danette Roe**, Evans Community Adult School, Los Angeles, CA; **Maria Roy**, Kilgore College, Kilgore, TX; **Jill Shalongo**, Glendale Community College, Glendale, CA, and Sierra Linda High School, Phoenix, AZ; **Laurel Owensby Slater**, San Diego Community College District, San Diego, CA; **Rheba Smith**, San Diego Community College District, San Diego, CA; **Jennifer Snyder**, Portland Community College, Portland, OR; **Mary K. Solberg**, Metropolitan Community College, Omaha, NE; **Rosanne Vitola**, Austin Community College, Austin, TX

Ventures Student's Book 3

Illustration credits

Photography credits

Assessment Audio CD/CD-ROM

What is the Assessment Audio CD/CD-ROM?

■ The Assessment Audio CD / CD-ROM contains the unit, midterm, and final tests (in both .pdf and customizable Word formats). In addition, it includes audio scripts, answer keys, instructions for administering tests, and the test audio for the listening portions.

■ The complete test audio can also be played using a conventional CD player.

Audio CD tracks:

Track 1:   Introduction
Track 2:   Unit 1 Test
Track 3:   Unit 2 Test
Track 4:   Unit 3 Test
Track 5:   Unit 4 Test
Track 6:   Unit 5 Test
Track 7:   Midterm Test
Track 8:   Unit 6 Test
Track 9:   Unit 7 Test
Track 10:   Unit 8 Test
Track 11:   Unit 9 Test
Track 12:   Unit 10 Test
Track 13:   Final Test

To access the assessment materials (including test audio):

Windows XP, Vista, 7

■ Insert the disc into a CD-ROM drive on your computer.

■ If Autorun is enabled, the application will start automatically.

■ If Autorun is disabled, open My Computer. Right-click the CD-ROM icon and then select "Open"or "Explore." Double-click "Cambridge-University-Press."

Mac OS X

■ Insert the disc into a CD-ROM drive on your computer.

■ Double-click the CD-ROM icon on the desktop to launch the application. Double-click the Audio CD icon to access the audio via iTunes.

System requirements:

■ Sound card. Speakers or headphones.
■ Media player.
■ PDF reader. Word processor.

Windows XP, Vista, 7

■ 400 MHz processor speed
■ 128 MB RAM

Mac OS X

■ 300 MHz processor speed
■ 64 MB RAM

Support:

If you experience difficulties with this audio CD / CD-ROM, please visit: www.cambridge.org/esl/support